WMU Studies in Maritime Affairs

Series Editors:

Maximo Q. Mejia, Jr.
Jens-Uwe Schröder-Hinrichs

For further volumes:
http://www.springer.com/series/11556

Proshanto K. Mukherjee • Mark Brownrigg

Farthing on International Shipping

Fourth Edition

With associate authorship contributions of

Jingjing Xu, Maximo Q. Mejia Jr., Abhinayan Basu Bal, Donald Chard, David Balston

 Springer

Proshanto K. Mukherjee
World Maritime University
Malmö
Sweden

Mark Brownrigg
UK Chamber of Shipping
London
United Kingdom

ISBN 978-3-642-34597-5   ISBN 978-3-642-34598-2 (eBook)
DOI 10.1007/978-3-642-34598-2
Springer Heidelberg New York Dordrecht London

Library of Congress Control Number: 2013941135

1st edition: © LLP Limited 1987
2nd edition: © LLP Limited 1993
3rd edition: © LLP Limited 1997

Printed on acid-free paper

Springer is part of Springer Science+Business Media (www.springer.com)

Foreword (Fourth Edition)

It was rightly said of the third edition of *Farthing on International Shipping* that it represented a general introduction to shipping which did not only explain the maze of regulations on shipping but also analyze the main issues facing shipping.

The fourth edition goes even further. In addition to offering what is still a first rate introduction to shipping in all its aspects, it is a mine of information for students of traditional maritime law as well as for many others who seek to understand the workings of the world's maritime services in general and shipping services, in particular. As with previous editions, the fourth edition retains the original purpose of elucidating and providing information on national and international policies and practices on shipping, including the age-old dichotomy between the concept of freedom of the seas and the persistent demands of States to control specific maritime areas, and the tension between, on the one hand, the claims of States to regulate and protect their shipping interests and, on the other hand, the abiding concern and unquestioned right of the international community to regulate the global shipping industry in order to ensure maritime safety, protection of the environment, and fair competition. But it also gives due attention to the many important changes that have occurred in international shipping since the publication first appeared in 1987. Particular mention may be made in this regard to, among others, the sections that describe the elaborate system of national and international technical rules and regulations designed to secure the safety of ships and lives at sea; the parts dealing with the interface of shipping and protection of the environment, including rules and mechanisms regarding liability for damage to the environment caused by the operation of ships; and the sections on emerging issues of maritime security, including measures to prevent and suppress unlawful acts that threaten the integrity of international shipping.

Unlike previous editions, this edition is the result of collaboration between several contributors. Nevertheless, the principal editors have managed to merge the different styles and orientations into a homogeneous whole that successfully presents a coherent picture, without in any way disguising the variety of approaches that have gone into it. The result is a compendium that provides a useful source of information and insights into many of the complex and developing problems which persons engaged or interested in various aspects of shipping will either encounter or deal with at one time or another. Clearly the book does not claim to answer all potential questions to the satisfaction of every reader; but it can at least be said with some justification that it has raised or touched on the main questions and issues that currently arise in the world and business of shipping. For that all who are engaged in shipping owe the authors and editors a debt of gratitude.

Indeed, this publication should be of interest to the global community as a whole. Shipping plays an indispensable role in world trade and commerce because it provides the medium without which the movement of goods needed for international commerce would not be possible. It is thus no exaggeration to assert that a treatise on shipping must be of undoubted significance to all States and to all peoples.

Hamburg, Germany   H.E. Judge Thomas A. Mensah
London, UK   International Tribunal for the Law of the Sea

Preface to the Fourth Edition

Most people in the shipping industry—when asked why they have stayed in the industry as long as they have, with all its volatility and uncertainty—point to its unique substance and meaning and the fact that it is an activity which adds value to the world. It combines intellect with practicality and spans every aspect of life— today, as it always has done. It is the one sector on which the modern world depends—for our trade (what we buy in our high streets), our food (for which ships are a major part of the supply chain) and our essential energy resources. The challenges, complexities and excitement of our association with this life-essential are both rewarding and addictive, at all levels of activity involving the sea and the industries which work with it.

The sea demands an elemental attachment, which can be difficult to describe to those who don't see or come into contact with it. It involves a scale and breadth of vision and reality, which shout importance out loud.

This fourth edition is the first since the original author of this work, Bruce Farthing, has died. The previous edition was already the product of a collaboration, but of necessity—with Bruce's encouragement—this one is even more so. It also seeks to move the book in a slightly new direction, taking it beyond the original concept of an introduction to the policy aspects of international shipping to a combination of that purpose and a basic textbook for students and other readers entering the world of maritime services. In the internet era, so much information is available that was not on offer before, that this shift of direction was probably inevitable.

The first and second editions were Bruce's alone. They were much slimmer and focused very specifically on what was then known by the term "shipping policy"— freedom of the seas, protectionism/liberalisation, trade and competition policy.

The third (in 1997), edited principally and developed by Mark Brownrigg, retained the spirit of the original but re-orientated and restructured the book, adding new chapters on broader aspects of policy such as ship registration, safety and the environment. Out of respect for Bruce's vision for his creation, we have reprinted the Foreword and Preface of the third edition as well, for readers to see.

In many ways, the range of international shipping policy issues has broadened again in recent years, with important new subjects coming to the fore particularly in relation to the environment and maritime security. And these areas have been exceptionally "busy". This fourth edition, under the principal editorship and direction of Professor Proshanto Mukherjee, together with Mark Brownrigg, again takes the book into greater detail on some of these—aspects of technical policy, maritime security, liability and more. This edition also draws more collectively on associate authorship contributions by Jingjing Xu of University of Plymouth, Max Mejia of World Maritime University, Abhinayan Basu Bal of Lund University and by Donald Chard and David Balston from the UK Chamber of Shipping. This means that there is no longer a single style to the different chapters and a small amount of duplication.

We are particularly grateful to H.E. Judge Thomas Mensah for contributing the foreword to this edition. We greatly appreciate his willingness to continue the tradition set by Sir John Nicholson, Lord Sterling and the then IMO Secretary General, Bill O'Neil, who wrote the forewords to the earlier editions.

Malmö, Sweden   Proshanto K. Mukherjee
London, UK   Mark Brownrigg
October 2012

Foreword (Third Edition)

Foreword

It has often been said that shipping is the most international of all industries—as well as being one of the oldest—and it is also one of the most complicated. Even the most skilled navigator in the world probably has difficulty in finding his way through the maze of regulations adopted by IMO and other international organisations, and how many people can explain the way liner freight rates are developed and then go on to talk about the growth of containerisation and the importance of the conference system and conclude by analysing the issues shipping faces to 2000 and beyond? The simple answer is that this book can.

It represents one of the best introductions to the subject that is currently available. The first two editions established the book's reputation and I am delighted to see that Bruce Farthing, Mark Brownrigg and the publishers have now produced a third. But it is far from being a reprint of the first two. The third edition contains much revised material and several completely new chapters dealing with such subjects as the importance of shipping to world trade and controversial matters such as free trade versus protectionism.

The book has the advantages of being comprehensive and concise, authoritative and readable all at the same time. It is likely to be of benefit to the student wanting an introduction to the subject and the experienced observer wanting a handy summary. I can thoroughly recommend it to both.

London, UK

William A. O'Neil
Secretary General, International
Maritime Organization

Preface to the Third Edition

The third edition of this book, like earlier editions, is neither a detailed academic study nor an authoritative legal textbook on the many complex issues it covers. It remains an attempt to provide, at not too great length, an introduction to, and an overview of the institutions and structure of the maritime world, together with an insight into the interplay between commercial freedoms and governmental policies. It is aimed, as previously, at those with an interest, but perhaps more importantly those who need to know—students, those entering any aspect of shipping or perhaps civil servants or academics suddenly confronted with the complexities of a fascinating industry.

It is equally more than just a third edition—an update of the earlier editions. Whilst drawing heavily on the previous editions it has been substantially recast, particularly those chapters which deal with major policy issues such as shipping nationalism and government involvement; freedom and protection—the spread of liberalisation; competition policy, liner conferences and cases; and ship registration, its context and practice. There are also entirely new—and separate—chapters on safety and on the environment. The final chapter attempts to set out priorities for the years to 2000 and beyond.

It is dedicated as previously to the leading figures, past and present in the shipping world with whom it has been the privilege of the authors to work, and to our respective wives, Moira and Deborah, without whose support, understanding and patience this work would have been impossible. The hope, as previously, is that it will kindle—or rekindle—in readers worldwide a deep and abiding interest in the intricacies and fascination of the international shipping industry.

London, UK   Mark Brownrigg
July 1997   Bruce Farthing

About the Authors

Bruce Farthing, MA (CANTAB) FIMgt, Barrister of the Inner Temple Deputy director general of the UK Chamber of Shipping, 1976–1983; rapporteur of the Maritime Transport Commission, International Chamber of Commerce, 1976–1996; consultant director of the International Association of Dry Cargo Shipowners (INTERCARGO), 1983–1999. Earlier positions included that of secretary of the Committee of European Shipowners (CES), 1967–1974 and secretary general of the Council of European and Japanese National Shipowners' Association (CENSA), 1974–1976, as well as others in the Chamber of Shipping and the International Chamber of Shipping (ICS).

He was an elected member of the Court of Common Council and subsequently an alderman of the Corporation of London, representing the Ward of Aldgate (the Shipping Ward) until his death, 1981–2007. He was also a council member of the City University and a governor of the School of Oriental and African Studies of London University.

Bruce was one of the founders of Maritime London, an organisation with the mandate of promoting the UK's maritime business services, serving first as chairman and then honorary president.

Mark Brownrigg, OBE BA Director-General of the UK Chamber of Shipping since February 2003.

After taking his degree at Emmanuel College, Cambridge, he first joined the Chamber in 1972. He was the assistant to the secretary general of the European Community Shipowners' Association, 1973–1976.

From 1976 to 1983, he was Secretary of the International Shipping Federation, dealing with maritime labour matters.

From 1983 to 2003, he held various senior posts within the Chamber starting with responsibility for international shipping policy and gradually adding responsibility for national trade and economic policy matters and communications, and then all policy aspects.

He has been closely involved in several national and international shipping campaigns, including particularly the development of the UK's successful tonnage tax regime (which has led to the remarkable revival of the UK fleet since 2000) and helping to establish two active cluster organisations—Sea Vision (focused on profile, education and careers across the broad maritime cluster) and Maritime UK (a coalition of maritime services sectors, providing one voice for shipping, ports and maritime business in the UK). He is also a founding board member of Maritime London, a trade promotion body for the UK's maritime business services.

Proshanto K. Mukherjee, LL.B. (Dalhousie) Ph.D. (Wales), Barrister and Solicitor, Notary Public (Ontario, Canada), FNI, AFRIN, Master Mariner Professor of maritime law and director of the postgraduate maritime law programme, Lund University; professor of maritime law and policy, World Maritime University; former vice president (research), World Maritime University; former senior deputy director and professor of maritime law, International Maritime Law Institute; former IMO legal adviser, Caribbean Region; former senior adviser, Maritime Policy and International Affairs, Canadian Hydrographic Service.

Professor Mukherjee served 16 years at sea from cadet to master on ships under various flags. He read law at Dalhousie University and obtained his Ph.D. from University of Wales. He is honorary research fellow at Swansea University and is visiting professor at Dalian Maritime University (China), Chung Ang University (Seoul, S. Korea) and National University of Juridical Sciences (Kolkata, India). He has drafted maritime legislation for some 25 jurisdictions worldwide and has published extensively on numerous public and private maritime law subjects. He is the author of *Maritime Legislation*, the only book of its kind addressing the theory and practice of the subject.

Acknowledgements

The authors are deeply grateful to Dr. Jingjing Xu, professor of maritime law and economics at University of Plymouth, Dr. Max Mejia, professor of maritime law and policy at World Maritime University, Dr. Abhinayan Basu Bal, lecturer in maritime law at Lund University and post-doctoral fellow at Gothenburg University; Donald Chard, formerly until retirement in 2012 was Head of Legal, Insurance and Documentary at the UK Chamber of Shipping and is now a maritime arbitrator; and David Balston, Director—Safety and Environment also at the UK Chamber, for their valuable contribution to the fourth edition. Their individual contributions have done much to ensure that the full breadth of the issues has been covered in an up-to-date way.

The authors also acknowledge the administrative and research assistance given by Carla Escalante Fischer, MBA, senior faculty assistant at WMU and Ying Fang, Jolyn Tay Ling and Bui Phi Bich Lien, Nadiya Isikova, M.Sc. graduates of WMU, Olena Bokareva, doctoral scholar at Lund University and Abhisaran Basu Bal, LL. M. graduate of Lund University.

Our appreciation extends to many friends, colleagues and others in the shipping world who have commented on texts and provided additional information and documents for this and/or earlier editions. These include the representatives of many of the various organisations mentioned in the book and colleagues past and present from a number of international and national shipping organisations—particularly Alfons Guinier and Herman de Meester (the European Community Shipowners' Association), Chris Horrocks (then with the International Chamber of Shipping), David Dearsley (then with the International Shipping Federation), Gavin Simmonds and Anastasia Frisk (the UK Chamber of Shipping), Steve Miller (US Department of State), Takashi Ishikawa (the Japanese Shipowners' Association) and Bruce's former colleagues at the International Association of Dry Cargo Shipowners. Without the sum of their help and cooperation, the book would not have been possible.

We are grateful to Springer Publications for editing and publishing the book and for compiling the index.

Contents

Table of Abbreviations

AIS	Automatic Identification System
ARPA	Automatic Radar Plotting Aid
ASC	Asian Shippers' Council
ASF	Asian Shipowners' Forum
BAF	Bunker adjustment factors
BIMCO	Baltic and International Maritime Council
CAF	Currency adjustment factors
CCI	Competition Commission of India
CENSA	Council of European and Japanese National Shipowners' Associations
CLIA	Cruise Lines International Association
CMI	Comité Maritime International
CO_2	Carbon dioxide
COFR	Certificate of Financial Responsibility
COPE	Compensation for Oil Pollution in European Waters Scheme
CRISTAL	Contract Regarding a Supplement to Tanker Liability for Oil Pollution
CSG	Consultative Shipping Group
DOC	Document of Compliance
DP	Designated person
ECASBA	European Community Association of Ship Brokers and Agents
ECC	European Cruise Council
ECDIS	Electronic chart display information system
ECJ	European Court of Justice
ECSA	European Community Shipowners' Associations
EEDI	Energy Efficiency Design Index
EEOI	Energy Efficiency Operational Indicator
EEZ	Exclusive Economic Zone
ELAA	European Liner Affairs Association

EMSA	European Maritime Safety Agency
EPIRB	Emergency Position Indicating Radio Beacon
ESPO	European Sea Ports Organisation
ETS	Emissions Trading Scheme
FASA	Federation of ASEAN Shipowners' Associations
FIATA	International Federation of Freight Forwarders Associations
FOC	Flags of Convenience
FONASBA	Federation of National Associations of Shipbrokers and Agents
FSI	Flag State Implementation
GATT	General Agreement on Tariffs and Trade
GHG	Greenhouse gas
GPS	Global Positioning System
GSF	Global Shippers' Forum
HELMEPA	Hellenic Marine Environment Protection Association
HSSC	Harmonized System of Surveys and Certification
IACS	International Association of Classification Societies
IAPH	International Association of Ports and Harbours
ICC	International Chamber of Commerce
ICC	Interstate Commerce Commission (US)
ICS	International Chamber of Shipping
ICS	Institute of Chartered Shipbrokers
ILO	International Labour Organization
IMB	International Maritime Bureau
IMCO	Inter-Governmental Maritime Consultative Organization
IMF	International Monetary Fund
IMIF	International Maritime Industries Forum
IMO	International Maritime Organization
INTERCARGO	International Association of Dry Cargo Shipowners
INTERTANKO	Independent Tanker Owners Association
IOPC Fund	International Oil Pollution Compensation Fund
IPTA	International Parcel Tankers Association
ISF	International Shipping Federation
ISU	International Salvage Union
ITC	International Tonnage Convention, 1969
ITCP	Integrated Technical Cooperation Programme
ITF	International Transportworkers' Federation
ITOPF	International Tanker Owners Pollution Federation
IUA	International Underwriting Association
IUMI	International Union of Marine Insurance
LMA	Lloyd's Market Association
LMAA	London Maritime Arbitrators' Association
LNG	Liquid natural gas
LPG	Liquefied petroleum gas
MAP	Mediterranean Action Plan
MBM	Market-based measures

MCA	Maritime and Coastguard Agency of the United Kingdom
MEPC	Marine Environment Protection Committee (IMO)
MET	Maritime education and training
MGO	Marine gas oil
MOU	Memorandum of Understanding
MSC	Maritime Safety Committee (IMO)
NITL	National Industrial Transportation League
NOX	Nitrogen oxides
OCIMF	Oil Companies International Marine Forum
ODMACS	Oil discharge control and monitoring system
OECD	Organisation for Economic Co-operation and Development
P&I Clubs	International Group of Protection and Indemnity Clubs
PSC	Port State Control
PSJ	Port State Jurisdiction
QSCS	IACS Quality System Certification Scheme
REMPEC	Regional Marine Pollution Emergency Response Centre
RO	Recognized Organizations
ROCC	Regional Oil Combating Centre
SDR	Special drawing right
SECA	Sulphur emission control area
SEEMP	Ship Energy Efficiency Management Plan
SIGTTO	Society of International Gas Tanker & Terminal Operators
SMC	Safety Management Certificate
SMS	Safety management system
SOPEP	Shipboard oil pollution emergency plans
SOX	Sulphur oxides
SSE	Shanghai Shipping Exchange
TEU	Twenty-foot equivalent units
TFEU	Treaty on the Functioning of the European Union
TOPIA	Tanker Oil Pollution Indemnification Agreement
UNCITRAL	United Nations Commission for International Trade Law
UNCLOS	United Nations Convention on the Law of the Sea, 1982
UNCTAD	United Nations Conference on Trade and Development
UNDP	United Nations Development Programme
UNFCCC	United Nation Framework Convention on Climate change
VOCs	Volatile organic compounds
WCO	World Customs Organization
WMU	World Maritime University
WSC	World Shipping Council
WTO	World Trade Organization

Chapter 1
Introduction: Freedom in International Shipping

Shipping, of all industries, is the most international. It has to be viewed, therefore, not from a narrow national or indeed nationalistic viewpoint, but against the broad sweep of world developments, particularly in the trade sector. After all, some 75 % of the world's surface is covered by the vast oceans, over 80 % of world trade moves in whole or in part by sea, and since time immemorial humankind has voyaged upon these oceans for the purpose of trading.

Indeed, ocean voyages were undertaken before land travel; there were sailors before farmers and shepherds; ships before settlements; and it was easier to transport goods, often over very long distances, by sea rather than over land. Methods of propulsion have, or course, evolved: originally the punt or paddle, then some 8,000 years ago the sail, then the steam engine and today the diesel engine and even nuclear power. There are also some who have seen the sail—wind power—as a supplementary means of propulsion in order to save energy. But this has yet to be proved a viable commercial option.

The central thread running through this book is the notion of freedom in international shipping. The narrow connotation of this phrase is manifested in one of the strands of the concept in public international law of freedom of the seas, namely, the ability for all to navigate the oceans and to enter and leave ports of other nations without let or hindrance. There is also the much wider connotation, namely, the freedom to trade one's ships without interference in commercial operations by others, particularly foreign governments. Both these dimensions, whilst distinct in themselves, often as subjects of public international law or private maritime law, respectively, have none the less been subject to various erosions. These are such that today the more technical aspects of shipping—navigation, safety, construction, stability, pollution control, to name but a few—are increasingly subject to governmental regulation, primarily international but also regional or national. The ability of shipowners to trade their ships from the commercial and economic standpoints free from governmental regulation has been, and continues to be, significantly eroded in various ways. This is seen to be for the general good.

In this book these erosions are traced and put into historical perspective. The origins and role of the various bodies, institutions and organisations of a governmental and a private nature are also explained. Through this, an understanding of the framework within which international shipping operates and the interface between governmental and commercial policies and practices will hopefully be gained.

Early Development of Maritime Law

Early maritime law, as with other branches of the law, was "custom-built"; it was a series of standards which survived the rise and fall of regimes and which eventually emerged as a codification. Its history is lost in antiquity but we know that it evolved from the customs and practices of early merchants and seafarers and was largely private and commercial in character. There is historical evidence that sea trade flourished in the ancient civilizations of India, China and the Middle East. In the late third and the second millennium BC, there was active sea-borne trade between the peoples of the Indus Valley civilization and the Sumerians and Akkadians of the Tigris-Euphrates basin. But there is little or no record of the maritime customs or laws of those pre-historic times. The earliest recorded mention of maritime law is in the Babylonian Code of Hammurabi dating back to the period between 2000 and 1600 BC. The rules which codified earlier Sumerian customs and practices, extended to marine collisions, bottomry and ship leases.

Certain elements of what today would be termed private maritime law are seen in the early Eastern Mediterranean civilisations of the Phoenicians. These include elements of insurance law, rules relating to salvage and to the carriage of goods by sea, compensation for seamen lost or injured and the like. A sketchy public law system also emerged in the form of protection by warships of merchant ships from pirates so as to enable them to continue to trade. In short, it constituted public protection of private maritime commerce.

In time the island of Rhodes became the main maritime power in the Eastern Mediterranean. To it we owe the first comprehensive maritime code. This not only regulated commerce in the region for a very long time but was also the foundation of sea law for the next 1,000 years. It was probably a codification of various ancient legal principles regarding navigation and commerce. It provided for exclusive jurisdiction over its own and adjacent seas. In short, it meant freedom for its own commerce and trade but necessarily therefore, a restriction on others. This is a concept, in part a dilemma, frequently seen during the history of maritime affairs. Even those who espouse freedom in shipping today, often really mean freedom for themselves on the back of restrictions on others.

Later, supremacy passed to the Greeks and a law governing maritime matters began to develop. This covered such elements as:

- The treatment of shipwrecked sailors.
- The jurisdiction of those courts dealing with maritime matters.
- Rules regarding blockade and piracy.

- The settlement of disputes arising under maritime contracts (early commercial courts).
- The role of prize courts, namely those to which recourse could be made in the event that persons felt they had been deprived improperly of their property (vessels, cargo, etc.).

There was a mixture of "private" law and "public" law elements—private in the sense that the rules governed relationships between private parties; public in the sense of governing the rights, duties and obligations of states. The Mediterranean, being bordered by many states, was common to all. The Greek policy was one of unmolested navigation, once enforced by vessels of war, later enshrined as a legal principle—an early stirring of the freedom to navigate encouched within the principle of the freedom of the seas.

The next stage in the evolutionary process was Roman maritime policy. As in English law, much of it was not codified although based on the Greek and Rhodian laws. Its strength stemmed largely from the *pax romana* which gave almost unchallenged security of commerce throughout the then known world. The Rhodian Sea Law was adopted by the Romans and evidence of this is found in two famous passages in the Justinian Digests regarding the law of jettison, the root of the peculiar maritime notion of general average. Piracy and brigandage had been banished and Roman commerce flourished. It is indeed most unfortunate that the menace of piracy has returned and is again rife in certain parts of the world. The contemporary problem of piracy is addressed in a later chapter under the topic of maritime security, which is a matter of major concern today.

The Roman maritime law covered *inter alia*:

- *The Sea*: this should be "open", but as it was under the strict control of the Romans, it lay within their ability to close it to others.
- *The Ship*: ships were classified, for example, into passenger, commercial/cargo and whether inland or sea-going. The law dealt with the rights, duties and obligations of those connected with the ship such as the owner, master, crew, pilot, shippers (cargo interests) and passengers.
- *The Cargo*: there was no obligation on the Roman ship (or shipowner) to receive cargo, but if he did then he was liable for its safety on board and for its safe delivery. It was during this period that the principle of general average probably emanated, namely that when it became necessary to jettison cargo in order to lighten the ship, this was regarded as for the good of all and accordingly compensation should be contributed by all parties to the common venture. On the other hand, no principle of salvage was known, namely payment to those assisting or saving a vessel in distress.
- *Responsibilities/obligations of those in shipping*: this covered the rules governing chartering (hiring) of the whole or part of a vessel, the implied authority of the master, for example, to effect urgent repairs, or purchase equipment in order that the voyage could proceed; and the general subject of special loans to those engaged in maritime ventures.

- *Settlement of disputes*: disputes arising under any of the above heads were subject to established rules of procedure and jurisdiction, but different procedures were applied depending on whether the acts or injuries were internal, namely committed or suffered on board, or whether they arose from external events such as collisions or damage by others.

Thus, an early system of law covering maritime affairs developed, much of it being relevant as the basis, in part, of the private law as we know it today.

The eventual breakdown and disintegration of the Roman Empire and the subsequent period of lawlessness and confrontation between Islam and Christianity (seen again today), gave way to another formative period in the history of maritime affairs. The growth of the Mediterranean littoral (coastal) states meant that there was need for new or redefined maritime laws and these were provided by a number of city states which today have, in the main, no interest or importance in maritime affairs. They included Venice, Amalfi, Trani (on the Adriatic Sea), Pisa (now inland but once an important trading centre), Genoa, Marseilles, Jerusalem (another important trading centre after the Crusades) and Oleron (a small island off La Rochelle, in France, once English territory and an important trading centre).

All these trading centres developed their own codified maritime laws, essentially based upon trust, which in an otherwise lawless period enabled commerce to continue. It should never be forgotten that shipping is the handmaiden of trade and commerce. Without trade, it is nothing. All these states in their way, made a contribution towards the development of maritime law as we know it today.

Oleron has a special significance in that the laws or customs of Oleron are contained in a fifteenth century illuminated manuscript known as the Black Book of Admiralty. This is preserved amongst the records of the High Court of Admiralty at the Public Records Office in London. The Black Book itself is a compilation of rules and precedents affecting the administration of maritime law and the functions of the Lord High Admiral of England and the officers of the Court.

The laws or customs of Oleron contained in the Black Book are amongst the oldest medieval sea laws known to survive. They are said to be the outcome of the privileges granted to the commune of Oleron by the Duke of Aquitaine before the marriage of his daughter, Eleanor of Aquitaine, to King Henry II of England, when the island passed into the possession of the English Crown.

It is of interest that a facsimile copy of the Laws of Oleron from the Black Book of Admiralty was reproduced in a special limited edition to celebrate the sixth centenary of the Admiralty Court in June 1960 and was presented to the people of Oleron by subscribers from the United Kingdom and the United States.

Further Developments: Fifteenth and Sixteenth Centuries

The previous section traced the early development of certain principles and concepts of maritime law with the emphasis on limited private rights, obligations and duties, and some stirrings about the public law concept of the freedom of the seas. It also covered the shift of maritime power and influence from the Eastern Mediterranean to Rome and then to the city states and the beginning of the move further west, even to the Atlantic coast of Europe.

During the remarkable period of European expansion and exploration in the fifteenth and sixteenth centuries, the emphasis was not only on the continued development of private commercial law, but more particularly, the development of the public law concepts regarding ownership of the seas that went hand in hand with trade and commerce.

Thus occurred the further development of commercial maritime law in new areas—Spain, the Hanseatic League and the Baltic—and the continued drift of the centres of power and influence from the east towards the west and then northwards into Europe and the Baltic states. Today that drift is reversed towards centres in the East such as the Middle East, India, Singapore, China, Hong Kong, Korea, and Japan.

Barcelona was a major trading and maritime centre from as early as the thirteenth century. By the fifteenth century the Maritime Code of Barcelona held the same position as had the Rhodian law in its day. Whilst, in essence, an updating of all Mediterranean laws, it had some 300 chapters setting out detailed answers to the many and manifold practical and legal difficulties of the times in maritime commercial and trading affairs.

The same period saw the development of the Sea Laws of Visby, a town situated in the island of Gotland in the Baltic Sea, which is now a part of Sweden, and the name has been commemorated in the twentieth century through the "Visby" amendments to the Hague Rules 1924 (which govern the conditions for the carriage of goods by sea). It also saw the rise of the powerful Hanseatic League towns, notably Hamburg, Lübeck and Bremen. The first and last of these have remained great maritime centres to this day, with Lübeck now being of less importance in that context.

With the exception of today's European Union (EU), the Hanseatic League was probably the strongest multinational alliance Europe has ever seen, comprising at its height nearly 80 cities. They banded together for the purpose of trade and commerce and to control piracy and other harmful activities. Their maritime law, the Hansa Towns Shipping Ordinance, was a comprehensive code covering essentially private law relationships.

Inevitably, for reasons of power and prestige, attempts were made by many of the shipping centres and groups touched on in this chapter, not only to lay down commercial principles but to exercise some measure of control over the seas adjoining their territories. And many were the claims, counter-claims and disputes. Examples can be seen in Venice claiming jurisdiction over the Adriatic Sea, Genoa over the Ligurian Sea and Norway over much of the North Sea and the area between it and the Shetlands, Iceland and Greenland.

But it was not until the great voyages of discovery by the new maritime superpowers of Spain and Portugal that attempts to close great tracts of the world's oceans for the exclusive use of one nation were seen. It is beyond the scope of this analysis of the principles of "freedom" and its "erosion" to recount the many and awe-inspiring voyages of discovery during this period. Suffice it to say that more than 500 years ago in May 1493, after the return of Columbus from his first voyage of discovery, a papal bull was issued (a decree constituting the highest form of legal direction at the time) which purported not only to divide between Spain and Portugal all lands discovered, or to be discovered, but also to set a line dividing the oceans between the two nations so as to give each exclusive use. Forces were thereby set in train which meant inevitably that, at some future date, an agreement would have to be reached on a public law regime for the seas.

It is no surprise that in both France and England the Pope's division of the seas was rejected. Indeed, when the Spanish complained to Elizabeth I of England about violations of the papal decree endorsing the principle of "mare clausum" espoused by Spain and Portugal, they were told that it was "contrary to the law of nations" to prohibit the English from carrying on commerce in those regions and that they would continue to navigate the oceans since "the use of the sea and the air is common to all: neither can any title to the ocean belong to any people or private man".

This must be regarded as one of the first recorded statements of the principle of the freedom of the seas, although in essence it was then no more than a unilateral assertion by one sovereign state. It was neither universally accepted, nor indeed formulated in any depth, however much the sentiment may be applauded today. This was not to come about until much later.

The Rise and Fall of Nations and Freedom in International Shipping

The fifteenth and sixteenth centuries saw the birth of many of the principles of today's maritime law. The years that followed marked the beginning of the rise of English maritime supremacy; the fall of the Iberian nations, Spain and Portugal, from their previous positions of eminence and strength; the rise and fall of the Dutch as a sea power; the development of a fully codified maritime law in France as a result of its growth as a trading and mercantile nation; and the first real attempt to enunciate the principle of the freedom of the seas.

It is not intended to attempt to trace these developments in any detail. The period up to the nineteenth century is extremely complex and requires specialist study. All that can be attempted is to highlight the most important features in the historical evolution of today's maritime world.

The early sixteenth century saw England as a maritime nation of little importance and modest trade. The Tudor monarchs, however, began a trend which eventually led to British dominance of seaborne trade. Henry VII (1485–1509) was a man who displayed a grasp of economic and commercial principles not normally found in British monarchs. It was he who saw the need for maritime commerce and who thus has a special place in history as the man who passed the first "navigation" laws, namely laws which gave a preferential position to English vessels in the carriage of cargo to and from Britain. Thus he created the principle of flag discrimination (a form of protectionism often termed cargo reservation or cargo preference) which has been, and remains, a matter of a major policy debate and conflict to this day. As such it is an erosion of free-trade principles and a maritime example of protectionism.

The sixteenth and seventeenth centuries also saw the Dutch developing into a major commercial, trading and maritime nation. It has been said that whilst the English were drawn to the sea (and still are today) the Dutch were "driven to it", because their small, loose-knit, country was unable to support its people and was in any event constantly being ravaged by wars. It was the growth of Dutch seaborne trade which led to conflict with others and to the pronouncements of their famous philosopher and jurist, Hugo de Groot ("Grotius" in latin), about freedom of the seas which essentially focused on freedom to navigate the seas and to engage in global trade through shipping.

In essence what Grotius, in his famous treatise *Mare Liberum* of 1605, sought to contest was the right which Portugal took upon itself to prohibit all others from engaging in seaborne commerce with the East Indies. The Portuguese took the position that they had proprietary rights over both land and sea as a result of the papal decree, in exercise of the Pope's spiritual powers, referred to earlier. Drawing on Rhodian and Roman law and practices in the Mediterranean, Grotius argued that the seas were *res nullius* and incapable of occupation, and further, that the Portuguese had not "legally" occupied the "Indies" (whatever the spiritual position might have been) and had no title to "occupy" the seas. In short, he was the first man to set out in any detail the legal principle (despite stutterings to somewhat similar effect in earlier years) that "navigation was free to all and that no one country could lay claim to the seas on the basis that their navigators were the first to sail on it". Thus, almost by accident, the great freedom of the seas principle was first enunciated. A cynic could well argue that Grotius' claim was no more, and no less, than a special pleading by a young lawyer—he was only 21 at the time—in support of his country's claim for freedom to trade Dutch vessels to the Indies. However, the principle caught the imagination of the times and gradually became accepted by custom. It was not until much later that the customary law became fully enshrined in public international law through treaty.

Ironically, it was an English legal scholar, John Selden, who opposed the doctrine of *Mare Liberum* in his responsive work in 1635 known as *Mare Clausum* in which he claimed that the seas were indeed capable of being enclosed and appropriated by exercise of maritime sovereignty.

The mid-seventeenth century also saw France developing new expansionist policies: increased home production in both agriculture and industry; expansion of its merchant shipping and the navy; and lastly, directly linked to shipping, the expansion of her colonies and the consolidation of world markets. However, wars and conflicts eventually stultified all these efforts.

What was left was a code of maritime laws which has been described as the "Maritime Code of Europe". This was the first comprehensive code developed by any major state at the time. It is not significant in the public law context, as illustrating the principle of the freedom of the seas; its significance lies in its comprehensive coverage of all aspects of maritime business and the fact that it drew heavily on earlier legal systems: Rhodian and Roman law as well as the Visby, Oleron and Hanseatic codes. It was incorporated in due course into the famous codification of French law known as the Code Napoleon of 1806.

This whole period, which marked the rise and fall of nations as maritime trading powers, underlined the importance of sea power, an importance which history has continued to show both in times of war and times of peace.

Growth of English Maritime Power and the Navigation Acts

As already explained, it was King Henry VII of England who first introduced a flag discriminatory law in favour of English vessels. It is a matter of historic fact—and very important for this whole historical analysis—to record that the real growth of British maritime power stemmed from the strengthening of the Navigation Acts in 1651 under Oliver Cromwell, and their subsequent development and enforcement.

The effect was that the significantly expanding trade to and from British colonies had to be carried in British ships. No foreign-built ships were to be used. Commodities of all sorts, particularly strategic commodities, had to be enumerated and their carriage regulated and controlled so that other nations could not participate in their carriage. Additionally, British shipowners were given special grants for the carriage of specified exports such as corn and other agricultural products.

After the restoration of the monarchy in 1660 the laws were further strengthened in favour of British ships and shipping. For example, colonial, namely American, ships had to be routed through English ports where a levy was imposed.

The seventeenth and eighteenth centuries in Europe were periods of great conflict and many wars. The battles between the English and the French in particular were largely either about the acquisition of new colonies or because of fears of expansion by one or other country. In all these, sea power was of paramount importance. At the beginning of the eighteenth century England was *a* sea power; at the end of the century she was *the* sea power. And, whilst seventeenth century England had few overseas possessions, by the early nineteenth century after the Napoleonic Wars, she had, despite the loss of the American Colonies, major new colonies, namely, Canada, the Cape Colony in South Africa, all of the Indian sub-continent, Australia and New Zealand. The Navigation Acts required all these extensive new possessions to be served by British ships. As a result of this, and the very substantial exports of coal, it is not surprising that the fleet expanded by leaps and bounds. Indeed, this continued at least until the First World War but not, during later years, as a result of a protectionist policy but of a free-trade expansionist policy, albeit from a position of great strength.

The pressures that led to this change of philosophy and indeed to the partial repeal of the Navigation Acts in 1841 and their final repeal in 1853, are complex and interrelated. Three factors, however, stand out. The first—and this is significant when we later consider pressures today for protection by whatever countries—was that Britain and British shipowners were so strong that they no longer needed protection. Rather, they wanted freedom, for example, to use non-British ships on certain of the more dangerous trades, and freedom generally. From the vantage point of commercial strength, freedom was obviously more desirable.

The second was that after years of conflict the new division of Europe, as a result of the Congress of Vienna in 1815, led to a more settled period in which governmental matters were seen as being increasingly for governments alone; and commercial (including maritime) matters for the commercial parties as long as commerce continued to provide a strong base for tax revenue. This was the beginning of the *laissez-faire* philosophy under which maritime/commercial affairs were left to their own devices.

The third factor was that, whilst shipping had a low priority in the minds of public servants and governments (as it still has to this day), commerce *per se* was the very foundation of British expansion and prosperity.

All these factors, coupled with improved agriculture, the development of a canal system and ports, coal and its use as an industrial fuel, and the new textile trade, led to increased demand for the carriage of every type of goods to an expanding world. The Navigation Acts were increasingly seen as restrictive to trade, against *laissez-faire* principles and, as already explained, were finally repealed in 1853. But they are significant historically and for any understanding of maritime issues today.

The Contemporary Public International Law Concept of Freedom of the Seas

What then is meant by the principle of the freedom of the seas today and, in particular, for the traditional freedom to navigate upon the high seas and other zones? The principles are set out in the United Nations Convention on the Law of the Sea, 1982 (UNCLOS) which, after many years of work going back over 20 years and in a sense even to the work of the League of Nations in the 1930s, came into force in November 1994 following the necessary 60 ratifications or accessions. The convention has been given effect domestically through incorporation into national legislation in most important maritime states.

The convention brings together and codifies the legal regime governing virtually every activity in, over or under the sea, including on and below the seabed, and in clearly defined sea areas offshore each coastal and archipelagic state including on and under the high seas. One of these is the 200 nautical mile Exclusive Economic Zone (EEZ) claimed by most countries since 1977 and accepted thereafter under customary international law.

The convention provides freedom of navigation or other rights of access or passage to merchant ships, as follows:

- *In internal waters* (that is, in bays, rivers, canals, estuaries and ports), a right of access subject to the coastal state's sovereignty. It is noteworthy that in practice rights to enter and leave ports are widely enjoyed under bilateral treaties or under the 1923 Ports Convention.
- *In the territorial sea* (that is, up to 12 nautical miles seawards of the territorial sea baselines), a right of "innocent" passage, namely, passage that is not prejudicial to the peace, good order or security of the coastal state and is in conformity with international law.
- *In straits* (namely, a natural waterway used for international navigation between one area of the high seas or EEZ and another), a right of transit passage. It is a wider right than innocent passage and provides freedom of navigation for the continuous transit of the straits.
- *In archipelagic waters* (namely, waters enclosed by archipelagic baselines, that are neither internal waters nor territorial sea, but are interconnecting waters which along with other natural features and islands constitute an archipelago), a right of innocent passage coupled with a right of passage through sea lanes designated by the archipelagic state in consultation with the "competent international organization", i.e. the International Maritime Organization (IMO).
- *In the contiguous zone* (namely, a zone contiguous to and beyond the territorial sea up to 24 nautical miles seawards of the territorial sea baselines), freedom of navigation subject to the coastal state's right to exercise the control necessary to prevent infringement of its customs, fiscal, immigration or sanitary laws and to punish such infringements committed within its territory or territorial sea.
- *In the Exclusive Economic Zone* (namely, a zone beyond and adjacent to the territorial sea extending up to 200 nautical miles seawards of the territorial sea baselines), freedom of navigation subject to the legislative and enforcement jurisdiction of the coastal state in relation to its sovereign rights over natural resources in the EEZ including rights over living and non-living and other economic resources, and jurisdiction with regard to the establishment and use of artificial islands, installations, and structures, marine scientific research and pollution control including the dumping of wastes and pollution from land-based and seabed activities. A coastal state may not, however, construct artificial islands, installations or structures which hinder international navigation in recognised sea lanes.
- *On the High Seas* (namely, all parts of the seas not included in the EEZ, the territorial sea, internal or archipelagic waters), freedom of navigation.

Thus the principle of freedom of navigation incorporated within the public international law doctrine of freedom of the seas remains virtually intact in the contiguous zone, the EEZ and the High Seas. It is to be noted in this context that the superjacent waters of the continental shelf, where the juridical shelf does not extend beyond 200 nautical miles from the territorial sea baselines, are part of the EEZ. Where the juridical shelf extends beyond that limit, the superjacent waters seaward of 200 nautical miles form part of the High Seas. In other waters, vessels have rights of access, innocent passage and transit passage. Such limitations as there are on the rights of navigation have been the subject of detailed and lengthy negotiation at the international level for the general good.

It is pertinent to note in the present context that the "juridical" continental shelf, by definition, comprises the seabed and subsoil of submarine areas beyond the territorial sea, that constitutes a natural prolongation of a coastal state's land territory. The coastal state may establish its outer limit in accordance with Article 76 of UNCLOS. If the shelf is geomorphologically narrow, the limit is fixed at 200 nautical miles from the territorial sea baselines. If the shelf is geomorphologically wide, options are available for the establishment of a limit beyond 200 nautical miles. In the continental shelf the coastal state enjoys sovereign rights over natural resources, some of which are exclusive, subject to the provisions of Part VI of UNCLOS.

Freedom of International Shipping Today

The concept of freedom in international shipping in its widest context does not necessarily mean an absence of regulation. What it does mean is that no one state has the right unilaterally to regulate an activity such as shipping that is inherently international in scope; any regulation must be for the good of all. There are many examples of this type of regulation which will be discussed later. Equally, there are many cases where individual nations have unilaterally sought to regulate for their own benefit. This latter type of regulation often covers the economic, trading and commercial aspects of shipping and is a clear erosion of the wider meaning of freedom in the context of international shipping. This includes:

- Freedom to trade with other nations either in the "direct" trades between two nations or as a third flag or cross-traders, that is, the freedom to trade between two nations neither of which is one's own.
- Freedom from governmental regulation in respect of the commercial/economic/operational aspects of shipping.
- Freedom to operate under a flag of choice, with crew of choice and with management and control where most convenient and economic.

It also connotes acceptance of the general principles of free enterprise, open competition and economic freedom; a principle which has gained considerable ground in recent years in the countries which previously favoured state control.

Chapter 2
Shipping as a Vital Service to World Trade

The Shipowning Business

A 100 years or more ago many shipowners started as ships' captains who had bought their own vessels and who sailed with them. Such men were complete masters of every aspect of the "shipowning" business; most were also traders, shipping and trade, then as now, going hand in hand. Later they remained ashore, employing their own captains as their fleets grew. Yet they retained full control of their businesses as indeed do some true shipowners today, notably in Greece and Norway, where they form a particular élite in their own countries.

During the second half of the twentieth century the true shipowner has become increasingly rare although by no means extinct, despite the fact that in the traditional shipping nations many of the famous shipping names have largely disappeared. Liner shipping especially, even before the change to containerisation, was increasingly run by the executives of shipping lines who, although afforded the title "shipowner" in industry parlance, certainly did not "own" any ship themselves although they may have been shareholders in the company. Thus shipowning has become increasingly, although not entirely, depersonalised.

With this change has come a change in approach. The true shipowner 50 years ago was in shipping because his father, his grandfather and often his great-grandfather, had been in it. Shipping was in his blood. He heard it talked about from his early childhood because shipping people tend to find it all-absorbing. In due time he joined his father and began to "learn the ropes"—itself a shipping expression from the days of sail—on board, in the office, at home and abroad. There was no question but that he would stay in the business and hand it on in due time to his own family. This was the pattern of the "true" shipowning family of which there were many in Western Europe, Scandinavia, Greece and elsewhere. Naturally there were many others who became shipowners, or chief executives, who were every bit as good, sometimes better than those born to it. The point is that shipowning was not so much a business as a way of life and, as history shows, frequently a very profitable one which carried with it much prestige, but equally much risk. To the

P.K. Mukherjee and M. Brownrigg, *Farthing on International Shipping*,
WMU Studies in Maritime Affairs, Vol. 1, DOI 10.1007/978-3-642-34598-2_2,
© Springer-Verlag Berlin Heidelberg 2013

new shipowning families and companies, particularly those in the Far East, the enterprise is very much a business, to make money but also to show the national flag.

But, while the romance of shipping remains, the always risky business of owning, operating and managing ships is today dominated by the balance sheet, the bottom line and quality control systems. These are perceived to be novel but in reality the true shipowner has always been vitally concerned with quality. Many shipping companies, let alone shipowners themselves, no longer own their ships. These have been financed by the banks or in other ways; or may very well have been repossessed because of defaults in repayment of loans. True ownership is thus often elsewhere than is assumed.

Old established companies in the traditional maritime nations have also increasingly turned to ship management and running the fleets of others, either at home or abroad, as their sole "shipping" activity. Ship management itself has become a new industry within the industry. Others have diversified so as to become not just shipping companies but companies involved in other aspects of transport, warehousing and the like. And some have diversified to such an extent that the shipping, or other aspects of the transport of goods ("transportation" to Americans and, today, to many others) is so small as to form only a peripheral part of their total operation. Others have, as the result of a conscious decision or through force of circumstances, simply left shipping entirely.

Shipowning, always an international business, is played on the liner side, very much with international partners and in fully international consortia or groups. But whatever the sector, other than home trades and generally the ferries, it is international pressures whether from government edict, famine, drought, failure of crops, insurrection—one could go on—which dominate the picture, coupled with a feel for what the market is doing. A fascinating, complex, intriguing, but above all, a risky business where fortunes have been, and will again be made. Equally many fortunes have been lost. It is not for the faint-hearted.

Vital to World Trade

A ship, whatever its type, size or flag, is nothing by itself; its purpose is solely to transport cargoes, be they manufactured goods in containers, bulk cargoes wet or dry in huge tankers and bulk carriers, specialised carriers for cars, livestock, cement, timber and other special cargoes, or passengers in cruise ships or ferries whether for pleasure or just to travel elsewhere. Equally world trade without shipping would quickly come to a halt. Lights would go out through power stations having no coal or oil; breakfast tables would be bereft of cereals; cars would be unavailable as exports or imports because of lack of iron ore to make steel and spares would be in short supply. As already stated, more than 80 % of world trade moves in whole or in part by sea.

Yet to much of the general public, shipping is seen only in the light of tragic incidents of whatever nature—lost lives, oiled seabirds or ruined beaches. To others it is seen as unnecessary since today "everything goes by air". Those who think this have not paused to consider the immense tonnages of oil, primary commodities and manufactured goods which are carried by sea day in day out, year in year out, over very long distances—safely, cheaply, efficiently without fuss or incident, in an environmentally friendly manner. Aircraft carry only a fraction of world trade. Casualties understandably catch the attention of the media and are often horrifying, certainly dramatic. But they are the exception, not the norm.

The shipping industry may in part be responsible for this and today it is trying by various means to achieve a better understanding of its importance. Perhaps for too long it has been content to be a silent service quietly getting on with its business. But there are other reasons. Ships nowadays are rarely seen in cities at all let alone in capital cities, apart from some exceptions like Hong Kong, Piraeus, Singapore, San Francisco, Cape Town and Sydney. Certainly ships are rarely seen today at the piers in down town New York and almost never in the Pool of London whereas 60 years ago, and even more so 100 years ago, both were scenes of tremendous shipping activity. Today ships invariably load and discharge at isolated terminals, sometimes miles offshore and certainly far from centres of population.

There was also a time when many young people dreamed of "going to sea", partly to travel, partly for adventure and often simply to earn some money and to have a job. Today seafaring has lost much of that appeal. Jet travel, even to the most exotic far away places is easy and for the package tourist comparatively cheap. The hunger of unemployment today is partly assuaged by social security benefits in the industrialised nations. Overall, the disadvantages of seafaring are given more prominence than the advantages. There is no getting away from the fact that a seafaring life inevitably means long periods away from home. This is especially difficult for those with a family. Yet conditions today are quite different from those endured by seafarers in earlier times. There are still adventures to experience and new places to be seen—many outside package itineraries. Responsibility is achieved early, promotion prospects are much better than previously and there are careers ashore in later life for the right people with seagoing experience. Today's seafarer also has control of very expensive ships and high-technology equipment demanding special skills from officers and crew.

The reality of shipping today is that:

- It is the prime method of carrying commodities, especially bulk commodities, over huge distances where all, or some element of sea passage is necessary.
- It is the most environmentally friendly means of transport.
- It is essentially safe: losses, groundings and collisions are the exception.
- It is the cheapest and most cost-effective means of transport for other than high-value, low-density cargoes.

Maritime Constituency

Shipping also provides employment and business opportunities for a wide range of people and shipowners require specialist technical and professional advice on a number of issues. Shipping is more than just ships. It is a joint venture among those directly involved as well as the involvement of a host of others essential for its operation. These include:

- Associations, either national or international, of shipowners devoted to their promotion and protection and trade unions concerned with the same on behalf of seafarers.
- Container building, leasing and operation.
- Financial services provided by a variety of banks and finance houses specialising in ship finance, mortgages, etc.
- Insurance provided by Lloyd's of London, insurance companies world wide and third party insurance provided by specialist Protection and Indemnity "Clubs".
- Legal services provided by lawyers specialising in various aspects of shipping, charterparties, bills of lading and litigation before Admiralty (Maritime) and Commercial Courts together with other methods of settling disputes through arbitration or conciliation.
- Navy/National Defence arrangements or associations.
- Operation and maintenance of ports, harbours and canals and related aspects, tugs, dredging, terminal equipment and maintenance.
- Provision of charts, both conventional and electronic, together with seafarers' almanacs, tables and so on.
- Salvage and emergency operations.
- Shipbreaking/demolition.
- Shipbroking on behalf of shipowners or charterers or engaged in the sale or purchase of ships.
- Shipbuilders/repairers responsible for the original construction and for repair and maintenance.
- Marine equipment manufacturers, who are responsible for up to 70 % of the cost of a ship.
- Social, charitable and other services provided by seafarers' welfare organisations.
- Supply services for victuals, stores, bunkers, waste disposal, recovery of used oil and all other ship's requirements.
- Technical and professional training for those entering, or thinking of entering the shipping industry or one of its related branches.
- Technical services provided by classification societies, naval architects, marine engineers and other technically qualified personnel.
- World wide communications and navigational networks through satellites and the provision of weather forecasting services.

- Whilst none of the above have—purposely—been put in any order of importance each are dependent either in whole or in part on ships and the shipping industry. Without shipping they would have no role.

Centres of Shipping

Although many ports and capitals world wide have significant elements of shipping activity, London has for years been regarded as the centre of the maritime world because it provides all the necessary services on a "one stop" basis. This goes back into history but especially to the seventeenth and eighteenth centuries when traders went to the City to buy their cargoes, to "rent" (charter) or purchase their ship, to insure the cargo and the ship, to set up a trading company and to find a book keeper. It also stems from the fact that, at the beginning of twentieth century, well over 50 % of the world fleet sailed under the Red Ensign. But there are today other factors:

- The International Maritime Organization (IMO) is located there. It is the only United Nations body in the United Kingdom.
- London is the home for many of the international shipping associations and organisations.
- London is the preferred centre for large expatriate shipping communities who find the welcoming attitude and tax regime better than elsewhere.
- The City contains a wealth of shipping expertise of all sorts available to the world maritime community—shipbrokers, Lloyd's, company insurers, consultants, P&I Clubs, average adjusters, lawyers, arbitrators, financiers, shipping accountants, etc.
- Institutions for shipping and transport related education, full or part-time.

The reduced size today of the British merchant marine, even after its remarkable revival over the last decade, raises the inevitable question as to how long the City of London can maintain its prominence in maritime business services over other shipping centres such as Oslo, Piraeus, Hamburg, Singapore, Hong Kong, Shanghai, Tokyo or New York, some of which have been aggressively promoting their offerings in recent years.

A less significant British merchant marine is not necessarily fatal in either the short or the long term, although the larger the fleet the easier it is for London to maintain its position. What would be disastrous would be if those many in the City of London, or the UK for that matter, with maritime or maritime-related skills which can only be acquired through seagoing experience or working in a shipping company, were to fail to respond to the romance of a great industry—a world wide industry—and were not to go out to that world with their expertise, flair and entrepreneurial skills. Although the City provides "one stop" services, those involved cannot afford just to sit in their offices. They must, can and do, travel frequently and extensively. The heritage of maritime London has been handed down to today's practitioners. It is in their hands. They must maintain and continue to improve their skills and service.

There is another factor. Too often is the City of London, with all its traditions, spoken of as "a leading" financial centre. This is far too narrow. The City from its early days has also been a great commercial, insurance, business and trading centre. The position of the City of London in the resolution of disputes is also important given the presence of the Admiralty and Commercial Courts and the many who practise in the area of maritime arbitration and conciliation.

It would take a great deal to dislodge London's pre-eminence in the maritime world. It will undoubtedly do its utmost to maintain that position even in this day of instant communications, based not only on the above factors but also the significant contribution it makes to the invisible earnings of the City and the UK economy.

Chapter 3
The Sectors of Shipping

Shipping does not comprise one industry but a number of them. The basic sectors are set out below. It is a peculiarity of shipping that each sector has its own clear character and style; and that those who work, even for a lifetime in one sector, often have little perception or understanding of others. Equally the sectors may well have different "political" perceptions even in the same country. Traditionally, deep sea operators will invariably have been for "freedom", while some in the cabotage or more localised trades may lean towards protectionism.

The container operator tends to believe that his sector is the only form of real shipping: and that those in the passenger sector, even in the days when there were scheduled services, were not "proper" shipowners. The bulk operator trading world wide on the open market "knows" that this is the only worthwhile type of shipping, and so on. There is also the factor that different nations, especially if one is thinking of the "traditional" shipping nations, tended historically to specialise in one sector or another. The Greeks and the Norwegians in bulk (or tramp) shipping, wet or dry; the British, Dutch, French, Germans, Italians and Japanese in the liner sector although the latter tend to be part of large diversified groups (descendants of the old Zaibatsu) which also includes ship yards, steel mills, car plants and sometimes even an airline. The typical Greek shipowner having several "one ship" companies for the carriage of the bulk cargoes, wet or dry, is poles apart from liner operators and rarely, if at all, do the twain meet in terms of philosophy, even if in the modern world they may meet socially or in other ways. US shipowners tended to operate in the subsidised liner trades, or in the tanker business whilst the newer shipowners from the Far East—Taiwan, Malaysia, Singapore and Korea—have broken into the liner trades. Those in Hong Kong, China (which has grown massively over the last 10–20 years), South Africa and South America have not sought to specialise in one sector or another but to meet perceived demands whatever the sector.

Since the initial editions of this book were written, there has also been substantial rationalisation in a number of sectors, which has seen the emergence of a few huge companies ahead of the pack. This is particularly the case in the container sector, where many of the older liner operators have disappeared; and no doubt further mergers lie ahead. The Maersk Company from Denmark is now the largest

P.K. Mukherjee and M. Brownrigg, *Farthing on International Shipping*,
WMU Studies in Maritime Affairs, Vol. 1, DOI 10.1007/978-3-642-34598-2_3,
© Springer-Verlag Berlin Heidelberg 2013

operator by a considerable margin, alongside the other very diverse interests in the group which include substantial tanker, dry bulk and off-shore support operations as well as ports and terminals. In the passenger sector, a similar thing has happened with the US-headquartered Carnival Corporation nowadays the largest operator, also head and shoulders above its nearest competitor. These and other developments, including the significant rise of new shipping involvements in all sectors in the Far East, particularly in China, mean that the nature of and approach to shipping in many countries has changed and is continuing to change, often in new ways which are not necessarily foreseeable.

Wet Bulk: The Tanker Sector

This sector is concerned with the carriage of "wet" cargoes—oil, chemicals, petroleum products—or anything in liquid form, in the tanks of specially designed vessels. Thus the phrase "tankers" or "tank vessels" as they were originally described. Vessels may range from the huge ultra-large or very large "crude carrier" tankers (ULCCs or VLCCs) of 250,000 tonnes or more deadweight (dwt), to small coasting or even canal and inland waterway vessels. Traditionally this sector was divided between those vessels owned by the oil majors (Exxon, BP, Shell, Total, Chevron, etc) and those owned by so-called "independent" shipowners (P&O, Bergesen, Mitsui, etc.). Indeed, it was this division which led to the establishment of the International Association of Independent Tanker Owners (Intertanko) as the voice of the "independent" tanker owner as opposed to the allegedly more powerful oil majors. Today this distinction is less obvious with the policy of many of the oil majors not to have their own ships but to charter (hire) those of others. Indeed, about half of all the oil shipped nowadays is owned by "oil traders" who charter tankers from the independent tanker owners.

The patterns of tanker trading are dictated by the main oil-producing and refining areas. Often tankers have long voyages from one relatively inhospitable oil-producing area to an equally inhospitable jetty miles from anywhere serving an oil refinery. But in common with their dry bulk counterparts, tankers trade where cargoes are on offer and not on any previously determined trade route. Although "wet" trading and "dry" trading have this common characteristic, the problems which confront them are by no means the same. The tanker operator, for example, is ever conscious of the need to avoid polluting the seas or beaches and the likely consequences if he does; the dry bulk shipowner is less concerned with this aspect (because by and large their cargoes do not pollute although their bunkers may) but is more concerned with the wider economic and commercial problems of the complex world trading patterns as regards the "dry" primary commodities. There is also a need to keep up with developments in the wider fields of law, finance, politico/economic changes and public relations.

During the last half of the twentieth century, specially constructed tankers with highly sophisticated containment systems have also been developed to carry liquefied petroleum and natural gas (LPG and LNG) for home usage and for power stations. Their carrying capacity is measured in cubic metres rather than tonnage and LNG ships in particular are now of substantial size. With declining oil reserves in the North Sea and other parts of the world and increasing public insistence on cleaner fuels, the demand for LNG has grown hugely in recent years. That demand and the numbers of LNG carriers are set to continue to increase well into the future.

Dry Bulk

This sector of shipping is concerned with the carriage in full shiploads of the world's primary "dry" commodities: coal, iron ore, grain, phosphates, fertilisers, sugar, etc. Again, as in the wet sector, the art is to find cargoes to match the ship and to cut ballast voyages to the minimum. But the world's trading requirements in the dry sector are far more complex than in the wet, and movements are very much dictated by the world economic situation. The dry bulk operator not only has to know his own market, but has to have a very keen eye for world developments, whether they be of an economic or political nature or a natural disaster or failure of a crop in one country or another.

As with the tankers, dry bulk shipping is of an essentially non-scheduled nature. Ships trade where cargoes are on offer and can be likened to the taxis of the shipping world plying for hire on the world's shipping exchanges, but primarily through brokers, mostly members of London's Baltic Exchange. Although some years ago there was a belief that ship sizes in the dry sector would increase dramatically, even up to 500,000 tonnes, this has not really happened. The typical bulk carrier trading world wide is somewhat smaller and in latter years there has been some emphasis on the so-called handy size (30,000–50,000 tonnes dwt) or the Panamax (the biggest ship that can transit the Panama Canal) of roughly 70,000 tonnes dwt. But there are also larger vessels, notably the Capesize of around 150,000 tonnes dwt and above for rounding the Cape. All these vessels are the real work-horses of the oceans.

Cargo Liners and Container Ships

Liners offer scheduled services on fixed routes at published—and generally stable—rates, unlike tramp ships, which ply for hire like taxis. They are the trains of international seaborne trade. They do not, in normal circumstances, offer the whole ship for hire (charter); they offer their customers (shippers) the facility of carrying individual packages, parcels, crates—or nowadays mostly containers—as part (less than full) ship loads. Traditionally, they advertise the days on which they will accept cargo for loading, when the vessel will close for loading and sail, together with the day on which she will arrive at her discharging port many thousands of miles away, indeed often at the far end of the world.

While the principle remains the same, practice has changed radically with the development of container services. A major difference has been in the size of the ships, which are measured in 20-foot equivalent units (TEUs) rather than by tonnage. While early container ships carried up to 1,000 TEUs (already performing the work of three to four earlier liner vessels), the scale of new buildings has increased massively over the years with the largest vessels today carrying up to 18,000 TEUs.

For more than 100 years, liner companies offering such services tended to form themselves into international associations, known as liner conferences, for the purpose of stability and rationalising the route (trade) in which they operated. This system and parallel forms of investment and operating co-operation called "consortia" will be explained later. Suffice it to say at this stage that while many liner companies operate as conference members, especially those from the traditional maritime states, this is by no means always the case. Any liner company may offer scheduled services outside the conference, as non-members; and many do so. But no line may offer services both within the conference and outside it.

Liner shipping, from the time of the change from sail to steam in the late nineteenth century until the middle of the 1960s, was seen by many as the cream of shipping. The liner companies vied with each other to produce visually attractive ships, dedicated to the service of one trade (or route), which sailed as regularly as clockwork whether full or empty. The stowage of all manner of different types of cargoes, largely manufactured goods, was an art. Not only had the right cargo to come out at the correct discharging port, and not be buried under a lot of other cargoes, but loading had to be such as to ensure the stability of the ship. It has been said, perhaps unkindly, that liner shipowners of former years were more concerned with the looks of their ships than with service to their customers, the shippers, although naturally good stowage was also to the benefit of shippers and the service itself increasingly an extension of the mass-production line.

The container revolution of the mid-1960s coupled with new political forces changed all that. While the conference system remained strong into the 1990s and still remains, albeit with significantly reduced scope and power because of regulatory changes, there no longer exist the large number of individual and individualistic liner owners of yesteryear. What we have today is a smaller number of family-owned or other large conglomerates—mostly multinational, made up from combinations of the original lines which operated container ships—alongside a number of newly emerging companies mainly in the Far East. The scheduling and regularity of service are still there and these fleets continue to assure the sea link in the international through-carriage of goods from one inland point to another inland point often thousands of miles away. They are a crucial part of the world's logistical supply chains, linking as necessary with land transport modes such as rail and truck.

The art of stowage of containers on board is now left to the computer. But not only that, the liner operation is still about customer service—punctual sailing, document accuracy, door-to-door service, local offices and trustworthy agents.

This has led to the development by lines of their own systems for electronic data exchange and equipment monitoring.

While the majority of the world's liner trades have today been containerised or have a facility for lorries/containers to be driven on and off (Ro/Ro), not all cargoes can be stuffed into containers, and some trades cannot support the massive capital investment necessary. There exists, therefore, a residue of liner services operating, largely as before the mid-1960s. But whatever the pattern, the essentials of liner trading still exist: fixed schedules, published rates of freight on a particular trade route for the carriage of individual parcels of largely manufactured goods. While liners carry the greatest proportion of the world's cargoes in terms of *value*, bulk ships carry the main burden in terms of *weight* and *volume*.

Coastal and Short Sea

Vessels operating in the coastal or so-called "short sea" (as opposed to deep sea) trades may operate either scheduled or tramp services. Their common characteristic is that they are small, or smallish, are specially designed for the particular circumstances and trades in which they operate or may operate, and their voyages are measured in terms of hours or days rather than weeks or months. As with their deep sea counterparts, they are essentially concerned with the carriage of a range of cargoes whether manufactured, specialised (for example, timber), or wet or dry bulk. This type of shipping is becoming increasingly favoured as a means of siphoning off cargoes from congested roads and from rail. The vessels naturally relate to barges and other craft operating in estuaries, canals and rivers.

Passenger Liners/Cruise Ships

Nowadays there are very few scheduled services by passenger vessels dedicated to a particular ocean route. Equally the cargo liner which carried 12 or more passengers as an ancillary operation to its main cargo-carrying role, is much rarer. The former is a direct result of the introduction of the wide-bodied jets, the latter the high cost of catering for the few. A contributory factor has been the whole development of the package tour and leisure industries.

On the other hand, the demise of the great passenger liners has given way to a remarkable growth in cruise ships. Whilst such ships may well make weekly or fortnightly cruises from, say New York or Miami to the Bahamas and back, or from Southampton to Mediterranean ports and return, from Far Eastern ports to Australia and back, they are not liners in the sense of shuttling back and forth across the Atlantic or down to Australia/New Zealand for the sole purpose of transporting passengers. The cruise ship is a floating resort dedicated to the leisure business. Whilst 40 years ago the belief was that the days of passenger ships were numbered, their reincarnation as part of the holiday resort business catering for the high-cost, largely but by no means entirely American market, has proved to be one of the few really profitable sectors in modern-day shipping. Another feature has been the development of so-called "fly/cruises". Passengers fly one way to join or leave the cruise ship. One or two shipping companies also offer very expensive round-the-world cruises, although it is possible just to join for a section of the cruise, another type of "fly/cruise". There are also educational cruises for children and others, for example, to see and learn about the antiquities of Greece and the Middle East or the ecology in places like the Galapagos Islands and the Antarctic.

Ferries

Ferries in the developed world have also changed out of all recognition in the last 40 years or more. Nowadays they are no longer small, cramped and uncomfortable, with little facility for carrying cars and vehicles. They are of substantial size—and growing—have high standards of comfort and stability but, above all, have the facility for cars and trucks to be driven on and off together with a considerable number of coaches and caravans, as well as catering for foot passengers. Indeed today, the carriage of "roll-on/roll-off" freight is in many cases the factor that facilitates the carriage of the passengers.

Strictly speaking, ferries perform scheduled liner services but their problems are quite different from those of deep sea, or even middle-range liner services. Neither do they operate in associations in the nature of liner conferences. Things have changed greatly also in some regions because of the new competitive situation brought about by the arrival of low-cost airlines, the building of alternative and often heavily subsidised land-based options such as bridges or tunnels (e.g. across the Channel), and the loss of duty-free sale revenues.

Generally, ferries show a sophistication and flexibility which was unknown 50 years ago and certainly prior to the Second World War. The 1987 *Herald of Free Enterprise* tragedy followed by the *Scandinavian Star* fire and the *Estonia* sinking in 1994 highlighted the difficulty of meeting the sometimes conflicting demands for quick loading and turn-round on the one hand and for stability and safety on the other. It was recognised that roll-on/roll-off ferries of this nature quickly became unstable following a large ingress of sea water onto the open car/lorry decks. This was a known danger against which every precaution had to be taken and new international safety and stability regulations were quickly adopted to prevent it. The problems for ferries in certain areas of the world, for example in Africa and South East Asia, are different, characterised by less sophistication, a tendency to overcrowding and sometimes different safety requirements.

Another newer type of ferry is the one described as "high-speed". Such ferries have been tried or come into use in some regions. Speed is achieved by newer designs and propulsion units such as catamarans, hydrofoils or jetfoils. Such ferries, although extremely powerful and speedy, can bring with them their own stability peculiarities and also high fuel costs.

Offshore Operations

There is today a relatively new sector of shipping known simply as "offshore". This embraces a wide variety of vessels of all sorts, many unknown in earlier days, connected with offshore as opposed to inland exploration for or mining of oil, minerals, gas or other valuable commodities lying on or under the sea bed. The basis of this sector is the rig from which mining or drilling operations are conducted. This may stand on the bottom, or float but with the capability of partly submerging. It may be fixed or movable either with its own or external power.

From this stems the need for ancillary support services which has generated a growing range of vessel types, many of them multi-purpose. These include conventional off-shore platform supply ships, anchor-handlers, emergency response and rescue (formerly called "stand-by") vessels, and accommodation platforms which are in fact modular offshore hotels. There is also today an increasing requirement for other specialist ships and boats to construct and maintain off-shore renewable energy installations at sea.

As with other sectors of shipping the offshore sector has its own distinctive character, problems and indeed dangers, as exemplified by the *Piper Alpha*, the recent *Deep Water Horizon* and other incidents. In policy terms, the central question of freedom, as perceived in this book, arises in this as in other sectors. But while the operations are offshore, compared with most other sectors of shipping, they are much closer to home and many of the operations are carried out either in, or close to, territorial seas and often adjacent to the coasts or zones of influence of others. This gives rise to the assertion by some that protectionism, whether in overt or covert terms, is appropriate and needed for the preservation of the national interest and influence.

General Considerations

The basic qualities of any ship, of whatever type, are determined by the sector in which it operates, and the area of trading or operation. While ships today are often more standardised and less purely custom-built than hitherto, it is easy to see that the variety is infinite. They all, however, have one thing in common. This is the need to be as economic, as fuel-efficient and—consistent with safety, environmental, human and governmental requirements and conditions—to operate with as few crew as possible. Significant changes have been made in recent years. In the early 1950s, for example, a typical 12,000 tonnes dwt cargo liner would have a crew of some 70–80. Today, with automation, crew numbers have been significantly reduced and some large vessels sail with as few as 15–18.

But whatever the size of crew, there inevitably remain many shipboard duties to be performed whether at sea or in the course of loading and discharging. For ships carrying cargo, which is the very essence of international shipping, the safe carriage and care of that cargo is paramount. Any failure to do so would be rapidly counter-productive in terms of substantially increased cargo claims and loss of shipper (i.e. importer/exporter) support. A balance therefore has to be struck.

Chapter 4
Private Shipping Organisations

The next two chapters are devoted to a description of the main organisations and institutions in both the private and public sectors internationally concerned with various aspects of shipping. Some understanding of their role and purpose is necessary for a meaningful appreciation of the more complex law and policy issues and political questions dealt with later in this book.

There are a great number of different private associations and organisations in the maritime sector—increasing year by year, both at international and national level. One might be forgiven for wondering why. There are many examples of associations where collaborative working and the promotion of maritime interests in common serves good purpose and assists in putting the maritime message across to governmental and public audiences. But inevitably, the proliferation of associations often serves to muddy that message and show the industry to be fragmented.

In previous editions, this chapter listed and described a range of such organisations in some detail, with a disproportionate emphasis on those based in and operating out of the UK. Two developments have changed our approach here: the increasing reliance on the internet and search engines for information on all subjects and entities in all walks of life; and the shift of the principal editorship of this book to an international rather than a British perspective.

Nevertheless—even in this electronic age—it may be helpful to give a brief reference point and onward links for the major known private organisations in the international shipping world as a starting point for further enquiry and research. With apologies to those which feel left out, that is what this chapter now sets out to achieve. One of the most comprehensive listings of these and other organisations can also be found at www.shipping-facts.com.

In a few instances, a brief summary is also given of organisations which no longer exist, but which have nevertheless played their part in the story of international shipping and appear elsewhere in this book.

P.K. Mukherjee and M. Brownrigg, *Farthing on International Shipping*,
WMU Studies in Maritime Affairs, Vol. 1, DOI 10.1007/978-3-642-34598-2_4,
© Springer-Verlag Berlin Heidelberg 2013

International Shipping Associations

BIMCO

www.bimco.org
mailbox@bimco.org

BIMCO (now known only by the initials of its original name, the Baltic and International Maritime Council) is the oldest of the international shipping associations, dating back to 1905. It represents shipowners controlling around 65 % of the world's tonnage—with members in more than 120 countries drawn from a broad range of stakeholders having a vested interest in the shipping industry, including managers, brokers and agents.

BIMCO's main objectives are to protect its global membership through the provision of quality information and advice and, while promoting fair business practices, to facilitate production, harmonisation and standardisation of commercial shipping practices and contracts.

The association is based in Copenhagen with a regional office in Singapore. It maintains a close dialogue with governments and diplomatic representations around the world including maritime administrations, regulatory institutions and other stakeholders within the areas of EU, the USA and Asia. It has NGO status with all relevant United Nations organs.

International Chamber of Shipping (ICS)

www.ics-shipping.org
info@ics-shipping.org

The International Chamber of Shipping (ICS) is the principal international trade association for merchant ship operators, representing all sectors and trades and about 80 % of the world's merchant fleet (in tonnage). Based in London, its members are the national shipowner associations in about 40 countries across the world, which are recognised by their governments as the representative industry bodies in their country.

Established in 1921, ICS is concerned with all technical, legal and policy issues that may affect international shipping. ICS is actively engaged and has NGO status with all relevant international bodies, including particularly: the UN's International Maritime Organization (IMO), other UN and international agencies whose mandate has an impact on shipping, and (through ISF) the International Labour Organization (ILO).

International Shipping Federation (ISF)

www.ics-shipping.org
info@ics-shipping.org

The International Shipping Federation (ISF) is an association of shipowners' associations acting on personnel, social and labour relations questions from the standpoint of the maritime employers. Founded in 1909 primarily as a means of co-ordinating opposition to the increasing threat of strikes by European seafarers and dock labour, ISF soon developed into the principal international employers' organisation with a similar membership to ICS. It has from the start co-ordinated the shipowners' position in preparation for meetings on relevant issues under the special maritime machinery within the International Labour Organization (ILO—see Chap. 5) and has led for the industry on training and manning issues within IMO.

In 2011, the International Shipping Federation, which already shared the same secretariat as ICS (Marisec), was brought formally into the ICS structure, although the ISF name is maintained in certain matters relating to international labour affairs, including representation within the ILO.

Independent Tanker Owners Association (INTERTANKO)

www.intertanko.com
info@intertanko.com

INTERTANKO membership is open to independent owners and operators of oil and chemical tankers, i.e. non-oil companies and non-state-controlled tanker owners. Independent owners operate some 80 % of the world's tanker fleet and the vast majority are members. The members' combined fleet comprises some 3,380 tankers totalling 285 million dwt.

INTERTANKO speaks authoritatively and proactively on behalf of tanker operators at international, regional, national and local level—promoting safe transport, cleaner seas and free competition. With its principal offices in Oslo and London, INTERTANKO also has offices in Singapore and Washington DC.

The International Association of Dry Cargo Shipowners (INTERCARGO)

www.intercargo.org
info@intercargo.org

Founded in 1980, INTERCARGO's 160 shipowner members in 26 countries operate predominantly bulk carriers in the international *dry bulk trades*—such as coal, grain, iron ore and other bulk commodities. Its main role is to work with its members, regulators and other shipping associations with the objective of creating a "safe, efficient and environmentally friendly" dry cargo sector.

To do this, INTERCARGO participates actively in the development of global legislation through the *International Maritime Organization* and other similar bodies.

INTERCARGO and INTERTANKO share a single secretariat structure within the same office in London, in order to provide an improved service for members in the wet and dry bulk sectors.

Council of European and Japanese National Shipowners' Associations (CENSA)

CENSA was formed in 1974 in London and was an association of national shipowners' associations from 11 nations in Europe plus the Japanese. At this time, the International Chamber of Shipping did not deal with international shipping and trade policy issues and this role fell to CENSA. Its main objectives were to:

promote and protect free market shipping policies in all sectors of shipping to meet market requirements under self-regulatory regimes in co-operation with the shipper community; and coordinate and present the views of its members to relevant intergovernmental fora, including particularly the Consultative Shipping Group of governments, the OECD, UNCTAD and also, in some instances, to individual governments directly.

Through its office in Washington DC, CENSA was very active in representing its members directly to US federal and state agencies and to members of Congress on the impact of US shipping policy and legislation on the international commerce of the US with its trading partners.

CENSA was disbanded in 2001, since many of its activities had either fallen away or were being pursued by other associations (e.g. ECSA, World Shipping Council and ICS); its residual functions were absorbed by ICS.

Cruise Lines International Association (CLIA)

www.cruising.org
info@cruising.org
The Cruise Lines International Association was formed in 1975 in response to a need for an association to promote the special benefits of cruising and in 2006 merged with the International Council of Cruise Lines (ICCL), a sister entity

dedicated to participating in the regulatory and policy development process of the cruise industry. CLIA exists to promote all measures that foster a safe, secure and healthy cruise ship environment, educate, train its travel agent members, and promote and explain the value, desirability and affordability of the cruise vacation experience.

CLIA is the world's largest cruise association and is dedicated to the promotion and growth of the cruise industry. It is composed of 26 of the major cruise lines serving North America representing 97 % of the cruise capacity marketed from North America. CLIA operates pursuant to an agreement filed with the Federal Maritime Commission under the Shipping Act of 1984 and has NGO consultative status with the International Maritime Organization. CLIA is headquartered in Fort Lauderdale, Florida and also has offices in Washington DC and Brussels (see CLIA Europe below).

Interferry

www.interferry.com

Interferry represents the ferry industry world-wide, with currently 225 members from 38 countries; its secretariat is based in British Columbia, Canada and is just opening a branch in Brussels. Originally formed in 1976 as the International Marine Transit Association, Interferry co-ordinates research and collects information on developments affecting the ferry industry, facilitates exchanges of technical data through its international network of members, and stimulates industry cooperation and advancement by providing a forum for people to share experiences and learn from others. It also represents its members on regulatory matters, including within the IMO.

InterManager

www.intermanager.org

With its head office in Cyprus and branches in the Isle of Man and London, InterManager is the international trade association for ship managers, crew managers and related organisations. Its members are currently involved in the management of nearly 5,000 ships and responsible for some 250,000 seafarers.

Originally founded in 1991 under the name ISMA—International Ship Management Association—InterManager is committed to improving transparency and governance in shipping. Its Code of Ship Management Standards is the foundation stone of the association, reflecting the highest standards of ship management practice. It has been drafted by practical ship managers and is based on the experience gained through their involvement in day-to-day ship management. All InterManager members are encouraged to sign up to the Code.

International Parcel Tankers Association (IPTA)

www.ipta.org.uk
mail@ipta.org.uk

Formed in 1987 and based in Lancaster, England, IPTA is the representative body for shipowners operating IMO-classified chemical and product tankers and is recognised as a focal point through which regulatory authorities, charterers and trade organisations may liaise with such owners. IPTA members have equal status within the association irrespective of the size of their fleets. They are committed to the enhancement of maritime safety, the protection of the marine environment and the reduction of atmospheric pollution from shipping.

International Salvage Union (ISU)

www.marine-salvage.com
isu@marine-salvage.com

The International Salvage Union is an association representing the interests of 58 salvors worldwide. Membership of the ISU is restricted to those companies with a record of successful salvage and pollution prevention. Members are required to have the high level of expertise expected of the professional salvor.

One of the ISU's primary objectives is to foster a wider understanding of the salvage industry's contribution to environmental protection and the recovery of property. The ISU also plays an active role in encouraging inter-industry debate concerning the many legal and commercial issues influencing the efficient performance of salvage and pollution prevention services.

Oil Companies International Marine Forum (OCIMF)

www.ocimf.com
enquiries@ocimf.com

OCIMF is an association of oil companies with an interest in the shipment and terminalling of crude oil, oil products, petrochemicals and gas. Its mission is to be the foremost authority on the safe and environmentally responsible operation of oil tankers, terminals and offshore support vessels, promoting continuous improvement in standards of design and operation.

OCIMF was formed in London in 1970, initially as 18 oil majors' response to growing public awareness of marine pollution, particularly by oil, after the "Torrey Canyon" incident. Incorporated in Bermuda in 1977 and with a branch office in London primarily to maintain contact with IMO, the current membership comprises 98 companies worldwide.

One of the most significant initiatives introduced by OCIMF is the Ship Inspection Report Programme (SIRE), which is a unique tanker risk assessment tool of value to charterers, ship operators, terminal operators and government bodies concerned with ship safety. It focuses tanker industry awareness on the importance of meeting satisfactory tanker quality and ship safety standards through a large database of up-to-date information about tankers and barges.

The "Round Table" of International Shipping Associations

www.shipping-facts.com

Not a separate organisation but a joint initiative bringing together BIMCO, the International Chamber of Shipping, INTERCARGO and INTERTANKO, the mission of the "Round Table" is to work together to serve, represent and advance the international shipping industry.

These associations seek to act in concert to avoid duplication on issues of consensus, where the combined effort of the Round Table can exceed the sum of the individual efforts. The website provides a useful portal into some of the major maritime issues of the day, the importance of the shipping industry to world trade, and lists of commercial and governmental maritime organisations.

Society of International Gas Tanker & Terminal Operators Ltd (SIGTTO)

www.sigtto.org
secretariat@sigtto.org

SIGTTO was formed in 1979 and now has more than 150 members representing nearly all the world's LNG businesses and more than half of the global liquefied petroleum gas (LPG) business. With NGO status at IMO, the Society is acknowledged as the authoritative voice of the liquefied gas shipping and terminals industries. Its purpose is to specify and promote high standards and best practices among all industry members throughout the world, and hence to maintain confidence in the safety of the liquefied gas industries and maintain their acceptance, by society at large, as responsible industrial partners. Registered in Bermuda, the main liaison office is in London.

World Shipping Council (WSC)

www.worldshipping.org
info@worldshipping.org

The World Shipping Council's goal is to provide a coordinated voice for the world's major liner shipping (mainly container) companies in their work with policymakers and other industry groups with an interest in international transportation. With container transport carrying more than 50 % of world seaborne trade by value, the WSC currently has 28 members across most continents, which operate approximately 90 % of the global liner ship capacity.

The main areas of the WSC's work involve maritime security, the environment (particularly the reduction of air emissions including carbon dioxide), cargo liability; enhanced customs information; and international technology standards for containers. The WSC routinely works with a broad range of stakeholders from the public and private sectors to advance policies and programs that will ensure adequate and efficient global transportation infrastructure capacity.

With its permanent secretariat in Washington DC and a small office in Brussels, the WSC was established largely to give a policy voice to the less formal International Council of Containership Operators (or the "Box Club"), which brings together the chief executives of the world's major container ship operators and whose secretariat is provided at any one time by the company of the Club's chairman.

Regional and National Shipping Associations

Asian Shipowners' Forum (ASF)

www.asianshipowners.org
info@asianshipowners.org

The Asian Shipowners' Forum (ASF) was founded in April 1992. With its permanent secretariat established in Singapore in 2007, ASF currently consists of eight members from the shipowners' associations of the Asia Pacific nations— Australia, China, Hong Kong, India, Japan, Korea, Chinese Taipei and the Federation of ASEAN Shipowners' Associations (FASA—itself consisting of Indonesia, Malaysia, Myanmar, the Philippines, Singapore, Thailand and Vietnam). Together, the membership is estimated to control about 50 % of the world merchant fleet.

ASF works through five standing committees dealing with: Shipping Economics, Ship Recycling, Seafarer issues, Safe Navigation & Environment, and Ship Insurance & Liability.

European Community Shipowners' Associations (ECSA)

www.ecsa.eu
mail@ecsa.eu

ECSA is the trade association for the shipping industries of the EU member states, which control more than 40 % of the world fleet. Formed in 1965 under the name of the Comité des Associations d'Armateurs des Communautés Européennes (CAACE), ECSA assumed its present name in 1990. It is based in Brussels and its members are the national shipowner associations of the EU and Norway.

The aim of ECSA is to promote the interests of European shipping so that the industry can best serve European and international trade and commerce in a competitive free-enterprise environment to the benefit of shippers and consumers.

ECSA is actively engaged, on behalf of its members, with all relevant EU and other international institutions, including particularly the European Commission, the Council of Ministers and the European Parliament.

CLIA Europe

www.europeancruisecouncil.com
info@cruisecouncil.eu

Since early 2013, CLIA Europe — formerly the European Cruise Council (ECC) — represents the leading cruise companies operating in Europe and has 29 cruise members and 40 associate members. CLIA Europe promotes the interests of cruise ship operators within Europe, liaising closely with the EU institutions including the European Maritime Safety Agency (EMSA). It also looks to protect the interests of its Members through close liaison with other European bodies such as ECSA, ESPO and the European Travel Agents & Tour Operators Association (ECTAA). The ECC also promotes cruising to a wider public audience to encourage expansion of the European cruise market and works closely in the pursuit of this objective with a number of regional cruise marketing bodies.

Federation of ASEAN Shipowners' Associations (FASA)

www.fasa.org.sg
office@fasa.org.sg

FASA was formed in 1975 as the organisation representing the shipowners' associations in the ASEAN (Association of South East Asian Nations) countries. Its objectives are to foster close cooperation and coordination among the members on shipping policy and other matters of collective interest; assist in improving shipping services and encourage the growth of ASEAN shipping and trade in the South East Asian region; and represent the members in their collective dealings with shippers' councils, port authorities, government, international and other organisations. It is also a member of the Asian Shipowners' Forum, see above.

National Shipowners' Associations

There are many national associations of shipping companies across the world. Through one or other of the international maritime bodies, all these associations tend to be in touch with each other. A good list of the main associations can be found under the "Useful links" page at www.shipping-facts.com.

Each such association has, of course, the same basic objective, namely the promotion and protection of its own members' fleets. But the size of the organisation and its relative strength depends largely on the number of members and the nature of the fleet. Some confine their membership to companies operating ships under the national flag only, while increasingly associations represent the full economic fleet in their country regardless of a ship's country of registration.

As an example, the UK Chamber of Shipping—www.ukchamberofshipping.com—is the trade and employers' association for UK-based shipping companies and as such is the voice of British shipowners on a very wide range of issues affecting the corporate interests of its members. Established in 1878, it is one of the oldest and has evolved substantially over the years. Its objectives have been to promote and protect the interests of its members in other than purely commercial matters. The UK Chamber operates nationally and internationally with respect to governments, government departments, Parliament and other bodies and interests including the unions, although nowadays, unlike previously, wage negotiations are handled at company level. Its role is to keep out of the marketplace, but to try to improve the overall competitive and regulatory environment for British shipping.

Its divisional and committee structures cover the areas of taxation, safety and the environment, employment and training of seafarers, security and defence, commercial and legal matters. Funding is essentially through members' subscriptions.

This pattern is reflected to a greater or lesser degree across the other associations in Europe, North and South America, Asia and the Far East.

Trade and Commercial Organisations

The Baltic Exchange

www.balticexchange.com
enquiries@balticexchange.com

The history of the Baltic Exchange spans more than 250 years and traces its origins back to a humble coffee house—the traditional meeting place of merchants and sea captains—in the City of London. The Baltic Exchange today is a membership organisation at the heart of the global maritime marketplace. It provides independent daily shipping market information; maintains professional shipbroking standards and resolves disputes.

Baltic Exchange members are at the heart of world trade, arranging for the ocean transportation of industrial bulk commodities from producer to end user. The bulk freight market relies on the co-operation of shipbrokers, shipowners and charterers to ensure the free flow of trade.

The Baltic brokers are bound by the Rules of the Exchange and its motto "Our Word Our Bond" sums up the trust and integrity which operates in the market.

The Baltic produces independent shipping market assessments. Using a panel of international shipbrokers, it provides daily assessments on over 50 dry and wet routes, weekly sale & purchase and demolition assessments as well as daily forward prices. It also produces daily cargo fixture lists and in-depth analysis of the main dry cargo markets. The Baltic Exchange also runs a series of shipping courses and workshops around the world, including on aspects of vessel chartering and freight derivative trading.

Institute of Chartered Shipbrokers (ICS)

www.ics.org.uk
enquiries@ics.org.uk

With 24 *branches* and 16 *distance learning centres* around the world, the members of the Institute of Chartered Shipbrokers (ICS) are part of an international network of shipping professionals who not only work towards high professional ethical standards of trust, but who also have proven knowledge, competence and understanding of the broad spectrum of shipping business.

Founded in 1911 and with its first Royal Charter in 1920, the Institute is the only internationally recognised professional body for shipbrokers, ship managers, agents and those involved in other aspects of shipping business. As a major provider of *education* and *training*, ICS sets and examines the syllabus for *membership*, providing the shipping industry with highly qualified professionals. It operates its own distance learning programme, *TutorShip*, and runs a variety of courses designed for both new entrants to the shipping industry and more experienced people looking for specialised knowledge.

Federation of National Associations of Shipbrokers and Agents (FONASBA)

www.fonasba.com
generalmanager@fonasba.com

Formed in 1969, FONASBA represents shipbrokers and agents by promoting fair and equitable practices, consulting and advising on matters of concern to its members, and co-operating with other international maritime bodies. Membership is open only to national associations of shipbrokers and agents and limited to one such association per country, although other shipping entities have access to associate membership. There are currently members (including associates) in 50 countries.

The Federation has three main focuses: liner and tramp matters, chartering and documentary affairs, and contact with directorates within the European Commission that have an involvement in shipping—this latter is pursued through the European Community Association of Ship Brokers and Agents (ECASBA) which acts as a sub-committee of the Federation.

International Chamber of Commerce (ICC)

www.iccwbo.org

The Paris-based International Chamber of Commerce is the voice of world business championing the global economy as a force for economic growth, job creation and prosperity. Its activities cover a broad spectrum, from arbitration and dispute resolution to making the case for open trade and the market economy system, business self-regulation, fighting corruption or combating commercial crime.

ICC has direct access to national governments all over the world through its national committees. The organisation's Paris-based international secretariat feeds business views into intergovernmental organisations (particularly within the United Nations) on issues that directly affect business operations.

Maritime affairs used to fall under the ICC's Commission on Transport and Logistics whose objective was to promote intermodal transport and competitive, efficient transport markets worldwide and elaborate global business positions on issues such as liberalisation, customs facilitation, competition and the environment. This work now comes under the aegis of a new and much wider ICC Commission on Customs and Trade Facilitation. It also contributes to the work of ICC International Maritime Bureau on combating maritime piracy.

International Maritime Bureau (IMB)

www.icc-ccs.org.uk/icc/imb
ccs@icc-ccs.org

The ICC International Maritime Bureau is a specialised division within the Commercial Crime Services department of the International Chamber Of Commerce. Established in 1981 and based in London, IMB acts as a focal point in the fight against all types of maritime crime and malpractice. The IMB has close relations with the IMO and the World Customs Organization (WCO), and observer status with Interpol (ICPO).

IMB's main task is to protect the integrity of international trade by seeking out fraud and malpractice identifying and investigating frauds, spotting new criminal methods and trends, and highlighting other threats to trade. A particular area of expertise is in the suppression of piracy. Concerned at the alarming growth in the phenomenon, the *IMB Piracy Reporting Centre* was established in 1992. The Centre, which is based in Kuala Lumpur maintains a round-the-clock watch on the world's shipping lanes, reporting pirate attacks to local law enforcement and issuing warnings about piracy hotspots to shipping. A live piracy map showing recent attacks can be found on its website.

International Maritime Industries Forum (IMIF)

www.imif.org
info@imif.org

The International Maritime Industries Forum was formed at the depth of the tanker crisis in 1975 following a report on the tanker industry commissioned by tanker owners, banks, shipbuilders and the "user" oil companies, all of whom were concerned about the massive imbalance between supply and demand in the tanker sector and its effects on the world's markets. IMIF allows shipowners, shipbuilders, cargo owners, bankers, classification societies, insurers and other interests the opportunity to meet for discussions on the many problems of their separate industries whose prosperity is inextricably linked.

It has no formal constitution but aims simply to re-establish and subsequently to maintain a healthy and profitable international maritime environment for all sectors of shipping. Specifically, it seeks to create a more balanced shipping market by encouraging the reduction of overcapacity through a determined policy of scrapping, the removal of government subsidies and an end to speculative building.

International Federation of Freight Forwarders Associations (FIATA)

www.fiata.com

FIATA (from the French name) was founded in Vienna in 1926 and today represents an industry covering approximately 40,000 forwarding and logistics firms, employing eight to ten million people in 150 countries.

FIATA has consultative status with several UN agencies and institutions and is widely recognised as the international representative body for the freight forwarding industry. Its main objectives include: to unite the freight forwarding industry worldwide; to represent, promote, and spread understanding about the sector; to improve the quality of freight forwarder services; and to assist with practical commercial aspects including vocational training for freight forwarders and liability insurance problems.

Shanghai Shipping Exchange (SSE)

http://en.sse.net.cn

The Shanghai Shipping Exchange was founded in 1996 by the Chinese Ministry of Transport and Shanghai Municipal People's Government and is the first state-level shipping exchange in China (although not a private organisation, the SSE is included in this chapter for convenience).

The basic functions of the SSE are "to standardise the transactions, to adjust the freight rates, and to communicate information on the shipping market". By performing these three functions and sticking to the principle of "Openness, Fairness and Justness", SSE seeks to regulate China's shipping market, maintain order in shipping transactions and encourage the healthy development of the China-based shipping market.

SSE is engaged in the publishing of shipping information, promotion of shipping conventions, exchange of shipping business, broking services, consulting and agency services, and formulation of sample documents.

Since 2009, the SSE has been responsible for implementing a nationwide freight rate filing system for international container shipping to and from China, for the purpose of "protecting the market order of China's international container liner services and the legitimate rights and interests of all related parties" and regulating unfair competition.

Shippers' Organisations

Shippers' councils represent cargo owners and freight transport interests (import and export by all modes of transport), whether manufacturers, retailers or wholesalers—collectively referred to as shippers. Their development owes its origin to a need for bodies to be established representative of the interests of shippers especially with regard to shipowners providing liner services and to a push in that direction given by the International Chamber of Commerce in the mid 1950s. Today shippers' councils are established in many countries across the world.

Different groupings have also emerged representing cargo interests on a global and regional basis. Examples include the:

Asian Shippers' Council (ASC)—www.asianshippers.org—which was formed in 2004 and now has its permanent secretariat in Colombo, Sri Lanka. The ASC seeks to integrate shippers' councils in all of Asia into a single entity. It comprises 20 shippers' councils from 16 countries and covers five geographical regions—China, South Asia, North Asia, Oceania and South East Asia.

European Shippers' Council (ESC)—www.europeanshippers.com—which represents the national shippers' councils in some ten European countries, together with the European paper and chemicals industries and a number of sizeable individual corporate members.

Global Shippers' Forum (GSF)—www.globalshippersforum.com—which was formally incorporated in June 2011, having been created in 2006 and with its origins in the informal Tripartite Shippers' Group dating back to 1994. The GSF represents the interests and shippers' organisations from Asia, the UK, North and South America, and Africa. Its secretariat is provided by the Freight Transport Association in the UK.

National Industrial Transportation League (NITL)—www.nitl.org—which is the oldest national association and has been the shippers' voice in the USA since 1907.

Worldscale Association (London) Ltd

www.worldscale.co.uk
wscale@worldscale.co.uk

This Association publishes, jointly with the New York based Worldscale Association (NYC) Inc, a tanker nominal freight rate schedule used as a standard reference in the chartering of tankers. It is available only on a subscription basis from the Worldscale Associations. This service has existed since 1969 and was based on freight rate schedules used during the 1939–1945 hostilities and in the post-war period. The Worldscale Associations in London and New York are both non-profit making organisations and each operates under the control of a management committee comprising senior tanker brokers from leading firms in London and New York.

Insurance

Lloyd's

www.lloyds.com
enquiries@lloyds.com

Unlike most other insurance brands, Lloyd's is not a company, but a market where its members join together as syndicates to insure and reinsure risk across all sectors.

Lloyd's is the world's oldest and leading specialist insurance market, conducting business in over 200 countries and territories worldwide—and is often the first to insure new, unusual or complex risks. It brings together a huge concentration of specialist expertise and talent, backed by strong financial ratings which cover the whole market.

Lloyd's insurance market had its origins—like the Baltic Exchange—in a London coffee house in 1688, where ships' captains, merchants, shipowners and others met to exchange intelligence and shipping news. London's importance as a trade centre led to an increasing demand for ship and cargo insurance. From this small beginning it grew to be a place where marine insurance risks could be placed with individuals or groups of individuals.

Today marine is a smaller but still significant part of its business, with most of the cover in this area for hull, cargo, marine, liability and specie (the insurance of highly valued items such as fine art while in transit). Marine makes up 7 % of Lloyd's business.

The Lloyd's Market Association (LMA), located in the heart of the Lloyd's Building in the City of London, provides professional, technical support to the Lloyd's underwriting community and represents their interests.

International Underwriting Association (IUA)

www.iua.co.uk
info@iua.co.uk

The International Underwriting Association exists to promote and enhance the business environment for international insurance and reinsurance companies operating in or through London and is the world's largest representative organisation for international and wholesale insurance and reinsurance companies.

Formed in December 1998, through the merger of the London International Insurance and Reinsurance Market Association (LIRMA) and the Institute of London Underwriters (ILU), the IUA brought together the representative bodies for the marine and non-marine sectors of the London company insurance market outside of the Lloyd's market. It is a trade association which does not have any regulatory authority over its members.

The ILU's history in the marine, aviation and transport insurance markets dates back to 1884, again starting through informal meetings of underwriters in a coffee house to discuss policy wordings and other matters of mutual interest.

The IUA today deals with questions of interest to the market as a whole and services joint IUA/Lloyd's committees which monitor topics of interest in particular fields such as hull and cargo insurance, carriers liability and war risks. These include the "Joint Hull", the "Joint Cargo" and the "Joint Technical and Clauses" Committees.

International Union of Marine Insurance (IUMI)

www.iumi.com

The International Union of Marine Insurance has its origins in an association established in Berlin in 1874 "where the members could discuss business matters of common interest with the purpose of agreeing upon principles concerning the management of marine insurance business". This broadened in the first half of the twentieth century into an international organisation which now has its base in Zurich.

Its objective is to represent, safeguard and develop insurers' interests in marine and transport insurance. IUMI is a professional body run by and for its members, which include 55 national associations across all continents. IUMI is not a decision-making body, nor is it involved in the formulation of rating schedules, clauses or conditions. Rather it is a forum to exchange experience, information and statistical data on marine insurance matters; to discuss legislative issues, loss prevention and safety measures; to debate, in an objective and conducive way, the challenges and opportunities facing marine insurers.

International Group of Protection and Indemnity (P&I) Clubs

www.igpandi.org
secretariat@internationalgroup.org.uk

P&I Clubs are associations of shipowners formed for the purpose of "protecting" and "indemnifying" themselves against claims by others on a mutual basis. As such they are different from Lloyd's and other commercial underwriters who write their business for profit and on fixed terms, but nevertheless they form an integral, yet distinct, part of insurance cover available to shipowners.

Each club is an independent, non-profit making mutual insurance association, providing cover for its shipowner and charterer members against third party liabilities relating to the use and operation of ships. Each club is controlled by its members through a board of directors or committee elected from the membership.

The International Group of P&I Clubs has its origins in a pooling agreement established in 1899 between six of the Clubs managed in England, under which they shared claims in excess of an agreed retention. The agreement continues today.

Based in London, the Group has 13 principal underwriting member clubs which between them provide liability cover for approximately 90 % of the world's ocean-going tonnage.

Clubs cover a wide range of liabilities including personal injury to crew, passengers and others on board, cargo loss and damage, oil pollution, wreck removal and dock damage. Clubs also provide a wide range of services to their members on claims, legal issues and loss prevention, and often play a leading role in the management of casualties.

Maritime Law and Arbitration

The London Maritime Arbitrators' Association (LMAA)

www.lmaa.org.uk
info@lmaa.org.uk

The London Maritime Arbitrators' Association is an association of practising maritime arbitrators and was founded in 1960 at a "meeting of the Arbitrators on the Baltic Exchange Approved List", but its roots and traditions stretch back more than 300 years over the history of The Baltic Exchange. "Over the years," membership of the association has been expanded so that the list of practising arbitrators now embraces a variety of disciplines, and a corresponding breadth of expertise.

The primary purpose of the association is to advance and encourage the professional knowledge of London maritime arbitrators and, by recommendation and advice, to assist the expeditious procedure and disposal of disputes.

More maritime disputes are referred to arbitration in London than to any other place where arbitration services are offered.

Association of Average Adjusters

www.average-adjusters.com
aaa@rtiForensics.com

The Association of Average Adjusters was founded in 1869 with its prime objects the promotion of correct principles in the adjustment of marine insurance claims and general average, uniformity of practice amongst Average Adjusters and the maintenance of good professional conduct. It was then and is now, a source of expertise in marine insurance and maritime matters.

The core membership comprises over 50 Fellows practising worldwide who have qualified by passing the Association's examinations. The association also has 350 subscribers from 26 different countries—these are maritime practitioners, insurance brokers, claims adjusters and lawyers, all of whom have in common a professional interest in maritime affairs.

Average Adjusters are expert in the law and practice of marine insurance and general average; they provide a professional and independent view on the claims arising from marine casualties.

The concept of general average is of ancient origin going back to Rhodian Law. Whilst the practice of average adjusting is complex, the principle is simple—namely that when action, sacrifice or expenditure is necessary to save a ship (for example, jettison of the cargo in whole or part), the expenses must be shared (i.e. adjusted) between those who have an interest. The association took a leading part in the codification of the laws on general average known as the York/Antwerp Rules.

Comité Maritime International (CMI)

www.comitemaritime.org
admini@cmi-imc.org

The Comité Maritime International was established in Antwerp in 1897 and is a non-governmental not-for-profit international organisation, whose object is to contribute by all appropriate means and activities to the unification of maritime law in all its aspects.

Its constituents are the maritime law associations of various countries originally from Europe, the United States and Japan but nowadays from over 50 developed and developing countries. The CMI was formed in Belgium with the object of "giving the sea, which is the natural tie between the nations, the benefit of a uniform law which will be rational, deliberated and equitable in its conception and practical in its text".

A major achievement of the CMI is the recent top-to-bottom reform of international maritime transport law. Working from the early 1990s, at first internally and subsequently hand-in-hand with UNCITRAL for a decade, the Comité is the acknowledged parent of the United Nations Convention on Contracts for the International Carriage of Goods Wholly or Partly by Sea, 2008 (the "Rotterdam Rules"). Other ongoing work—primarily with IMO—involves a number of important issues including Places of Refuge for vessels in distress, Fair Treatment of Seafarers, and Guidelines for National Legislation on Piracy and Serious Maritime Crime.

Technical/Safety/Navigation/Operational

International Association of Classification Societies (IACS)

www.iacs.org.uk
permsec@iacs.org.uk

The International Association of Classification Societies makes a unique contribution to maritime safety and regulation through technical support, compliance verification and research and development. More than 90 % of the world's cargo carrying tonnage is covered by the classification, design, construction and through-life compliance rules and standards set by the 13 Member Societies of IACS.

IACS traces its origins back to the International Load Line Convention 1930 which recommended collaboration between classification societies to secure "as much uniformity as possible in the application of the standards of strength upon which freeboard is based...".

This prompted a series of conferences and working parties involving the major societies over the next years and eventually, in 1968, led to the formation of IACS by seven leading societies. The value of their combined level of technical knowledge and experience was recognised in the following year with the granting of IMO consultative status; IACS remains the only non-governmental organization with observer status which is able to develop and apply rules. Its secretariat is in London.

Compliance with the IACS Quality System Certification Scheme (QSCS) is mandatory for IACS membership.

Many of the members of IACS are substantial organisations in their own right. They currently comprise: American Bureau of Shipping (ABS), Bureau Veritas (BV), China Classification Society (CCS), Croatian Register of Shipping (CRS), Det Norske Veritas (DNV), Germanischer Lloyd (GL), Indian Register of Shipping (IRS), Korean Register of Shipping (KR), Lloyd's Register (LR), Nippon Kaiji Kyokai (ClassNK), Polish Register of Shipping (PRS), Registro Italiano Navale (RINA), and Russian Maritime Register of Shipping (RS).

International Tanker Owners Pollution Federation (ITOPF)

www.itopf.com
central@itopf.com

The International Tanker Owners Pollution Federation is involved in all aspects of preparing for and responding to ship-source spills of oil, chemicals and other substances in the marine environment.

It was *established* in London in 1968, in the wake of the Torrey Canyon incident, to administer a voluntary compensation agreement ("Tanker Owners' Voluntary Agreement concerning Liability for Oil Pollution – TOVALOP"), which assured the adequate and timely payment of compensation to those affected by oil spills.

When TOVALOP came to an end in 1997, the remit of the Federation changed and ITOPF now devotes considerable effort to a wide range of *technical services*, of which the most important is responding to spills of oil and chemicals. ITOPF's small response team is at constant readiness to assist at marine spills anywhere in the world. This service is normally undertaken on behalf of its members (tanker owners) or other shipowners and their oil pollution insurers (normally one of the P&I Clubs), or at the request of governments or international agencies such as the

International Oil Pollution Compensation Funds (IOPC Funds). Other technical services provided include damage assessment, contingency planning, training and information.

International Association of Ports and Harbors (IAPH)

www.iaphworldports.org
info@iaphworldports.org

The International Association of Ports and Harbours was founded in 1955 and has since developed into a global alliance of ports, representing today some 230 ports in about 90 countries. These include public port authorities (national, state, or municipal), private port/terminal operators, and government agencies responsible for ports. The member ports together handle well over 60 % of the world's sea-borne trade and nearly 80 % of container traffic. It is headquartered in Tokyo and maintains a European office in the Netherlands.

Its principal objective is to foster good relations and cooperation among all ports in the world by providing a forum to exchange opinions and share experiences on aspects of port management and operations. IAPH promotes the fact that ports form a vital link in the waterborne transportation and play such a vital role in today's global economy.

The founding fathers of the IAPH believed that ports could contribute to create a more peaceful world by helping world trade grow and develop, as explicitly shown in its motto, "World Peace Through World Trade – World Trade Through World Ports".

European Sea Ports Organisation (ESPO)

www.espo.be
mail@espo.be

Founded in 1993 in Brussels, the European Sea Ports Organisation represents the port authorities, port associations and port administrations of the seaports of the member states of the European Union and Norway, with observer members in several neighbouring countries to the EU.

ESPO's mission is to influence public policy in the EU in order to achieve a safe, efficient and environmentally sustainable European port sector, operating as a key element of the transport industry, as far as practicable operating under free and undistorted market conditions.

With 90 % of Europe's cargo trade and more than 400 million ferry and cruise passengers passing through 1,200 seaports in the 22 maritime member states of the EU every year, ESPO provides the voice of seaports in the European Union and is engaged with all relevant European stakeholders in the ports and maritime sector.

Marine Manufacturing Associations

Surprisingly, there do not seem to be any significant associations representing shipyards, ship repairers, or marine equipment manufacturers at a global level, although these do exist at regional and national level. International examples include, in Europe, the Brussels-based Community of European Shipyards' Associations (CESA)—www.cesa.eu—and European Marine Equipment Council (EMEC)—www.emec.eu—both of which have been established for some decades.

Social and Charitable

International Transport Workers' Federation (ITF)

www.itfglobal.org
mail@itf.org.uk

The International Transport Workers' Federation brings together some 780 unions representing over 4.5 million transport workers in 155 countries across all transport sectors.

It has been helping seafarers since 1896 and today represents the interests of seafarers worldwide—over 600,000 are members of ITF-affiliated unions. Here, the aim of the ITF is to improve conditions for seafarers of all nationalities and to ensure adequate regulation of the shipping industry to protect the interests and rights of these workers. It pursues this both directly and through intergovernmental organisations. The ITF helps crews regardless of their nationality or the flag of their ship.

At the heart of the ITF's work for seafarers is its longstanding campaign against so-called "Flags of Convenience" (FOC), a campaign which has two main objectives:

To establish international governmental agreement on a "genuine link" between the flag and ship and the nationality of domicile of its owners, managers and seafarers with the aim of eliminating the flag of convenience system entirely.

To ensure that seafarers who serve on flag of convenience ships, whatever their nationality, are protected from exploitation.

Seafarers' Welfare Organisations

There are a range of international and national welfare organisations which have been set up to minister to the pastoral needs of active seafarers. Some are linked to particular religious denominations, and these are increasingly seeking to work together ecumenically and to rationalise and optimise the use of resources; others are secular.

These organisations mostly focus on seafarers who find themselves in foreign ports a long way from their homes, possibly with little or difficult access to shore facilities where they can find relaxation away from their place of work, the ship. They seek to provide spiritual and/or practical support and assistance with any problems crew members may be facing. Some run centres in or near ports where the seafarers can find a "home from home" and contact their loved ones from whom they may be separated for months on end.

There are also many charities and voluntary organisations which help former merchant and naval seafarers, who have fallen on hard times after leaving the sea, but these are not dealt with here.

The following three organisations are among the most active in this context:

Mission to Seafarers—www.missiontoseafarers.org
Apostleship of the Sea—www.apostleshipofthesea.org.uk
Sailors' Society—www.sailors-society.org

Professional/Educational Institutions

A number of international institutes exist to support and accredit nautical and marine engineering professionals, both seagoing and shore-based. Among these are:

IMarEST (Institute for Marine Engineering, Science and Technology)—www. imarest.org—which was established in London in 1889 as a learned society for marine professionals on the engineering side. It has a strong international presence with an extensive marine network of over 15,000 members in 50 international branches and affiliations with major marine societies around the world. IMarEST provides access to its Library Collection (held by Lloyd's Register's Information Centre), a catalogue of specialist eBooks covering various marine disciplines, past issues of IMarEST publications, its archive comprising bibliographic information and summaries from major marine technical publications, its International Directory of Marine Consultancy, and online communities.

The Nautical Institute (NI)—www.nautinst.org—which is the international professional body for professional mariners, providing a wide range of services to enhance the professional standing and knowledge of its members. It is devoted to promoting high standards of nautical competence and knowledge and improving the safety and efficiency of shipping. The Nautical Institute has over 40 branches worldwide and more than 7,000 members in over 110 countries. Its monthly journal "Seaways", books, web services and projects help to provide real solutions to problems facing the industry and provide mariners' input to decision-makers internationally and nationally.

Hellenic Marine Environment Protection Association (HELMEPA)

www.helmepa.gr
helmepa@helmepa.gr

HELMEPA, founded 1982, is a joint voluntary association of Greek shipowners and seafarers with initiatives in the areas of safety and the protection of the marine environment by focusing on the human factor. Its objective is to create environmental consciousness and upgrade safety within the maritime community through a concerted voluntary effort to inform, educate and motivate all, from shipowner to the last seafarer. It was inspired by the leading Greek shipowner, George P. Livanos, who urged the Greek shipping community to adopt a new approach to the human element of ship-generated pollution.

HELMEPA's success has led to the creation of sister organisations in a number of other countries.

Chapter 5
The Interface with Governments: National and International

Government ministries, departments and agencies and intergovernmental bodies which interface with shipping described in this chapter are grouped as follows:

- The departments and machinery of a national government and national law (this chapter takes the United Kingdom as one example of a major maritime nation).
- The European Union.
- The United States.
- The main United Nations organisations and regional agencies.
- The specialised intergovernmental groups.

Reference has already been made to the main UN bodies—the IMO, ILO and UNCTAD—involved significantly in shipping. There are others but they are of less importance to shipping. This chapter aims to describe their origins and role in more, but hopefully not too much, detail.

Ministries, Agencies and the Law of the United Kingdom

The responsibility for shipping issues of both a policy and technical nature falls to different ministries in different countries—it may be treated under foreign affairs, trade, transport, or sometimes have its own dedicated department. Although for many years in the UK the "Board of Trade" was the main government department responsible for shipping, it and its successors are by no means the only departments concerned with this key sector. Indeed the responsible departments are subject to frequent name-changes reflecting changes and combinations with other fields such as energy or the environment.

The same is reflected in most other countries with a parliamentary democracy. The position in the UK can, therefore, be taken as a good example of how governments at national level involve themselves in shipping.

The main "shipping" department in the United Kingdom today is the Department for Transport (DfT). Following a recent restructuring, shipping and ports policy fall

P.K. Mukherjee and M. Brownrigg, *Farthing on International Shipping*,
WMU Studies in Maritime Affairs, Vol. 1, DOI 10.1007/978-3-642-34598-2_5,
© Springer-Verlag Berlin Heidelberg 2013

under one of four Directors General, who deals with "International, Strategy and Environment". Under this post, the Maritime Director and his staff handle policy questions across the whole shipping field, both international and domestic, and including training, ports and navigation. Specifically, they are responsible for the development of policies and programmes which support a healthy UK maritime sector (including both the business climate and the safeguarding of the necessary skills), promote maritime safety, prevent maritime pollution, and provide for the development and oversight of related security policies and programmes.

This Directorate General also sets policy guidelines for the Maritime and Coastguard Agency (MCA)—itself a product of re-organisation in recent years to bring together the previous organisations dealing with operational safety matters and the Coastguard. The MCA has responsibility for technical standards in shipping and for implementing the government's maritime safety policy in the UK, working to prevent the loss of life on the coast and at sea. It inspects and surveys ships to ensure that they are meeting national and international safety rules, provides certification to seafarers, registers ships, and responds to pollution risks from ships and offshore installations.

The DfT is the sponsoring body for British shipping and as such maintains a close relationship with the UK Chamber of Shipping and other trade associations within the UK maritime cluster. It is also the spokesperson for, and champion of, British shipping and maritime interests in all interdepartmental discussions on shipping questions.

Other departments concerned from time to time with shipping, or specific aspects of it, include:

- *HM Treasury*: tax and fiscal.
- *Foreign & Commonwealth Office*: shipping relations with other countries, bilateral agreements, international agreements and international affairs generally.
- *HM Revenue & Customs*: the entry and clearance of ships, the levying of dues of one sort or another on imports and exports, the administration of VAT.
- *Home Office*: immigration, repatriation, refugees.
- *Ministry of Defence*: shipping defence and strategic issues including NATO, and more recently also piracy.
- *Energy & Climate Change*: industry requirements relating to carbon emissions and the development of offshore renewables installations.
- *Environment, Food & Rural Affairs*: protection of the resources of the sea and environmental control within UK territorial jurisdiction.
- *Business, Innovation & Skills*: Office of Fair Trading and competition policy, apprenticeship programmes, shipbuilding and general industrial policy as it impinges on shipping, international trade policy.
- *Work & Pensions*: various aspects of the work conditions and pension arrangements for seafarers.
- *Education*: aspects concerning education programmes.
- *Justice*: various aspects of contractual law, jurisdictional, and governance.

- *Health & Safety Executive*: safe working practices and the control of noise levels.
- *Hydrographer*: concerned historically with the surveying of seas and coastlines and the production of "admiralty" charts.
- *Scottish Government*: the UK now has three devolved governments, which retain responsibility for coastal matters. The most active of these is that of Scotland.

While the above departments, through their Secretaries of State, Ministers and permanent officials, are the executive arm of government, it is to Parliament that they are responsible, and it is Parliament that is responsible to the electorate for the policy they implement under the various Acts and regulations passed over the years and amended from time to time.

Aside from its legislative function through the upper House of Lords and lower House of Commons, Parliament also has a number of committees which operate as standing committees of either house on particular subjects (for example, European Union legislation). A number of these (for example, the Transport Committee) consider shipping questions from time to time.

On occasion, *ad hoc* Committees of Inquiry may be established in order to report to Parliament. These are not committees of Parliament, as are standing committees, but committees of non-Parliamentarians appointed under an eminent person to report to Parliament. One such committee was that established in 1967 under the chairmanship of Lord Rochdale to look into "the UK shipping industry, its methods of operation and any other factors which affect its efficiency and competitiveness". This had implications for shipping, not only nationally, but world wide. Parliament also from time to time has debates which wholly or in part concern themselves with general or specific shipping issues. The Committee of Inquiry chaired by Lord Donaldson following the sinking of the *Braer* is an example of such procedure.

The machinery of Parliament is known colloquially as "Westminster" and that of the Departments of State as "Whitehall" from those parts of London wherein they are located, although today many government departments and especially the Executive Agencies are outside the strict confines of "Whitehall."

In the United Kingdom, although not so universally, the courts and the judiciary are entirely separate from Parliament and the executive arm of government.

For shipping, the English courts have a special significance because of their role over the years in the hearing and settlement of "commercial" maritime disputes and other cases stemming from "maritime" causes such as collisions, strandings, salvage, prize, etc. The first type of dispute is heard before the Commercial Court (or list), the second before the Admiralty Court. Both are nowadays part of the Queen's Bench Division of the High Court.

Both the Commercial Court and the Admiralty Court have much wider significance than might be assumed in that the disputes coming before them invariably have a very distinct international connection with parties and interests widely spread around the world.

To summarise, cases before the Commercial Court normally stem from disputes under charterparties and bills of lading, claims for freight and demurrage and for contribution in general average, disputes under marine insurance policies, claims for damage to, or short delivery of, cargo, etc. Those coming before the Admiralty Court arise out of disputes regarding the vessel itself and include those arising out of such incidents as collisions, strandings, salvage, arrest of sea-going ships and claims for prize money. In cases involving collisions and salvage, the judge is usually assisted by two Elder Brethren of Trinity House (one of the three "General Lighthouse Authorities" with responsibility for navigational aids around the UK and Irish coastlines) on matters of fact and seamanship. The jurisdiction of the Admiralty Court as we have seen earlier, is of considerable antiquity; that of the Commercial Court is more recent.

Arbitration, often under the arbitration clause in charterparties, is another method frequently resorted to for the settlement of disputes which would otherwise go before the Commercial Court. The advantage is that it cuts costs and time and gives the parties greater autonomy over the process of the dispute. Appeals on points of law are to the Commercial Court, although the criteria are tightly set to avoid the situation where every case is challenged, as this would defeat the object of referring a dispute to arbitration.

The European Union (EU) and Its Institutions

Today, the European Union represents 27 European countries in a unique economic and political partnership. It is progressively building a single Europe-wide market in which people, goods, services, and capital move among the member states as freely as within one country.

The Union originated with the European Coal and Steel Community founded by France, Germany, Italy and the Benelux countries in 1952. The European Economic Community (EEC) came into being with the Treaty of Rome of 1957 to which the original signatories were the same six founding members as above. Denmark, Ireland and the UK joined in 1973, Greece in 1981, Spain and Portugal in 1986 and Austria, Finland and Sweden in 1995. Ten other countries joined the Union in 2004 (Cyprus, Malta and many East European countries—Czech Republic, Estonia, Hungary, Latvia, Lithuania, Poland, Slovakia and Slovenia); and two more (Bulgaria and Romania) in 2007. Applications for membership are also currently pending from Croatia, Iceland, Macedonia Montenegro and Turkey.

The initial principles under which the European Union operates are set out in the early Articles of the Treaty of Rome. From the standpoint of shipping and this book, the following are important:

- The elimination of customs duties and restrictions on the import and export of goods as between Member States.
- The establishment of policy towards third countries.
- Freedom of movement for persons, capital and services.
- A common transport (which includes shipping) policy.
- The institution of a system to ensure that competition is not distorted.

The relevance of these will be seen later. Whatever criticisms (bureaucracy, slowness, another layer of government, loss of sovereignty, etc.) may be levelled against the Community, one thing stands out above all others. For those who grew up in the shadow of the 1939–1945 War, the great achievement of the European Union is that it is inconceivable that there should ever again be a war between EU Member States.

A sequence of institutional acts and treaties has been adopted over the last 20 years which have sought to consolidate and deepen the processes of co-operation and integration within the EU. The Single European Act of 1987 amended the Treaty of Rome and promoted the completion of the Single European Market and the lowering of barriers between EU nations to form a truly open market from 1993. The Maastricht Treaty 1991 extended the powers of the European Parliament and provided for increased voting by majority (rather than unanimity) in the Council of Ministers. The Maastricht Treaty also established a single European currency—the Euro—which would become in January 1999 the new official currency of the participating states, replacing their old national currencies. Currently, the Euro has been adopted by 17 countries, with new-entrant states introducing it gradually and three earlier Member States (Denmark, Sweden and the UK) remaining outside the system.

In an endeavour to respond to ever-evolving new issues relating to globalisation, the environment and security, the EU has continually sought to modernise its institutions and processes in order to ensure it has effective, coherent tools to perform the tasks required of it. The Treaty of Nice in 2003 brought in further reforms of the EU's institutional structure in preparation for the EU enlargement planned at that time. In particular, it provided for an increase of the number of seats in the European Parliament and suggested a reduction in the size of the European Commission.

The Treaty on the functioning of The European Union signed in Lisbon in December 2007 known as the Lisbon Treaty, adopted new rules defining what the EU can and cannot do and improving the structure of the EU's institutions and how they work. The Treaty entered into force in December 2009.

Before an explanation of the institutions of the Community is given, several preliminary and important points must be made:

• Whenever a country joins the European Union it thereby gives up some of its own sovereignty over shipping as well as in other ways. Full sovereignty is no longer with the national parliament.
• The Union has the power, and uses it, to make laws which override those of the Member States. There are gradations of enactments. Regulations are binding in their entirety and are directly applicable to Member States. Directives are binding but the method and form of implementation are not stipulated. Decisions are binding only on those to whom they are addressed. Recommendations and Opinions are merely advisory.

- The Union has a powerful voice in shipping matters and works over an increasingly wide area. Most measures affecting shipping take the form of Regulations or Directives.

The EU Institutions and Other Bodies

According to the EU Treaties, there are now seven EU institutions. These are:

- The European Commission
- The European Council (heads of state)
- The Council of the European Union or "Council of Ministers"
- The European Parliament (EP)
- The European Court of Justice (ECJ)
- The Court of Auditors
- The European Central Bank.

More traditionally, however, when talking about the EU institutions, three of these institutions are recognised as—together—holding the executive and legislative power of the Union: the Council of the European Union, representing national governments; the European Parliament, representing citizens; and the European Commission, the initiator of EU legislation. This "institutional triangle" produces the policies and laws that apply throughout the EU. In principle, it is the Commission that proposes new laws, but it is the Parliament and Council that adopt them. The Commission and the Member States then implement them and the Commission ensures that the laws are properly taken on board.

Although not an institution as such, a brief description is also given of the Economic and Social Committee and the European Maritime Safety Agency.

The European Commission

The Commission has three main responsibilities. Generating legislation, all of which is initially drafted by Commission officials; enforcing the treaties governing the EU and ensuring that the decisions of the institutions are upheld; administration of the Community Budget and all funding.

The 27 Commissioners, one from each EU country, are appointed for a 5-year term. Each Commissioner is assigned responsibility for specific policy areas by the President of the Commission. The President is nominated by the European Council, which also appoints the other Commissioners in agreement with the Commission President. In both cases, however, the nominations have to be approved by the European Parliament.

The work of the Commission is currently divided between 33 departments or, as they are termed, Directorates General (DGs). For shipping, the Directorate General of immediate concern is that dealing with transport issues, DG MOVE (Mobility and Transport), but many others are also important. These include DGs; CLIMA (Climate Action), COMP (Competition), DEVCO (EuropeAid Development and Co-operation), EEAS (European External Action Service or "foreign relations"), EMPL (employment and labour affairs), ENTR (Enterprise and Industry), ENV (Environment), JUST (Justice), MARE (Maritime Affairs and Fisheries), MARKT (Internal Market), RTD (Research and Innovation), and TAXUD (Taxation and Customs Union).

All proposals by the Commission are developed by individual DGs with the responsible Commissioner, but have to be approved by all Commissioners before submission to the Parliament and the Council of Ministers.

The European Council

The European Council comprises the heads of states or government of the EU Member States, along with the President of the European Commission (currently José Manuel Barroso), and the President of the European Council (currently Herman Van Rompuy). The High Representative for Foreign Affairs, currently Catherine Ashton, also takes part in its meetings. While the European Council has no formal legislative power, it is charged with defining "the general political directions and priorities" of the Union. It is thus the Union's strategic body. The summit meetings of the European Council are chaired by its President and take place at least twice every 6 months. The European Council should not be confused with the Council of the European Union—another EU body (see next paragraph)—or the Council of Europe, which is a separate international organisation and not an EU body at all.

The Council of the European Union

The Council of the European Union (also known as the "Council of Ministers", or informally as just "the Council") is the second of the three main European institutions, representing the governments of the EU Member States. It is composed of 27 national ministers (one per state). The exact membership depends on the topic. In other words, it is not one Council but in fact several different Councils dealing with their respective portfolios (e.g. Transport) and made up of the Member States' ministers responsible for the area under discussion. The Council has no power to initiate proposals although it can instruct the Commission to bring forward proposals. It acts on proposals presented to it by the Commission, considering the opinions of the European Parliament and the Economic and Social Committee.

The chair of the Council rotates between Member States every 6 months and for that period the Member State holds the Presidency of the European Union. Following the changes introduced by the Treaty of Lisbon, successive Council presidencies—known as "presidency trios", i.e. the current presidency working together with the last and the next governments holding the presidency—are now expected to cooperate for an 18-month period to provide continuity by sharing common political perspectives and programmes.

The Council is served by COREPER (Committee of Permanent Representatives) comprised of Permanent Representatives in Brussels of the Member States. COREPER II is comprised of Ambassadors; COREPER I of Deputy Ambassadors who deal, amongst other things, with transport (including shipping) issues. Both COREPERs meet weekly to prepare items for discussion in the Council of Ministers. COREPER is supported by a plethora of working groups attended by Member State officials. Their main role is detailed discussion of Commission proposals before decisions are taken by the Council. Advisory or management committees are often established which meet under Commission chairmanship to assist in the implementation of directives and to keep them up to date so as to reflect, for example, changes in international agreements or other relevant developments.

European Parliament (EP)

The European Parliament is an EU institution, which is directly elected by the citizens of the EU Member States. The Parliament is composed of 736 Members (MEPs) who are subject to election every 5 years. MEPs are grouped by their party political affiliation rather than by country. The Parliament comprises seven political groups. At present, the European People's Party (EPP—Christian Democrats) are the largest, followed by the Progressive Alliance of Socialists and Democrats (S&D), the Alliance of Liberals and Democrats for Europe (ALDE), the European Conservatives and Reformists (ECR); the Greens/European Free Alliance (Greens/EFA), the European United Left (GUE-NGL); the Group for Europe of Freedom and Democracy (EFT), as well as a number of non-attached members.

The Parliament has 20 standing committees that deal with legislative proposals in specific policy areas. The Committees meet twice a month to debate and adopt reports on the Commission's legislative proposals. Once adopted by the relevant Parliamentary committee, these reports are to be presented for the adoption in plenary. When it comes to shipping, a number of the Parliamentary committees could be involved in debating legislative proposals. The main committees concerned are those dealing with Transport, the Environment, and Legal Affairs.

The European Parliament has the following main roles:

- Debating and passing European laws, with the Council
- Scrutinising other EU institutions, particularly the Commission, to make sure they are working democratically
- Debating and adopting the EU's budget, with the Council
- Electing the President of the Commission, and approving (or not) the appointment of the Commission as a whole

The EU's standard decision-making procedure is known as "co-decision". This means that the European Parliament has to approve the EU legislation together with the Council of Ministers. The Treaty of Lisbon increased the number of policy areas where "co-decision" is used. The European Parliament now also has more power to block a proposal if it disagrees with the Council.

European Court of Justice

This court may be compared with the highest court of appeal in any Member State. Its judgments not only settle the particular matters at issue, but spell out the precise construction to be placed on disputed texts in the EU's basic treaty. Actions may be brought by the Commission against governments for alleged infringements of the treaty: by governments against decisions of the Commission; and, less frequently, by individuals. The court also increasingly gives preliminary rulings on matters referred to it by national courts. This is the result of the increased intermingling of national and EU laws.

Since 1986, a lower "Court of First Instance" (CFI) has also been established. Its role includes cases involving competition law, anti-dumping and complaints against the EU institutions.

The Court of Auditors

This body, set up in 1977 to take over the duties of previous boards, is in charge of the external auditing of the Union's general budget. It has wide powers of investigation and reports annually. The European Parliament attaches considerable importance to this body as reinforcing its own watchdog powers.

The European Central Bank

The European Central Bank is the Central Bank for the Eurozone (the states which have adopted the Euro) and thus controls monetary policy in that area with a mandate to maintain price stability. It is at the centre of the European System of Central Banks which comprises all EU national banks. The bank is governed by a board of national bank governors and a President.

The Economic and Social Committee (ESC)

This consists of representatives from various sectors of economic and social life. It has to be consulted before decisions are taken on a wide range of subjects. It is also free to submit opinions on its own initiative. Its members are business and professional people with wide experience in various fields who belong to one of three groups: employers, trade unions and other interests. Its role is to give a general, non-political, layman's view on proposals under discussion and not to give "expert" opinions on the matters in question (though it frequently does).

European Maritime Safety Agency (EMSA)

The EU has a number of specialised EU agencies which were established in order to provide support to the EU Member States in some specific policy areas. Those policy agencies are bodies governed by European public law; they are distinct from the formal EU institutions and have their own legal personality. They are set up by an act of secondary legislation in order to accomplish a very specific technical, scientific or managerial task.

The key player in the field of maritime safety at Community level is the European Maritime Safety Agency. Created in the aftermath of the foundering of the Erika, EMSA contributes to the enhancement of maritime safety in the Community. In general terms the Agency provides technical and scientific advice to the Commission in the field of maritime safety and the prevention of pollution by ships in the continuous process of updating and developing new legislation, monitoring its implementation and evaluating the effectiveness of the measures in place. The Agency works closely with Member States and is required to respond to their specific requests in relation to the practical implementation of Community legislation.

Division of Competence Between the EU and the EU Member States

The division of competence between the European Union and the Member States is set out in the Treaties. There are three main types of EU competence:

- Exclusive EU competence—the areas where national governments have relinquished their powers in favour of the European Commission include state aids, common trading policy, competition rules, and negotiation of international agreements.
- Shared competence with the Member States—however, Member States may exercise their competence only in so far as the EU has not exercised, or has decided not to exercise, its own competence. Some examples of the areas where the EU shares its competence with the Member States are: the internal market, social policy, environment, consumer protection, and transport (including shipping), Trans-European networks, energy, research and technological development.
- Supporting competences—the EU can only intervene to support, coordinate or complement the actions of Member States.

The EU's competence and powers have expanded greatly in recent years. The European Court of Justice has developed a doctrine of "implied powers", by which the EU not only has the powers expressly laid down in the Treaties but also powers which may be implied from particular provisions. Moreover, according to recent case law (in particular, an ECJ judgment in 2002 on freedom to conclude bilateral agreements), the EU acquires exclusive external competence in those areas, where it has already acted by proposing and adopting relevant regional legislation.

Over the last decade, the EU has produced extensive legislation in the areas of maritime safety, security, environment and social conditions. Hence, it would be difficult to envisage a situation where the subject matter of an international agreement would still remain outside the framework of competence of the European Union institutions. This has had a dramatic effect on the negotiating powers of the Member States in international organisations such as the IMO. In practice, this means that the Member States are—strictly speaking—no longer allowed to negotiate individually in those areas that affect existing EU regional legislation. The term "affect" is defined as "cover the same subject as". Moreover, as suggested by the ECJ in *Commission* v. *Greece* (Case C-45/07) and *Commission* v. *Sweden* (Case C246/07), Member States may be in breach of European law (duty of loyalty) if they act individually in the IMO. However, understandably, this suggestion is strongly contested by a number of the Member States.

Governmental Machinery in the United States Relevant to Shipping

The United States, because of its size and importance (although not the size of the US flag merchant marine) and because of certain policies it has espoused over the years, is of great importance in any study of shipping policies and politics. It is thus necessary to have some understanding of the role of Congress and the various departments of government as they impinge upon, or may affect, shipping.

The basic points to remember about the US machinery of government are the following:

- The division of power between the President (the executive), the judiciary and the Congress (the legislature). The President has no in-built majority and cannot "tell" Congress what to do; indeed the majority in either or both houses may not belong to the President's party.
- The powerful committee structure in both the Senate and the House of Representatives and the important part played by the "staffers" (the not-so-permanent officials of the various committees). "Hearings" are much more politicised than elsewhere and some regard them as almost inquisitorial.
- The difficulty the various departments of state have in reaching a common policy on shipping questions.

- The fact that the Federal Maritime Commission has been purely an independent regulatory body that reports only to the President and not to any of the executive departments or Congress.
- The very deeply felt need to uphold the "antitrust" principles of US law. This comes from fear steeped in US history of major conglomerates (or trusts) and their previous monopolisation of markets.
- The very political approach to all matters and the infiltration by lawyers, many of whom are young, seeking to make their way in life through working as an aide to a Congressman or as a staff member of a committee "on the Hill".

More specifically, we should note the following as being involved in shipping in one way or another. That involvement has frequently strayed far outside the territorial bounds of the United States into the shipping affairs of other nations.

US Congress

The main committees concerned with shipping are:

Senate

- Commerce, Science and Transportation Committee and its Sub-committee on Surface Transportation and Merchant Marine
- Homeland Security and Governmental Affairs
- Judiciary Committee
- Finance Committee (Tax and Fiscal Issues)

House of Representatives

- The Transportation and Infrastructure Committee and its Sub-Committee for Coast Guard and Maritime Transportation for regulatory matters. Promotional matters are now the responsibility of a maritime panel of the Homeland Security Committee
- Judicial Committee
- Ways and Means Committee (Tax and Fiscal Issues)

Departments

Department of Transportation

Since 1981, the Secretary of Transportation has been responsible for maritime policy and officials from that department normally take the lead on shipping questions in international intergovernmental discussions. The department also has a division known as the Maritime Administration (MARAD) which is responsible for the promotion of the US Merchant Marine through, *inter alia*, its programme of subsidies and the implementation of cargo preference laws.

Department of Homeland Security

Created in 2003 by the Homeland Security Act in response to the 9/11 attacks, the Department of Homeland Security (DHS) integrated 22 separate agencies into a single organisation to safeguard the country against terrorism and to respond to any future attacks. Within DHS, the US Coast Guard, formerly in the Department of Transportation, has the duty of publishing and implementing safety, environmental protection, and security regulations made under basic legislation (for example OPA'90). Customs and Border Protection has the responsibility for overseeing security arrangements for ocean freight and for managing supply chain security.

Department of Justice and the Antitrust Division

This department is concerned, *inter alia*, to maintain the US antitrust laws and to be a watchdog in all antitrust matters. Its role with regard to shipping has diminished somewhat since the enactment of the US Shipping Act 1984. This will be discussed later.

Department of State

This department is concerned with foreign affairs and foreign relations including those in the shipping sector. Other departments may become relevant to shipping from time to time, for example those concerned with tax law and its administration, the environment and health.

Regulatory Agencies

The Federal Maritime Commission (FMC) and its predecessor agencies have been responsible, over the years, for the "regulation" of shipping under the various

Shipping Acts, notably those of 1916 and the 1961 (Bonner) Amendments as well as the Shipping Act of 1984. The FMC makes regulatory policy through interpretation of the applicable statutes and rulemaking decisions on individual cases. Commission members, or members of its staff on the other hand, frequently participate in international discussions. But, strictly speaking, the role of the FMC is regulatory alone and in that capacity it has a quasi-judicial role.

Foreign Representation in Washington

The shipping attachés from the embassies of the traditional maritime nations in Washington have for many years had an informal grouping known as the "Cotton Club". This vehicle has been used frequently to assist parent national governments on matters pertaining to shipping and the United States and for the presentation of joint notes of protest or other observations (*aides-mémoire*) to the US Administration through the State Department. The chairmanship of this group was originally in UK hands but nowadays it rotates.

The Main United Nations Intergovernmental Bodies and Regional Agencies

Reference has already been made on a number of occasions to the IMO (IMCO), UNCTAD and the ILO. It is now necessary to explain their origins and role in more detail as well as that of the UN regional bodies. These latter are of much less importance to shipping than the former three bodies.

International Maritime Organization (IMO): Originally Known as Inter-Governmental Maritime Consultative Organization (IMCO)

The first International Maritime Conference held in Washington in 1889 suggested the establishment of a permanent international commission on maritime affairs but although then regarded as desirable it was seen as premature. Two further unsuccessful attempts were made by the International Law Association in 1926 and by the Institute of International Law in 1934. It was not until immediately after the Second World War that some progress was made. This was under the aegis of the then newly formed United Nations as the successor to the pre-War League of Nations.

The basic aims of the United Nations were established in its Charter by a conference of "United Nations" held in the shadow of the war in 1945. They were to:

- Save succeeding generations from the scourge of war.
- Reaffirm faith in fundamental human rights.
- Establish justice and respect for international obligations.
- Promote social progress and better standards of life.

All these were undertaken in the names, not of any one state or groups of states, but of "the peoples of the United Nations".

The UN system as then conceived comprised the principal organs; the subsidiary organs on particular aspects of UN policy, the specialised agencies; and a number of *ad hoc* global conferences dealing with specific important issues. It was under the aegis of this new system that a full Maritime Conference was convened in 1948 and entrusted with the task of preparing a Convention on the establishment of an Intergovernmental Maritime Consultative Organization (IMCO). This was adopted and opened for signature in March of that year.

The main purposes were:

- To provide machinery for co-operation between governments on technical matters affecting shipping in order to encourage high safety standards.
- To encourage the removal of discriminatory and restrictive actions by governments and thereby to promote the free availability of shipping services for the benefit of world trade.
- To enable the Organization to consider unfair restrictive practices by shipping concerns.
- To consider shipping matters referred to it by other organs of the UN.
- Generally to assist in the exchange of information between governments on maritime issues.

Whilst the comparatively small number of states then involved, largely from the traditional maritime world, were by this time prepared to see the establishment of a global maritime organisation, this was only on the basis, first, that it would be "consultative" and would therefore have no teeth; and second, that it would confine itself to the discussion of technical matters. Governments themselves, as well as their shipowners, were still basically unready to give up much, if anything, in the way of sovereignty. Shipowners were certainly not prepared to see governments involved in the commercial, competitive, operational, managerial and economic aspects of shipping. In the event, the necessary number of ratifications for the Convention to come into force were not achieved for some years and the Organization did not come into existence functionally until March 1959. Because, however, of the reservations described earlier about the scope of work of the Organization, there was a gentleman's agreement that it would restrict itself to technical matters.

This is a very important point. It demonstrates how fearful the founder nations led by the UK and Norway, aided and abetted by their shipowners, were of government involvement in other than a limited technical field; and how, despite the provisions of the Convention, a small group of traditional maritime nations were able to suppress part of its work. It also raises the very interesting question, which cannot now be answered, as to whether UNCTAD would ever have become involved in the non-technical aspects of shipping had IMCO (IMO) been ready, or enabled, to carry out its full remit. It also raises the question as to whether the IMO today would still be the relatively non-political and technical body which it has managed to remain. Politics, as we shall learn, was never far below the surface in UNCTAD, although post-UNCTAD VIII things are different.

The original organs of the IMO were:

- The **Assembly**: comprising all member states.
- The **Council**: originally comprised 16 member states elected by the Assembly but this has now increased to 40.
- The **Maritime Safety Committee (MSC)**: originally comprised 14 elected members of which not less then 8 were to come from the largest shipowning nations. This committee was to be the principal technical organ empowered to consider all aspects of maritime safety. Today, however, all member states are entitled to seats on the MSC.

It is historically interesting that in the early days when membership of the MSC was restricted a dispute immediately arose as to which nations were in fact "the largest shipowning nations". The original elections had resulted in a Maritime Safety Committee comprising the US, the UK, Norway, Japan, Italy, the Netherlands, France and the then Federal Republic of Germany representing the shipowning group. Liberia (which ranked third in terms of shipping tonnage) and Panama (which ranked eighth) both contended that they should have been elected. Both were "flag of convenience" states which accepted ships from other states on their registers. The traditional maritime states contended that they were as a result not truly "shipowning" nations.

The matter was submitted after lengthy debate for an advisory opinion of the International Court of Justice at The Hague. By a nine-to-five majority the court decided that the non-election of Liberia and Panama was contrary to the relevant article of the IMCO Convention. In short, "largest shipowning nation" meant just what it said, namely the largest by reference to tonnage on the national register.

In this decision we see the seeds of the very long-lasting controversy which was only partially resolved in 1986, namely the question of "genuine link" between the ship and the state and whether or not nations should be free to fix the conditions for grant of nationality (and thereby flag). This is an issue in shipping which remains at once contemporary and controversial.

The IMO's involvement in pollution and environmental matters stems from its taking over responsibility for the 1954 Convention for the Prevention of Pollution of the Sea by Oil which had resulted from a UK inspired conference and which had come into force in 1958. And, as a result of the *Torrey Canyon* incident, the **Legal Committee** and the **Marine Environmental Protection Committee (MEPC)** were established.

Another committee established after the IMO came into being was the Facilitation Committee. This Committee is concerned with improving governmental documentary and physical requirements and procedures for the entry and clearance of ships, their passengers and cargo.

It is impossible to give complete details of the many areas of work and responsibility which nowadays fall to the IMO but the following list gives some indication:

- Navigation and marine engineering in all aspects.
- Ship design, construction and equipment.
- Sub-division, stability and load lines.
- Tonnage measurement.
- Radio communications and Global Maritime Distress and Safety System.
- Search and rescue.
- Casualty investigations.
- Navigational safety including prevention of collisions.
- Life-saving appliances.
- Carriage of dangerous goods.
- Carriage of dry and liquid bulk cargoes including oil and chemicals.
- Fire safety.
- Ship-source marine pollution caused by oil cargo and bunkers.
- Marine pollution caused by other noxious or hazardous cargoes.
- Training and certification of seafarers.
- Facilitation of international maritime traffic.
- Quality in management.
- Human element in shipping.
- Responsibilities of flag states.
- Port state control.
- Piracy and other violent and unlawful maritime acts.

All these subjects and others feature in the very long list of international treaty instruments which the IMO has generated and administered since its inception. Relevant aspects of these have been mentioned in this book, however, for details the reader is advised to resort to the instruments themselves and other related literature.

Mention must also be made of two other aspects of the IMO's work:

Technical Assistance

Many of the IMO's member states are emerging maritime nations. Consequently, they lack the centuries-old commercial seafaring traditions of the established countries and lack the qualified personnel and other resources needed to play a full part in the maritime world although this is now rapidly changing in some quarters.

Thus the establishment of the IMO's Technical Assistance Programme under the guidance of its Technical Co-operation Committee. As such the IMO is one of the executing agencies for the United Nations Development Programme (UNDP). The IMO programme includes advisory services, assistance with specific projects, a fellowship programme, advice on obtaining equipment, the arrangement of seminars, workshops and so on.

World Maritime University (WMU)

The experience of the IMO has shown that there is a continuing need in developing countries for high-level, specialized education for shipping personnel, particularly those in senior positions and professional and management levels, in both the public and private sectors. In its endeavour to facilitate such education, it has established three institutions of higher maritime learning. The World Maritime University (WMU) established in Malmo, Sweden in 1983 is IMO's apex institution. The fact that this initiative was only mooted in 1981 is evidence of the real thrust given to this side of the Organization's work. Whilst the WMU was established by the IMO, it has a partially autonomous status by virtue of its Charter and is independently financed and administered. The governance of the University is carried out by its Chancellor, the Board of Governors and the Executive Board. The members of these two boards are mandated to act in their personal capacities. The Chief Executive of the University is the President, who is responsible for the administration of the University. Under the Charter, the Board of Governors provides directions and guidelines as necessary to the President and the Executive Board advises on University policies and programmes.

The WMU provides postgraduate education leading to the degree of Master of Science (M.Sc.) in Maritime Affairs. Six areas of specialisations within maritime affairs are currently offered. WMU also has a doctoral programme in Maritime Affairs. As part of its academic outreach initiatives, the University has an M.Sc. programme in Maritime Transportation Management and Logistics at Shanghai Maritime University and another M.Sc. programme in Maritime Safety and Environmental Management at Dalian Maritime University, both in China.

The IMO also established an International Maritime Law Institute in Malta and the International Maritime Academy in Trieste, Italy.

IMO and Other UN Maritime-Related Bodies

In the course of its work the IMO naturally has working relationships with other bodies within the UN system. An example is its co-operation with the Secretariat of the Law of the Sea officially known as the Division of Ocean Affairs and the Law of the Sea in the Office of Legal Affairs. The areas of mutual interest include:

- Rights and obligations of flag states, coastal states and port states.
- Powers and responsibilities of states in the newly established exclusive zones.

- Rights and obligations of states regarding transit for international navigation.
- Conditions for use of artificial islands, installations, *etc.*

Thus the IMO has come a long way since it was first established. Its membership now stands at 170. There are also three associate members, namely Hong Kong (China), Macau (China) and Faroe Islands (Denmark). It has a fine building (the only UN body located in London), a substantial staff and an extremely full work programme which keeps meeting rooms constantly in use. Above all, it has high standing world wide as an efficient body which gets on with its programme of practical work and has little time, despite its very wide spread of membership, for politics. It prides itself on the "IMO spirit" which even in the most difficult situations usually results in a solution being found.

United Nations Conference on Trade and Development (UNCTAD)

The period following the Second World War saw a complete change in the world economic and political situation and also the first real attempt, at intergovernmental level through UNCTAD, to consider, and intervene in, the economic and commercial aspects of international shipping. This resulted during the 1970s and 1980s in high tension and confrontation between the traditional shipping interests in the Western (Group B) countries and those from the emerging "Group of 77" countries (established on 15 June 1964 at the end of the first session of UNCTAD).

The period also saw, in varying degrees, the awakening of a public conscience in the Western nations to the needs of the developing countries and the desire to give a new impetus to trade and aid and thereby to assist the development process of the underprivileged nations. Historically a number of UN Resolutions provided the stepping stones for government involvement in the commercial and economic aspects of shipping:

- A programme of expanded technical assistance (1949).
- The first UN Development Decade (1961); there have subsequently been further Development Decades.
- The World Food Programme (1961).

and importantly; the establishment of the United Nations Conference on Trade and Development (UNCTAD).

The first meeting of UNCTAD in Geneva in 1964 established a Shipping Committee with 45 members under the "invisibles" division and subject to the general policy direction of the senior UNCTAD Committee, the Trade and Development Board. Formal machinery was thereby set up for in-depth discussion and debate of shipping, not from the technical standpoint, but so as to cover the commercial and economic aspects. It marked a watershed in this study of the erosion of the "freedom" principle.

Following this, aspects of shipping came up at main UNCTAD meetings: New Delhi (1968), Santiago (1972), Nairobi (1976), Manila (1979), Belgrade (1984); and at shipping committee meetings held in Geneva every 2 years. The 1987 UNCTAD Conference was the first at which shipping did not come up—a sign of changing times.

The following list indicates some of the main topics which have been discussed within UNCTAD.

- Liner conferences, a code of conduct and various detailed aspects of liner conference operation and pricing arrangements.
- Multimodal transport, i.e. where more than one mode of transport is involved in carrying goods.
- Ports, their development, adequacy and efficiency.
- Protection of shipper interests.
- Development of merchant marines, especially from the standpoint of developing nations.
- Co-operation in merchant shipping.
- Imbalance between supply and demand.
- The bulk trades, wet and dry.
- Conditions for registration of ships.

UNCTAD, in the same way as the IMO (and indeed the ILO, see below), are involved as members of the UN family in its Technical Assistance Programme funded by the UN Development Programme (UNDP). Examples from the UNCTAD standpoint are the TRAINMAR programme designed to assist the training of all types of managers from developing countries; and the JOBMAR programme designed to assist the training of seafarers from developing countries including "on the job" training in developed nations.

It must be underlined that UNCTAD's Shipping Committee arose out of a perceived need at the time for a new approach to international shipping as part of a new impetus to world trade and aid. It was not established for the benefit of the developed world as such; it was established to facilitate the growth of developing countries in a variety of ways including shipping. However, UNCTAD was reputed to be impartial, but not necessarily unbiased in its overall approach. In other words, it tried to examine issues impartially from the standpoint of establishing the facts; but when it came to proposals for action then it was unashamedly biased (as it was required to be) towards what it perceived as the best interests of developing countries. Whether or not certain of UNCTAD's shipping initiatives in fact improved things for developing countries is something history will have to judge. There may well be conflicting views.

In the late 1980s and into the early 1990s the mood within UNCTAD member governments on shipping questions began to change. The period of confrontation between developed and developing nations was also drawing to a close although as the UNCTAD Secretariat in its Review of Maritime Transport for 1990 pointed out the developed world owned 67 % by deadweight of world tonnage as against a slightly increased tonnage by developing countries of 21 %. Yet developing nations generated nearly 50 % of world trade.

This changing mood was demonstrated at the full UNCTAD VIII meeting in Cartagena, Colombia in early 1992. This marked a turning point in UNCTAD generally and as regards shipping, in so far as member governments came to accept not only the concept of the free and open market-place but that this was the way forward also for developing countries: a marked change in direction. All existing committees, including the Shipping Committee and its satellite committees were disbanded. Shipping was put under the aegis of a new Standing Committee on Developing Services Sectors and its work programme, whilst lengthy, was of a largely technical nature and concerned with evaluating trends albeit from the standpoint of developing countries.

Since then the UNCTAD structure has been further reorganised into three very broad "commissions" (on Trade in Goods, Services and Commodities; Investment, Technology and related Financial Issues; and Enterprise, Business Facilitation and Development). There is much less focus on sectoral issues. Shipping questions could in theory arise under any of these commissions, but in practice any UNCTAD work on shipping is likely to be confined to training, development, co-operation and other essentially uncontroversial matters.

International Labour Organization (ILO)

The ILO was founded in 1919 as a product of the Paris Peace Conference of that year and its constitution enshrined in the Peace Treaty. This set out its objectives broadly as follows:

- The establishment of peace based on social justice.
- The alleviation of various social injustices in hours and conditions of work, through the establishment of a maximum working day and week and in other ways.
- The prevention of unemployment and the provision of an adequate living wage.
- The protection of workers against sickness, disease and injury arising out of their employment.
- The protection of children, young persons and women.

The ILO is divided into three parts: the General Conference, the Governing Body and the Permanent Office. Uniquely, it is a tripartite organisation bringing together representatives of governments, employers and workers.

The General Conference normally meets once a year and each member state is entitled to send four voting delegates: two from government and one each from the employers' and workers' organisations. These conferences can cover all social questions and result in either conventions (which are binding when adopted) or recommendations (which are not). Recommendations may well pave the way for future conventions.

The Governing Body, also tripartite, meets three times a year. It controls the work of the Office, it draws up the budget, and is generally responsible for the programme of the organisation, including that in the maritime sector.

The main function of the Office is to provide a permanent secretariat, to collect and distribute information on all aspects of industrial life and labour, to assemble technical material as a basis for future conventions and to prepare for conferences. Nowadays the secretariat is large and the different areas it has to cover are very broad indeed.

Maritime affairs are treated differently in the ILO from other sectors, no doubt recognising the special characteristics of employment at sea (for example, since seafarers are at their place of work 24 h a day, 7 days a week for long periods at a time). This is manifested in two ways. First, a large number of dedicated maritime instruments have been adopted alongside the general labour standards that apply to other sectors. While most of these were established by separate ILO Maritime Conferences convened every 10 years or so according to need, maritime matters have recently been brought within the General Conference. Over the years, the ILO has adopted over 30 international conventions and 25 recommendations dealing exclusively with maritime labour conditions. These figures compare with the total of 189 conventions and a similar number of recommendations adopted by the ILO in all.

Second, uniquely in the ILO, a specialist body—the Joint Maritime Commission—is responsible for covering maritime matters between Conferences, including preparation of the conferences. The JMC is bipartite, comprising employers' and employees' representatives only.

This clearly gives the two sides of industry considerable power of decision, not least in setting the agendas of the conferences. The secretariat of the Shipowners' Group in the JMC and the ILO is provided by the International Shipping Federation, that of the Seafarers' Group by the International Transport Workers' Federation.

The treaty instruments generated by ILO have often been criticised for being grossly outdated. However, during the last decade, a major effort has been made to update older conventions or replace them with new instruments. This challenge was picked up actively by the maritime community and a long, ambitious and comprehensive exercise was undertaken to consolidate all seafarer standards in a single mandatory instrument. This resulted in 2006 in the highly successful adoption of the groundbreaking Maritime Labour Convention, which can now be held up as a model to the rest of the ILO. In view of its serious consideration of contemporary and topical issues relating to seafarer welfare, worldwide acceptance of it has been evidenced by the fact that the required number of ratifications for entry into force was reached in August 2012.

World Trade Organization (WTO)

The decline in the role of UNCTAD as regards shipping coincided with the rise of the role of the General Agreement on Tariffs and Trade (GATT) and latterly of the World Trade Organisation (WTO).

The GATT was a world wide process which had the aim of imposing multilaterally agreed disciplines on governments regarding the conduct of trade in goods. Formally, it had no institutional establishment, only a small secretariat. It was a set of rules based on an international agreement. Although it lasted for nearly 50 years, it operated only on a "provisional basis". Its objective was to provide a business environment which encouraged trade, investment and job creation, as well as choice and low prices. It started from the premise that such an environment needed to be stable and predictable and that was best assured by a system which allowed free market access limited only by tariffs or customs duties. The principal aim of the GATT was then to reduce those tariffs progressively, which it did rather successfully. Its scope also included the settlement of disputes and an anti-dumping code.

The GATT operated through a series of "rounds" of multilateral trade negotiations. The seventh and last of these which began in 1986 and ended in December 1993, was called the Uruguay Round. Its commitments covered more than 120 countries. One of its distinguishing features was that it extended the GATT process into a number of new areas including trade in services and intellectual property rights.

Following the end of the Uruguay Round, the World Trade Organisation was established to carry on and develop further in a permanent institution the GATT's functions of administering the multilateral trade agreements and providing a world wide forum for future trade negotiations.

The WTO, based in Geneva, is the legal and institutional foundation of the multilateral trading system. It provides the principal contractual obligations determining how governments frame and implement domestic trade legislation and regulations. It is the platform on which trade relations among countries evolve through collective debate, negotiation and adjudication. The WTO was established on 1 January 1995 following the conclusion of the Uruguay Round of negotiations and the adoption of the Marrakesh Declaration which affirmed that the Round would "strengthen the world economy and lead to more trade, investment, employment and income growth throughout the world". Not only does the WTO have a potentially larger membership than the GATT, it also has a much broader scope. The GATT only applied to trade in goods; the WTO covers trade in goods, services and "trade in ideas" or intellectual property. Its essential functions are:

- Administering and implementing the multilateral and plurilateral trade agreements which together made up the WTO.
- Providing a forum for multilateral trade negotiations.
- Seeking to resolve trade disputes.
- Overseeing national trade policies.

- Co-operating with other international institutions involved in global economic policy-making.

The structure of the WTO is dominated by its highest authority, the Ministerial Conference, which meets every 2 years. The day-to-day work, however, falls under its Secretary General through a web of other bodies notably the General Council, the Trade Review Body and the Dispute Settlement Body together with Councils for Trade in Goods, Trade in Services and Trade Related Aspects of Intellectual Property Rights.

For shipping, the importance of the WTO lies in the strengthening which it gives to trade without discrimination, predictable and growing access to markets, the promotion of fair competition, and the encouragement of development and economic reform. Part of the WTO's ongoing work covers negotiations on maritime transport which were scheduled to end in June 1996 but were carried forward with no end date. The aim was to improve on the commitments already included in the three main areas: access to and use of port facilities; auxiliary services; and ocean transport. However, with progress on the wider trade negotiations faltering over recent years, progress has effectively halted on maritime issues and it is uncertain when or whether they will be reprised.

The preamble to the WTO Agreement also recognises the relationship between trade and the need to protect the environment and to promote sustainable development.

Other Specialised Intergovernmental Groups

Organisation for Economic Co-operation and Development (OECD)

This is the intergovernmental body, established by Treaty and based in Paris, of the developed nations. As such it has traditionally been the group which, on matters before many international intergovernmental bodies, coordinates and formulates the policy of the Group B nations within the United Nations bodies. That role has however diminished, particularly as regards maritime issues, with the decrease in confrontational discussion based on specific international groupings. Two panels traditionally advise the OECD: the Business and Industry Advisory Committee (BIAC) comprising business experts from the private sector and the Trades Union Advisory Committee (TUAC), the role of which is obvious. Until recently, for maritime issues, the OECD had an active Maritime Transport Committee (MTC) discussing policy developments on matters such as competition policy, support measures and economic issues arising out of non-compliance with international safety and environmental rules and standards. Most notably, perhaps, the MTC adopted a set of common principles of shipping policy which it subsequently promoted more widely through dialogue with non-OECD countries. While the MTC has now been disbanded, there remain maritime-related obligations, through the common principles and adherence to specific OECD codes, and the opportunity exists to raise maritime-related issues within the other structures of the organisation.

The Consultative Shipping Group (CSG)

This started as an informal group of the maritime administrations from the European traditional maritime nations together with Japan. It emerged in the early 1960s in response to those governments' concerns about shipping issues vis-à-vis the United States and a desire to discuss and co-ordinate their policy responses.

The CSG still exists and continues to evolve to meet the needs and wishes of its members. Its membership has grown to 18 countries which adhere to the liberal principles of open and unrestrictive access to international shipping markets and free and fair competition on a commercial basis. These include: Belgium, Canada, Denmark, Finland, France, Germany, Greece, Italy, Japan, the Republic of Korea, Norway, Poland, Portugal, Singapore, Spain, Sweden, The Netherlands and the United Kingdom. Nowadays its remit is somewhat wider than just US shipping policy and the focus has shifted to include greater dialogue and cooperation with the US as necessary on issues of mutual concern.

Initially, the chairman and secretariat of this group was provided by the UK Department responsible for shipping, but these roles are today held by the Danish Maritime Authority in Copenhagen.

World Customs Organization (WCO)

This Brussels-based organisation is the International Association for National Customs Authorities and deals solely with customs and related matters on an international basis. It involves itself in technical questions about standardising and improving customs formalities, including documentation pertaining to the entry and clearance of ships and their cargo, and to developing co-operative programmes between customs authorities and trade interests in anti-drug smuggling initiatives. Over the years it has shown itself to be a pragmatic organisation ready to listen to the views and concerns of the private sector.

Chapter 6
Shipping Nationalism and Government Involvement

From early times, "authorities"—whether local, regional, national or international—have never been far from involvement in one aspect or another of shipping. Sometimes that involvement is for the good; sometimes it is not. Indeed, one of the main themes of this book is to trace the ebb and flow of the involvement of these authorities and to put this involvement in perspective in today's world against the background of the principle of freedom in shipping.

This chapter and the next look at the ways in which the aspirations of national authorities have created impositions and obstacles for other countries' shipping interests and then at the conflict between those aspirations and what may be termed the international or multilateral imperative, without which chaos and economic war would ensue. They consider the many different forms of present-day protectionism and its confrontation with policies based on liberalisation.

Later, it is explained how governments have become involved—in some cases heavily—in the important areas of safety, the environment and pollution control, security, liability and management quality. Their involvement in crewing and other labour issues is also covered briefly.

The Backdrop

The end of the Second World War and the dismantling of the different European colonial regimes led to a growth of nationalism in those countries which had previously come under the control and protection of others. Many of those countries saw the creation of a national airline—and, as an extension of that philosophy, of a national shipping line—as a necessary demonstration of their newly found national autonomy and prestige. The "wind of change" in the 1950s and 1960s, to quote the famous phrase of Britain's then Prime Minister, Harold Macmillan, blew as fiercely in the shipping world as elsewhere. This should not be a surprise. We have already seen protectionist attitudes from early times in different nations: Spain, Portugal, the Netherlands, France, along with Britain and its Navigation Acts, which for nearly 300 years helped to protect and promote British shipping.

The natural tendency of all nations, including the traditional maritime countries, has been to look at shipping from their own national perspective and to see where they could gain an advantage. In the United States, shipping in the early twentieth century was regarded as an industry to be maintained at any price if it was a benefit for the nation; but not at any price for the sake of shipping itself. Greece and Norway, both major shipping nations and with shipping their largest single industry, saw their greatest benefit in the maintenance of an open-trading, free-enterprise environment. This same philosophy has now come to be held widely by maritime states because it is considered to be to their benefit as both shipping and trading states. It is difficult to see this trend changing with the increasing globalisation of the national and world economies, although the risk is still present with the emergence of regional country groups.

In Germany, Italy and Japan, during the uneasy days prior to the outbreak of the Second World War, shipping was not seen purely in a trading context but as an arm of a nationalistic and expansionist regime. The period following the Cuban crisis in 1962 through to the early 1980s saw the expansion of the Soviet merchant marine as an extension of that country's political aspirations, in order to ensure a presence in various parts of the world, to correct its previous lack of sea power and maritime prestige and to earn hard currency. This, to an extent, was also the policy of other Eastern Bloc countries, which blazed the trail for the developing countries in shipping nationalism.

Some West African countries, India, Sri Lanka, the Philippines and others followed suit, with the result that a number of developing countries built up much bigger merchant fleets than some of the developed states.

This process was actively encouraged following the establishment in 1964 of UNCTAD, which from the start gave special consideration to the problems and interests of developing countries and to the growth of their merchant marines. The 1950s had seen an explosion of nations joining the newly formed United Nations. By the early 1960s, there were up to 50 from Asia, Africa and Latin America. UNCTAD provided a timely platform for many of these countries to express their concerns and grievances. In their minds, shipping had long been the preserve of a handful of developed states, operating under a legal and commercial system which had been designed by them and worked essentially for their benefit.

The pattern of history has begun to repeat itself and the distinctions have become blurred in a number of cases. Many of those states who built up their fleets on the back of protectionism of one sort or another now espouse free-trade principles because, as Britain found in the mid-nineteenth century, protectionism is no longer in their best interests. That is the mood of recent years as demonstrated by the changing nature and direction of UNCTAD and by the growth in importance of the GATT and the WTO.

This chapter explains the principal mechanisms which governments have used to bend economic, commercial and free-trade principles to the benefit of their own national merchant marines. These may be broadly categorised as follows:

- National (unilateral) regulations or requirements
- Subsidies (overt or covert)
- Bilateral, government-to-government, arrangements
- Regional arrangements
- International agreements and conventions.

Any governmental action under one or more of these heads, which is protectionist or restrictive, tends to erode free competition in terms of price, cargo availability and the ability to trade and to limit the freedom of exporters and importers to choose their service-provider.

The next chapter describes some of the specific issues which are of importance today and how some individual countries or country groupings have responded to these mechanisms. It also touches on some of the current initiatives at regional and international level to bring together the thinking of governments in this area.

National Regulations or Requirements

Given that all forms of national or unilateral regulation under this head are for the purpose of protecting and promoting the national merchant marine, they are restrictive on others and examples of what may be called "anti-freedom". There are many categories. Historically, they have included:

Denial of Access to National Shipping Markets

- National (unilateral) legislation, which reserves all or part of a nation's export or import cargoes to national-flag ships.
- Other forms of discrimination in favour of the national flag—through the use of a freight booking centre or bureau which allocates cargoes on a preferential basis; or through the inclusion of clauses in import licences, or letters of credit, which give preference to the national carrier.
- Cabotage, whereby a country's domestic (coastal or inter-island) trade is reserved to ships flying the national flag.
- Boycotts, whereby ships are debarred from operating in a certain region or trade, for political or economic reasons.
- Domination of the national-flag carrier by a requirement that all goods exported are sold on *cif* (cost, insurance and freight) terms; and that all goods imported are purchased on *fob* (free on board) terms.
- Other administrative provisions which have the effect of debarring non-national lines from participating in the trade.
- Requirements that military, strategic, aid or other government cargoes are carried by national-flag carriers.

• Unwritten pressures or campaigns to ship by the national flag, whether government-sponsored or as a result of national sentiments.

Restrictions on Operations by Non-nationals

• Restrictions on the allocation of berths or anchorages through priority treatment for the national flag.
• Requirements that national-flag vessels be given priority use of loading or discharging equipment, port or navigational equipment or other aids.
• Restrictions on the acquisition or importation of spare parts.
• Requirements that excessive (and expensive) ship repairs are carried out locally in order to support national interests.

Restrictions on the Freedom of Non-nationals (Shore-Side)

• Difficulties or prohibitions for non-nationals wishing to establish branch offices or agencies.
• Restrictions on the operation of inland haulage.
• Impediments in obtaining necessary licences, work permits or visas for non-nationals.
• Restrictions on inward investment or on the repatriation of profits.
• Requirements that national agents, firms or organisations be used in preference to non-national interests.

Extra-Territorial Application of National Laws

• Attempts to extend purely national or regional legislative requirements, for example, US or EU antitrust concepts, into other jurisdictions on the basis of the "effects" doctrine.
• Endeavours to extend to shipowners and shippers of other nations national requirements as to the terms and conditions upon which trade between them is done.
• Unilateral requirements that national laws on practical, operational issues which go beyond the accepted international standards (for example, concerning safety, stability, fire protection, pollution control, and health standards) apply equally to foreign vessels entering national ports or otherwise coming within national jurisdiction.

Restrictions on the Charges for Shipping Services

- Restrictions or pressures on the level of freight rates or the amount or frequency of rate increases, or other interference with commercial pricing policies.
- Powers to disallow freight rates or rate increases on the basis of national criteria such as the "interests of the commerce" of that country.

Subsidies and Other Forms of Assistance

Within this category fall various forms of assistance to shipowners and also to shipbuilders as well as those which, although directed to shipbuilders, are in fact disguised assistance for shipowners.

Shipping

- Investment subsidies, designed to encourage national carriers to invest in new or second-hand tonnage, whether or not the ships have been built at home.
- Construction subsidies based on the principle of putting the national carrier, building a new ship at home, on equal terms with its foreign competitor building either at home or abroad.
- Taxation arrangements designed to assist investment by national carriers.
- More beneficial credit arrangements for national owners building in their own country than for foreigners building in the same yard or yards. These facilities may be provided either by governments, yards, or banks and finance houses.
- Operating subsidies designed to put national carriers on an equal footing with their international competitors, on the argument that national operating costs are, for various reasons, higher.
- Income tax and/or social security alleviations designed to encourage the training and employment of national crews.
- Politically motivated arrangements, some of them covert, for providing national shipowners with an advantage. Although not subsidies in the true sense, they have similar effect.

It is probably the norm rather than the exception for governments to try to assist their shipping through taxation measures, although shipowners in any one country are often heard to complain that the taxation advantages elsewhere are greater. It is a fact that international shipping markets are generally low-cost and low-tax. Many higher-cost countries try to match or offset those conditions for their national operators. It is often difficult to quantify the benefits as between different countries in what is a constantly changing situation.

Depending on the country in question, some measures may be tied to operations under the national flag; others may apply to investment or employment relating to ships owned and operated from the country regardless of where the ship is registered.

Shipbuilding

Historically, governments have sought to aid and bolster up their shipbuilding yards through a wide variety of methods. Although these frequently have a knock-on effect which benefits shipowners indirectly in terms of the price and financing arrangements, they should be distinguished clearly from subsidies or other assistance to the national shipping industry. These aids have the primary aim of assisting the national interest in terms of manufacturing and they benefit any shipowners, whatever their nationality, purchasing a vessel from those yards.

It is a fact of the world maritime scene that, in most countries, shipbuilding has traditionally had a political importance, because it can be labour-intensive and thus means votes. Shipping has tended to have less influence in political terms because it commands fewer votes concentrated in particular areas. Such political leverage as it has stems from other factors, which include its importance to the national economy and skills-base, defence and strategic considerations, and—in some cases—the need to show the flag internationally.

Among the wide range of methods national governments have used to provide assistance to their shipyards come the following:

- Straight financial grants or other financial assistance;
- Government-sponsored schemes for selling ships at non-commercial prices to others for political reasons;
- Schemes for building ships for stock;
- The promotion of scrapping or "scrap and build" schemes, both of which provide, or may provide, employment for shipyards.

The main international forum engaged in the overview of competition-distorting government support in world shipbuilding since the 1960s has been the OECD Working Party on Shipbuilding (WP6).

Most of the measures described above were outlawed by the OECD agreement on shipbuilding subsidies ("Agreement respecting normal competitive conditions in the commercial shipbuilding and repair industry"), which was adopted in 1994. This provided a set of binding, legally enforceable disciplines addressing both subsidies and injurious pricing practices. Specifically, it required all parties to eliminate all existing support measures or practices which "constitute obstacles to normal competitive conditions" in the industry and not to introduce any new ones. It also contained a ban on "injurious pricing"—i.e. the selling of ships to the nationals of another party to the agreement at less than the normal value of the vessel—and allowed the imposition of equalising charges to remedy any material harm caused.

The agreement was concluded after many years of highly sensitive negotiations between the authorities of the USA, the EU, Japan, and other OECD member states. Some other major shipbuilding nations then outside the OECD membership (such as Korea) were also involved. However, one of the main protagonists of the agreement during the early stages of its negotiation, the USA—under pressure from some of its hitherto highly subsidised national shipyards—has never ratified it; as a result, it has never come into force.

In 2002 the signatories to the agreement reached the view that the agreement was most unlikely ever to come into force and the OECD Council created a Special Negotiating Group (SNG) to undertake detailed negotiations on a new world-wide agreement. In contrast to the composition of the negotiations leading to the 1994 agreement, the SNG was directed to invite all non-OECD economies with significant shipbuilding industries to participate in the negotiations on an equal footing with OECD member countries. Eventually, Brazil, China, Croatia, Malta, the Philippines, Romania, the Russian Federation, Chinese Taipei (Taiwan) and Ukraine participated in the negotiations—bringing the proportion of world shipbuilding capacity represented to around 95 %.

The negotiations were "paused" in September 2005 for an unspecified period, in order to allow the parties to reflect on their positions, to talk to each other and to observe developments in the market. The intention was to resume the negotiations when the environment for success had improved. In the meantime, pending their resumption and in an endeavour to maintain interest and stimulate momentum, the OECD's Working Party on Shipbuilding organised a number of workshops together with non-OECD countries and industry which allowed an informal stock-taking of the global industry. It began a series of reports on the industries in both OECD and non-OECD economies, with the full participation of the countries in question. The situation in China and Vietnam was examined and the reports for both countries were issued in 2008.

Despite these efforts and lengthy endeavours to restart the negotiations, the differences between some of the participants could not be overcome and the OECD Council terminated the negotiations in December 2010. Nevertheless, the Working Party on Shipbuilding continues its work in accordance with its original mandate.

Bilateral Government-to-Government Arrangements

There is nothing wrong in principle with bilateral agreements which may well serve a good purpose in establishing an agreed approach to key shipping matters. By its nature, most shipping takes place between two or more countries and therefore a mutual understanding on practical issues affecting the interface between the two countries may be necessary. Ideally this should be done on a multilateral, world-wide basis as far as possible, but in some cases that understanding may be best achieved on a bilateral basis. Whether they are restrictive or non-restrictive depends entirely on the provisions in the particular agreements.

Instinctively, shipping people shy away from bilateralism because they see parallels with air transport where the world's airlines are governed as to landing rights and terms and conditions of their services by a whole network of bilateral, government-to-government agreements.

For shipping, with its vastly more complex patterns of trading, its completely different sectors, and by and large its open-market, free-trade philosophy, such a system would be quite impractical, wasteful of resources and inefficient. Yet, to a limited extent, bilateral agreements between governments do exist, especially as regards regular liner services. Their nature may be either protectionist or defensive. Bilateral agreements often also govern certain administrative aspects of shipping such as consular matters or travel of crew members to or from their ship, which do not affect the market.

Protectionist agreements are designed to promote the national fleet. They no longer seem to be as prominent or as active as they were in the 1970s and 1980s though they may still persist today, particularly in longstanding arrangements. In the past these sought to divide the shipping market between the two countries on some agreed basis. Various formulae were designed to keep carriers from other nations, i.e., cross-traders, completely out of the trade or to limit their share. The split could therefore be 50/50; or 40/40 allowing a 20 % share for cross-traders or 33/33/33. Whatever their nature, they are all restrictions on the principle of the freedom of shipping.

Defensive agreements may be found where one state seeks unilaterally to reserve to its national flag a substantial proportion of its trade with another state, or to impose other restrictions. In such a case, a bilateral agreement may be the only way for that other nation to defend its carriers and enable them to trade effectively.

Examples have been found at various times in different parts of the world. Typical examples in earlier times included the trades between a number of South American states and the USA, the former approaching them from the standpoint of promoting their national interests, the latter in order to defend the interests of its national lines. The most recent US agreements were concluded with Brazil in 2005 ensuring equal treatment in maritime-related services and facilities including shipping taxes, and equal access for each country's national-flag carriers to the other country's government-controlled cargo; and with Vietnam in 2007 allowing US carriers to open wholly-owned subsidiaries in that country, in the face of government monopoly positions in its growing maritime trade. Currently the US has only a few agreements; the others are with China (2003) and Russia (2001), as well as an exchange of letters on port services with Japan (2007) that also has the effect of an agreement.

Other examples of defensive bilaterals were in the relations of individual EU member states and other countries with state-trading countries, particularly the former Soviet Union and, more recently, China. However, these have been overtaken in recent years by the growing number of EU agreements, which do not contain cargo-sharing provisions, and by the entry of a number of the former Eastern Bloc countries into EU membership.

Regional Arrangements

In the same way as individual governments seek to promote, protect or defend their national shipping interests, so may several governments join together for the same purpose in a regional context.

The European Union's common shipping policy is particularly illustrative of the way governments, on a regional basis, may attempt to promote and protect their joint shipping and trading interests. The EU governments have, since December 1986, adopted a common approach to their maritime external affairs, also based on free-market principles. The interesting point is that the EU has shown a readiness to use its collective governmental muscle to defend the liberal principles on which its shipping policy is based.

In contrast, for at least a quarter of a century until fairly recently, the South American countries together pursued restrictive policies in an endeavour to promote their merchant marines. Until the breakdown of communism in the late 1980s, all the centrally-controlled economy states in the Eastern Bloc (COMECON) banded together in the same way. Much the same happened in West Africa in the 1970s and 1980s where a few countries established a series of ministerial meetings in order to co-ordinate their shipping policies for the benefit of their common trading and shipping interests and adopted openly protectionist policies based on cargo reservation. Now, under the aegis of the more liberal Maritime Organisation of West and Central Africa for Maritime Transport (MOWCA), which has 25 state members, the trend is more towards liberalisation with member states becoming signatories to the General Agreement on Trade in Services (GATS) and focusing their energies more on expanding private-sector participation, developing coastal shipping networks and strengthening maritime education and training institutions.

International Intergovernmental Arrangements

While government involvement in the commercial aspects of shipping has long been widespread at national levels, and to a lesser extent at regional levels, it is only during the second half of the twentieth century that governments began to intervene in these aspects on a fully international basis. Groups of like-minded states such as the Consultative Shipping Group or the OECD have exchanged views and acted in a co-ordinated way on these issues. They are wider than regional groupings, but are not fully international. Both of these groupings have been concerned with promoting an open competitive environment.

In the case of the OECD, this is changing. On the one hand, new members have joined in recent years from Eastern Europe, the Far East and Central America. The OECD, has its own Code covering the invisible service interests—such as shipping, insurance, banking, and tourism—which is again directed to the maintenance of open competition. Unfortunately, the United States maintains a different position on the key aspect of the Code as it applies to the shipping sector, insisting on its own freedom of action. In addition, for a period of about 10 years during the 1990s, the OECD was very active—in the absence of progress within the GATT/WTO discussions—carrying the liberal message to different regional groups of countries in a similar way to what it was trying to do in shipbuilding.

On the other hand, the OECD is no longer involved in this area, having disbanded its Maritime Transport Committee in 2005.

The following are some examples of global involvement through international initiatives:

- The agreement in 1993 on trade in services, within the General Agreement on Tariffs and Trade. The basic GATT principles of liberalisation apply to shipping in principle, but there has been no agreement yet on how they should be implemented.
- An extensive range of labour conventions and recommendations, adopted within the International Labour Organisation over the last 90 years, on matters relating to the employment of seafarers. These are unusual in that they are agreed on a tripartite basis, since governments, employers and employees all vote at ILO conferences. As mentioned earlier, most of these have now been revised and subsumed in a major new consolidated instrument, the Maritime Labour Convention, adopted in February 2006. This is expected to be widely supported.
- The United Nations Convention on Conditions for Registration of Ships, 1986, sponsored by UNCTAD, which sought to define the elements necessary to establish a genuine link between a state and the ships flying its flag in the areas of manning, management, control and ownership. This Convention has not entered into force and is unlikely ever to do so.
- The United Nations Convention on the International Multimodal Transport of Goods, 1980, another UNCTAD-sponsored Convention, which laid down the terms and conditions applicable to the international carriage of goods under the responsibility of a single transport operator, when more than one mode of transport is used. This Convention, too, has not entered into force and may well be overtaken by the newly adopted UNCITRAL-sponsored instrument, the United Nations Convention on Carriage of Goods Wholly or Partly by Sea, 2009, known as the "Rotterdam Rules".
- The United Nations Convention on a Code of Conduct for Liner Conferences, 1974, generally referred to as the "UN Liner Code" was also sponsored by UNCTAD. It covered a number of aspects previously considered purely commercial matters, such as conference market shares, pricing policy, relationships between lines and their customers, the shippers, and membership criteria for

liner conferences. This Convention entered into force in October 1983, but rapidly became overtaken by events and is now ineffectual in practical terms.
- The general provisions of early UN plans to the effect that developing nations should have greater participation in shipping, to the extent of at least 20 %.

In all these ways, governments, through their political and bureaucratic machinery, have been drawn into the discussion of shipping issues of an economic and commercial nature.

Chapter 7
Demise of Protectionism and Rise of Liberalisation

Although protectionist practices are less prevalent today, they often remain in the statute books and are still an impediment to world trade; and new instances continue to arise from time to time. At a time of economic downturn and uncertainty such as the world is experiencing today, the danger and fear of a resurgence of protectionism remains very real, as local economies try to gain or maintain an involvement in commerce and create or safeguard local employment.

There are encouraging signs, in that states and economies across the world are working together more frequently and effectively to discuss and find solutions to key issues in the global economy—including through the G20 (the group of the major industrialised nations spanning both developed and developing countries, together with their national bank governors and the World Bank, which has over the last 10 years sought to promote global economic co-operation). In their communiqué following a meeting in September 2009, the G20 leaders committed themselves to stand together to fight against protectionism. Specifically, they promised to keep markets open and free and refrain from imposing barriers to trade in goods and services. They expressed their determination to seek an ambitious and balanced solution during 2010 to the Doha Development Round in the WTO negotiations (see below).

This is therefore very much a current issue, whether active or just under the surface.

Until the late 1970s, protectionism in shipping—in the many forms listed in the last chapter—was widespread. Although, in terms of the overall volumes transported, most liner cargoes were carried between the countries which were members of the OECD at that time (which generally espoused liberal principles), there was a feeling in many parts of the world that, if a country generated cargo, it had in some way a "right" to carry it, or at least to control its carriage. This sense was common among many of the developing countries, driven by the understandable wish partly to exercise greater autonomy over their own affairs, partly to try to find sources of commercial income, and partly also to have a symbol of national and economic prestige.

P.K. Mukherjee and M. Brownrigg, *Farthing on International Shipping*,
WMU Studies in Maritime Affairs, Vol. 1, DOI 10.1007/978-3-642-34598-2_7,
© Springer-Verlag Berlin Heidelberg 2013

The same applied to bulk cargoes, albeit to a lesser degree.

At that time, for the developing countries, shipping was a public matter. They drew no great distinction between commerce and government. Shipping was seen as necessary to safeguard trade and earn foreign currency. In UNCTAD, within the "Group of 77", they argued in favour of government regulation based on a concept of international shipping as a public utility (and not a profit-making commercial service), in which they should have adequate participation. This could only be achieved by governments laying down rules about, for example, the activities of liner conferences and the share of the trade companies should carry. The socialist bloc nations ("Group D") tended to side with the developing nations.

This contrasted with the general approach of the countries from the developed or Western world, namely the OECD countries represented in "Group B". For them, commerce and shipping had long been regarded as private for commercial interests and as an area that should not be subject to undue government interference or regulation. Access to international markets should by and large be free and not subject to any form of discriminatory treatment.

This is not to say that all the Group B countries pursued totally liberal policies at that time. A number of them reserved government cargoes (often broadly defined), development aid cargoes, or cargoes said to be of "strategic" importance (which could include oil or even water) wholly or partly to ships under their national flag. Restrictions were applied by some in bilateral trades with former or existing colonies, or on their domestic shipping routes (cabotage), or both.

In the "Common Measure of Understanding" which resulted from the first UNCTAD conference in 1964, one of the main elements was that the growth and development of the merchant marines of developing countries should be based "on sound economic criteria". In the minds of the Group B countries, this meant that no special preferences should be given to them. History was to show other aspirations, as, in the short term, there was a rash of promotional and discriminatory measures in developing countries—cargo reservation, cargo-sharing, subsidy in its various forms, and other preferential treatment.

One product of this trend was the heavy emphasis, in the UNCTAD debates leading up to the adoption of the UN Liner Code, on the issue of the "cargo generator's rights" on particular routes. The Common Measure of Understanding and the UN Liner Code are discussed in greater detail in the chapters on competition policy.

Protectionism Today

There is nowadays a different balance. With the emergence of China in particular as one of the world's major trading partners and the rise of intra-Asian trade, intra-OECD-country trade is no longer dominant. Over the last 30 years, the world's nations—East and West, North and South—have developed a greater understanding of each other's problems and there is now a greater realism in all countries, coupled with a wide acceptance of free-market principles. Many countries in South

America, Asia, Eastern Europe and North Africa no longer have—or at least apply—discriminatory practices against other countries' shipping, although some still retain "sharing" arrangements between neighbouring countries (e.g. in South America).

There has always been a distinction between the formal regulations in a particular country and its practical capability to put them into effect. For example, a country which has no significant merchant fleet may nevertheless retain a formal national policy which reserves 50 % or even 100 % of its imports/exports to a weak or non-existent national shipping line. In some circumstances, this type of anomaly persists today. But generally, the problem of protectionism is nowadays of a different degree. It turns more frequently on the creation of administrative and bureaucratic obstacles with a cost impact, rather than fundamental positions of policy.

The most common examples in international shipping have been:

- *Cargo reservation to national-flag ships.* Usually of 40 % or 50 % of all trade in and out of the country concerned. In some cases, this may result from an incorrect interpretation of the UN Liner Code's conference 40-40-20 cargo-sharing provisions. Again, such a provision may not necessarily be applied in practice, but its existence has been used as a pretext for charging for cargo reservation "clearances" or "waiver rights".
- *Central freight bureaux or booking offices.* Originally set up by a number of countries (mostly in East and West Africa) in order to implement their cargo reservation policies, these were responsible for allocating cargoes to national-flag ships, granting waivers for shipments to be carried by foreign ships, and imposing penalties for non-compliance. Although they do not exist in the same form today, arrangements may still remain for "tracking" import and export cargoes, operated on behalf of government-sponsored "shippers" councils' by an agent in the port of loading, who oversees and approves the transport movement against payment required, prior to the loading of the cargo.
- *Discriminatory charging arrangements.* These are also less common today, but may still apply in some countries to freight or other taxes, use of port facilities, pilotage, tonnage dues or other cargo-handling activities.
- *Restrictions on landside activities.* These may apply to the use of existing infrastructure or the ability for foreign companies to set up their own local handling, inland agency or haulage arrangements.
- *Administrative obstacles.* These may include delays in the remittance of freight revenues and cumbersome licensing requirements for local offices.
- *Restrictions on or preferential treatment for the carriage of government cargoes.* These may also relate to development aid or "strategic" cargoes.

It is interesting that, in some of the countries mentioned (particularly in West Africa), there have been moves towards greater liberalisation in recent years, following pressure from the World Bank in the interest of securing efficient transport chains for the carriage of world trade. This approach has been supported by the EU.

Trade Defence Instruments

National

Individual countries that consider themselves essentially free-trading have long had defensive legislation designed to protect their national trade and shipping interests from harm caused by other countries' protectionist measures.

United States

The United States grants wide-ranging powers to the Federal Maritime Commission (FMC) to respond to "general or specific conditions unfavorable to shipping in the foreign trade", whether in any particular trade or upon any particular route or in commerce generally of the US, under section 19 of the Merchant Marine Act 1920. These were supplemented in the Shipping Act of 1984 by a provision for action against a shipping line or a foreign government which has "unduly impaired access of a vessel documented under the laws of the United States to ocean trade between foreign ports". They were further expanded in the Foreign Shipping Practices Act 1988 in regard to laws or actions of foreign governments or carriers that create conditions which "adversely affect the operations of US carriers in US oceanborne trade and do not exist for foreign carriers" from the country concerned in the US. Again, under both these Acts, the FMC is charged with investigating and taking the necessary action.

Remedies against the shipping interests of another country may include limiting sailings to/from the US ports, limiting the amount or type of cargo carried, suspending their antitrust immunity (where applicable), suspending any preferential arrangements that may apply, the imposition of a fee of up to US$1 million per voyage, or any other necessary and appropriate action.

The US attaches considerable value to the strength and autonomy that these national countermeasures secure and they have been used successfully on several occasions against a wide range of countries.

During 1997, they were activated to put pressure on the Japanese government to eliminate exclusionary licensing requirements and to restrain the Japan Harbour Transportation Association (JHTA) (a non-governmental body) which was imposing burdensome prior-notification requirements and other trading hindrances on US and other shipping companies. The FMC found that JHTA practices created unfavourable conditions and that the Japanese Ministry of Transport established licensing requirements that were discriminatory and protectionist in effect and bore ultimate responsibility for the actions of the JHTA, which operated under its regulatory authority. In response, the FMC assessed heavy fees on Japanese carriers visiting US ports. After high-level negotiations, the two governments signed a Memorandum of Consultation committing the Japanese government to introduce reforms, which it did in 1999. The FMC suspended the sanctions and ordered US and Japanese shipping companies to issue periodic reports. This last requirement ended in 2011.

The US action was an example of the latitude allowed by the US legislation and contrasted with the reaction of the EU, which was to seek discussions within the multilateral, WTO disputes procedure.

Japan

As another example of national powers, Japan has a law providing for Special Measures against the Unfavourable Treatment of Japanese Oceangoing Ship-operators by Foreign Governments and Others. When Japanese carriers face less favourable treatment than the carriers of the country in question (for example, through cargo reservation, imposing unreasonable fees on Japanese vessels, or any other measures which affect the competitiveness of the Japanese carriers) and suffer harm as a result, the Minister of Land, Infrastructure and Transport may take countermeasures. Following an amendment in 1999, the Minister is bound to warn the foreign carriers of his intention and to give an opportunity for the position to be rectified within 6 months. The countermeasures must not go beyond what is necessary to correct the situation, but may include the denial of the right of the foreign carriers' ships to enter Japanese ports and restrictions on the loading and unloading of cargo. Failure to observe these orders can result in imprisonment or a fine up to 5 million Yen (currently about US$65,000).

The European Union

In Europe, the governments which are members of the EU have a co-ordinated approach to countermeasures.

The Treaty on the Functioning of the European Union (TFEU) provides for the development of a common transport policy. However, under Article 100, the Council has authority to decide whether, and to what extent, sea and air transport should be included. For a number of years, no endeavour was made to formulate any common shipping policy. Such steps as were taken were *ad hoc* in relation to a specific situation. However, by the early 1980s, there was a strong mood in favour of developing a common policy, particularly covering three key aspects: the Community's external relations with third countries; the question of free access to shipping trade between the Member States (within the internal market, which was only then being established in a practical way); and competition policy (which is dealt with in detail in the next chapters).

Four important regulations were adopted in 1986. Throughout their lengthy and often difficult gestation, the industry's views were co-ordinated by the European Community Shipowners' Associations (ECSA).

All the regulations applied to shipping companies established in the EU operating their ships under any flag, unless otherwise stated. The one on the competition rules went further, applying also to non-EU lines trading to the EU. Special provision was made to cover the particular position of Greek nationals and Greek-controlled companies operating, for example, out of New York or any other non-EU country, if their ships were registered in Greece in accordance with Greek legislation. Such owners also benefited from the regulations.

Two of the regulations are relevant here.

Regulation 4055/86 Applying the Principle of Freedom to Provide Services to Maritime Transport Between Member States and Between Member States and Third Countries

The effect was to remove any remaining restrictions on the international carriage of cargoes both in intra-EU trade and in the bilateral trades between individual Member States and third countries.

The regulation provided a clear legal commitment on Member States not to enter into new cargo-sharing arrangements with third countries and, where they existed, to dismantle them within a prescribed timetable. The liberalisation within the EU was implemented over a 6-year transitional period, with the abolition of restrictions in intra-EU trading for national-flag vessels (i.e. registered in the Member States) by the end of 1989; the abolition of restrictions in trades with third countries, also for national-flag vessels only, by the end of 1991; and the abolition of all trading restrictions for "other ships" operated by EU nationals under any flag or registry by the end of 1992. The latter date was deliberately timed to coincide with the formal establishment of the Single Market.

Progress on this particular regulation was difficult. Some of the restrictions were long-standing and deeply embedded in the national policies of the individual Member States concerned. They argued that some protection was necessary for strategic, defence or purely trading reasons; opponents argued that such restrictions should be eliminated quickly, or over a period of not too many years.

The question of the "beneficiary" from Community policy was also contentious. A number of Member States held strongly to the view that a ship should have to be registered in the EU to derive advantage from EU policies. The majority recognised that the world was changing and that, increasingly, it was the fact of ownership (rather than registration) that was important in commercial, trading, and wider economic terms. This view prevailed and the whole of the 1986 package of four regulations is predicated on this approach. Hence, in this regulation, the transition period ends with a definitive opening-up to EU-owned ships under all registers.

Subsequent analyses by the European Commission of the impact of this regulation show that, while its implementation was initially slow, this liberalisation has been successful. Almost all of the unilateral restrictions and of the offensive elements in bilateral agreements have now been removed.

Regulation 4058/86 Concerning Co-ordinated Action to Safeguard Free Access to Cargoes in Ocean Trades

This regulation provided a framework for co-ordinated joint resistance to discriminatory practices by third countries which restricted, or threatened to restrict, free access by EU shipping companies to liner, bulk or passenger services in trades to and from the EU. It laid down a carefully orchestrated, step-by-step procedure to be applied in the event of such action—first, through diplomatic representations and then, if necessary, through the use of specific countermeasures. These include, separately or in combination, requirements to obtain a permit to load or unload cargoes, and the imposition of quotas or special taxes.

The regulation—and indeed the whole 1986 package—was a clear demonstration of the EU's determination to ensure free and non-discriminatory access to cargoes for EU shipowners and to secure fair competition on a commercial basis in the trades to, from and within the EU. The Community had begun the process in 1977 with a decision which set up a consultation procedure between affected Member States on developments in relations between the Member States and third countries on shipping matters and on shipping questions dealt with in international organisations. Regulation 4058/86 accordingly elaborated and expanded on that earlier policy.

This regulation has been a useful and effective part of the EU's armoury in the development of its maritime external relations activity, although the fact that the initiative must come from the member states has been a limiting factor, since it means that other economic concerns of individual member states may reduce the willingness to take action. The regulation nonetheless led to the European Commission, on behalf of the member states, taking an active approach in third-country relations and international trade discussions. The shipping industry has been happy to see a planned and visible purpose in this area of EU policy, which is clear and evident to other countries.

Unfair Pricing Practices

While the last section dealt essentially with problems relating to access to trades and discriminatory treatment, powers were also taken, for example in the US and in the EU, to respond to unfair pricing practices or the "dumping" of freight rates. These were directed at carriers in the liner sector whose assets are owned, controlled or heavily subsidised by the government of the flag state and which engage in non-commercial pricing to the detriment of other nations' economic interests. The nature of these instruments was that they are vague and imprecise, leaving considerable scope for subjective interpretation.

United States

In addition to the broad powers already described, so-called "controlled carriers" are subject to section 9 of the Shipping Act of 1984. This debars rates or charges which are "unjust or unreasonable", defined as resulting or being likely to result "in the carriage or handling of cargo at rates or charges that are below a just and reasonable level". The assessment of this is at the discretion of the Federal Maritime Commission and the burden of proof is on the controlled carrier.

Factors that have to be taken into account include:

- Whether the rates are below a level that is fully compensatory, based either on the carrier's actual costs or, if not available or trusted, on constructive costs (i.e. based on those of another carrier, other than a controlled carrier, operating similar vessels and equipment in the same or a similar trade).
- Whether the rates are similar to those of other carriers in the same trade.
- Whether they are required to ensure the movement of particular cargo, or to maintain the necessary continuity or level of service, in the trade.

If the FMC so determines, it may disapprove the rates.

The provision does not apply where there is a bilateral agreement between the state in question and the US providing for most-favoured-nation or national treatment. The Ocean Shipping Reform Act of 1998 amended the Shipping Act of 1984 to eliminate the former exemption from the Controlled Carrier Act for carriers of countries that have subscribed to the shipping statement in the OECD Code of Liberalisation of Current Invisible Operations (see later in this chapter.) The Ocean Shipping Reform Act of 1998 also amended Section 19 of the Merchant Marine Act, 1920 explicitly to identify pricing practices as one of the possible factors creating unfavourable conditions in the US foreign trade, which the Federal Maritime Commission has the authority to adjust or meet with rules and regulations affecting foreign shipping.

European Union

The EU position is governed by the third of the 1986 regulations—Regulation 4057/86. This laid down the procedure to be followed in the event of third-country liner shipowners engaging in unfair pricing practices which cause, or threaten to cause, serious disruption of the freight pattern on a particular trade route to, from, or within the Community and consequently harm either to EU shipowners engaged on that route or to Community interests in general.

An "unfair" pricing practice was defined as a rate lower than the "normal" rate charged for at least 6 months previously and only made possible as a result of some "non-commercial" advantage granted by a non-Community state (for example, state-ownership, subsidy or other form of government assistance). A "normal freight rate" was not easy to define but had the same broad meaning as a "just and reasonable" rate under the US Shipping Act—a comparable rate charged for a comparable service, derived from actual or constructive costs.

To understand the origins of these provisions, it is necessary to look back to the most prominent state-trading nation during the years which preceded them—the then USSR—and to the Cuba crisis in 1962. This had changed the Soviet Union's whole attitude towards merchant shipping and led it to pay far more attention to the development of its own merchant fleet. In the eyes of the Western maritime nations, it began a period of aggressive expansion not justified in trading terms and supported by practices which had political as well as commercial objectives. In particular, there seemed to be a clear strategic desire to support a Soviet presence in certain sensitive areas of the world such as the Horn of Africa and Central America.

This expansion was felt mainly in the liner trades where the Soviet lines, working outside the conferences, were beginning to draw off cargo from the established lines. The latter were by then well embarked on the changeover to containerisation and anxious that their cargo base should not be eroded. In order to win cargo, the Soviet lines drove down the freight rates to such an extent that the rate structure on which the conferences depended was severely threatened. The lines in the Far Eastern Freight Conference—UK/Continent to and from the Far East—were also concerned about the way the competition from the Trans-Siberian Railway was increasingly making inroads as a result of equal or lesser transit times at rates which bettered those of the conference.

The Soviet interests denied excessive expansion. They argued that their rates were commercial, in their terms, and that they had to make a profit like any other shipping line. There was no argument on that point. The difference was, however, that in addition to any wider political or strategic purpose, they were operating within a central-economy, state-trading regime. This had two effects. First, the contribution of hard currency income-earners was particularly valuable to that regime. Second, there was a significant cross-subsidy between different economic activities. For example, the Soviet companies had their vessels provided by the state; this meant that they had no financing costs and that they did not have to insure them other than for P&I purposes.

The base-line from which they operated was therefore quite different from that of the Western lines. This is also relevant today to an understanding of relations with other state-trading regimes, to the extent that similar circumstances apply.

Various attempts were made to resolve this issue during the late 1970s, but there was little progress until the early 1980s, when attempts were made by five nations (France, Belgium, the Netherlands, the then Federal Republic of Germany and the United Kingdom) to reach an agreement with the Soviet Union. Two meetings were held, centred around the possibility of a better understanding leading on the one hand to the Soviet lines playing the game according to normal commercial rules and on the other hand perhaps to some form of conference membership for Soviet lines in three principal trades (from Europe to, respectively, Central America, East Africa and the Far East) where they had established a strong and, from the Western standpoint, destabilising presence. When these ended in failure, the Western nations pursued a tough line and indeed introduced n nitoring of Soviet carryings and rates charged in the trades in question. The conc ns of the five-nation group were instrumental in ensuring that, when the pack ge of four regulations was developed in the EU, one of them dealt with unfai pricing. As evidenced in discussions within individual national bilateral joint commissions with the Soviet Union at that time, it was clear that the Soviet Union was concerned at the possibility of legislation of this nature.

Ironically, when Regulation 4057/86 was applied for the first time, it was not against a Soviet carrier, but against Hyundai Merc nt Marine of Korea. This involved a complaint lodged in 1988 by ECSA on b half of the EU conference lines in the Europe/Australia trade (supported by the one EU non-conference line) that Hyundai, a non-conference competitor, was:

- Benefiting from non-commercial advantages, through direct subsidies and substantial writing-off and re-financing of debt from the Korean government, as well as from the Korean government's policy of cargo protection;
- Engaging in unfair pricing practices by charging unrealistically low rates in the southbound trade and thereby dragging down the rates on the route to uneconomic levels; and
- Causing significant injury both to the EU lines involved (through loss of revenue and threat of loss of market share) and to the EU's wider economic interest, in the form of likely reduction in the service offered and loss of jobs.

After an in-depth investigation the Commission, through its transport directorate, decided that Hyundai was undercutting the "normal freight rate" by US$450 per TEU (20-foot equivalent unit container), or about 26 %, and imposed a corresponding "redressive" duty on containers lifted by Hyundai in EU ports. Shortly afterwards, the Korean Line suspended its service, but its ships continued to be traded on charter by a new French company, which also used the same agents, ports and schedules. However, the Commission considered the new service to be too closely connected with Hyundai and effectively extended the duties to the containers it carried. In due course, the French line severed its connections with Hyundai and agreed both to pay outstanding duties and to raise its rates over a period. The redressive duties on Hyundai were reviewed after 5 years and removed, since the problem had disappeared.

From the standpoint of ECSA and the EU lines, the outcome was a success because it resulted in liner rates returning to a more economic level and demonstrated the outward effectiveness of the regulation. It was a clear warning (a "spear on the wall") against state-supported shipping activity combined with substantial undercutting of rates.

After that case had shown the regulation to be effective, preparations were begun to invoke it in the West Indies trade against the Soviet Baltic Shipping Company. However, this was not followed through, since by that time the threat that had existed previously was already fading away and a much more commercial approach to shipping was emerging in the Soviet Union. Shortly afterwards were to be seen the beginnings of the break-up of the USSR and the retreat of its international shipping presence, both politically and commercially.

Cabotage

The reservation of national coastal and inter-island shipping services—or "cabotage"—is still widespread in both developing and developed countries. A key distinction that needs to be made in any consideration of cabotage is whether the cargoes in question are genuinely domestic cargoes or are trans-shipped international cargoes which are being carried between two ports in the country of origin or destination. This is particularly relevant for containerised cargoes.

Where the coastline is short or there is little domestic transport volume, cabotage may not have a significant impact. But where there is a substantial internal trade or where restrictions impinge on the onward movement of international cargoes, the impact may be substantial.

One prominent example of a country with a long tradition of applying cabotage restrictions is the US, where the Jones Act (Merchant Marine Act 1920) restricts the carriage of cargoes between the US mainland and say Hawaii or Alaska and even the trans-shipment of containers in international trade. Coastal cargoes are required to be carried in ships which are not just registered, but also owned, built and crewed in the US.

Many countries that adopt otherwise liberal policies in terms of market access in international trades find extending that philosophy to the domestic trade a step too far. This was the experience of the EU, which left it out of its first shipping policy package in 1986, returning to it only later. As we have seen, Regulation 4055/86 was forward-looking and trenchant when dealing with the trade between Member States. The cabotage issue proved long, difficult and complex, involving as it did the defence and national interests of several EU countries including France, Greece, Italy, Spain and Portugal. An uneasy compromise was reached in 1992 with the adoption of Regulation 3577/92/EEC, under which existing restrictions would be phased out for EU-based carriers progressively over a period of 12 years. Although the restrictions on coastal cargo movements along the mainland were abolished almost immediately, temporary exceptions were enacted for "strategic cargoes" (mainly oil and water) until January 1997 and for inter-island traffic in some cases until January 1999 (in Greece, extended for regular passenger ferry services to 2004).

Two particular points of principle remain:

- The liberalisation extends only to ships registered in the EU Member States. It does not open up national cabotage trades within the EU in any way to non-EU companies. While that may be understandable in a regulation essentially orientated towards the internal market, the liberalisation does not even open up these trades to the same beneficiaries as Regulation 4055/86—i.e. to all ships

operated by shipping companies established in the EU states, including those
under non-EU flags. It is extraordinary that, within the same internal market, two
inconsistent regimes still apply. This is an anomaly which persists today and it is
disappointing that it has not been addressed during one of the regular reviews
required by the regulation.

- Crewing restrictions persist on foreign ships involved in island cabotage trades.
  Breaking a cardinal principle of international law that the flag state should have
  jurisdiction over operational matters on board its registered ships, here foreign
  ships may still be required to apply the local state's requirements.

While the whole issue of cabotage liberalisation was considered sensitive, not
least because of the social implications in some of the countries concerned, studies
undertaken for the Commission indicate that there have been no severe
consequences to date. Indeed, at one point this fact led the Commission to propose
a further relaxation of the crewing restrictions, but this was overruled by the
Mediterranean member states at the time.

The experience of many countries which operate cabotage restrictions is that
they can encourage high domestic freight costs and old and inefficient fleets—and
can therefore be unhelpful to the local economy. For these reasons, there are
pressures from time to time in a number of countries, such as Australia, Brazil,
and the US, to relax their restrictions. From the viewpoint of the freedom of the
seas, cabotage restrictions, however understandable, are objectionable, not just
because of their protectionist impact on domestic markets but because of the
cross-subsidy which they can provide for companies which also trade
internationally.

International Activity and Legislation

There are four main reference points for the pursuit of these issues, which go wider
than regional groupings.

US/CSG Dialogue

Despite their deep-seated philosophical differences, the United States on the one
hand and the governments of the Consultative Shipping Group (currently comprising 13 EU member states, Norway, Canada, Japan and—recently joined—Republic
of Korea and Singapore) on the other, began in the early 1980s to try to reach a
better understanding and *modus vivendi* on a range of issues. At the start, a large
number of debating papers were exchanged between the two parties, each side
probing the foundations and consistency of the other's policy stance. This was

followed by meetings of senior shipping officials and became known as the US/CSG Dialogue.

The basis of the Dialogue was the common desire to safeguard and promote competition in all sectors of shipping and to maximise the amount of cargo subject to competitive access. The formal framework of consultation under the agreement required co-ordinated action on the following:

- Joint methods of resisting protectionist measures
- Means to improve competition in shipping and
- Means to overcome restrictive commercial practices which inhibit or restrict trade, especially those that give rise to restrictive shipping policies by third countries

Among other things, it was agreed—whether or not the UN Liner Code applied to their trades—to avoid the introduction of new governmental measures and to resist measures by other countries which restricted the access of their own shipping to international cargoes. Over the years, a number of joint diplomatic representations (démarches) have been made by the US and the CSG countries with regard to third countries.

The other important aspect was the agreement of both parties to co-operate and consult closely on the application of existing "regulatory" (i.e. competition or antitrust) arrangements and on their future development.

The Dialogue continues today, with its secretariat now held by the Danish maritime authority, and covers a wide range of topical issues.

Organisation for Economic Co-operation and Development (OECD)

Brief mention has already been made above of the OECD's Code of Liberalisation of Current Invisible Operations (CLIO). Its purpose, as indeed that of the companion OECD Code of Liberalisation of Capital Movements, is to enable residents in the different member countries to do business with each other as freely as with other residents in their own country. The invisibles code was adopted in 1961 and covers a wide range of service sectors, including banking, insurance, tourism and transport. Shipping is governed by Note 1 to Annex A of the code, which commits OECD member governments to abolishing any national restrictions on the provision of maritime transport services between their countries.

In 1987, culminating some years of work by the Maritime Transport Committee, the OECD Council adopted a recommendation setting out 13 "Common Principles of Shipping Policy for Member Countries" together with detailed guidelines for liner shipping. These principles remain in place today. They are all designed to complement the obligations arising under the invisibles code and to roll back protectionist policies in the shipping sector by way of example and by the use of collective power.

Among other commitments, the OECD member governments emphasised the importance of CLIO for shipping and that the "principle of free circulation of shipping in international trade in free and fair competition . . . forms a guarantee of adequate and economic world shipping services and of maximum economic benefit for shipowners, shippers and consumers". They agreed to:

- Refrain from introducing new or additional measures restricting competitive access to international trade and cargoes.
- Oppose actively restrictive regimes operating in other countries.
- Consult with the other governments, in the event of their being subjected to pressure from a non-OECD country to accept cargo-sharing, or cargo-reservation measures, with a view to defending the aims and principles set out and to exploring the possibility of a co-ordinated response.
- Make available and use countervailing powers in the event that any problems with the non-OECD country cannot be resolved through diplomatic processes.
- Ensure that their domestic policies and measures were consistent with the OECD Code of Liberalisation.
- Safeguard open and fair competition, and avoid conflicts of law, in the application of competition policy to liner shipping.

This policy is wholly compatible with the philosophy underlying the US/CSG Dialogue. Of note is the fact that the recommendation does not apply to the sensitive area of cabotage.

The OECD, having established its policy clearly, then proceeded to take it in a practical way to other groups of countries which historically had not shared the same liberal philosophy. It did this both in the criteria that it applied when admitting new countries to membership and in direct discussions at international level.

This was significant, because during the mid-1990s several Eastern European countries were admitted into membership (including the Czech Republic, Hungary and Poland, all of which have since become EU member states), as were Mexico and Korea. It is probably not a coincidence that Korea during this time abandoned its waiver system for liner cargoes and removed its last restrictions on the carriage of bulk cargoes.

Further, since the early 1990s, and echoing OECD actions on the wider economic front, the Maritime Transport Committee held a number of rounds of discussions with the then New Independent States of the former Soviet Union (NIS) and the Central and Eastern European Countries (CEECs), with the People's Republic of China, with the Dynamic Asian Economies of the Far East (DAEs), and with Latin American countries.

The first—with the Eastern European countries—quickly produced an Understanding on Common Shipping Principles in 1993. This followed closely the philosophy of the OECD's 1987 recommendation, with all parties affirming their commitment to a freely competitive environment in international shipping, to the progressive elimination of any current discriminatory treatment, to fair market pricing, and above all to continued consultation on any problems of implementation and on further developments in their shipping policies.

The discussions with the Asian non-member states (Hong Kong, then Korea, Malaysia, Singapore, Taiwan and Thailand) proceeded more cautiously, but were also positive. Informal consultations in 1991 were followed by informal workshops in Yokohama in 1994, and by a further session in Paris in 1996. For the latter, the parties were also joined by three South American countries (Argentina, Brazil and Chile) in a grouping re-named the Dynamic Non-Member Economies (DNMEs).

In 2003 and 2004, workshops were organised covering a wide range of subjects (e.g. security) which brought together the OECD Governments with all the "Non-Member Economies" involved. Overall, these actions were effective in encouraging the non-OECD countries to pursue more free-market policies in shipping and in helping those countries already tending in that direction to consolidate their progress along that path.

2004 also saw deeper questioning of the role and value of the OECD's Maritime Transport Committee against the backdrop of ongoing cost reviews across the organisation as a whole. It was clear that it had lost its way. Opinions were divided—both between governments and within the industry associations—as to the practical value of its deliberations. This view was particularly felt by those who had found the way in which the organisation had approached the competition policy issue in the early 2000s either untenable or damaging. Others still retained the belief that there was a need for governments to have a truly international (as opposed to regional) forum in which to be able to exchange views and experiences on maritime trade policy issues.

In 2006, a formal decision was taken by the OECD Council to cease funding this dedicated activity and it was disbanded.

While the existing instruments remain in place, it is clear that—without the constant monitoring and renewal that comes from an active and specialist body—their impact will inevitably diminish in time. Some miss its earlier key contributions in international debates particularly in UNCTAD and in the contacts with the Non-Member Economies. This will be particularly true for as long as the WTO is unable to make progress in underpinning a liberal approach to access to trade in shipping. Others have been pleased to see an end to their dissatisfaction with the OECD's maritime activity ...

In practical terms, its role in shipping has now been superseded by the actions of the EU, and by the Consultative Shipping Group and its dialogue with the USA.

UNCTAD

Although, as we have seen, UNCTAD played a key role in allowing protectionist attitudes to find their expression at an international level, its significance for shipping issues is nowadays much diminished. The eighth session of UNCTAD, held in Cartagena, Colombia in 1992, confirmed the shift. It took place against the background of a rapidly changing world, a general feeling within the UN family that economies and rationalisation were necessary and a new readiness on the part of the UNCTAD secretariat to work with private sector interests.

Shipping as such did not feature on the agenda for UNCTAD VIII but came within the discussion on the services sector. What was significant, not only for shipping but world trade and development as a whole, was that there was a new mood of recognition of the importance of free-market principles not just for the developed world but also for the developing nations. This marked a historic change in the direction of UNCTAD, with consequential reforms to its machinery. All of its existing committees, other than those on preferences and restrictive practices, were suspended. This included the Committee on Shipping which had existed since the first meeting of UNCTAD in 1964.

Nowadays, shipping no longer has a separate identity within UNCTAD and indeed, as mentioned earlier, the former shipping division was disbanded by the mid-1990s. Shipping-related activities that have remained are in the areas of training, development co-operation, and business facilitation.

World Trade Organization

The decline in the role of UNCTAD in this area coincided with the rise of the role of the General Agreement on Tariffs and Trade (GATT) and of the World Trade Organisation (WTO).

The General Agreement on Trade in Services (GATS), which was one of the main achievements of the Uruguay Round (1986–1993), set out a range of disciplines covering services drawing on the GATT principles already applicable to trade in goods. It comprised a framework of general rules, supplemented by "annexes" which qualified those rules for certain individual service sectors (for example, financial services, telecommunications and air transport—none was agreed for maritime transport) and by country-specific "schedules" under which each contracting government set out any limitations on its commitments to the general rules.

The basic principles contained in the framework include:

- *National treatment (NT)*: whereby each government commits to treat service providers from other countries in the same way as its own.
- *Most-favoured-nation treatment (MFN)*: whereby each government commits to treating all foreign providers equally, but not necessarily in the same way as its own.
- *Transparency*: all relevant national laws must be published and openly available.
- *Progressive liberalisation*: the Agreement provides for a further round of negotiations aimed at liberalisation within 5 years. Specifically, any MFN

exemptions recorded in individual-country schedules must be reviewed within 5 years and are in principle only valid for a maximum of 10 years.

There was a strong insistence by governments that no service sectors should be excluded from the GATS, for fear of the number of excluded sectors growing uncontrollably. Hence the compromise of the annexes. Some of these effectively excluded the heart of their sector, for example the annex on air services which excluded traffic rights and related matters. When the Uruguay Round was concluded, only three sectors were left open, with separate, sector-specific negotiations continuing. Two were already covered by annexes and have since been resolved: telecommunications and financial services. The other was maritime transport services, which was not covered by an annex but was carved out and made subject to a "standstill".

Over the earlier years, the international shipping industry—through its representative organisations including ECSA and CENSA—had called for any action on shipping to be clearly based on the concepts of "standstill" (i.e. no further restrictive measures of any kind) and of early and effective "rollback" i.e., the removal of existing restrictions within a fixed time-table. Received wisdom was that, while the first was a possibility (assuming anyone considered that it would happen in practice), the second was not achievable at this stage of the negotiations. The industry therefore took the view that, although it supported the basic principles of the GATS, shipping stood to lose more than it stood to gain from allowing its relatively liberal regime to be the subject of regulation through the GATT mechanism. This was considered unwieldy and to favour the lowest common denominator.

Moreover, this was the one international body dealing with maritime affairs that did not allow shipping industry representatives to participate, even as observers. Scepticism led the shipping industry to fear that its interests would be in some way traded off against the interests of one or other sector, which might be more high-profile or considered more important. There was also little control, in its eyes, over the schedules of individual countries and the fear was that protectionist measures which had been confined to individual countries (and were often not implemented in practice) would have to be recorded in the schedules and would thereby be given a new and more harmful life.

Although they appreciated the dangers, this view was not shared by all the EU governments, nor indeed by all the EU shipowners' associations. The EU, through the European Commission, made its position very clear through schedules which contained no limitations except a technical one relating to the Brussels Package, explained in a later chapter.

At that stage, the US—both government and industry—was negative, but not necessarily acting from the same motivation. It refused for a long time to put any formal position down on the table and, when it did, made no commitments in regard to the ocean leg of maritime transport, i.e., "blue water", confining itself to access to port facilities and landside activities. There are two views. The US side argued again that it could achieve greater and more effective liberalisation through the existing US countermeasures legislation. It is important to note here that adherence to the GATT or the GATS means that individual countries forgo their ability to invoke their unilateral measures in favour of the multilateral disputes procedure. The US is understandably sensitive to this possibility. In 1997, the then Chairman of the Federal Maritime Commission said in a speech that: "The Commission's authority to move unilaterally to counteract the laws and actions of foreign governments is unique. Obviously, this is an important authority and the Commission is judicious in its use. Had the US agreed to include maritime services in the World Trade Organization, the Commission would have lost this authority and not been able to take these actions."

More cynical observers, however, were suspicious that there may have been ulterior motives connected with the desire not to become embroiled in a process which, at a later stage (although not then, since both were excluded from the scope of the negotiations), might place the spotlight on the USA's own restrictive measures, for example concerning government cargoes and cabotage.

Whichever view one takes, there is no doubt that the unwillingness of one of the world's largest trading powers to take a leading role has had a material impact on the development of these negotiations.

However, since the early 1990s, the history of the services negotiations generally and the maritime negotiations in specific has been "stop and start". There has been repeated build-up of pressure from the main interested parties for progress—at last—towards some text or structure that might stand a chance of attracting agreement, only to be followed by frustration and disappointment. Progress in the general negotiations has been bedevilled mainly by deep-rooted policy differences between the EU, the USA, and the developing world on the approach to agriculture and its relationship to non-tariff barriers to trade and sectoral subsidies. Summit after summit has tried to break the deadlock, each time apparently with greater momentum and hope than before but ultimately without success. There is now, in shipping policy terms, a very embedded sense of déjà-vu and cynical observers of the maritime dimension will not be optimistic that any positive outcome can be achieved.

The most that one can conclude today is that the principles governing trade in maritime transport services are contained, as for all services, in the GATS. However, no detail has yet been agreed and the most that has been achieved is the collective definition by WTO members in 2005 of sectoral and modal objectives for negotiations on maritime transport and the request by a number of liberal WTO members, led by Japan, that 24 other WTO members participate in plurilateral discussions and offer liberalisation commitments on the basis of the so-called "Maritime Model Schedule". Progress since then has been uncertain and this action remains a long way short of actual commitments.

Other Aspects

Also relevant to the question of freedom and protectionism are subsidies and fiscal or other treatment designed to improve the position of a particular national fleet whether in regard to investment or employment or for some other benefit. This is a broad and potentially very complex area which has given rise to mixed emotions and judgements over the years.

When developed countries have raised the subject of protectionism over the years, the developing countries have tended in turn to accuse them of distorting competition through subsidy programmes. The truth is that all kinds of countries and governments operate with subsidies and favourable taxation arrangements. Often they are complicated and concealed by the fact that one country's normal tax regime is another's subsidy. Certainly, the ability to grant subsidies or to relieve part of its economic and business earning power of standard taxation is dependent on the government in question having sufficient wealth to afford them, since they can be expensive.

Governments that are otherwise oriented towards the free market justify favourable treatment of this nature on the grounds that they need to help their operators match the lower taxation or costs levels in competitor countries. Others adopt a more Keynesian approach on the basis that the measures sustain themselves through the additional economic contribution and employment that they bring to the national economy. The latter theory is not as popular now as it once was, although it does apply in some cases.

These themes underlie actions which have been taken over the years in the US and in Europe, as well as elsewhere. In Europe, for example, following the 1986 regulations, a debate ensued on the development of so-called "positive measures" which could enable EU fleets to be more competitive in world shipping markets; in other terms, on a positive industrial policy. The focus has been mostly on enabling the employers of EU seafarers to reduce their costs closer to those of lower-cost crews from say the Far East or Eastern Europe. There were two imperatives for the European Commission, as guardian of EU policies: first, to promote the fleets of Member States and the employment of their nationals and, second, to control government support measures by the application of the EU's "state aid" policy.

Additional complexity arises from the fact that the Commission has responsibility under EU law for sector-specific measures, direct and indirect, which are considered to be state aid, while general taxation or fiscal treatment is the jealously guarded competence of individual member governments.

In July 1997, EU guidelines were published by the European Commission on state aid in the maritime transport sector. Although essentially an internal EU initiative, they took as their yardstick the competitive position in international shipping markets and reflected the Commission's view that "support measures may nevertheless be required for the present to maintain and develop the Community's shipping sector ... In principle, operating aid should be exceptional, temporary and degressive. In the case of maritime transport, however, the problem of competitiveness of the EU fleet on the world market is a structural one, deriving in large part from external factors". As a result, the guidelines set out effectively to enable individual Member States to create a tax-free environment for their shipping, subject to a number of constraints.

The guidelines debarred net direct subsidies. However, they allowed the Member States to make available to shipping companies a range of fiscal allowances (such as accelerated depreciation and tax-free reserves) and explicitly permitted the application of tax regimes based on the tonnage of the fleet operated by the shipping company, rather than its actual earnings or profits. With the aim of reducing the costs and burdens of EU operators and seafarers towards levels in line with world norms, income tax and social security contribution alleviations were allowed, with the objective of safeguarding and expanding the employment of EU seafarers. Training assistance was also addressed.

The Commission's guidelines were reissued in 2004 and reaffirmed the same positive approach, although a number of additional constraints on member state actions were introduced. These focused mainly on the required demonstration—in order to justify the exceptional treatment under the EU's state aid policy—of the economic benefit to the EU, for example through stricter monitoring processes and through tightening up some linkages to member state flags. Within the EU, the guidelines are deemed to have been a success combining encouragement with the imposition of practical constraints. Although there have been issues surrounding the consistency of their application, overall, industry shares that view.

The guidelines will remain in place until or unless they are changed. They are the subject of a review at the time of writing.

The issue is live elsewhere too. For example, in the 1990s, the US disbanded two systems of direct subsidy—the Construction and Operating Differential Subsidy schemes—which were designed to offset the higher costs of building ships and employing seafarers in the US. On the other hand, in addition to the cargo preference measures which have already been mentioned, it introduced during 1996 an extensive direct subsidy scheme for the operators of a substantial number of designated ships under US registry, ostensibly for defence reasons. This still continues and the Maritime Security Act of 2003 authorized expenditure under the Maritime Security Programme up to 2015. In 2012, the annual cost was US$186 million spread over 60 US-flag ships.

This chapter has dealt with the issue of freedom of access to markets. The area is grey, in the sense that the difference between freedom and protection is often one of degree rather than substance. This is true of the question of subsidies and other assistance, but also of protectionism generally. While the European Union's four regulations in 1986 had as their basic objective the preservation of an essentially open, commercial and competitive regime, at least one of them (4057/86) and possibly another (4058/86) could be regarded as protectionist. But they must be seen in the context of defending EU shipping against restrictions or unfair practices by other countries. In contrast, Regulation 4055/86 (applying the principle of freedom to provide services within the EU) was a true expression of liberal principles in so far as it sought, consistent with the general thrust of EU policy, to break down internal barriers.

The so-called "competition" regulation (4056/86) has presented a dilemma like all legislation establishing antitrust immunity for liner conferences. On the one hand, it sought to control conferences and to preserve them from process under the standard prohibition of cartel and monopoly activity. On the other, its aim was to preserve a system which did distort competition to an extent, yet which was for decades regarded generally as necessary for the carriage and service of world trade. However, in recent years, this whole area has faced fundamental changes and is the subject of the next chapters.

Chapter 8
Co-operation in Liner Shipping

The application of competition or antitrust policy to sea transport is probably the most developed and complex area of international shipping policy. The central question which has confronted governments for 120 years is whether, and to what extent, co-operative ventures between liner shipping companies should be exempted from the prohibition of cartel and antitrust activity which applies to business generally under national and international laws; and, if so, under what circumstances and subject to what alternative requirements.

This chapter explores the origins of co-operative agreements, starting with conferences and their origins and what they are allowed to do in practice. It also sets out and examines the position since the early 1980s up to the end of the twentieth century in Europe, the USA, and other major jurisdictions. Further explanations of governments' perception of such arrangements and their reactions, investigations and the later development of international policies, are elaborated in the next chapter.

It is important, however, to be aware that the conference system has frequently been under the microscope in Europe. The changes have encouraged similar reviews in other major jurisdictions. Despite carriers' reasoned case that the unique attributes of liner shipping argue for a special regime to permit co-operation and avoid a return to the economic chaos of the pre-conference era, the European Commission has been less disposed to any provisions which are incompatible with its philosophy of uninhibited competition, a position supported by many shipper representatives.

The Conference System

The modern conference system emerged in the Indian trade in 1875, although similar arrangements can be traced back to the Hanseatic League in medieval times. Following a period of instability, over-capacity and cut-throat competition, the British lines in the trade homeward to the United Kingdom from Calcutta agreed to charge the same rates for carrying cargo. This arose as much from the desire of

P.K. Mukherjee and M. Brownrigg, *Farthing on International Shipping*,
WMU Studies in Maritime Affairs, Vol. 1, DOI 10.1007/978-3-642-34598-2_8,
© Springer-Verlag Berlin Heidelberg 2013

importers and exporters of such commodities as tea for a stable rate of freight as from the shipowners' need for more rationalised earning power in an increasingly capital-intensive industry.

In the tea-exporting ports, huge variations in freight rates would result from the over- or under-supply of space. These were inevitable when the supply of vessels was subject to immense variations, owing to the vagaries of weather on the performance of sailing ships. Thus, often only one vessel would be in port at a given time and able to charge premium rates.

This might be followed shortly afterwards by a spate of vessels. The surplus space available after the previous famine would substantially depress freight rates. The less delay there was in the shipment of a valuable cargo, the greater the profit for both the shipowner and the cargo owners, especially if the goods reached market during a period of shortage of the commodity involved.

With the expansion of trade in the second half of the nineteenth century and the change over from sail to steam, liner companies were able to provide an increasingly regular service. Traders accepted the idea of a group of lines co-operating on the numbers and frequency of ships and charging common rates of freight. It removed a number of risks for them and gave a degree of certainty and stability, coupled with the assurance that they were receiving the same treatment as their trading competitors and that their goods would arrive in the market when required.

Thus emerged, albeit in a rudimentary form and in a sense out of necessity, the first liner conference. Others followed until by the beginning of the twentieth century the world was covered by a comprehensive system of liner services operating under the same basic practice and philosophy. A world-wide network of conferences continues to operate today but changes in form and substance have for some time now called their future in to question.

The major liner trade routes are: trans-Pacific, Europe–Far East, trans-Atlantic, intra-Asian, and the so-called "long thin" trades serving Europe–South America, Europe–Australia/New Zealand and Europe–Southern Africa. There are, in addition, many local conferences serving for example Mediterranean Europe, the Middle East and North Africa, and the Baltic Sea and adjacent ports.

A liner conference is a free association of lines operating in the same trade or route who agree on certain basic principles, the fundamental one being that the more closely space available can be equated to cargo flow, the more efficient and competitive the operation. In short, agreement on capacity and on common rates of freight.

Unlike commodities or manufactured goods which have a continuing or residual value even if unsold, surplus shipping space loses its value immediately the vessel sails. Thus a service that rationalises, and as far as possible equates, supply to the requirements of traders, and which assures both regularity and certainty, provides benefits for both the user and the supplier of the service.

The principal benefit to the shipper or transport-user (including freight forwarders)—and therefore for the economies of individual countries—is stability. This manifests itself in the availability of regular and reliable services which are responsive to customers' needs. Traditionally, it has been the role of the conference to "cover the berth"—in terms both of cargo types and of geography. In return for the privilege of being permitted to co-operate commercially, there has been a clear understanding that conferences on a particular route will ensure that all major areas are served and that a pricing structure is applied which will enable most cargo types and values to be moved. This obligation is undertaken in good times and in bad, whether cargo is offered or not.

What regular shippers (or transport-users) want is:

- Frequent services and regularly interspersed sailings.
- Full coverage for all cargo types, attractive or unattractive, easy to handle or difficult.
- A reasonable and stable price. This is of course subjective.
- Freedom of choice of carrier although shippers have argued that the workings of a particular conference may not allow them to choose the carrier.

All this is achieved by the conference mechanism.

The term "conference" is generic and covers a wide variety of different associations. Some are formal with written agreements and permanent secretariats, some looser agreements about frequency of service, others purely informal associations of lines covering only general working arrangements. The distinguishing feature for all is the published tariff of common or uniform rates of freight. However, as we shall see later, the growth of individual service agreements has resulted in the tariff assuming the role of a benchmark only for the growing number of one-to-one negotiations between carriers and individual shippers.

In practice, little has changed since the classic explanation of the conference system in 1958 by Sir Donald Anderson, the then Chairman of P&O: "Shippers want to be able to buy or sell large or small quantities at short notice with knowledge that shipping space will be available. They want their goods to be carried in large or in small lots, regularly or irregularly, in season or out of season, at ordinary temperatures, or chilled, or frozen or deep frozen. Their shipments may be dry or liquid, dirty or clean, safe or dangerous, live or dead, animal, vegetable or mineral. The essence of the liner conference system is that it constitutes a real service, as essential to trade and commerce on the route it serves as rail and bus services combined are to an isolated community."

Today, this could equally be taken as a description not only of conferences, but of customers' needs generally. Although shippers and some governments argue increasingly that the conference system is no longer acceptable, shippers' commitments to their customers still require the certainty and stability of regular and reliable services—or failure to meet "just in time" obligations will mean lost business.

Common Elements

The traditional common elements which applied, wholly or partly, depending upon the degree of sophistication of the association, were:

• Common freight rates and conditions of carriage;

and probably one or more of the following:

• Regulation of the carrying capacity offered by the individual lines;
• Agreed frequency and allocation of sailings, incl ding co-ordination of time-tables;
• Common approach to membership;
• Arrangements for concluding joint "service contracts" with individual shippers on the basis of a quantity or frequency discount;
• A common approach to surcharges;

and in the more formalised, sophisticated conferences:

• Pooling of cargo; and/or
• Pooling of revenue possibly, but not always, through some integrated joint service arrangement.

However, legislative and regulatory changes in the USA and Europe have resulted in changes in the extent to which conferences today exert their influence.

Conferences operating on the basis of these common elements to some degree restrict competition. However, while they are cartels, they are not monopolies. This is because the member lines are open to competition both internally within the conference, as to quality of service and nowadays increasingly on rates linked to the service package they provide, and externally from non-conference or independent operators (sometimes called "outsiders") in the same trade. There is also competition from other forms of shipping (for example, bulk ships carrying liner-type cargo), from airlines for high-value/low-volume commodities, from other maritime routes involving a different mix of sea and land legs, and in some cases from other transport modes such as rail, road or inland waterway.

Liner Freight Rates

The underlying principle of the liner conference system was that the members agreed to charge the same rate for the same commodity to the same destination, whether or not the vessel is fully loaded by sailing day. This was originally supported by shippers who knew that competitors were largely paying the same rate for the same route and commodity. However, shipper representative bodies later actively campaigned for an end to carrier immunity arguing for individual negotiations.

A significant factor is that conferences try to quote rates which will remain the same for a period, frequently 6 months or more, although when conditions are unstable this is not always possible.

It is up to the lines in the conference to set the level of freight rates over the vast range of commodities they may be called upon to carry. A rate is not set, as might be supposed, just on the basis of the distance the cargo is carried. There are many factors taken into account including value of the goods, weight/measurement ratio, nature of the cargo, ports and their facilities and other competitive factors.

The basic desire of the liner carrier is to maximise trade both for itself and for its customers. Traditionally, the endeavour was to ensure that the relatively lower volumes of high-value manufactured goods were supported by the greater volumes of lower-value goods. The freight earnings/costs of the latter were effectively subsidised by the higher relative freight earnings/costs of the former. This mix of high- and low-value cargoes with high- and low-bulk factors, each freighted (priced) using the elements set out above, provided the opportunity to maximise the trade—and thereby cover the berth in terms of cargo—on a particular route.

Basic freight rates are set out in the conference tariff, a published document which conferences are nowadays required to make freely available. The tariff gives a broad indication of the actual freight price and of the surcharges which apply, but may well not reflect the actual rate charged in the market-place. That will be a product of negotiation in the light of the competitive pressures at any one time and of the situation of individual shippers. Increasingly, the tariff is the starting point for individual carrier/shipper negotiations on individually tailored contracts.

Membership

Traditionally, there were two types of conferences—"closed" and "open". Most were "closed". Their member lines were like members of a club. They did not necessarily wish to let in others in a way that upset the carefully balanced coverage achieved by existing members. Nor did they particularly wish to see their share of the market reduced to accommodate others. Thus there was a constant battle over the years to achieve a balance between existing members and those who would like to join but who were currently operating as independent lines. Applicant lines had to have certain qualifications, mainly as to size and quality, including ownership (as opposed to chartering-in of ships); long-term commitment to the trade; proven ability to bring business to the trade; mutual benefit; and sufficient resources.

Membership was therefore not a matter of course. Lines usually gained membership by demonstrating that they had the right qualifications through operating on the same route as the conference and by attracting cargo away from the conference lines, thereby creating a situation in which it was mutually beneficial for there to be a joining of forces.

From the viewpoint of governments, the key factor in the right of closed conferences to operate was that there should be sufficient actual or potential competition in practice in a particular trade outside the conference. The key concept was "closed conferences in open trades". Up until the 1970s, non-conference lines rarely lifted more than 5 % or 10 % of liner cargo on their trade-route. However, the competitive environment subsequently intensified and with the growth of very large carriers which operate alone in most trades, it became not infrequent for as much as 50 % or more to be carried by independents.

The contrasting system was that of open conferences, which was that accepted by the world's largest trading power, the United States. This was important because the US lay then at the heart of two of the largest liner trade routes in the world—the trans-Atlantic and the trans-Pacific. It secured freedom of trade by requiring conferences to admit any applicant into membership subject to reasonable and equal terms and conditions; and to allow any existing member to withdraw from membership of the conference on reasonable notice without penalty. The fact that the UN Liner Code endorsed the closed conference system was one of the major factors that lay behind the US's adamant opposition to that convention.

The whole question of conference membership was, for many years, a matter of considerable sensitivity. At different times, there have been pressures for liner conferences to admit as of right the national shipping lines of any countries they served. While 50 years ago such lines rarely achieved membership, eventually there were few trades where true national lines, where they exist, which were not in membership. These pressures reached their peak at the time of the UN Liner Code, but faded somewhat as more market-oriented trade philosophies spread to many of the developing countries.

The structures in liner shipping changed, with the increasing focus on co-operative arrangements other than conferences (for example, consortia, alliances and trade-lane agreements) and the declining trade shares carried by conferences compared to the growing number of large independents. As a result, the differences between closed and open conferences became far less relevant resulting in few being closed in the traditional sense of the word.

Loyalty Arrangements

In return for offering regularity, frequency and stability in good times as well as bad, conferences generally expected their customers, the shippers, to support them with a measure of "loyalty". This was the origin of what is known as the "loyalty" system which gave shippers who regularly supported the conference a rate advantage.

Two options were available. The contract system required support for all shipments unless a dispensation was granted to use non-conference carriers in special circumstances. Under the deferred rebate system, a percentage discount would be returned after a period of 3 or 6 months "loyalty" to the conference but repayment would be forfeited if an outsider was used without authorisation.

Deferred rebates were made unlawful in the United States in 1916. In Europe, specific rules laid down in 1986 governing the use of loyalty agreements required a choice to be offered between immediate and deferred rebates. With the general weakening of the loyalty concept and increase in service contracts, loyalty arrangements became rare, existing only in the smaller trades.

Time/Volume Agreements and Service Contracts

The 1970s and 1980s saw the emergence in the US trades and then elsewhere of time/volume agreements and of liner service contracts—to the extent that these are now the principal forms of loyalty or regular service arrangement that apply. In 1984, the Shipping Act of the US was amended to mark the beginning of the deregulation process. Shipping lines were permitted to offer rates based on time and volume of cargo so that the rates varied with cargo volume tendered over a specified period.

Service contracts were a deliberate endeavour to get away from the severe, traditional loyalty ties. In response to customer pressure, conferences offered discounts to exporters who shipped a certain volume of cargo within a specified period and they varied in proportion to the volumes involved. By using service contracts, it was envisaged that the shipper would secure preferential freight rates as well as a host of other positive returns such as shipboard guarantee of space, orderly sailings and over-all reliability of service. Often these contracts would provide coverage of service extending to shore side transportation; in other words, the entire logistical chain could be rendered undivided in so far as billing was concerned. Liquidated damages provisions in the contract were permissible under the legislation for failure of performance of obligations.

The Shipping Act of 1984 in the US also permitted a departure from the published conference rates through "independent action." Tariffs published under independent action averaged 11–25 % below standard conference tariffs with respect to a specified commodity. These independently generated rates could force conference carriers to bring down their own published rates in order to compete. Thus the Act engendered a system whereby shippers could freely negotiate rates to their advantage but the necessary terms of a contract had to be made public without discrimination. The hallmarks of common carriage were thus preserved in conjunction with a considerable degree of deregulation of economic transactions between carriers and shippers such as discrimination in relation to volume of cargo. Although the Shipping Act of 1984 permitted service contracts, the effect of that permission was very limited, because of the requirement in the statute that the terms and conditions of the contract had to be publicly available and could be demanded by other similarly-situated shippers. But, it was often not clear what attributes constituted a "similarly-situated" shipper. Of course, the market forces reacted; when a shipping line offered a rate reduction from the conference rate, several small volume shippers wanted to jump on the bandwagon with the so-called "me too" contracts causing carriers to recoil so that only large volume shippers who quickly moved in on the action succeeded. Thus, the 1984 Shipping Act by legitimizing rate discrimination was viewed as favouring large shippers against the interests of their smaller counterparts. It would appear that technically the service contract concept endorsed and supported by legislation largely benefitted the major shippers who had considerably more bargaining clout. However, the conditions under which such discrimination took place was conceivably narrow which made the possibility of such discrimination not widely practical. In fact, it is argued that the "me too" provision in the statute really re-established with the left hand the antirate discrimination policy which the service contract provision in the Shipping Act tried to give with the right hand.

Finally, the Ocean Shipping Reform Act enacted in 1998 allowed confidentiality of rates in service contracts and abolished the requirement for carriers to cater to small shippers who wanted similar rates. The new Act by removing the "me-too" requirement and providing for confidentiality fulfilled the formal promise that was in the Shipping Act of 1984 but which was never actualized by the restrictions in that Act. As a result, service contracts came into more frequent use and virtually became the norm through which rates were set. These contracts could cover even a unit as low as a single container. Removal of all of the regulatory strictures made possible by this Act, including the legitimization of confidentiality and elimination of the compulsion to offer similar terms to similar shippers, became most advantageous for the mega shippers who had negotiating power far in excess of small shippers.

The reduction in barriers to world trade and the emergence of international production centres in Asia impacted the flow of global trade and strategic approaches to international maritime transport. The reforms in 1998 enabled globalized manufacturers and retailers to gain advantageous contractual arrangements which were based on market reference points. While the cost to the shipping line was the base for these arrangements, they were essentially according to market reference points. In other words, the price set was the cost to the manufacturer as the floor, but the actual price established was often well above this level; as high as the market would bear. This shift in philosophy was largely seen as benefitting the major players among the shippers simply because they were the ones who could on a temporal basis supply large volumes of commodities. This, in turn, enabled carriers to benefit from lower costs. A relevant question in this regard was whether the arrangements engendered by the service contract concept, strongly endorsed by legislation, exemplified a balance of bargaining power between carriers and shippers or whether it manifested itself as an enhancement of the commercial powers of large shippers. Information itself became a valuable commodity for both parties concerned since rates were no longer required to be published and confidentiality became the rule of the day. Again, it was the larger shippers who were better equipped to access information pertaining to the market better than their smaller counterparts. The information in turn became a formidable bargaining tool.

While it is recognized that the service contract concept has benefited large shippers, there has been a strong complementary trend that has benefited smaller shippers through the growth of large consolidators such as FedEx, UPS and DHL as well as others, on the international scene. Some of these consolidators have evolved from small entities operating out of a basement or small office to large and sophisticated shipping, logistics management and supply chain management service providers with operations and offices all across the globe. There is considerable competition among these consolidators which has given them every incentive to negotiate major discounts with asset-based ocean carriers and to pass a good portion of those savings on to their own customers. These have enabled many smaller shippers to get at least part of the benefit of the volume discounts experienced by large shippers. Moreover, as indicated earlier, these large consolidators often offer supply-chain management services as well, to the benefit of smaller shippers.

Surcharges and Adjustment Factors

Over the years, conferences have sought to maintain their revenue by putting surcharges, often known as "adjustment factors", on rates in various special circumstances. These include currency movements (currency adjustment factors—CAFs); or sudden and unexpected increases in the price of fuel oil (bunker adjustment factors—BAFs); or periods of port congestion when, through no fault of the shipowner, or indeed the shipper, a vessel is expensively held in a port.

Often, the imposition of such surcharges has taken place in response to corresponding developments in the world economy. For example, CAFs largely date from the late 1960s when the fixed exchange rate system collapsed. Essentially, with most liner earnings in US dollars and with costs arising in several different currencies, CAFs were established to avoid unforeseen gains or losses to both carriers and shippers, when there were significant fluctuations in the tariff currency compared to the basket of other currencies in which the costs were incurred. The currency adjustment—which could go up or down—would be triggered by a given percentage change in the value of the tariff currency.

BAFs were introduced after the first world oil crisis in 1973, in response to fluctuations in the price of bunker fuel. They operate in broadly the same way. There may, also, be a need when port or terminal facilities are under strain during busy periods to impose a port congestion surcharge. Such costs have been justified by shipowners on the basis that the events that have given rise to them are sudden and unexpected; often they are not imposed until long after the losses have been occurring for a sustained period. Shippers on the other hand have been critical, seeing them as an unjustified attempt by the lines to cushion themselves against events to which all in business are subject.

Pools

These are only found in the most sophisticated conferences. Where cargoes are pooled, a balance is struck at the end of a given period between those in the conference who have overcarried their agreed share of the trade and those who have undercarried. In a revenue pool the same principle is applied, but the working out of agreed shares of the revenue pool means precise record-keeping and much work for the conference secretariat.

Pooling in this way is well known in liner shipping and was formerly permitted under European legislation, but it has been criticised as protecting the less efficient carrier at the expense of the more efficient and putting a damper on competition in quality of service, which has always been one of the advantages of the conference system. However, fierce competition between conference member lines, coupled with the growth of individual service contracts and the use of slot-chartering and similar arrangements under the Consortia regulation (see below), has probably reduced the effective extent of pooling arrangements.

The Change to Containerisation and Liner Consortia

This was a revolutionary change, which was to affect not just methods of transport, but the whole way in which much of world trade was carried.

The invention of the container ranks with the invention of such objects as scissors and cats' eyes. It is universally credited to Malcolm McLean, an American trucker, who recognised in the late 1930s that the then system of moving goods from their point of origin to their destination involved several different transport movements and that the interface between each of these entailed the risk of damage, pilferage and loss of time. Carrying cargo between Pittsburgh and Paris required at least eight operations:

- Truck from factory to railhead,
- Rail to port town,
- Truck to dockside,
- Handling on to the ship and into the hold, mostly by sling, and
- All four in reverse at the other end of the trade.

His revolutionary thought was simple: the risk of loss at every stage of the movement would be drastically reduced and efficiency hugely increased if the initial trailer drawn by the truck could be lifted directly on to the ship and carried all the way to the cargo's destination—without its contents being disturbed.

It took more than 20 years to put the idea into practice. The technology of the container was developed from the basic road transport trailer into a unit which was reinforced with steel cornerposts, underpinning and twist-lock fasteners at the corners. The first movement of containers by sea took place in April 1956 when a converted tanker with specially installed decks carried 58 containers on a coastal voyage from Newark to Houston. This was followed by other experimental voyages in the US domestic trades, including from the West Coast to Hawaii.

Initially, loading and unloading was effected by a gantry crane on board the ship itself (normal on general cargo ships of that time), but very soon the advantage of using specialised container cranes and terminals ashore was recognised. The first dedicated container facility was established at Port Elisabeth in the port of New York and New Jersey and the first terminal occupied by Sea-Land in 1962. The first acclaimed international containership voyage was by Sea-Land's *Fairland* on 23 April 1966, carrying 236 containers from Port Elisabeth to Rotterdam.

From the start, it was recognised that the savings—over traditional break-bulk operations—would be huge. Time in port was cut from a week or more (with traditional cargo-handling methods) to less than a day, with a consequent reduction in labour costs. Transit times across the Atlantic were halved. There was a 90 % drop in damaged cargoes and pilferage was almost eliminated, leading to lower insurance costs. By the late 1960s, it was clear to all that containers were the direction of the future in the liner trades. Door-to-door transport had taken off, allied increasingly to the "just in time" concept of distribution.

It did, however, require enormous amounts in new investment—the ships themselves, containers, land and equipment in the shore-side terminal, and increasingly sophisticated logistical planning.

While containerisation was a US creation, it was four leading British shipowners (P&O, Ocean, British & Commonwealth and Furness Withy) who introduced it in a big way into European shipping, closely followed by others in Europe and Japan. These owners took the unprecedented step in 1965 of pooling the liner interests of their four groups—originally in the Europe/Australia and New Zealand trade only, but later in other trades as well—through the formation of a new company named Overseas Containers Ltd (OCL). Although not itself a consortium (since it was a company with a separate identity from its shareholder lines, in which their liner interests were merged), OCL set the trend for other mergers and looser groupings. In the same year, five of the remaining six major British liner companies—Ben Line, Blue Star, Cunard, Ellerman and T & J Harrison—followed with the establishment of Associated Container Transport (ACT). Other mergers and groupings soon appeared on the Continent, in Scandinavia, in Japan, the US and elsewhere.

Within a period of few years, the large liner groupings began to take over the many individual liner companies whose titles went back many years as household names. Moreover, the new container groups began to work together, mainly internationally but not always, as even bigger groupings or consortia in their particular trades.

Consortia

The standard dictionary definition of a consortium is "an association of companies for a particular purpose". In liner shipping, that purpose is essentially operational, bringing together the fleets of the companies concerned within a single fleet for purposes of providing the service. In the knowledge of the broader scale of operation which would be achieved as a result, the individual lines would be in a better position to commit a share of the investment required to run the service. Mostly, consortia have traded within conferences, combining the operating activities of two or more of the conference lines. Historically, their role has complemented that of the conference, which had a broader perspective regarding such matters as sailing schedules and rationalisation, and of course which had the rate-making authority.

However, consortia arrangements are of a practical nature and quite distinct from conference arrangements. Consortia may have differing degrees of integration, covering the full spectrum from loose operational arrangements to tightly knit commercial combinations. While the ships in many consortia are still owned or chartered in by the constituents, it is the consortium that deals with the liner operations in the trade or trades in which they are involved. While the lines within a conference remain clearly separate entities, the closer operational relationship of lines within a consortium could extend into more commercial activities such as joint marketing, the issue of joint bills of lading and the pooling of revenues. In a few cases, the size of the consortium in a particular trade could be such that its membership mirrors that of the conference.

Prior to the EU regulation on consortia, adopted in 1992, the term was used freely. Indeed, consortia had not been regulated explicitly under any international or national legislation, presumably on the basis that the objectionable elements of a liner operation were already covered under the conference legislation.

Other Co-operative Arrangements

Various other forms of co-operation have emerged at different stages of evolution of the modern-day liner shipping sector. Some are akin to conferences or consortia under other names or guises. Others are genuinely new developments, where liner companies are responding to changing global trends and customer demands. Some, such as container slot-exchange or slot-charter arrangements, are straightforward commercial arrangements which should give rise to little interest or concern from a competition policy viewpoint, but which nevertheless may come under scrutiny because of the wider antitrust concern which attaches to liner shipping activities.

Discussion Agreements and Trade-Lane Agreements

After the milestones of the 1984 Shipping Act in the US and the European Union's competition regulation in 1986 (and faced with a continuing and alarming decline in freight rates, not just in real terms, but frequently in terms of the monetary value of the day), lines in some of the biggest trades combined in groupings often wider than the conferences to discuss rate-setting and capacity management. These arrangements were given different names, such as, discussion agreements, trade-lane agreements, stabilisation agreements and tolerated outsider agreements; and all had different nuances which some competition authorities argued distinguished them from conferences or consortia.

The so-called *discussion agreements*, Eurocorde 1 and the Eurocorde Discussion Agreement, emerged on the trans-Atlantic route in 1985, shortly to be followed by at least one other. They enabled the lines in the eastbound or westbound (or both) conferences across the North Atlantic to engage in discussions with non-conference lines and to agree on rates and capacity. While these were initially accepted by the Federal Maritime Commission (FMC), the European Commission soon made it clear that it did not regard them as valid.

In the other major liner trades—the trans-Pacific and Europe–Far East—there was also an endeavour to reverse the decline in rates through what became known as *stabilisation agreements*. However, these did not involve rate-setting and could not be construed as extensions of conference activity. Arrangements emerged in both these trades, whose emphasis was on tonnage rationalisation alone. The first of these was the Trans-Pacific Stabilisation Agreement (TSA), which began in 1988 and provided a straight 10 % capacity reduction on eastbound routes. It was required to be terminated in 1995, because conditions had changed. A subsequent application to re-introduce a capacity management programme, submitted to the FMC towards the end of 1996, was also withdrawn.

Alliances/Global Partnerships

The containerisation of liner services was only the beginning of a further, continuing process in the evolution of scheduled liner services. As well as bringing together individual lines in consortia, since the 1970s, there has been a continuous shaking out of lines in the traditional maritime countries. These structural changes have proceeded against the background of a rapidly changing world in political, economic and trading terms. They have intensified over the last 10 years and continue today.

In the mid-1990s, companies began once again to feel their way, both individually and in new groupings, towards yet further cost rationalisation and economies of scale in order to ensure their survival. These pressures were driven by the examples of the largest carriers whose vision had become multi-trade, whether in the form of round-the-world services or of a presence in all or most of the major trades around the world. A number of groupings or "alliances" emerged with very definite global ambitions. The first examples included the "Global Alliance", which brought together American President Lines, Mitsui OSK Line, Orient Overseas Container Line and Nedlloyd, in some trades with Malaysian International Shipping Company; and the "Grand Alliance", which comprised Nippon Yusen Kaisha, Neptune Orient Line, Hapag-Lloyd and P&O Containers (the successor to OCL, after P&O bought out the shares of the other partners).

In 1996 the "Global Alliance" was renamed "New World Alliance" consisting of three major participants: American President Lines/Neptune Orient Line of United States/Singapore, Mitsui OSK Line of Japan and Hyundai of South Korea. The "CKYH Alliance" comprised the Sino Japanese Alliance and what was formerly known as TRICON. The Sino-Japanese Alliance comprised COSCO of China, K-Line of Japan and Yang-Ming of Taiwan of which COSCO was the lead carrier ranking fifth in the world. K-Line and Yang-Ming were also among the leading container carriers. TRICON was formed out of a strategic partnership combining Hanjin Shipping of South Korea, Cho-Yang of Kuwait and UASC of South Korea. A number of permutations and combinations followed, at the end of which the CKYH emerged as the leading alliance consisting of Hanjin, COSCO, K-Line and Yang-Ming.

Others also appeared, some of which proved to be developing relationships which would soon lead to takeovers or mergers: e.g., Maersk/Sea-Land and Hanjin/DSR Senator. Many lines now co-operate on a multi-trade rather than single-trade basis. The huge increase in the numbers of ships available to the alliances enables individual lines to introduce ships of larger size and thereby gain economies of scale while at the same time improving the service offered.

In 1998, P&O Containers established a jointly owned company with Netherlands-based Nedlloyd to become P&O Nedlloyd, retaining its headquarters and commercial base in London, and the fleet and technical management function in Rotterdam. Following a number of intervening acquisitions, the company was the subject of a reverse-listing on the Dutch stock exchange, using the vehicle of Royal Nedlloyd, with P&O retaining a 25 % shareholding and positions on the board. This created the third-largest container company in the world. However, the new company was the subject of an uncontested takeover by the Maersk Line of Denmark in 2005 and totally absorbed into that company in February 2006, giving Maersk (which was already the largest, following its acquisition of Sea-Land) a substantial lead in terms of capacity over its closest rivals (Mediterranean Shipping Company and Evergreen). Elsewhere, the French liner company CMA-CGM bought out Delmas and Hapag Lloyd of Germany bought out CP Ships.

With the consolidation of the container trade through various mergers, acquisitions and alliances across the world, the flow of containerised cargo in world trade is now controlled by a few major entities. As of 21 October 2009, the cargo flow worldwide puts the AP Moller Maersk Group in the lead with 11.6 % followed by MSC at 9.8 % as individual shipping conglomerates. Among the alliances, CKYH controls 12.2 % and New World Alliance 6.5 %. A considerable portion of the market is held by other relatively small container lines (see Containerisation International Yearbook 2010).

Contemporary Perspectives

Growth and Opportunity

From the first container movement in 1956, volumes have grown beyond all expectations. By 1973, the annual carryings were about four million TEUs. Ten years later, with most of the world beginning to be containerised, carryings were 12 million TEUs. By 2004, total trade was recorded at 96 million TEUs. By end 2010 it was about 140 million TEUs and in 2011 it rose to an estimated 154 million TEUs which illustrates the continuing growth of this phenomenon.

Containership operators are sometimes accused of irresponsible overcapacity, which merely perpetuates the prospect of low freight rates and overall returns. However, as we have seen, there has been extensive real growth over the years in the number of boxes shipped, supported by positive projections for the future. The rewards for lines and groupings which are successful in anticipating and meeting future demand are likely to be great.

The container is without doubt key to the transport, and therefore also expansion, of world trade in manufactured goods. Over 90 % of general (i.e. non-bulk or non-specialised) cargoes are moved by containers. It is essential that the world's regulators bear these facts in mind when considering and reviewing this crucial sector.

Investment

Liner shipping has always been capital-intensive and this has been a major factor in the reasoning of governments in granting antitrust immunity. For example, a 56-day round trip from Europe to the Far East, calling at 11 or 12 ports during the voyage, requires eight or nine ships to maintain a weekly service.

But this is in the container era. Depending on the size of the ship, each container ship in today's world has replaced between 7 and 25 earlier general cargo or break-bulk ships. In pre-container times, the transit time would have been at least double and, with smaller ships, many more were needed.

The technological revolution of containerisation was also expensive to introduce and continues to be expensive to refine and extend. The hardware costs alone can exceed well over US$ 100 million. In addition an amount equivalent to at least US$ 50 million would constitute a substantial investment on the containers themselves. That amounts to an investment of almost US$ 1.5 billion for the fleet required to operate a single weekly run from Europe to the Far East. To that has to be added the cost of operating the ship (bunker fuel, repairs and maintenance, insurance, port and other charges, crew wages and victualling, and so on), the cost of investment in and use of specialist equipment in container terminals and of the practical land-side operation, namely, interface with the importers and exporters and with the different linking transport modes, and increasingly the cost of logistical systems support for tracking each individual container, securing its return, maintaining it; and general rationalisation of the complex land-side relationships.

Profitability

Yet historically, and despite occasional periods of better than average profitability, returns in the deep-sea liner sector have been lower than would normally be acceptable in industry or service businesses ashore. This probably has a lot to do with the sector's capital intensity. Nevertheless, it is not necessarily attractive to the often short-term approach taken by investors. The average rate of return on net assets of nine of the major container companies over the period 1988–1995 was reportedly less than 4 %. With the increasing focus in all business on ensuring that each element of a business operation is economically viable in the short as well as the long term, there is pressure on some containership operators to achieve a rate of return of say 15 %, which would be comparable with expected returns from shore-based activities. All lines have therefore continued to review their cost structures fundamentally, paring costs to the bone while either seeking the maximum cost advantages of large-scale operations, and therefore, increasingly, mergers, or specialising in particular markets (geographical or cargo). Even in 2004, which was an exceptionally good year, average returns for the top 29 major liner companies were only 11 %, well below the 25-year average for the S&P 500.

Single-Trade/Multi-Trade/"Round-the-World"

Conferences and consortia are mechanisms that have traditionally operated within individual trades. Although inherently international, they do not have a global dimension, by definition.

An important development in the early 1980s was that of the round-the-world service which introduced the multi-trade concept for the first time. This mode of operation suits only non-conference lines of sufficient size, which swoop around the world picking up cargo in the main loading/discharging areas, but having no commitment to cover a particular trade let alone the way-ports they pass en route. They can thus afford to carry such cargo at marginal costings at the expense of those conference lines whose tariff structure is based on serving the total trade on a particular route. This to an extent has had a destabilising effect on the major conference trades. But it has been accepted as part of competition.

It has however fed another tendency which has grown up in recent years for conferences/lines to concentrate on a few hub ports, with an increased number of feeder services. It is self-evidently an integral element of any round-the-world service.

Another response to the new global requirements of world trade has tended to be favoured by the more conference-oriented groupings and the new alliances. Their services are a more complex interweave of separate "strings" or "loops" across the three inter-continental ocean trades. They blend the advantages of genuinely global co-operation with the ability to serve more ports directly, since each string will, like a normal conference operation, serve several ports at each end. However, by focusing energies very strongly on the three East–West, round-the-world legs and by interconnecting their operations where necessary, they achieve global coverage.

The lines involved often maintain their involvement in the North–South trades outside the groupings or alliances. Here, they continue to compete with those lines which concentrate on such niche trades. The "long thin" trades to Australia and New Zealand and to the South Pacific are examples of this.

Competition External and Internal

Competition in liner trades is as strong today as ever. Despite accusations from some regulators and shippers that the conference system is harmful to business and outmoded, the self-regulatory approach and the flexibility allowed within the system itself has not in any way inhibited the evolution of other co-operative mechanisms or mergers. Indeed, in many ways, it has laid the ground for that evolution and provided a relatively stable framework within which it could happen. Equally, whatever may have happened in earlier days, it is not justifiable to suggest that in recent years shipping costs have been unduly high. As we have seen, for the most part, profitability is far lower than in land-based businesses and the share of the total cost of the end-product represented by shipping costs is very small; indeed the land transport component is frequently much higher proportionately.

Chapter 9
Development of Competition Policy and Its Historical Evolution

In the first part of this chapter, an examination is made of the investigations which took place into the conference system during the early years and also political actions at national, regional and international levels which helped shape that landscape. This is followed by a discussion on US and EU policies which were applied in the trans-Atlantic trade since the 1990s depicting a close focus for activity as the conference lines tried over a 10–15 year period to adapt their processes to the new era of increasingly intensive regulation. The second part of this chapter focuses on competition policy and legislation in the US and EU followed by developments in other jurisdictions including Australia, Canada, Japan and Singapore.

Early Inquiries and Investigations and Their Consequences

Royal Commission on Shipping Rings, 1909 (UK)

This was the first major inquiry into the liner conference system, its advantages and disadvantages, at a time when conferences had been in operation for little more than 25 years. It examined the system, its historical background, its operation in practice, including the level of freight rates charged and the justification for some tying arrangement with shippers, in particular the deferred rebate system. Its terms of reference required it to report on "whether liner conferences caused, or were likely to cause, damage to British or Colonial trade and, if so, what remedial action by legislation or in any other way should be taken".

A majority report accepted that conferences were subject to sufficient competition to avoid their being in a monopoly situation and that a tie with shippers, including the use of the deferred rebate system, was justified. A minority, however, were critical of the system, on the grounds particularly that the interests of shippers, the customers, were not sufficiently protected. This cry has been echoed over the years.

The important and interesting recommendations were that:

- While it was undesirable for the state to intervene in terms of legislation, shippers and merchants in a particular trade should form themselves into an association, registered with the Board (Ministry) of Trade, as a counterweight to the conference.
- Tariffs should be published.
- Conferences should deposit confidentially with the Board of Trade their basic agreements, rebate particulars and agreements with commodity groups or associations of merchants.
- The Board of Trade might possibly involve itself in the settlement of disputes.

The first and second of these recommendations were adopted not long afterwards in a few trades, but it was to be some 50 years before they were fully implemented.

The Alexander Committee Report, 1914 (US)

The House Merchant Marine and Fisheries Committee of the US Congress, under the chairmanship of Mr Joshua Alexander, held hearings and took evidence in much the same way as the 1909 Inquiry in the UK. Although it looked broadly into the nature of conferences and their effect, it paid particular attention to the following aspects, at least one being peculiar to the US trades:

- Deferred rebates which, while unlawful in US outward trades, were at that time accepted inbound (although this would later change).
- The role of fighting ships (i.e. charging very low rates) to drive away non-conference competition.
- The idea of quantity discounts for big shippers.
- Whether rate levels were reasonable.

The evidence supported the position that completely free and open competition could not be countenanced, largely because of the instability that would ensue (rate wars, bankruptcies and general uncertainty); but that, while the advantages of the conference system were recognised, conferences should nonetheless be brought under a measure of governmental control. This was a first step towards governmental regulation of conferences, albeit by one powerful nation alone.

The Recommendations of the Alexander Committee were subsequently enacted in the US Shipping Act 1916. Conferences in the US trades were thus brought under regulation in return for immunity from US antitrust laws which made combines or trusts unlawful if they monopolised or otherwise interfered with open-market forces.

US Shipping Act 1916

The new legislation brought conferences under the regulatory control of the Interstate Commerce Commission (ICC) among others, as to rates of freight, terms of contracts and other agreements. It also prohibited rebates or special discounts favouring or discriminating against a particular shipper or port; required equal rates for all shippers regardless of size; prohibited fighting ships; and made deferred rebates unlawful for outbound shipments.

The Interstate Commerce Commission was given authority:

• To disapprove agreements filed with it if they were found to be discriminatory or unfair or detrimental to the commerce of the United States.
• To investigate, on complaint, any rates which were alleged to be unfair or unreasonable and, if it thought fit, to disapprove the rate—but not to set a new rate.

This was a turning point for conferences and indeed for shipping. It was the first occasion on which a governmental authority had been empowered to intervene in basic commercial decisions concerning the charge for a shipping service and the conditions on which the service was offered.

Regulation of US liner trades, albeit in very different terms, rests today with the Federal Maritime Commission.

Imperial Shipping Conference, 1921

This further inquiry, instituted by British Commonwealth governments in 1921, covered much the same ground as the 1909 investigation but from the standpoint of the shipping requirements of the Commonwealth countries. The Committee:

• Accepted that some tying or loyalty arrangement with shippers was appropriate if conference lines were to maintain a regular service with sufficient tonnage to meet the ordinary requirements of the trade at stable freight rates and with no distinction between large shippers and small shippers;
• Did not condemn the deferred rebate system but suggested an alternative such as the contract system used in the South African trade;
• Recommended greater consultation with shippers before freight rates were altered and the setting-up of associations of shippers to represent the interests of shippers with respect to conferences.

US Congressional Inquiries 1958–1961

The *Isbrandtsen Case* in the 1950s was the catalyst for renewed US interest in the conference system. One of the main pillars of the conference system at that time was the ability of the conference lines to tie shippers through some loyalty arrangement. With the demise of the deferred rebate system as a result of the 1916 Shipping Act, the normal method used was the dual rate contract system. Contract shippers were given the lower of the two rates quoted by the conference: generally the discount was 10–15% below the normal rate. The *Isbrandtsen Case* decided that the dual rate system was contrary to the Act and therefore unlawful. At the same time doubts began to arise about the ability of the regulatory agency to provide conference lines with immunity from antitrust process merely by the approval, under section 15 of the Act, of agreements required to be filed.

Conference lines in Europe began to close ranks and established a pressure group, the Committee of European Shipowners (CES). At the same time, governments in Europe, both for themselves and at the behest of their liner conference members, began to take note. This led to the establishment of the Consultative Shipping Group of Governments (CSG).

In 1958, moratorium legislation was enacted by Congress in order to enable lines to continue, legally, to use the dual rate system pending hearings in Congress. The hearings were extensive and involved Congressmen travelling to Europe and both European shipowners and their governments putting forward views in Washington. The Congressional hearings were not just on the legality or otherwise of the dual rate system, but also on whether the objectives of the 1916 legislation were being met.

The Bonner Amendments, 1961

The subsequent Bonner Act, which amended the 1916 legislation, established a new regime, partly confirming previous principles, but also providing the Federal Maritime Commission (FMC) with increased regulatory teeth.

The broad purpose was, according to the preamble, "to authorise common carriers and conferences thereof serving the foreign commerce of the United States, to enter into effective and fair dual rate contracts with shippers and consignees and for other purposes". It required, *inter alia*, that conferences to and from the USA must be open to all qualified operators as in the open conference system. It also required lines to file, and the FMC to approve, agreements which had to comply with US anti-trust legislation; and confirmed the longstanding position that the deferred rebate system should not be used. However, all agreements had to be in a standard FMC-prescribed format and the FMC was required to ensure that freight rates to and from the US were fair and non-discriminatory and not detrimental to US commerce. These requirements, which were applied to agreements wherever concluded, were offensive to shipowners outside the USA and their governments.

The FMC approached its newly enhanced regulatory role with fervour, spurred on by the prevailing Congressional suspicion of the effect of conferences on US trade interests.

Over the next 3 years, the FMC implemented the provisions of the Bonner amendments. However, as well as seeking to regulate the detail of conference line operations, including agreements entered into outside the USA, demands were made for the production of documents, information, records, and notes of meetings from companies situated outside the United States. The purpose was to support investigations into allegations that rates of freight were set at levels which impeded US commerce.

Governments in Europe and Japan reacted to protect their shipowners and traders from this excess of regulatory zeal. The Consultative Shipping Group of Governments (CSG) emerged as an informal yet cohesive group. The UK Government enacted the Shipping Contracts and Commercial Documents Act 1964 to prohibit lines from giving information in the UK which was sought by the FMC in pursuance of its regulatory role on the grounds that its disclosure would not be in Britain's public interest. Other countries in Europe adopted similar defensive legislation.

Developments within the shipping industry pointed to the need for a representative body of national shipowner associations to discuss and formulate policies with governments and shippers' councils (which following an initiative by the International Chamber of Commerce were becoming increasingly influential). The Council of European and Japanese National Shipowners' Associations (CENSA) eventually emerged to fill this role. It was based in London and mirrored CSG nations on the government side.

CSG Ministers' Resolution, 1963

In a resolution adopted in 1963 (following a series of meetings to consider the US position and a growing worldwide tendency for governments to interfere with the free operation of international shipping in pursuit of purely national objectives), the CSG ministers reaffirmed the underling tenets of the conference system with self-policing rather than government controls. They further resolved to take steps to ensure that conferences of which the shipping companies in their countries were members provided a mechanism for discussing grievances and resolving disputes between lines and shippers or groups of shippers.

This was a further endorsement of the conference system by a powerful group of governments. At the same time, it made it clear that conferences seeking help in response to hostile actions must first put their own house in order.

European liner conference shipowners responded through CENSA with a memorandum to ministers dealing specifically with two aspects of their resolution.

On the first, during 1963, the lines drew up a note of understanding with the European Shippers' Councils which proposed that there should be regular discussion on matters of principle and broad issues of mutual interest; and improved machinery for dealing with grievances. This became the foundation stone for corporate consultations between CENSA and the European Shippers' Councils (although they subsequently faltered) and also for the explicit legal consultation requirement which was built into the UN Liner Code and other national and regional legislation.

On the second, the European lines pointed out that the inclusion in conference agreements of provisions dealing with malpractices (namely unfairness between one member line and another) was the rule rather than the exception. Nonetheless, they drew up—through CENSA—a list of suitable model clauses for inclusion in new or amended conference agreements.

Further Activity in the US

The growth of containerisation and the through movement of goods from inland points in the US to inland points elsewhere gave rise to new jurisdictional problems as well as to the purely commercial difficulty that the US laws prohibited conferences (but not individual lines) from quoting shippers a composite "through" rate.

Even more menacingly, two further legal decisions undermined what little degree of certainty existed: the *Carnation Case* (1966) and the *Svenska Case* (1968). The first decided that the antitrust immunity, which the FMC approval gave, was not universal—as had been thought—but only extended to actions that fell four square, and lawfully, within the terms of the approved agreement. Thus, there were fears that actions taken which were perfectly lawful under national law, or which were thought incorrectly to be covered by the agreement, could give rise to antitrust suits, both civil and criminal. These fears were subsequently proved to be only too well founded.

The *Svenska Case* introduced a new test which had to be satisfied if agreements were to be approved and thereby at least a measure of antitrust immunity achieved. This was that the carrier had to demonstrate that there was "a serious transportation need, necessary to secure important public benefits". This test was unclear and difficult to meet. The result was delay, expense and difficulty, especially under the US adversarial system whereby competing interests were only too ready to oppose approval on the basis of one of these criteria.

Rochdale Inquiry, 1967–1970 (UK)

The Rochdale Inquiry, set up following the 1966 seamen's strike, was asked to review the whole organisation and structure of the UK shipping industry. In an examination of liner conferences, it concluded, on balance, that it would not be in the public interest to prevent liner companies banding themselves together in order to regulate and rationalise trade; and further that the closed conference was desirable for most deep-sea routes. Its assessment was that, on any other basis, there would be insufficient volume of traffic to make it economic for the shipowners to continue to provide efficient services to shippers with a reasonable profit. Nevertheless, it proposed a policy of greater openness on the part of conferences.

Rochdale recommended that conferences should accept a published code of practice covering provisions for admission; publication of tariffs; arrangements for freight rate negotiations; and consultations with shippers and governments. In practice, this devolved onto CENSA and the European Shippers' Councils.

While the recommendations were put forward in a national context, it was recognised that they would only be effective if developed subsequently on an international basis and then essentially as a self-regulatory code, and not one imposed unilaterally by government. The committee was fully aware of the problems induced by attempts at governmental level to regulate both inward and outward conferences. The British Government was accordingly urged to take an international initiative on the whole matter.

CENSA/ESC Code

Substantial progress had been made in the development of consultation machinery by shipowners and shippers since the 1963 CENSA/ESC note of understanding. By 1970 (when Rochdale reported), the rudiments of a code were in place through jointly agreed recommendations on a number of the points suggested.

A further meeting of CSG ministers was held in Tokyo in 1971 to consider a range of shipping developments including US policy and liner conferences (in the new light of containerisation). The ministers re-affirmed their support for the liner conference system. Shipowners, in consultation with shippers, were requested to elaborate the details of a code of practice for conferences, incorporating a number of the proposals put forward by Rochdale.

The CSG governments did not, in principle, wish to involve themselves in the commercial aspects of shipping although they wished to receive progress reports from time to time. In turn, shipowners and conferences would do their best to ensure that the code, when prepared, was properly implemented. Ministers clearly saw the early development and implementation of a code as a pre-emptive strike against those from the developing countries and elsewhere who were beginning to think along similar lines in the context of UNCTAD.

Intense consultation was undertaken between CENSA and the European Shippers' Councils. Because of the reasonable working relationship between these two bodies and because certain of the elements had already been agreed, it was possible to submit the code to governments by the end of 1971. In political terms, the stage was thus set for the forthcoming battles in UNCTAD.

United Nations Conference on Trade and Development

UNCTAD Shipping Committee, 1964–1974

One of the subjects discussed at the first UNCTAD Conference in 1964—for the first time on a world-wide basis—was liner conferences. These were seen by the developing countries as a key element of the shipping scene and were heavily criticised in relation to the fixing of freight rates; discriminatory practices; offering inadequate opportunities to lines from emerging nations; and maintaining private maritime law to the benefit of industrialised states.

Despite all this, the specialised working group to which shipping was remitted in 1964 did manage to reach, at least on the surface, certain areas of general agreement, embodied in the "Common Measure of Understanding on Shipping Questions". This understanding, which expressed general support for the conference system while at the same time acknowledging the issues of concern to the developing nations, was an important first milestone in the consideration of shipping questions in UNCTAD.

The criticisms voiced by developing countries and others subsequently culminated in the first international convention on liner shipping. This in turn would lay the ground for a far more precise regulation of the activities of conferences than ever before.

The UN Liner Code

The United Nations Convention on a Code of Conduct for Liner Conferences was adopted at a UN Diplomatic Conference in 1974. It is sometimes referred to—wrongly—as the "UNCTAD" Code because all the preparatory work was done in various groups under the aegis of UNCTAD.

At the same time as Rochdale in the UK was suggesting a code of practice, the UNCTAD secretariat was working on a much more detailed regulatory code, and various elements within the Group of 77 (developing nations) were also working out their own ideas. As expected, the subject proved controversial. The CENSA/ESC code, which reflected normal commercial conference practice and had been generally accepted by the CSG governments, was quickly brushed aside as not going nearly far enough for the Group of 77 who now put forward a unified text. Despite the wide gaps between the groups, and intense and difficult negotiations, general agreement was achieved on certain subjects to be included in a universally acceptable code. However, deadlock remained over the system of implementation. The Group of 77 wanted a legally binding instrument which could be enforced; the Group B (OECD) nations favoured less formal provisions which governments would use their best endeavours to see implemented.

Following a resolution at the UN General Assembly and after four, often difficult, preparatory sessions reflecting free-enterprise self-regulation versus governmental regulation, a Convention (somewhat loosely drafted because of the unusual absence of referral to a legal vetting group, thus rendering the content vague and often ambiguous) was eventually adopted, partly because of a split within the developed nations. The adoption of the Convention took place at the end of two conferences of plenipotentiaries in November/December 1973 and March/April 1974 chaired by none other than Mr. C.P. Srivastava of India who subsequently became Secretary General of the IMO. The UK and the USA were among the handful of States which voted against the Convention.

Although the CENSA/ESC code had been rejected at an early stage, some 70 % of the UN Liner Code was in fact based on its principles. The Code was also an endorsement of the conference system as such; and indeed of closed (as opposed to open) conferences.

The main elements of the Code covered conference membership; acceptance of loyalty arrangements; self-policing; consultation machinery; fixing and revision of freight rates; application of surcharges; and dispute resolution provisions. Arrangements for participation gave national lines of the two countries served equal rights to participate in the conference trade with third-country lines entitled to a significant share such as 20 %. This was the genesis of the so-called 40/40/20 rule. But, it was not a rigid rule; the share of national lines depended upon third-country participation, and then "unless otherwise mutually agreed". The principle of formula cargo shares did not exist in the CENSA/ESC code and was hotly contested by most Group B countries.

The Code eventually entered into force in 1983.

It is questionable whether the Code has ever really been implemented in practice. It has been prayed in aid by some developing countries in the justification of national legislation, usually restricting access to cargoes for non-national lines. However, by 1983 the nature of the liner industry had changed significantly with the growth of containerisation and consortia and the fact that lines operating outside conferences were carrying an increasing share of liner cargo in many trades.

The Brussels Package, 1979 (EC Regulation 954/79)

Many of the Code's critics were intrinsically opposed to any government interference in liner shipping. However, when the dust began to settle, it was seen that it was not as inflexible as had originally been believed and many of its principles began to seep into liner conference operations world-wide.

France, Belgium, the then Federal Republic of Germany and Japan had voted with the developing countries to adopt the Convention. The three EU nations considered that, despite the Code's imperfections, it was politically and commercially expedient to take steps to ratify and begin the process of implementation at national level. However, the European Commission said that all EU countries had to act together on such issues and threatened legal proceedings to restrain any action by individual Member States. The Commission was also concerned, as were others, about the protectionist nature of the 40/40/20 principle.

However, shipowners in other EU States began to come round to the views of the three supportive countries. British lines remained unhappy with the Code but they, too, eventually had to accept the need to find ways with governments to overcome the more offensive elements.

This resulted in EU Regulation (954/79) known as the "Brussels Package" which was designed to enable all member states to proceed towards implementation on the basis of a common reservation at the time of the deposit of instruments of ratification. This was based on the "disapplication" or "redefinition" of certain principles which would otherwise have applied to EU lines (or those of like-minded OECD countries) at the European end of liner trades. There was also a growing acceptance of the idea that the Code might help to contain some of the worst excesses of cargo reservation practised by developing countries and others.

A significant factor in the Brussels Package was the disapplication of the conference cargo sharing (40/40/20) provision between EU nations and between like-minded OECD nations who agreed to join the arrangement on a reciprocal basis. Shares would continue to be determined on the basis of commercial principles. As a result, the EU effectively succeeded in excluding the application of the most objectionable aspects of the Code from about 70 % of the world's liner trades.

However, repeal of Regulation 4056/86, removing the liner conference block exemption, meant that EU Member States could no longer fully comply with their obligations under the Code. As a result, Regulation 954/79 became inapplicable and was repealed with effect from 18th October 2008 when conferences ceased to be lawful in European trades. It seems that while Member States were not automatically required to denounce the Code since participation in conferences in third party trades should be unaffected, there are arguably treaty law implications surrounding partial application. The UK has denounced the Code.

Reviews and the Future of the Liner Code

To date, 79 nations have ratified. However, the USA remains implacably opposed arguing that the protectionist nature of the 40/40/20 principle, the acceptance of the closed conference system and other elements are not compatible with the US Shipping Acts. Elsewhere, specific agreements to circumvent the content mean that the Code is rarely applied as written. These facts—together with the lack of progress at the two review conferences in 1988 and 1991, the failure to arrange subsequent review conferences, the decreasing protectionist tendencies in some developing countries, the reducing role of UNCTAD in shipping issues and, most recently, the EU's decision to abolish the conference block exemption, all call into question the Code and its future relevance.

Development of Competition Policy in the USA and the European Union

General

The evolution of US antitrust policy concerning sea transport and the parallel development of the EU's competition policy during the 1980s and 1990s is set out in chapters 8 and this chapter. This section provides further detail on how these were applied in the trans-Atlantic trade, which was a close focus for activity as the conference lines tried over a 10–15 year period to adapt their processes to the new era of increasingly intensive regulation.

The North Atlantic Saga

The North Atlantic trade is third in size after the trans-Pacific and Europe/Far East trades. In 1984, the then nine conferences were replaced by the North Europe–USA Rate Agreement (Neusara) and USA–North Europe Rate Agreement (Usarera) for westbound and eastbound traffic respectively. The agreements were based on traditional principles of published tariff rates, service contracts between the conference and individual shippers and, reflecting the US Shipping Act 1984, conference members' right to take independent rate action. However, rates, which had been in general decline since 1980, continued to fall and in 1985 the Eurocorde and Gulfway agreements were concluded as non-binding arrangements for facilitating discussions with the main independent carriers on rates, tariffs and conditions of carriage.

Faced with continuing weak rates a new mechanism, known as the Trans-Atlantic Agreement (TAA), was established as a means of restoring stability and enabling freight rates to be raised. TAA members comprised the former Neusara and Usarera members and the major independent operators. There were 15 operators at the time.

The key elements were:

- Fixing in common tariffs applicable to the maritime sector and inland carriage, with restrictions on independent rate action;
- Arrangements for service contracts; and
- A capacity management programme (CMP).

Membership recognised a difference between former conference members, where more highly disciplined actions, including a prohibition on entering into individual service contracts, were regulated by committee; and the greater flexibility granted to former independent operators.

TAA was notified to the European Commission in August 1992. It was subsequently examined by the Commission pursuant to Council Regulation 4056/86 regarding maritime transport and in accordance with Regulation 1017/68 in the application of the Competition Rules to inland transport. Complaints were also lodged by port, shipper and forwarding interests.

In a decision (94/980/EC) dated 19 October 1994, the Commission concluded that TAA was not a liner conference agreement contemplated by Article 3 of Regulation 4056/86 because:

- It established at least two rate levels; and
- It provided for non-utilisation of capacity.

In its detailed analysis, the Commission rejected TAA's interpretation that carriers could jointly, i.e. in common, agree differentiated rates between themselves but categories of carrier must uniformly apply their agreed rate level to shippers. The Commission took the view that "The real purpose of the introduction of differentiated rates... such as that of the TAA is to bring independents inside the agreement" (Recital 341) and "This type of agreement seeks to disguise as a conference what is really an agreement with outsiders, independents wishing to maintain price flexibility. This is not a genuine liner conference ..." (Recital 343).

The Commission was equally critical of the CMP noting that the regulation of carrying capacity permitted under Article 3(d) of Regulation 4056/86 must be incidental to conference price-fixing and not intended to change freight rates substantially. The CMP was not a capacity regulating tool but, rather, "intended primarily for suspending unused capacity so that it can be artificially maintained, and the trade and prices for European exports artificially increased" (Recital 370).

Inland price fixing was also examined. TAA argued that Article 5(3) and (4), relating to conditions and charges for services not covered by freight charges, applied the block exemption to multi-modal transport organised by a liner conference. This was rejected by the Commission on the grounds that "the scope of the block exemption cannot be wider than the scope of Regulation (EEC) 4056/86 itself. According to Article 1(2) of the Regulation 'it shall apply only to international maritime transport services from or to one or more Community ports'" (Recital 373). This was a significant conclusion in the Commission's restrictive approach to the block exemption, a line followed in subsequent cases and generally upheld by the Courts.

It was not, therefore, surprising that the Commission rejected an individual exemption for the maritime sectors arguing that there was insufficient outside competition and that TAA provided its members with considerable power to eliminate competition. An application for an individual exemption under Regulation 1017/68 for inland haulage price-fixing was equally refused. Carriers had argued that this was necessary to ensure stability of multi-modal transport provided in conjunction with conference price arrangements which might otherwise be undermined. However, the Commission was not persuaded, questioning how quality and stability could be improved when carriers bought-in haulage on individually negotiated terms but resold the services at uniform rates.

As well as taking immediate action to end the infringements, and refrain from further similar activities, the 15 TAA members were instructed to offer their customers the opportunity to renegotiate or terminate existing contracts or other TAA agreements.

The lines appealed. However, it was not until February 2002 that the Court of First Instance delivered its judgment, together with similar issues arising from the subsequent TACA case and the Commission's findings regarding the FEFC.

Trans-Atlantic Conference Agreement (TACA)

In 1994, a new Agreement at that time comprising 17 lines—TACA—was notified to the Commission to come into force from October that year. The parties maintained that this was a liner conference falling within the block exemption in Regulation 4056/86. In the alternative, the parties applied for an individual exemption. The number of participants varied over the years, eventually and after various mergers settling at 14 companies; and TACA itself was modified from time to time.

Significantly, TACA abandoned the TAA's capacity management programme; eliminated the different categories of membership and two-tier tariff structure and withdrew from membership of the Gulfway and Eurocorde Discussion Agreements.

The principal features of TACA were:

• The price agreement relating to maritime transport;
• The price agreement relating to inland transport as part of a multi-modal (carrier haulage) service to shippers;
• Agreement between the carriers concerning terms and conditions for offering service contracts to shippers; and
• Agreement between the carriers regulating maximum levels of freight forwarder compensation.

The application was scrutinised over the next 3 years. Contrary to the understanding that notification would provide immunity from fines until a decision was taken, in November 1996 the Commission removed the TACA parties' immunity in relation to inland rate-fixing in the Community. A decision (case number IV/35.134) was issued in September 1998. Once again, this reflected the Commission's policy of narrowly construing the scope of exemption arrangements. The Commission separated Article 85(1)—subsequently Article 81(1) and now Article 101—agreements between maritime transport services under Regulation 4056/86, which covered only the maritime sector and a limited number of other ancillary activities, out from inland transport services under Regulation 1017/68. It argued that, where an agreement covered maritime and inland transport, it must be dealt with under both regulations, while non-transport services fell to be determined under the procedural provisions of Regulation 17 [Recital 285]. Accordingly, the agreements under the last three bullets above fell outside the block exemption provided in Regulation 4056/86.

The main conclusions of the Commission's detailed decision were that:

- The price agreement for inland transport services under the tariff (and despite the existence since November 1995 of arrangements to facilitate the inland positioning of empty containers) supplied within the Community to shippers as part of a multi-modal operation, did not lead to an improvement in the quality of these services, did not allow shippers a fair share of the resulting benefits and contained restrictions of competition which were not indispensable. The conditions for an individual exemption under Regulation 1017/68 did not, therefore, appear to be fulfilled (Recital 424);
- While, as the result of separate discussions with the FMC, TACA had been modified from 1996 to remove the prohibition on individual service contracts (prior to that, only conference service agreements had been permitted), the contract was still required to comply with certain conference imposed conditions (Recital 502);
- As with the tariff rates, inland price setting for carrier haulage under a service agreement fell outside of the liner conference block exemption and was, by the same criteria, incapable of individual exemption (Recitals 503/4); and
- The agreement to regulate freight forwarders' conditions was a restriction of competition which fell to be determined under Regulation 17 and not Regulation 4056/86 or Regulation 1017/68. However, the agreement did not fulfil the conditions for an individual exemption (Recitals 509/510 and 518).

Issues connected with a dominant position under Article 86 were then examined. The Commission asked whether the TACA parties were capable of being jointly dominant and whether they were in fact dominant in the relevant markets. An analysis looked at the theory of dominance where the TACA parties had a share of up to 70 % of some market sectors, giving rise to a "strong presumption of a dominant position". The discriminatory price structure, whereby rates are based on cargo value with a fivefold difference between high- and low-value commodities, was questioned. This, it was argued, was a means of maximising revenue where an undertaking had "a substantial degree of market power" (Recital 535).

However, it is not clear what alternative system might have been advocated by the Commission. A single rate would deter the transport of low-value commodities. The result would be to distort trade either through the unavailability of goods no longer entering trade or the inappropriate use of resources to manufacture goods which would previously have been traded.

The Commission was particularly concerned about TACA members' agreement to place restrictions on the availability and contents of service contracts. This, it was argued, deprived shippers of additional services which individual TACA parties might have been able to offer. Concern was also expressed that arrangements for potential competitors to enter the market as TACA parties had distorted the competitive structure of the market to reinforce TACA's dominant position.

The TACA parties were instructed to put an immediate end to the infringements relating to inland pricing, fixing freight forwarder remuneration and setting freight rates and conditions for service contracts with shippers. At this stage, fines were not imposed for inland rate-fixing pending a court ruling on the scope of Regulation 4056/86.

However, abuse of a dominant position is prohibited per se. On the objective evidence, the TACA parties were found to have infringed Article 86. In a very critical commentary on the TACA parties' actions, the Commission rejected any basis for mitigation and imposed (then) record fines totalling Euro 273 million based on turnover and ranging from Euro 6.88 million for the smallest company to Euro 27.5 million for AP Møller-Maersk Line and Sea-Land Service Inc. P&O Containers and Nedlloyd, which as separate companies would each have each been fined Euro 23.6 million, had by that time merged their operations and were required to pay the combined amount of Euro 41.26 million.

Finally, the parties were required to offer their customers the opportunity to renegotiate or terminate forthwith existing joint service contracts.

The TACA parties appealed.

The Court of First Instance delivered a series of inter-connected judgements in 2002.

The first case (T-18/97) related both to the TAA and to similar TACA appeals regarding the Commission's withdrawal of immunity from fines for inland price-fixing arrangements. The Court noted that Regulation 17 and Regulation 4056/86 each contained provisions whereby fines for infringements could not be imposed in respect of acts taking place after notification to the Commission and before the Commission's decision allowing or refusing an application under Article 85(3), now Article 81(3). However, there was no similar immunity in Regulation 1017/68 and the Court declined, in the absence of such express provision, a right of immunity as a general principle of Community law. The appeal was dismissed.

The second case (T-395/94) requested the Court to annul the original TAA decision. In the alternative, the Court was asked to annul the provisions prohibiting inland rate-setting as part of inter-modal transport and annul the requirement to offer shippers the opportunity to renegotiate service contracts.

Once again, the carrier case was dismissed, almost in its entirety. The Court upheld the Commission's findings that TAA restricted competition for the purposes of Article 85(1). Moreover, TAA was not a liner conference under Regulation 4056/86 because it established at least two rate levels through the differentiated tariff scheme for the two categories of members and did not apply uniform or common freight rates applicable to all (Recital 176). At the same time, the capacity management programme was considered to be an activity outside the scope of the liner conference block exemption. The Court then examined, but rejected, the TAA request for individual exemption. However, the applicants' case for annulment of the requirement to renegotiate existing service agreements was upheld on a technicality.

Multi-modal Rates: FEFC Case

In parallel with the TAA/TACA appeals, the Court of First Instance also ruled (Case T-86/95) on an appeal concerning similar issue brought by the Far Eastern Freight Conference (FEFC). The conference tariff, which had taken effect from 1990, included collectively set prices for inland carriage covering door-to-door container transport. German shipper representatives had lodged a complaint arguing that only the sea transport sector fell within the block exemption in Regulation 4056/86 and that inland carriage must be considered under Regulation 1017/68.

In a decision (94/985/EC) issued in December 1994, the Commission had agreed that FEFC had infringed Article 85 and the conditions for an exemption under Regulation 1017/68 had not been fulfilled. The Conference was ordered to put an end to the infringement with token fines of ECU 10,000 levied on each of the 14 members.

The issues were explored in detail by the Court. Significantly, the Court supported (Recital 345) the Commission's view in the original decision that the advantages of intermodal transport in general were not in dispute. However, the argument centred on the legality, under the Competition Rules, of collectively fixing the price of inland services in multi-modal transport.

Relying on the *travaux préparatoires*, general rules of interpretation and the wording of Regulation 4056/86, the Court dismissed the applicants' case that such Conference activities fell within the liner block exemption. The Court also rejected the application for an individual exemption under Regulation 1017/68.

In this connection, the Court (as in the TAA decision) noted that FEFC members bought in inland transport services individually to be resold at a collectively agreed rate, in contradiction to similar services individually offered by independent lines and freight forwarders. Collective inland price-fixing was not therefore indispensable to the supply of inland transport services (Recital 380).

While issues of principle had been lost by the lines, the Court annulled the Commission's original, albeit token, fines.

More Developments Concerning TACA

In 2003, the Court of First Instance upheld the substantive provisions of the Commission's findings that TACA had infringed the Competition Rules (because the service contract restrictions constituted an abuse) and the Commission's refusal to grant an individual exemption for the TACA arrangements. However, the Court:

- Set aside the fines of Euros 273 million imposed for the abuse of a collective dominant position, partly owing to lack of evidence and infringement of the rights of the defence and partly because of immunity conferred by notification to the Commission; and

- Set aside, owing to lack of evidence and infringement of the rights of the defence, the Commission's decision concerning measures inducing competitors to join the conference.

The Commission did not appeal the Court's decision.

Following the Commission's rejection of the original TACA in 1998, and in the light of discussions with the Commission on the principles of future arrangements, a Revised Trans-Atlantic Conference Agreement (TACA 2) came into existence and was notified in 1999. It comprised eight member shipping companies. The main features were:

- Rate-setting only within the provisions of Article 3 of Regulation 4056/86;
- Complete freedom for carriers and shippers to agree the content of individual service agreements;
- Provisions covering conference and multi-carrier service agreements;
- No inland price-fixing but an agreement for carriers not to charge less than their out-of-pocket expenses (the "not below cost" rule); and
- Arrangements, with appropriate safeguards, for compiling and exchanging information.

The "not below cost" rule was approved in August of that year, although a complaint was subsequently lodged with the Court of First Instance by the European Shippers' Councils. However, the Commission expressed reservations about the information exchange arrangements and the competitive effects on individual service contracts.

It was to be more than 3 years before TACA 2 eventually received Commission clearance in 2002. The final agreement included strict limits on the nature of information exchanges with the Commission monitoring aspects of the arrangements. Tightly defined provisions were also agreed to ensure that freight rates could not be increased in response to any temporary withdrawal of vessel capacity.

By the time of the TACA 2 clearance, discussions between the Commission and carriers had defined the scope and limited extent of acceptable provisions in conference agreements. An essential feature was that there could be no restriction on conference members' rights to agree confidential service contracts with individual shippers. Individual service contracts became the rule with only a very small percentage of cargo moving under the published conference tariff. Nevertheless, conference rates continued to have a value as they provided a benchmark starting point for rate negotiations.

TACA 2 represented the end of a chapter, but not the end of the story. The outcome of the Commission's review of Regulation 4056/86 has resulted in far-reaching changes.

Far East Trade, Tariff Charges and Surcharges Agreement (FETTSCA)

FETTSCA was drawn up in 1991 as a means of introducing greater transparency in relation to maritime charges and surcharges. Details were provided to the Commission but the arrangements were not formally notified (which would have conferred immunity) because the parties believed it to be a technical agreement benefiting from Article 2 of Regulation 4056/86. In its later Statement of Objections, the Commission admitted that the scope of Article 2 had been unclear at the time and it was only subsequent legal advice which paved the way for the Commission to impose fines in the absence of non-notification.

FETTSCA was short-lived with only three meetings, the last in 1992. The Agreement was terminated in 1994, shortly after receiving the Statement of Objections. Attempts to settle the case were made, with the lines offering to agree a set of legal principles to meet the concerns expressed. Nevertheless, in May 2000, the Commission imposed fines, based on the individual turnover of the 15 member companies, totalling Euro 6.8 million. Fourteen of the companies subsequently appealed on substantive grounds and on the grounds that even if there had been an infringement (which was denied), the fines were excessive and disproportionate to the facts. In 2003, the Court of First Instance annulled the fines because of the length of time between the proposal to act and the decision to impose monetary sanctions. The Commission appealed for the fines to be re-imposed but this was rejected by the European Court of Justice.

The United States

US Shipping Act 1984

Against the somewhat torrid background to US policy towards conferences, set out above, this section focuses on developments after the flurry of antitrust suits in the 1970s and early 1980s against European and other lines and their individual shipping company executives. These resulted in very heavy damages as well as fines, even the threat of imprisonment. This arose, not out of negligence or wilfulness on the part of the lines or their executives, but as a result of continuing uncertainty about the scope of antitrust immunity afforded by the Bonner amendments to the 1916 Shipping Act, following the *Carnation* and *Svenska* cases, and the general mood of strict antitrust enforcement.

This uncertainty, together with the general policy of deregulation and an acknowledgement in particular that co-operation was after all necessary to facilitate intermodal or door-to-door services, led to improvements in the previously strained relationship between the US and Consultative Shipping Group (CSG) governments and proposals for new shipping legislation.

This was finally enacted as the US Shipping Act 1984 and resulted in:

- Clarification of the antitrust position of lines.
- A new approach to the establishment of joint ventures and other methods of rationalisation.
- A shift away from the "presumptive illegality" of agreements.
- Authority to approve intermodal conference agreements and new forms of contracts with shippers.
- Conferences being enabled to quote a through rate, inland point in the US to inland point abroad, but not to negotiate the inland rate. This could only be done by individual lines.
- Conferences being required to permit any conference member to take independent action on any rate or service on 10 days' notice, after which that new level or agreed item would become available to other shippers also.
- The authorisation of service contracts with individual shippers or shippers' associations, subject to the filing of their essential terms, which would then also become available to other, similarly situated shippers.
- Streamlined procedures for the approval of agreements.
- The establishment of procedures to maintain access to foreign trades for US carriers.

Apart from the provisions on independent rate action and service contracts, both of which tended to weaken the position and coherence of the conference in regard to rate-making, the contents of the 1984 Act were encouraging. They confirmed more clearly than ever before in the US the validity of liner conferences, including their overall rate-making role; and they endorsed explicitly for the first time, the intermodal, door-to-door concept.

At this time, a Presidential Advisory Commission was established to review the working of the Act after 5 years and to consider whether to continue, revise or eliminate conference antitrust immunity; whether open or closed conferences were to be preferred; tariff-filing and service contracts arrangements; and conference relationships with shippers and non-vessel-operating common carriers (NVOCCs).

The review was protracted, with participation by foreign and US lines, evidence from more than 100 witnesses and testimony from in-depth interviews with 120 industry and government representatives.

The Commission finally reported in 1992 that no meaningful consensus could be reached on the main issues. Consequently, no changes were recommended.

As stated, the governments covered by the US/CSG Dialogue had agreed to consult in future on each other's regulatory practices; they had also undertaken to maintain the ability of commercially operated non-conference lines to compete freely. The Dialogue was undoubtedly helpful in preparing the ground for the rapprochement between the thinking in the US and in Europe on competition policy in the 1984 Act.

Nevertheless, further changes just over the horizon would lead to a fundamental review of the conference system resulting in even greater individualism in the relationship between carriers and shippers.

Deregulation was the mantra when the Republicans took control of Congress in 1994. This provided a focus for continuing shipper opposition to the liner conference system giving rise to far-reaching proposals by the National Industrial Transportation (NIT) League for ending carrier anti-trust immunity and abolishing the Federal Maritime Commission (FMC).

Initial opposition to the Republican-backed shipper proposals, co-ordinated through a carrier coalition, was moderated after the NIT League agreed not to press for abolishing anti-trust immunity in July 1995. It took a further 2 years of discussions before proposals were put forward as a final Senate compromise in March 1998. Despite strong objections from non-vessel-operating common carriers (NVOCCs) aggrieved that they remained unable to enter into confidential service contracts with shippers (but this has now changed—see below), the reform legislation was passed by the Senate and the House of Representatives. The outcome was seen as a broadly acceptable compromise which:

- Retained anti-trust immunity and maintained the FMC;
- Prohibited conferences and other agreements from banning the negotiation of individual service contracts by any of their members;
- Allowed conferences to have voluntary Guidelines relating to the terms of individual service agreements;
- Eliminated tariff filing with FMC but required carriers and conferences to make tariffs and essential terms publicly available;
- Required only minimum information to be made available (either publicly or to other members) for service contracts covering: origin and destination port ranges, commodity(ies), minimum volume and duration of the contract;
- Reduced the notice period required for individual conference members to take independent rate action from 10 to 5 days; and
- Allowed groups of ocean carriers to negotiate with non-ocean carriers for rates and services for inland transportation, provided that there was no conflict with US anti-trust laws.

Ocean Shipping Reform Act 1998

The *Ocean Shipping Reform Act 1998* (OSRA) came into force in May 1999.

The workings of OSRA were examined by FMC 2 years later, described as a "sufficient period of time for those in the industry to begin to adjust to the new regulatory environment and for the FMC to make an initial candid assessment of how the impact of the legislation appears to be unfolding". Responses to the FMC's Notice of Inquiry were described as voluminous. FMC also conducted a comprehensive examination of pricing and service behaviour based on random samples of filed service contracts. The findings were published in September 2001.

The Report concluded that OSRA's objective for promoting a more market-driven and efficient liner shipping industry had generally been achieved.

OSRA's most enduring change was to provide carriers and shippers with the right to conclude individual and confidential service contracts. The 1984 Act had given conferences control over their members' use of independent service agreements. Even where they were permitted by a conference, the main provisions had to be made publicly available with similarly situated shippers able to demand the same "me too" rate. Only limited information was now required to be made publicly available and Conferences or Agreements could no longer impose restrictions on or dictate the content of their members' individual contracts. Carrier rights for setting a separate rate independently of the conference tariff had also been relaxed.

The result has been a significant shift away from the traditional conference tariff to upwards of 80 % of cargo moving under service contracts. Anti-trust immunity is now centred on discussion agreements with non-binding rate authority and members' adoption of voluntary, but non-enforceable, service contract Guidelines.

A review of the FMC analysis suggests that, although not necessarily in equal measure, carriers and cargo have obtained advantages, particularly the ability to tailor contracts to individual circumstances. However, there are shipper concerns that discussion agreements can be used to undermine contract confidentiality provisions while carriers point out that their competitors' rate quotes are used by some shippers as a bargaining tool.

Carriers thus regard the ability to exchange information as essential to promoting stability and avoiding a return to the destructive competition of the pre-conference era. Stability is aided by bench-mark rates where the market knows the price as a starting point for discussions.

The reformed US system is of direct benefit to large and multi-national shippers whose market power can be brought to bear during contract negotiations. It remains to be seen whether small- and medium-sized enterprises will be able to secure a similar competitive advantage through a suggested resurgence of shipper associations and their buying power.

An interesting, but possibly unplanned, side-effect of the new confidentiality regime has been the demand by some shippers for terms requiring the carrier to reduce or surrender traditional contract defences and accept increased liability levels. Voluntary erosion of internationally agreed provisions abrogates liability cover and carriers accepting such demands incur higher costs to cover the uninsured risks.

Two groups did not welcome the changes and were opposed to OSRA. Congressman Henry Hyde, Chairman of the House Judiciary Committee, made subsequent efforts to remove anti-trust immunity from carrier agreements—arguing that OSRA placed NVOCCs, freight forwarders and smaller shippers at a disadvantage. Non-vessel-operating common carriers, who at one point during the OSRA legislative process expected change, had remained prohibited from entering into service contracts with shippers, although they could agree such contracts with ocean common carriers. As a result of subsequent efforts, these strictures were later relaxed as explained below.

Under the United States regulatory scheme, both NVOCCs and forwarders, defined as "Ocean Transportation Intermediaries" under OSRA, were subject to certain licensing and financial responsibility requirements. As mentioned above, NVOCCs were prohibited from offering "service contract" rates to shippers. Eight petitions were filed with the FMC in 2003–2004, relating to NVOCC Service Contracts by Third-Party Logistics Providers. The petitioners included UPS, FedEx, BAX Global, and DHL-Danzas, each calling for service contract authority or reform of tariff publication requirements. In conjunction with these petitions, the NVOCCs stressed that authority to contract was a major issue for the international shipping community. They called on the FMC to further the deregulatory spirit of OSRA by extending confidential contracting authority to intermediaries. The NVOCCs stressed that such authority was necessary to meet the demands of their shipper-clients, the continuing integration of logistics services across all modes, and to respond to the age-old demand for confidentiality of ocean rates.

In response to these petitions, the FMC accepted a staff recommendation that NVOCCs should be allowed to enter into confidential service contracts and decided in October 2004 to authorize "service arrangements" for NVOCCs to provide parity with service contracts. The so-called NVOCC Service Arrangement (NSA) rule thus provided "service contract parity" to NVOCCs acting as carriers, when dealing with their shipper-customers. The NSA rule was allowed under section 16 of the Shipping Act and is still in effect. It exempts NVOCCs from tariff publication and adherence to the enforcement requirements of the Shipping Act, subject to certain filing and publication requirements. In contrast to the service contract rules, the NSA rule prohibits shippers' associations which include NVOCCs as members from entering into an NSA. This restriction is similar to another aspect of the NSA rule which prohibits NVOCC-to-NVOCC NSAs, where one NVOCC acts as carrier and the other as shipper. In each instance, the FMC determines whether permitting such behaviour might eventually lead to anti-competitive activities on the part of the NVOCCs without any effective regulatory oversight by either the FMC or other United States federal agencies such as the Department of Justice.

The NSA rule represents one of those rare occasions when the regulated and the regulator understood the significance of an issue and came together to address it effectively. The FMC has commented that "[t]he [NSA] rulemaking will provide shippers with a broader range of service options, and greater opportunities for integrated supply chain solutions... [A]s the use of NSAs develops over time they will ultimately lead to greater competition and a more efficient shipping industry." Some shippers' associations have pointed out the NSA rule's prohibition on NVOCC-to-NVOCC arrangements is unnecessary and counter-productive.

Until recently, NVOCCs had to additionally publish and maintain a tariff. The critics of the NSA rule were long emphasising that the real issue involved tariff publication and enforcement. In a decision of the FMC issued orally on 18 February 2010, the Commission ruled that NVOCCs would not have to publish tariffs.

The 3-1 decision largely approved a petition submitted by the National Customs Brokers and Forwarders Association, Inc. (NBBFAA) that sought an exemption from the Commission under the Shipping Act of 1984 as amended that would exempt rate tariffs from being published. This is a major development with respect to NVOCCs, as it will make it considerably easier for them to operate and respond to market conditions. It makes it even more likely that such companies will be able to serve their function of providing the benefits of competition to smaller shippers.

In its decision the Commission said it would issue a rule within 30 days to the public that would permit licensed NVOCCs to be exempt from the requirement and associated costs of publishing rates under the Shipping Act. The rule will be issued pursuant to the Commission's authority under the Act and is based on the Commission's finding that granting the exemption within certain parameters and conditions will not result in substantial reduction in competition or be detrimental to commerce. In taking this action, the Commission noted that the exemption is voluntary in that NVOCCs may choose whether to utilize the exemption which only applies to licensed NVOCCs; and the exemption which is limited to rates as tariff rules must continue to be published.

For those NVOCCs that choose to use the rate tariff exemption, the following conditions would apply:

- Notice of the rate exemption must be published in a permanent place with the rules tariff that the NVOCC has chosen to operate under the exemption and opt out of publishing tariff rates;
- Public access to the rules tariff must be granted free of charge. In lieu of free public access, an NVOCC may provide a copy of the rules tariff with each of its rate quotes or proposals; and,
- Unpublished rate agreements must be agreed to and noted in writing, including the applicable rate for each shipment, by the date the cargo is received by the common carrier or its agent.

Inland hauliers (teamsters) were also unhappy, alleging that carrier immunity in rate-setting discussions had been used to the disadvantage of drivers whose salaries and conditions had been adversely affected.

Nevertheless, in overall terms, OSRA has achieved the strategy of combining free market conditions with limited controls over that freedom. This, therefore, provides a generally workable solution acceptable to carriers and cargo. It remains to be seen whether similar elements will be embraced in liner conference reviews taking place in other jurisdictions.

Europe

Note: Articles 85 and 86 providing the framework mechanism for application of the EU's competition rules in the original Treaty of Rome, were subsequently renumbered Articles 81 and 82 respectively, as a result of amendments to the

Treaty. Another revision was put into place through the Treaty of Functioning of the European Union of 2009 (TFEU) and the renumbered articles are 101 and 102 respectively. The article numbers in the text below are the current ones.

EU Competition Policy: Liner Conferences

After a European Court decision in 1974 which confirmed that the general articles of the Treaty of Rome applied to sea and air transport, it became evident that liner conferences were strictly unlawful under the EU competition (or antitrust) rules. Article 101 of the Treaty contains a general prohibition of concerted practices which may affect trade between member states and which have as their object or effect, the prevention, restriction or distortion of competition. Article 102 prohibits abuses of a dominant position, generally defined in case law and in interpretations of the position of shore-based businesses as a share upwards of about 25–40 % of the market in which the undertaking is trading, depending on the specific case.

A specific regulation was, therefore needed to apply the Treaty principles to sea and air transport, the only sectors to which they did not yet formally apply.

Action on this imperative had been deferred during the evolution of the EU's overall competition policy through a series of instruments adopted by the Council of Ministers. First, transport as a whole had been exempted from the regulation applying Articles 101 and 102 generally to business activity (Regulation 17/62) by Regulation 141/62. Then sea and air transport had been excluded from the regulation applying them to rail, road and inland waterway transport (Regulation 1017/68). The 1974 Court decision, once digested, meant that direct application to liner conferences was only a matter of time.

Conferences, if they were to continue to be lawful, had therefore to be given an exemption under the competition (or antitrust) articles of the Treaty of Rome. The matter had to be regularised through a formal exemption from the general ban on cartel activity under Article 101 (there is no corresponding possibility of exemption from Article 102). There were also other issues which needed to be addressed.

Following consultations, the European Commission put forward formal proposals in March 1985. They were part of a wider package of proposals for what became known as the first stage of the Common Shipping Policy, themselves in turn part of a comprehensive set of proposals for the development of a common transport policy as requested by the European Parliament.

The period up to the adoption of these proposals was one of intense activity by governments, the Commission, the shipping industry and shipper (now named "transport-user") interests within the then ten Member States. The leading voice for the shipping industry was the Comité des Associations d'Armateurs des Communautés Européennes (CAACE)—since renamed the European Community Shipowners' Associations (ECSA). Differences of view persisted right up to the last minute when compromises had to be struck, not just within the competition proposal itself but also across the other shipping policy proposals.

Regulation 4056/86

The so-called "competition regulation" was adopted in December 1986 laying down detailed rules for the application of Articles 101 and 102 of the Treaty to maritime transport. It was very detailed and laid down the conditions and obligations under which liner conferences might continue to operate.

The final version of the regulation met with disquiet from both sides of industry. There was reluctant acceptance of the principle with concern about what it would mean in practice because, as in the US trades, the price for immunity from process was a measure of regulation. This was an important feature in that a number of member states, including the UK, effectively exchanged very wide-ranging exemptions in their national legislation for a much more explicitly defined exemption under EU law which was directly applicable in their countries. No-one then saw the EU regime as being intended to be as bureaucratic as that administered by the US Federal Maritime Commission. Indeed, both government and industry representatives frequently stressed that one of their objectives was to avoid creating a European FMC. However, later events were to change that perception.

Regulation 4056/86 was—although it took some time for the shipping industry to acknowledge it—a unique regulation in the context of EU competition law, for four reasons. First, it enacted a "block" or "group" (i.e. sector-wide, as opposed to individual) exemption for horizontal price-setting agreements—which had never been done before (and has not been done since). Price-setting is considered one of the most objectionable anti-competitive practices. Second, the exemption was established directly in the implementing regulation adopted by the Council of Ministers, rather than through the normal channel of a Commission regulation. Third, unusually, the regulation was based not just on the competition articles of the Treaty of Rome, but also on the then Article 84(2)—now 100(2) of TFEU—which dealt with how transport policy issues should be applied to sea transport. This emphasised the instruction to take account of the distinctive characteristics of maritime transport. Fourth, the exemption was not time-limited. The norm is for exemptions, group or individual, to terminate or be reviewed after a fixed period, usually 5 years.

The regulation built on the basic philosophy underlying the UN Liner Code, albeit in the context of an instrument which had a more focused antitrust, regulatory intent. The preambular clauses made clear the EU governments' support at that time for the concept of liner conferences and their recognition of the wider social benefits they brought.

The main elements of the regulation were as follows:

- *Scope*. It applied to "international maritime transport services to or from a Community port". The question of inland carriage would be an issue in later Commission decisions.
- *Coverage*. The regulation specifically excluded tramp vessel services. This was consistent with the general contention of bulk operators that their markets were open and free. Any regulation of bulk shipping was therefore effectively left to

national authorities and courts. However, the Commission subsequently also referred in decisions to an undefined specialist sector.

- *Liner conferences.* A group exemption was enacted for "agreements, decisions and concerted practices of all or part of the members of one or more liner conferences" which operated on the basis of "common or uniform rates" and also engaged in one or more joint activities such as scheduling of sailings and the regulation of the carrying capacity offered by the member lines.
- *Condition.* The exemption was subject to one condition not to discriminate between ports, transport-users and other relevant parties unless the action can be economically justified. Failure to comply with a condition means that the agreement is deemed to have been void *ab initio*.
- *Other requirements.* Attaching to the exemption were a series of obligations which were interesting in the context of earlier examinations of the liner conference system and laws (for example, in the US). Non-compliance with an obligation only gives rise to sanction if and from the time the offender is instructed to terminate an infringement. The next four elements listed the main obligations:

  - *Consultation.* There had to be "consultation" (not "negotiation") on matters of general principle between providers and users on rates, conditions and quality of scheduled services.
  - *Loyalty.* Arrangements based on the contract or other lawful system were to be permitted, subject to consultation and other detailed rules. These could extend to cover 100 % of cargoes, but such coverage could not be unilaterally imposed. Deferred rebates were permitted, but in that case shippers had to be offered a choice between immediate and deferred rebates.
  - *Tariffs.* Tariff rates, related conditions, regulations and the like had to be made available to users. They also had to set out all the conditions concerning loading and discharge including the exact extent of the services covered by the freight charge, showing the proportions for the sea leg and the land leg, and by any other charge made by the lines.
  - *Inland haulage.* On the land leg of a multimodal movement, users had to be offered a free choice of whether to use haulage arranged by the shipping line (carrier haulage) or arranged by themselves (merchant haulage).

- *Agreements between conferences and transport-users.* A further group exemption was enacted for certain agreements concerning rates and conditions of service.
- *Enforcement and penalties.* Detailed provisions were made, including, most importantly, for a staged imposition of warnings and sanctions and for proportionality. As in other sectors, the maximum penalties were potentially very high, rising to 10 % of the total turnover of the company in question (not just that generated by shipping activities).
- *Entry into force*: a 6-month transitional period was envisaged until July 1987, by which time conferences were expected to have adjusted their arrangements in line with the requirements of the regulation.

Because of the difficulty of reaching full agreement both on this regulation between governments, the transport directorate and the competition directorate, and on the shipping policy package as a whole (mainly between the individual governments), all recognised from the start that the regulation was imperfect, but it broke new ground at least in Europe. Continuing the approach of the individual member states, it appeared on the face of it to be largely self-regulatory, intentionally relying for its enforcement not on tariff-filing as in the US, but on transparency of behavioural requirements.

It had been hoped that a period of relative stability would follow the adoption of Regulation 4056/86, but it was not to last more than a few years. Soon, the Commission was to begin chipping away at the exemption through a number of cases which arose as a result of complaints. In time, some of these would challenge certain of the fundamental precepts upon which the exemption had been based.

Application of EU Implementing Rules

Before turning to the review of Regulation 4056/86 and the events which led to it, it is appropriate to pause and note a further development in the EU affecting, in particular, non-liner shipping, i.e. bulk and specialist trades.

Article 101 of the TFEU sets out general rules applicable to restrictive practices. Paragraph 1 prohibits all agreements between undertakings designed to prevent, restrict or distort competition between member states. All such agreements are automatically void. However, in accordance with paragraph 3, where an otherwise prohibited agreement contributes to an improvement in the production or distribution of goods or promotes technical or economic progress while allowing consumers a fair share of the resulting benefits, and does not impose indispensable restrictions on the undertaking or substantially eliminate competition, the provisions of paragraph 1 may be declared inapplicable.

Article 102 prohibits, *per se*, any abuse by undertakings of a dominant position. This includes the imposition of unfair purchase or selling prices or trading conditions; limiting production, market or technical development to the detriment of consumers; and discriminatory practices.

Article 103 empowers the Council to give effect to the principles laid down in Articles 101 and 102 through appropriate regulations or directives.

Regulation 17, adopted by the Council in 1962, was the first implementing provision, laying down a centralised system of supervision and enforcement procedures. The Commission and national authorities could all declare a practice prohibited under Article 101(1) but only the Commission could grant an exemption under paragraph (3). Applications for exemption of prohibited practices had to be notified to the Commission under Regulation 17, where Article 15(5) provided immunity from fines from the time of notification until any decision by the Commission found that the activities were not capable of exemption. The system of notification and immunity was an important safeguard for industry and undertakings.

However, given efforts to establish a common transport policy, Regulation 141 of 1962 disapplied Regulation 17 to agreements, decisions or concerted practices in the transport sector having as their objective or effect "the fixing of transport rates and conditions, the limitation or control of the supply of transport or the sharing of transport markets; nor shall it apply to the abuse of a dominant position within the meaning of Article 102 of the Treaty...".

Transport by rail, road and inland waterway was subsequently brought back within implementing provisions through Regulation 1017/68. Significantly, and unlike the provisions of Regulation No 17 and Article 19 of Regulation 4056/86, Regulation 1017/68 did not confer immunity from fines from the date of notification of a prohibited practice. As discussed elsewhere, this had implications for the respondent undertakings in the TACA case.

As part of a package connected with EU trade and treaty commitments, including the UN Liner Code of Conduct, Regulation 4056/86 applied competition implementing rules to "international maritime services ... other than tramp vessels". This created the block exemption allowing liner conferences to jointly agree tariffs.

The block exemption was developed to reduce the number of individual exemptions being notified as a means of securing immunity. A block exemption was also later granted to liner companies working together in consortia (see below).

In 1999, the Commission put forward proposals for reform arguing that, after some forty years' experience, the original objective of establishing and harmonising competition provisions throughout the Community had largely been achieved. The Commission's responsibility for considering exemptions had led to large numbers of notifications being submitted. This was creating severe administrative delays, which would become even more acute when accession states joined the European Union in 2004, and detracted from the Commission's efforts to eradicate hard core cartels.

Streamlined arrangements were therefore proposed and developed as Council Regulation (EC) No 1/2003 of 16 December 2002 on the implementation of the rules on competition, laid down in Articles 101 and 102 of the Treaty. The main provisions:

- Replaced the system of notification (and its accompanying immunity from fines) with directly applicable "self assessment" exception arrangements;
- Abolished the Commission's sole preserve in overseeing implementation of the competition rules by empowering national competition authorities to apply Article 101(3) provisions;
- Allowed the grant of block exemptions to continue under the Commission's exclusive competence *but* with national competition authorities empowered to withdraw the benefit in their territory;

- Devolved powers back to national authorities to apply Articles 101–102 as a whole, together with arrangements to ensure the uniform application of Community competition law;
- Replaced the industry-specific Advisory Committee on Agreements and Dominant Positions in Maritime Transport with a General Advisory Committee on Restrictive Practices and Dominant Positions;
- Expressly excluded the application of the Regulation to international tramp vessel services and cabotage services; and
- Repealed Regulations 17 and 141 and introduced consequential amendments, *inter alia,* to Regulation 1017/68 (Inland Transport) and Regulation 4056/86 (Liner Conferences).

It is submitted that rather than removing an administrative burden, abolition of the notification system will potentially create uncertainty for business undertakings. A view (no matter how carefully considered), which concludes that a prohibited practice is capable of an exemption, might be contradicted at a later stage by regulators who might view the practice as an infringement, which should not benefit from the protection of immunity from fines. It remains to be seen whether guidance issued by the Commission on the methodology for the application of Article 101(3) will provide the degree of confidence essential to the smooth functioning of businesses.

OECD Activity

As part of an examination of regulatory regimes across the whole spectrum of member countries' activities, an OECD secretariat report on Regulatory Reform in Maritime Transport was issued in 1999. The Report is examined at this juncture because of its place in the chronology of developments and its eventual impact on the evolution of EU policy. Its central thesis argued for reassessment of anti-trust protection and, controversially, suggested replacing automatic immunity for setting common rates with specific approval to be given against a "public benefit" test. It also argued for outlawing discussion and capacity stabilisation agreements.

Carriers were critical of the content arguing that it was devoid of any meaningful economic analysis; overlooked regulatory changes, such as confidential contracting; did not appreciate that normal competition regulations were inappropriate to the unique conditions of liner shipping; and failed to recognise that block exemptions and immunity were balanced by tightly regulated and enforced obligations. Timing was also unfortunate because recent changes in a number of jurisdictions, where the underlying principles of immunity had been reaffirmed, meant that there were now settled arrangements for conferences after a long period of uncertainty. It was not, therefore, unreasonable for carriers to expect an era of calm whereas change, or the prospect of change, would be likely to create yet further legal uncertainty.

Not surprisingly, shipper representatives welcomed the proposals.

An OECD workshop was held in Paris in May 2000 when none of the governments present showed any enthusiasm for the report. Several, including representatives from the USA, Japan and on behalf of the European Union, made it clear that they did not wish to change the position at that time.

The report was remitted for further work. A second report, issued in advance of a subsequent workshop in December 2001, maintained the abolitionist stance and suggested a "second best" way forward, using as a basis the arrangements in the USA under the Ocean Shipping Reform Act, 1998. Carriers again criticised the content for its paucity of data, the assumptions made, and the analysis used to reach the conclusions.

Predictable positions were taken by industry representatives at the workshop. The USA, Australia and, in particular, Japan, repeated their opposition to change. However, this time the European Union representative noted that the secretariat report would be seen as a point of departure for further work by the EU. This comment was to have far-reaching implications, unleashing a review of Council Regulation 4056/86.

The final report, with the conclusions unchanged, was issued in May 2002. This remained a secretariat publication and was not official policy agreed by OECD member states. Unfortunately, this important distinction was not universally recognised.

Review of Regulation 4056/86

Liner Shipping

It has been mentioned that, over the years, the Commission sought to restrict the interpretation of what was viewed as a very generous provision in relation to liner shipping conferences. We have also seen that, in the 18 months between the two OECD workshops, the Commission's position shifted from one of taking no immediate action to a pro-active review.

The review process started with a consultation paper issued in 2003. This reached the preliminary conclusion that the regulation needed to be brought up to date. It suggested that the liner block exemption (described as controversial) appeared open to challenge and questioned the continuing exclusion of tramp services and cabotage from competition implementing regulations. The practical value of the provisions covering technical agreements and conflicts of law were also questioned.

Despite carrier views to the contrary, the Commission attempted to place the burden of proving the continuing need for a maritime regime squarely on carriers. This is not to say that carriers were on the defensive but it was less than satisfactory that cargo interests were not called upon to prove their case for removing the block exemption. There was also some surprise when, despite the Commission's indication that it had an open mind on future arrangements, the then Competition Commissioner, Professor Monti, ruled out US-style discussion agreements before the opening consultation period had expired.

ECSA co-ordinated the views of its constituent members based in the European Union and Norway, and worked closely with national associations outside Europe, particularly the Japanese Shipowners' Association, and with other international shipping organisations including the International Chamber of Shipping (ICS), BIMCO, Intertanko and Intercargo. Nevertheless, as liner aspects dominated the first part of the review, the major liner companies came together to form the European Liner Affairs Association (ELAA) with an original membership of 24 lines world-wide which had interests in conference trades to and from Europe.

Responses to the consultation paper were divided along partisan lines. Carriers argued that the block exemption was a necessary means of providing stability in an inherently unstable market, bedevilled by the unpredictability of trade levels and chronic imbalances according to seasonal and directional demands and the varying economic health of countries served. Yet, despite everything, liners always provided regular services meeting advertised sailing schedules. The European Shippers' Council (ESC) expressed a contrary view, repeating their members' longstanding call for repeal of the block exemption and a totally deregulated market for freight rates.

A mixture of views came from forwarder interests with, in general, qualified support for the value of the conference system but concerns expressed about the lack of consultation on surcharges and capacity changes. However, UK and Swedish organisations reflected shipper arguments for total abolition.

The majority of governments that responded favoured the principle of liner shipping exemptions with some calls for simplification. One state noted the need for consistency with other regimes such as in the USA, while others questioned the need for exemption arrangements.

A public hearing was hosted by the European Commission in December 2003. This provided industry with an opportunity to put forward views on the conference system and, particularly, on the pre-announced themes of stability of prices, reliability of services and indispensability of the arrangements. Presentations by the different interest groups were followed by general exchanges and the opportunity for member states to put forward questions. Few, if any, new arguments emerged on that occasion. An offer by carrier representatives to work with shippers, freight forwarders and the Commission, under appropriate legal privilege, to try to agree terms of reference for collecting empirical data of actual prices, was not taken up. Shipper representatives questioned the objectives of price stability arguing that competition, or yield management, were preferable to price administration within opaque tariffs and short-notice changes. They argued that rates should be left for individual agreement to reflect more closely carrier cost levels and indicated that they could live with the resulting consequences of supply and demand.

In response to calls for alternative arrangements to Regulation 4056/86, ELAA put forward a set of proposals in August 2004, emphasising that its membership remained of the view that changes were neither necessary nor justified. It offered an alternative basis for liner co-operation to preserve stability in the supply of services to users. The proposals were predicated on a new legal instrument allowing: the collection and dissemination of aggregated and historic information between lines on trade, capacity utilisation, commodity developments and forecasts; a publicly available past price index; and the development of formulae for surcharges and ancillary charges. Significantly, there would be no reference to collective rate-setting or capacity regulation.

ELAA's proposals were set out in some detail in a White Paper issued by the Commission in October 2004.

Tramp and "Specialist" Shipping

It is now necessary to take a step backwards and focus specifically on the issue of tramp shipping services. While subject to Community competition rules, tramp shipping remained outside the competition implementing rules. As a result, operators using bulk shipping pools and carriers working together in dedicated trades for the carriage of, for example, cars, chemicals and liquid gases, could not protect themselves under the former notification arrangements. The exclusion, which might have been seen as casting carriers into a legal wilderness, was also deemed a protection in that the Commission had no power to demand information or take enforcement action in the event of alleged irregularities. The exclusion continued under Regulation 1/2003. However, proposals in the review of Regulation 4056/86, would bring this to an end, while at the same time creating potential new uncertainties.

Article 3 of Regulation 4056/86 distinguishes between "liner conferences" which come within the ambit of the block exemption and its accompanying rules; and "tramp vessel services" which do not. As noted earlier in this chapter, the TAA decision created a new category of "specialist transport", a term which has never been properly defined (*TAA decision 94/980/EC Recital 33*). The proposed removal of the exclusion from the implementing regulations was seen by the industry as almost inevitable once the only other exception, relating to air transport, had been removed early in 2004.

ECSA's response to the proposal was to open a dialogue with the Commission to explain in greater detail the workings of non-liner services. Cabotage arrangements attracted very little comment and efforts were therefore concentrated only on the tramp sector. A tramp shipowner, operating in total isolation, is the very embodiment of textbook competition. In most cases the firm is too small individually to have any influence over a market populated by dozens, and often hundreds, of charterers. A study undertaken for the industry identified some 4,800 shipping companies in the tramp sector with only four having over 300 ships (2 % of the market share) and an average number of five ships per company.

However, isolation is not always an effective answer and bulk operators often work through shipping pools as an efficient means of administering and marketing their vessels. Pools are created for the purposes of facilitating chartering and husbandry. Rates set themselves in response to market mechanisms of supply and demand.

The other affected category, specialised transport, embraces a variety of trades using high-cost, purpose-built vessels, such as chemical carriers, car carriers, reefer vessels and forest product carriers. Trade routes may be determined by the availability of specialist terminals or dedicated infrastructure provisions or there might be an element of flexibility in the routes served. Specialist trades can share characteristics of liner services but they do not enjoy the, albeit limited, protection afforded to conference operators.

Removal of the exclusion would bring the non-liner sectors into unknown legal territory. Despite the competitive environment, certainty would be essential in relation to co-operative arrangements in areas such as pools. The abolition of the notification arrangements under Regulation 1/2003 would mean that pools, which could not be notified in the past because of the sectoral exclusion, would be subject to self-assessment requirements. Guidance was therefore needed on the criteria to be applied in future to assist operators seeking to determine whether any actions potentially giving rise to a prohibition under Article 101(1) would be eligible for an exemption under Article 101(3).

Subsequent Events and Developments

The next major event was the Commission's White Paper in October 2004 which, not surprisingly, recommended:

• Repeal of the block exemption for liner conferences; and
• Lifting the exclusion applicable to tramp (including specialist) shipping and cabotage services.

Views were invited on the recommendations, on potential alternative arrangements for future application, and on the ELAA's proposals.

Responses again mirrored the parties' known positions. Carriers questioned the need for any change but took the position that if change was inevitable, a new regime for liner shipping should be built on ELAA's proposals. In contrast, shipper interests advocated reform. Government views were mixed. There was less comment on the proposal to lift the tramp exclusion although ECSA responded emphasising the importance of providing guidance as a means of enhancing certainty for shipowners.

In December 2005, the Commission adopted the following proposals:

• *Repeal of the liner conference block exemption*: this was said to benefit EU exporters by lowering transport prices while maintaining reliable services and in turn enhance the competitiveness of EU industry.

    However, carrier representations for limiting the extent and speed of change had been heeded with the Commission proposing that repeal should not take effect until 2 years after adoption of the required Council decision. The transitional period would enable carriers to adapt to new market conditions and Member States time to review their international obligations including, no doubt, treaty implications under the Code of Conduct for Liner Conferences and bi-lateral trade agreements.

- *Tramp Shipping*: the exclusion from the implementing provisions set out in Regulation 1/2003 would be lifted thereby bringing the sector within Community competition rules. This will mean that the Commission, rather than individual Member States, would have competence to apply the powers and instigate enforcement measures.
- *New Guidelines*: nevertheless, account had been taken of industry representations for guidance on the future practical application of the rules. Guidelines would be issued on the application of competition rules to all forms of co-operation across the maritime sector. It was hoped that they would include elements of the alternative arrangements governing liner shipping operations advocated by ELAA and also advice particularly in relation to bulk shipping pools. On the latter, the Commission maintained its stance that formal guidance could not be issued until it had been granted the necessary oversight powers, but acknowledged the need for informal advice in advance of the changes taking effect and the issue in due course of the definitive and comprehensive Guidelines.

The European Parliament was broadly supportive of the industry approach and need for Guidelines but, although consulted, had no decision-making powers in this area.

The Commission's proposals were adopted unanimously by the Competitiveness Council in September 2006. The liner conference block exemption was repealed but a 2-year transitional period meant that it would not take unconditional effect until October 2008. However, and despite representations by the industry for a similar transitional period, the sectoral exclusion for tramp shipping was lifted when the implementing Regulation 1419/2006 took effect in October 2006—although it was generally understood that the Commission would be unlikely to use its new enforcement powers until the promised Guidelines had been issued.

At the same time, an Issues Paper was published by the Commission as a first step in the development of Guidelines. It dealt almost entirely with liner shipping including a preliminary assessment of ELAA's proposals. However, a brief introductory comment noted that tramp operations, particularly bulk pool arrangements, would also be addressed. The industry hoped that this would recognise the purpose and rationale for pool co-operation which had been explained to Commission officials at a series of meetings hosted over the summer by individual shipowner associations in the main European centres.

A consultant report, drawn up on behalf of the European Commission, published early in 2007, examined the workings of tramp shipping. Its main focus was on the compatibility of bulk pools with competition legislation. The consultants' preferred view was that if pools were seen as production joint ventures with an integrated distribution function, they would not be caught by the prohibition in Article 101(1). Accordingly, the extent to which pools represented an integrated whole and not a separate function of supply by owners and fixing (i.e. selling) by pool managers, was crucial to determining how pools should be assessed. As far as owners were concerned, this was the position. Owners provide one or more vessels and remain responsible for technical safety issues but pool managers undertake all commercial activities including planning vessel movements, instructing vessels, nominating port agents, liaising with charterers and shippers, concluding fixtures, issuing freight and demurrage invoices, ordering bunkers and resolving problems or disputes. Pool managers will also be scanning markets for new opportunities. In other words, this is production of the service.

It was, therefore, disappointing that draft Guidelines issued in September 2007 took an alternative approach and applied a narrower interpretation characterising shipping pools as joint selling coupled with some features of joint production. This would mean that every pool would have to be analysed to determine whether it fulfilled the criteria for a claimed exemption under Article 101(3).

Further representations were made over the following months on the importance of maintaining a stable environment for bulk pool operators while emphasising that the system had never been challenged by charterers. At the same time, liner interests called for clarification of the Guideline contents to ensure certainty in future information exchange arrangements, noting that such arrangements were essential to the continuing provision of competitive and efficient services for customers.

The final Guidelines were adopted by the Commission in July 2008. The approach towards pools is not quite so uncompromising as originally suggested and acknowledges that the greater the joint production element, the less likely it is that the pool will be caught by the Article 101(1) prohibition. However, this will not absolve pool managers from having to self-assess their arrangements. Anecdotal evidence suggests that some pools have decided to cease operations, not because they are acting unlawfully but, rather, because they have no desire to be pinpointed for a test challenge. Commission officials have hinted that they will not be targeting pool agreements for their own sake.

The Guidelines also address future co-operation in liner trades. Advice is set out in broad terms and it will be for undertakings to determine the compatibility of their arrangements with the legislation. The Guidelines suggest factors which should be taken into account such as market structure, including number of operators and any structural links between competitors; whether information exchanged is already in the public domain; sensitivity of the information; whether it is individual or aggregated; whether it is historic, recent or future; frequency of exchanges; and how, and to whom, it is circulated. Discussions and information exchanges can be conducted in a trade association but the association must not be used for undertaking prohibited or anti-competitive practices or to remove the uncertainty of market operations or competitors' behaviour. In other words, the market must be capable of offering price-based vibrancy to customers. The Commission is in the process of consulting interested parties on a proposal to remove the guidelines altogether as from September 2013.

On 18th October 2008, and after an existence of more than 125 years, the conference system in Europe slipped quietly into history. It remains to be seen whether the Commission's success in Europe to restrict the extent of co-operation in liner shipping will open up a new era of uncertainty by reference to untried criteria. Moreover, changes in Europe might have implications for the future shape of anti-trust arrangements in other jurisdictions. Some governments outside Europe are beginning to look with interest at the direction taken by the EU. Only time will tell whether the process gains momentum and heralds the eventual demise of conference arrangements throughout the world.

Liner Consortia

As explained earlier, liner consortia working both within and outside of conferences have become an essential part of the liner shipping scene. It is through them that European (and other) carriers have been able to rationalise and combine their services in order to meet competition from the massive, and sometimes subsidised, single operators. Nevertheless, from a policy standpoint, consortia also raise issues about their effect on competition.

Detailed discussions on whether liner consortia (not liner conferences) were in conformity with the Treaty of Rome, or whether some special regime for them was necessary, were in train between governments, the industry and the Commission's competition and transport directorates prior to the adoption of Regulation 4056/86. They continued into the early 1990s.

The shipowners' view was that, since the primary restrictive practices in the liner shipping industry—rate-setting and capacity rationalisation—had been addressed in Regulation 4056/86 in regard to liner conferences and since consortia as then formed did not have those functions, no further regulation was needed. In this thinking, they drew on Article 2 of Regulation 4056/86 which defined certain types of agreement as "technical" and then excluded them from the regulation; in other words, they were considered not to have contravened the prohibition of cartel activity in Article 101 at all. The shipping industry through ECSA argued that agreements between consortia members—where they were not covered by the full conference exemption—were technical agreements in that sense.

There was a major definitional problem with the industry being compelled to define a concept which, although some consortia had been in existence for more than 10 years, was flexible and varied. The competition directorate on the other hand, insisted that an exemption could only be established in respect of agreements which were clearly defined and indeed only for specified activities. This period marked the beginning of a much tougher approach by the European Commission to the application of competition policy to the maritime sector and also reflected a deliberate intention to re-assert Commission—as opposed to Council (i.e. governments)—competence in this key area of EU policy-making.

In 1992, the EU governments agreed in Council Regulation 479/92 to grant a group exemption for consortia and instructed the Commission to develop an implementing regulation taking the utmost account of agreed Guidelines which they set out in an annex. This decision marked the end of the possibility that governments might themselves continue to regulate competition issues in other areas of the maritime sector as they had in Regulation 4056/86.

The Commission's Regulation (870/95) was adopted in 1995, at least 20 years after the establishment of the first consortium—a European invention—and about 10 years after work on it had begun.

The main features of the regulation were the following:

- *Definition.* This encompassed a number of agreements which would have been traditionally regarded as technical or operational, and therefore unexceptionable in competition terms. Consortia had to be involved in container operations, a limiting factor thus ruling out co-operation between, in particular, specialist operators in the non-liner sector, although it was not clear to what degree. They had to improve the service offered by each of the member lines and rationalise their operations, but that service could not include price-fixing.
- *Exemption.* This was applied only to a list of specified activities, many of which recalled technical or other functions mentioned in the conference regulation (4056/86). They were grouped under the broad headings which had featured in the matrix developed during the consultation stage: operation of liner services, use of port terminals, participation in pools, and joint marketing.
- *Pre-requisites.* The application of the regulation was dependent on one of three situations applying: price competition within the conference within which the consortium was operating through the ability to take independent rate action in the trade in question; or sufficient competition between the conference members through the ability for the consortium to offer its own independent service contracts/arrangements; or the consortium members had to be subject to effective competition from lines outside the consortium. All three options were extremely vague, and their full meaning was difficult to assess and potentially inconsistent with the application of Regulation 4056/86.
- *Market share.* There was a complicated and somewhat arbitrary requirement that the consortium should not have more than a specified share of the trade. For consortia within conferences, the maximum limit was 30 %; for those not, 35 %. This was helpfully amended from share of trade to share of the full market when the Regulation was renewed in 2000.
- *Consortium membership.* Those consortia with a market share of between 30–35 % and 50 % were subject to a further limit on the numbers of members they could have, namely, six. Nothing was said about such consortia where one or more members decided to leave, for whatever reason.
- *Further requirements.* Conditions and obligations were also established, among others, regarding:

- Individualised service contracts by lines within the consortium;
- Notice periods for withdrawal from part or all of the consortium agreement;
- Non-discrimination between ports, transport users or carriers (as in Regulation 4056/86);
- Consultations with transport-users "on all important matters ... concerning the conditions and quality" of the services offered by the consortium. These did not of course include rate-fixing.
- A *grandfathering clause* concession to those consortia in existence at the time of the adoption of the regulation, which had more than the permitted market share and/or numbers of member lines.

The Commission subsequently dealt with, and for the most part cleared, applications from consortia in different trades.

The renewal of Regulation 870/95 in 2000 for a further 5 years was not contentious. The main difference was the change from trade share to (the generally wider) market share for determining whether a consortium fell within the block exemption criteria but this was threatened in proposals for renewal of the Regulation from 2010 (see below). Automatic exemption would apply where a consortium operating within a conference had under 30 % market share, or 35 % outside a conference. Until Regulation 1/2003 replaced the notification system, the Commission had 6 months in which to oppose a consortium beyond the block exemption limits but not exceeding 50 % of market share. However, the opposition procedure was repealed in Regulation 463/2004, so that undertakings would have to self-assess any claim for an individual exemption beyond the block exemption limits.

The Regulation was further renewed from April 2005. Nevertheless, this was no more than an interim renewal pending completion of the review, and repeal, of Regulation 4056/86.

At this juncture, it is appropriate to recall that, in contrast to the rate-setting provisions under the former Regulation 4056/86 (and it should be pointed out that as a result of legislative and trade changes, conferences had already ceased to apply and police rigid tariff-setting long before the demise of the block exemption), consortia activities do not involve commercial dialogue. Consortia are predicated on technical co-operation with the benefits being passed on to customers through lower costs. It is a mistake to view consortia and their objectives as being ancillary to conferences or a cover for anti-competitive practices.

It was against this background that the industry approached the Commission in the summer of 2008 with recommended issues to be addressed as part of the process in the lead-up to the 2010 renewal. Industry proposed:

• Broadening the concept of a consortium beyond an agreement between two or more vessel-operating carriers which fails to take account of other forms of co-operation such as vessel sharing, slot charters, swap agreements and container service agreements;

- Removing the restrictive chiefly by container as this would open the way for co-operation in specialist liner trades such as chemical parcel, timber and car carriers;
- Abolishing market share limits, or at least significantly increasing, the 35 % maximum for automatic coverage under the block exemption, because individual lines, and not the consortium, are discrete market parties and in fierce competition with each other to offer a better and differentiated service;
- Extending the period for members to give notice of withdrawal from a consortium beyond the laid down maximum of 36 months to a more realistic timescale of up to 10 years for the recovery of new building and operating investment costs.

Formal consultation launched by the Commission in October that year largely failed to take account of the industry position. A certain amount of flexibility was added to the definition of consortium but even so it remained open to subjective interpretation by reference to "economic reality" rather than legal form. This would be far from ideal and could lead to legal challenges putting operators in mind of the early days of Regulation 4056/86 when the legislative boundaries were constantly tested by the Commission. The container restriction would be maintained and while it was argued by the Commission that consortia operating (cargo) ro–ro and semi-container vessels would not be excluded, the scope remains restrictive to the detriment of other liner-type services.

The biggest surprise, and disappointment, was a reversal of the market share test which would be reduced from the maximum 35 % (previously applicable to consortia operating outside of a conference) to 30 % (which had, prior to the repeal of Regulation 4056/86, been the maximum for operations within a conference). Furthermore, new, and restrictive, criteria had been introduced for determining the threshold figure based on market reality and the need for effective external competition. DG Competition argued that the threshold reduction was to bring the figure into line with the relatively few block exemptions permitted in other industries. It quickly became clear, not only to carriers but also to some shippers, that the provisions would be restrictive, difficult to assess and could perversely reduce available choice if operators were forced to withdraw tonnage to bring a service within the allowed percentage trade share. Consortia above the 30 % qualification would not be unlawful but would have to be justified by individual self-assessment, a time-consuming and expensive undertaking especially where carriers operated on multiple trades.

Industry responded to the formal consultation, largely repeating the initial submission while harbouring a degree of pessimism about the direction being taken.

Regulation EC No 906/2009 was subsequently adopted by the Commission in September 2009 and reaffirmed the underlying principles of consortia activities. Contrary to expectations, the Commission accepted the industry case for broadening the application of consortia operations to all liner type services and removed the longstanding "chiefly by container" restriction. It was also satisfactory that a degree of recognition was given to industry arguments for extended notice periods for withdrawal from a consortium, although the longer periods granted still, arguably, fail to recognise the length of time needed for investment recovery programmes.

While not unexpected, it was disappointing that the concept of a market share maximum for automatic coverage under the block exemption was maintained but set at 30 %, a level below the minimum advocated by the industry in the event that a figure was applied. Market share is to be determined by reference to volumes carried within a particular consortium and must also take account of participants' involvement in other consortia and any non-consortia services over the same trade route. Consortia exceeding the limits must self-assess the compatibility of their operations with competition legislation to demonstrate that any restrictions are outweighed by the wider benefits to users.

Finally, as the provision requiring consortia and customers to undertake consultations on conditions and quality of services has never been used, it has been removed from the Regulation.

Time will tell how the updated Regulation, which took effect for 5 years from April 2010, will function in practice, especially the interpretation of the market share tests. It will, also, be interesting to see whether liner operators in non-container trades take advantage of the newfound opportunity to streamline their services through the establishment of consortia.

Other Jurisdictions

North America

Canada

In Canada, conferences operating to and from the country's ports must comply with the Shipping Conferences Exemption Act 1987. This includes filing a copy of the lines' agreements setting out aspects of jointly agreed services and pricing arrangements. Conferences are prohibited from collective price-setting with inland carriers but individual lines may agree their own contracts. A consultation paper, issued in 1999, raised the prospect of phasing out immunity. However, this was rejected and amendments, introduced through the Canada Shipping Act 2001, permit conferences to continue but encourage greater competition by allowing individual shippers and carriers to negotiate confidential contracts. The notice period for independent rate action has been reduced from 15 to 5 days and administrative requirements eased, including the abolition of tariff filing with the Canadian Transportation Agency. Enforcement is administrative, rather than through the Courts, with greatly increased fines for non-compliance. Canada's move to introduce greater competition stems from reasons of comity and the competitiveness of the Canadian industry which seems to be generally following the United States' deregulatory lead.

Asia

Asian shippers have been pushing for repeal of antitrust immunity among Asian nations but with mixed success. The Asian countries have different dominant roles in liner services, which partly explain the respective position of these countries with respect to liner conferences. China and India are net users of liner services, Japan is a net provider of liner services, and Hong Kong and Singapore are primarily facilitators of liner services. The focal point over rate-setting practices in Asia has been the assessment of terminal handling charges that were instituted by the liner carriers starting in 2001.

China

In China, maritime regulations are under the jurisdiction of the Ministry of Commerce which allows collective agreements among shipping lines. However, in March 2007, China's Ministry of Communication issued a requirement that shipping lines first discuss any proposed rate increases with their customers and that they file their conference and discussion agreements with the Ministry 15 days before they become effective, raising speculation that the government will be scrutinizing the liner conferences more closely. Moreover, China passed a competition law in August 2007 that came into force in August 2008. The new law does not exempt liner conferences from the law's antitrust provisions. China's policy in this area appears to be in a state of flux, but it is not clear as yet what the exact implications will be for liner carriers calling at Chinese ports.

Recently, China has issued new maritime regulatory rules which require liner carriers that move container cargo from China to file tariff rates and negotiated rates with the Shanghai Shipping Exchange (SSE). These SSE rules state that liner service must be provided at a normal and reasonable price and must not be performed at a zero or negative freight rate. Tariff rates are to be published as a range containing a maximum and minimum freight quote. Negotiated rates according to the SSE should be filed if they are at a level that falls outside of the tariff ranges and must include, *inter alia*, the code of agreement, consignor, route, port of loading, port of destination, duration, the quantity of containers and the freight rate.

India

India is purportedly moving in the direction of outlawing collective rate-setting. The Competition Commission of India (CCI), created by a law passed in 2002 but whose actions have been delayed by litigation, appears to be in favour of banning collective-rate setting and has advised India's Ministry of Shipping to curb the practice. However, India's Ministry of Shipping appears to favour further oversight of current shipping practices rather than an outright ban on conferences.

Japan

Japan appears to favour the *status quo* allowing the conference system to continue. The position is governed by the Marine Transportation Law 1949 (as subsequently amended), which sets out an overall framework for the regulation and promotion of shipping, including the competition aspects. It adopts a common carriage approach, requiring all liner carriers to establish and make public their tariffs and any changes before they take effect. Agreements between two or more carriers relating to freight rates and other conditions of transport, routes, sailings, etc, are exempted from the Act Concerning Prohibition of Private Monopolisation and Maintenance of Fair Trade 1947 unless unfair trade practices are employed or user interests are unduly impaired by the effective restriction of competition in trade. A "report" of any such agreement must be filed in advance with the Ministry of Land, Infrastructure and Transport. Japan may prove to be a holdout for the conference system due to the fact that large shippers are linked to large ocean carriers in Japan through the *keiretsu* or "group system" of business organization. Also, Japan may favour the carrier's perspective because Japanese ocean carriers rely more on trade outside Japan than they do on trade to or from Japan. Japan does not wish to forego the maritime exemption as liners pump substantial monies into its national economy. Therefore, Japan will probably be the last state internationally to move towards a more market-based system.

Hong Kong and Singapore

Hong Kong and Singapore, like Japan, are also home to major ocean carriers and are world rivals as container transfer hubs, but neither is home to large producers or importers of liner cargo. Understandably, a concern of the Hong Kong and Singapore governments is that they not be too far out of step with the maritime regulatory regimes of the major trading nations using their transport services. Hong Kong's strong tradition for *laissez faire* policies may explain its lack of competition legislation, but it appears to be evaluating the need for a competition policy in the liner sector. Hong Kong has lost some of its market share to mainland Chinese ports, partly because of higher terminal handling charges that are applied across the board by the shipping lines calling at Hong Kong.

Singapore granted a 5 year exemption for liner carriers from its new Competition Act passed in 2004, which took effect from January 2006 and a block exemption for an initial unspecified period for conference and discussion agreements, but subject to review in the light of local and international maritime industry developments. Detailed provisions were subsequently worked out and the Competition (Block Exemption for Liner Shipping Agreements) Order 2006 was given retrospective effect from January of that year. The block exemption has since been extended for a further 5 years to 2015. The Singapore Competition Commission stated that "it was seeking to create a regulatory environment for shipping lines operating through Singapore that was broadly aligned with that in other major jurisdictions."

Australia

In Australia, liner conferences are permitted under Part X of their Trade Practices Act 1974, as amended by the International Liner Cargo Shipping Act 2000. The interpretation is broad and covers traditional conferences and discussion agreements. Shipping lines are allowed to co-operate in the provision of services, capacity agreements, service levels, rates and technical agreements. Exemptions are limited to liner shipping activities covering ocean transport and loading and discharging operations at cargo terminals, including inland cargo terminals. As far as possible, protection available to cargo interests is extended to cover importers' inward shipments. Powers are available to the Minister for Transport and Regional Services and the Australian Competition and Consumer Commission to respond to conduct likely to cause an unreasonable increase in freights and/or an unreasonable decrease in services. No unreasonable restrictions must be placed on new parties seeking to join a conference. Recently, the Australian Productivity Commission, an independent government agency charged with reviewing the economic effects of government policy, has undertaken a further review of the arrangements to determine the continuing justification of the Acts or any changes required to improve their effectiveness. The Commission reported in 2005 that its strongly preferred option is to repeal the ocean liner shipping exemption under Australian competition law. While cargo interests appear to be reasonably satisfied with the principles of the current system, it appears that regulators might take a less benign view.

Chapter 10
Maritime Governance

Introduction

This chapter is about maritime governance focusing on the roles of a state in its capacity as flag state, coastal state and port state, respectively. The notion of governance is addressed from the wider national perspective including the constitutional implications of statehood and the interaction with law-making at the international level through treaties. The discussion is of course in the maritime context, and therefore, it centres on the structure and functions of a typical maritime administration in relation to the above-mentioned roles of the state.

In relatively recent times it has become plainly apparent particularly from investigations into maritime casualties, that maritime affairs and activities contain a hard and a soft dimension. The so-called hard aspects consist of legal regimes and prescriptions whereas the soft pertain to their compliance and execution by humans, or rather, the failure or inadequacy of the relevant human effort in certain instances. This chapter addresses this topical and important issue under the rubric of the human element otherwise variously referred to as the human factor or human error consequences, in tandem with the hard aspects loosely referred to as regime requirements in relation to maritime governance.

Governance at the National Level

Within a national context, governance consists of the so-called three estates, namely, the legislature, the executive and judiciary. In perfunctory terms, the function of the legislature is to make law, that of the executive to execute the law, and the judiciary to interpret the law, all for the benefit of the citizenry and consequently, the state. As an extension of the foregoing functions, it is to be understood that the law made by the legislature is written law ostensibly reflecting the will of the people, the citizenry; the executive is the supreme decision-making

P.K. Mukherjee and M. Brownrigg, *Farthing on International Shipping*,
WMU Studies in Maritime Affairs, Vol. 1, DOI 10.1007/978-3-642-34598-2_10,
© Springer-Verlag Berlin Heidelberg 2013

entity otherwise generally referred to as the government. Its decisions are implemented or carried out by the administration which is notionally subsumed in the executive and is the manifestation of government. The judiciary, in interpreting the law often makes law indirectly, or admonishes the legislature to repeal or change the law if the judiciary pronounces it to be *ultra vires* the constitution, the supreme law of the land which is virtually unchangeable.

A fundamental premise of the liberal democratic tradition of governance is that the three estates operate independently of each other. The principle is expressed in the notion of "separation of powers". In practice and reality, however, interaction among the three estates in unobtrusive ways is unavoidable, inevitable, and in many cases, desirable. The principle of separation of powers in the Westminster system of government, historically attributed to Oliver Cromwell's political ingenuity, is in juxtaposition to another fundamental tenet of liberal democracy, namely, the supremacy of Parliament. In generic terms this principle is expressed as the supremacy of the legislature. In other words, the voice of the electorate manifested in the legislature is supreme; indeed it is empowered to alter a decision of the executive or the judiciary through appropriate legislative action, if it deems it necessary. However, in its law-making prerogative, the legislature must act in conformity with the constitution, the supreme law of the land. As alluded to above, whether any enactment of the legislature or other legislative or executive instrument is *ultra vires* the constitution is for the judiciary to determine through judicial review or an advisory opinion rendered by the highest court of the land on a referral. It is apparent from the interrelationships among the three estates of governance that they do not operate in isolation. Even though their powers are separate, it is the inter-dependency that makes the system of liberal democratic governance ideal and exemplary.

In any system of government, the administration or bureaucracy is an integral part of the executive although in the hierarchy the executive is higher than the administration. In practical terms, the two components together comprise the government in which the executive makes the decisions and the administration is responsible for administering or putting them into effect. The administration, while it comprises the main machinery of government, is essentially subservient to the executive which is a political institution.

Maritime Policy and the Role of the Administration

It is important to appreciate that in the law-making process the deliberations of the legislature are preceded by development and formulation of policy which is then transformed into law. However, not in all cases is legislation necessary to effectuate a particular policy initiative of the government. Usually policy is initiated at the senior functional echelons of the administration. In the development of maritime policy, the object is not only the promotion and protection of national interests but also their international implications. The expertise of officials involved in maritime affairs should be multi-faceted embracing the relevant technical and scientific disciplines, and perhaps more importantly, the disciplines of law, economics, finance and management principles in the maritime context, particularly the combined discipline known as economic analysis of law.

The substantive subject elements of maritime policy are largely based on safety, environmental, and security concerns spanning unlawful criminal acts of violence from terrorism to piracy on the high seas or in coastal zones. The typical maritime administration is largely staffed by technocrats. This has evolved naturally given that the regulatory tasks of administration officials are predominantly technical in nature comprising surveys, inspections and certification under the various technical IMO conventions and administration of seafarers' welfare, training and certification under the relevant IMO and ILO conventions. Their contribution towards initiating maritime policy is indispensable given their technical expertise and management experience. They are able to identify faults, gaps and shortcomings in the existing regimes from a technical perspective which is crucial to the formulation of rational policy and planning for consideration by the executive.

Efficiency of shipping, which comprises a commercial element, is rarely on the agenda of the typical maritime administration. Usually it falls within the mandate of the government ministry or department involved in trade and commerce matters. The lack of connectivity with the maritime administration often creates inertia and stifles the rational development of maritime policy in many jurisdictions. In some governments, however, there is a system of inter-ministerial or inter-departmental bodies that are tasked with considering maritime policy in a holistic manner from the perspective of the government's overall priorities and strategies. At any rate, given that the maritime administration is where maritime policy is initiated, it is important that among its officials there is some appreciation for the commercial aspects of maritime affairs and economic implications of policy proposals.

The dynamics of the law and policy process are illustrated in Fig. 10.1. The seeds of maritime policy sprout at the senior functional echelon of the maritime administration. The subject matter may involve one or more of the substantive issues mentioned above and may relate to an existing or proposed international convention or other treaty instrument. In the case of an existing convention, the policy in question may be regarding whether or not the government should ratify or accede to the convention. Obviously national interests in the field must be considered as well as the international implications of joining or not joining the convention. If the policy is regarding a proposed convention, again the same considerations will feature in its formulation. Assuming a diplomatic conference or meeting is due to be convened, a decision will have to be made as to whether the government will participate in the deliberations. It may well be that the government finds it in its interest to instigate the convening of a convention or meeting. Regional interests may be at stake and appropriate consultations will have to take place before a national position is formulated. The maritime administration will no doubt consult other national stakeholders in both the public and private sectors.

As far as the mechanics of the process is concerned, usually a policy document is first generated and circulated to all parties within government as well as external to

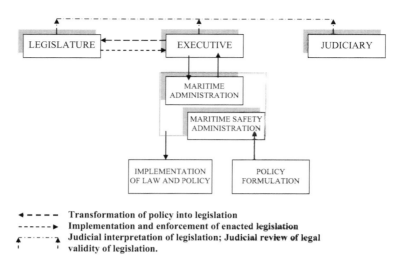

◄ - - - -   **Transformation of policy into legislation**
- - - - - -►   **Implementation and enforcement of enacted legislation**
◄·-·-·-·▲   **Judicial interpretation of legislation; Judicial review of legal**
'   '   **validity of legislation.**

Fig. 10.1   Governance through international instruments and their national implications

it to determine the benefits and possible detriments of going forward with the
proposal. After consideration by the maritime administration of the inputs received,
the policy document is refined and submitted to the upper echelons of the Ministry
from where it may eventually reach the Cabinet for approval. If legislation needs to
be drafted Cabinet instructs the Parliamentary Draftsman's office staffed by
specialists in legislative drafting to initiate draft legislation in consultation with
the maritime administration. It may be that legislation is not needed and the policy
in question may be effectuated simply through administrative action of the
government.

Figure 10.1 illustrates how the initial policy proposal first moves vertically
upwards from the maritime administration to the Executive and then horizontally
to the Legislature to be transformed into law. After legislation is enacted the
movement is back horizontally in the direction of the Executive and then vertically
downwards to the maritime administration for implementation. It is important that
enacted legislation promptly enters into force through a prescribed constitutional
process; otherwise it remains dormant in the statute books and is not effective
as law.

The implementation process will likely entail the making of subordinate, subsidiary or secondary legislation, usually in the form of regulations, otherwise
referred to as statutory or legislative instruments which derive their authority
from the parent principal instrument, the act of parliament itself. In the maritime
field, the substance of subordinate legislation is characteristically of high technical
content; and such legislation is usually drafted by technocrats who are adequately
experienced and knowledgeable both in the subject matter as well as in technical
draftsmanship.

It may well be that the legal validity of the enacted maritime legislation or its secondary counterpart is subject to legal challenge in the course of some administrative or judicial legal proceedings, or it may be otherwise subjected to statutory interpretation by a court of construction. Thus, maritime law and policy is liable to undergo a lateral sideward movement within the framework of Fig. 10.1 in the direction of the judiciary box in instances exemplified above.

It is apparent from the foregoing discussion that interaction among the three estates is an essential attribute of maritime governance. The shifting dynamics of the maritime law and policy process within the framework of governance can be at once complex and challenging for maritime administrators and decision makers at the executive echelons of government.

The Hardware Components

Having provided a thumbnail sketch of the basic tenets of maritime governance at the national level, it is now incumbent upon us to look at its interaction with law-making at the international level which is essentially carried out through the vehicle of treaties. The most important treaty in the maritime domain is the United Nations Convention on the Law of the Sea, 1982 (UNCLOS) variously referred to as the constitution of the seas or a framework or umbrella convention governing all matters maritime from the perspective of public international law. UNCLOS provides the blueprint for the various specialised regulatory conventions generated by the IMO and ILO addressing the subjects of maritime safety, marine environmental protection and seafarers' affairs. It must of course be appreciated that there are numerous other maritime subject matters covered by UNCLOS which is a uniquely comprehensive convention but a detailed consideration of all of them is beyond the scope and context of this discussion on maritime governance.

Article 94 of UNCLOS contains the blueprint provisions for all the relevant IMO and ILO conventions ranging from ship registration to regulatory matters covering maritime safety and training, certification and welfare of seafarers. Part XII of the convention includes regulation of marine environmental matters. IMO conventions provide the detailed regulatory regimes. It is said that "necessity is the mother of invention" and IMO conventions largely exemplify this adage. Under the auspices of the IMO have been created several instruments and effectuating procedures out of necessity to reach the objectives of safe, secure and efficient shipping and cleaner seas. The cynical view has been that reform of maritime regulatory regimes has traditionally taken place *ex post facto* in reaction to major disasters. Critics have voiced the opinion that the IMO and its conventions have no teeth. But in recent years it is evident that the IMO has assumed a dynamic proactive role exemplified by the adoption of such instruments as the ISM Code, STCW 1995, the Code for the Implementation of Mandatory Instruments, the Flag State Self-Assessment Scheme and the Voluntary IMO Member State Audit Scheme.

The international regulatory regime now directly impinges on the private sector of shipping, exacting increasing responsibility for maintenance of standards and eradication of sub-standard ships. Similarly, maritime administrations are being made more accountable to the world maritime community, sometimes by imposition of hard law, at other times by "arm twisting" devices such as voluntary schemes. The two schemes mentioned above and several other Guidelines and Recommendations testify to this relatively recent development in the IMO domain.

Implementation of International Maritime Treaties

While international law-making is the province of bodies such as the IMO and ILO, the law generated through a convention then needs to be given effect nationally in state parties to it. There are two dimensions to the notion of giving effect to a convention domestically. The first is implementation which involves making the treaty a part of the national legal domain; the other is enforcement. Domestic implementation of an international treaty is carried out through one of two processes in accordance with the constitutional law of the jurisdiction. In the monistic system of implementation the treaty may at once become a part of the law of the land upon the state's formal expression of consent to be bound by the treaty either through signature, ratification, accession, acceptance or approval as provided in the Vienna Convention on the Law of Treaties, 1969. However, if the treaty in question is not "self-executing" or "directly applicable", then express legislation is needed to implement it domestically. By contrast, in the dualistic system, express legislation is necessary in all instances regardless of the nature of the treaty.

There are two aspects to the enforcement of the implemented treaty. There is the practical aspect which essentially involves technically oriented activities such as surveys and certification under conventions such as SOLAS and MARPOL, and policing activities typified by such activities as surveillance, monitoring, inspections and the like under those same conventions. The latter activities may also require technical expertise. These enforcement measures are largely preventive in nature. The other aspect involves administrative or judicial enforcement through appropriate sanctions in the event of a violation of the implemented convention law. This aspect of enforcement is obviously remedial in nature.

Flag State, Coastal State and Port State Roles

The discussion here focuses first on the flag state, coastal state and port state roles of the state and the structure and functions of a typical maritime administration. As a preliminary matter it is necessary to have a clear conception of the definitional significance of each of the terms flag state, coastal state and port state in relation to a ship. The flag state is that state whose nationality is held by a ship by virtue of which the ship is entitled to display the national flag or merchant ship ensign of that state and in fact displays such flag or ensign. Nationality is conferred by the flag state on the ship through the process of registration. Where a ship is not registrable under the national law because its size is below a certain threshold or because it trades only in internal waters or in close proximity to its coast, it is deemed to possess the same nationality as its owner. When a foreign ship is physically located in a maritime zone of a state, that state is the coastal state in relation to that ship. For the purposes of this definition, the maritime zones are the internal waters, territorial sea, contiguous zone and exclusive economic zone. The port state is that state in whose port or off-shore terminal a foreign ship is physically located at a given time. In relation to a foreign ship, a state may at once be a coastal as well as a port state and may exercise the appropriate jurisdiction.

Maritime Administration

The administration of matters maritime is a part of the wider domain of maritime governance as illustrated in Fig. 10.1. Whereas governance involves the formulation of policy and its transformation into law from a macro perspective at the executive level and directing the implementation and enforcement of law and policy, administration involves providing advice to the executive on law and policy and the functional execution of the directions received from it. Administration thus operates at the micro level. The delivery of a state's mandate under most maritime conventions is primarily executed through its Maritime Administration. In several instances maritime matters relating to trade policy and commercial issues, marine environmental concerns and security enforcement measures fall within the respective mandates of the government department or agency entrusted with the administration of those subject matters. Ideally, however, a sound operational and consultative link should be maintained with the Maritime Administration in such cases.

The makeup of a state's Maritime Administration is largely dictated by the area or areas of focus of its maritime interests and its geographical configuration. Coastal state interests predominate in states with long coastlines, offshore resources and fragile marine environments. Port state interests are in the forefront in states with large and busy ports and terminals catering to a multiplicity of numbers and types of ships, and consequently, safety and security concerns are high. The maritime interests of some states are primarily in the area of crew supply where maritime education and training (MET) and welfare of seafarers are the main preoccupations of the Maritime Administration. In major maritime countries all of the above interests prevail at once and the Maritime Administration therefore is structured accordingly. A basic generic organization chart of a typical Maritime Administration is presented in Fig. 10.2 reflecting the maritime interests described above.

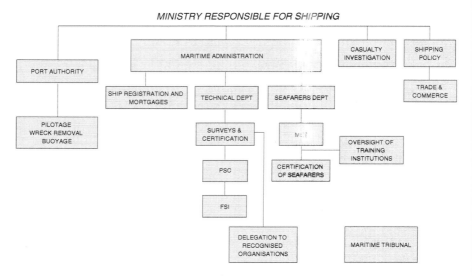

Fig. 10.2 Flag state role: model organisational structure for administration of maritime affairs

It must be appreciated that IMO and ILO conventions are largely flag state conventions although there are provisions in these conventions relating to port state rights and responsibilities in the context of the subject matter of the particular convention. The coastal state role is hardly addressed in these predominantly flag state conventions. Flag state implementation of IMO and ILO conventions is at the centre of considerations involving the role of the flag state in maritime matters. The principal features of the flag state role and how these are delivered through a typical Maritime Administration in the current international milieu can be gleaned from the organization chart depicted above.

The flag state role of a state pertains to the ships flying its flag and the crews of those ships. In essence, the flag state must effectively exercise its jurisdiction and control in administrative, technical and social matters over ships flying its flag. This fundamental role of the flag state is manifested in mandatory terms in Article 94(1) of UNCLOS and represents an expression of what constitutes "genuine link". The remainder of Article 94 sets out the various areas of responsibility of the flag state in sufficient detail. These include:

- Maintaining a register of ships holding its nationality except those ships that are unregistrable by reason of being small in size and engaged exclusively in near-shore operation;
- Ship safety matters including construction, equipment, communications, safe manning and seaworthiness;
- Navigational safety matters including provision on board of navigational equipment, nautical charts and publications and prevention of collisions;
- Training, certification and qualifications of crews, seafarer welfare and labour conditions;

- Surveys and certification pertaining to maritime safety and protection of the marine environment; and
- Investigation of maritime casualties.

What is important in respect of all of the above-mentioned matters is that in discharging its mandate, the flag state must ensure conformance and compliance with generally accepted international regulations, standards, practices and procedures. These are, for the most part, dictated through international maritime treaty instruments mainly generated through the IMO and ILO. The above is simply a synoptic representation of the contents of Article 94 of UNCLOS. Needless to say, flag state administration officials should be more than familiar with the precise provisions of that Article, and be well-versed in the individual maritime treaty instruments dealing with the respective subject matters.

Enforcement being the essential counterpart to implementation, it is important for flag states to ensure that its ships comply with international maritime standards. Among the major enforcement elements of a flag state's mandate are the following:

- Ship surveys, initial, periodic, intermediate and annual primarily under SOLAS and MARPOL;
- Regulation of certification regimes under MARPOL, LOADLINES and SOLAS including the ISM and ISPS Codes and various other mandatory instruments;
- Regulation of construction, equipment and seaworthiness of ships under SOLAS;
- Enforcement of safe manning, certification and watchkeeping requirements under SOLAS, STCW and relevant ILO conventions;
- Maritime labour related matters under relevant ILO conventions and SOLAS including hours of work and rest;
- Occupational safety and crew welfare matters under SOLAS and relevant ILO conventions relating to crew accommodation, medical care, wages of seafarers, employment conditions, etc.

Flag states are obliged to apply appropriate sanctions for non-compliance and violations of convention provisions including detention of ships. Before sanctions can be applied, states must transform convention violations into offences through the enactment and promulgation of appropriate domestic legislation.

It is frequently alleged, especially since the rapid proliferation of open registries, that flag states are not discharging their responsibilities and statutory mandates under international conventions with the diligence required of them. The rise of substandard shipping is largely attributed to the failure of flag states to properly regulate the ships flying their flags. To deal with this problem, some years ago a Flag State Implementation (FSI) Sub-Committee was established under the Maritime Safety Committee of IMO. This new body was expressed to have as its primary objective, the identification of measures necessary to ensure effective and consistent global implementation of IMO instruments, and consideration of the difficulties faced by developing states in this regard. Initially the mandate of the FSI Sub-Committee included the following elements:

- Identification of the range of flag state obligations under IMO instruments;
- Assessment of current level of implementation of these instruments by flag states;
- Identification of areas of difficulties with regard to such implementation and their reasons;
- Assessment of problems encountered by states acting in their port and coastal state capacities and their reasons;
- Proposal for assistance to be given to developing states to fulfill their implementation obligations as flag states;
- Monitoring of flag state performance of actions taken.

Through the FSI Sub-Committee, a system of self- assessment of flag states was instituted which involved flag state administrations documenting their levels of compliance with IMO conventions to which they were parties, according to a standardized "Flag State Performance Self-Assessment Form" and submitting the forms officially to IMO. To assist the administrations of developing flag states, IMO engaged several experts to visit these states and advise them on substantive and procedural details regarding the scheme as part of its technical cooperation programme. The self-assessment scheme was not a huge success because there was no definitive way of verifying the accuracy of the information provided by the administrations. Nevertheless, it exemplified the growing proactive stance of IMO and its efforts to force the hands of flag states to exercise more responsibility over their ships.

Another scheme that was subsequently adopted by IMO to meet the problem of flag state implementation in relation to substandard shipping was the IMO Member state Audit Scheme. Originally it was called the Flag State Audit Scheme but then it was agreed at IMO that singling out flag states might be counter-productive and unfair simply because there are many states which are parties to a few or several IMO conventions but are not really flag states as such because they have very few sea-going ships, or in some instances, none at all, but are bound by the provisions of IMO conventions which pertain to the port or coastal state roles of a state. Initially, problems were encountered with the scheme as many states felt that binding submission to an audit conducted under IMO auspices might be an impingement on their sovereignty and construed domestically as a constitutional violation. It was therefore decided to make the scheme entirely voluntary, and it is now referred to as the Voluntary IMO Member State Audit Scheme, otherwise referred to as VIMSAS. There is a move afoot at IMO to make the scheme mandatory. Whether that will succeed remains to be seen.

The audit scheme documentation generated by IMO consists of the Framework document, the Procedures document and a Memorandum of Cooperation. The salient features of the Framework document are, *inter alia*, a vision statement, the objective of the scheme, the principles on which the scheme is based, the IMO mandatory instrument, obligations and responsibilities, member states' areas to be covered by the scheme, and obligations of member states. In the Procedures document, the important noteworthy features are the definitions of "audit" and "verification", provisions on preparation for an audit including a pre-audit questionnaire, opening meeting, assistance to audit team, accompanying the auditor and closing meeting. The corrective action plan for the member state is also an important feature. The Memorandum of Cooperation (MOC) deals with member states' responsibilities regarding cooperation with the audit team pursuant to the scheme.

Under the audit scheme, certain responsibilities are set out pertaining to those of the IMO Secretary General, member states and the audit team.

The Secretary General is responsible for:

- The implementation of the audit scheme;
- Formal appointment and maintenance of a list of audit team leaders and auditors;
- Establishment of an audit team for each participating member state;
- Ensuring that audit team leaders and auditors are competent as per section 4 of the Procedures;
- Ensuring that auditors meet requisite training standards to achieve consistency in audit quality;
- Entering into an MOC with participating member state prior to the audit;
- Ensuring that audits are planned according to the IMO audit timetable;
- Liaising with and assisting developing member states to access external sources such as the Integrated Technical Cooperation Programme (ITCP);
- Ensuring that a participating state is afforded the opportunity of a visit by the lead auditor prior to the actual audit and be briefed on the purpose of the scheme, the scope and process of the audit, and information relevant to better understanding and cooperation between the state and the audit team;
- Communicating the agreed audit summary to all member states;
- Consolidating audit summary reports, identifying lessons learnt and issuing them periodically in standard form;
- Maintaining records of the findings of audits;
- Managing the audit scheme including follow-up actions.

Under the scheme, the participating member state must do the following:

- In accordance with the MOC, facilitate the audit by providing access to the building, adequate office space, access to office equipment and internet, access to relevant documentation and personnel for conducting interviews;
- Agree with the Secretary General on the composition of the audit team and its leader;
- Respond to the findings of the audit team by establishing and implementing an action plan;

The audit team leader is required to:

- Prepare a detailed plan of the audit;
- Conduct meetings and interviews according to the Procedures and exercise supervision over the audit team;
- Prepare the interim and final audit reports and the mission report;

- Prepare the audit summary report in agreement with the member state and submit it to the Secretary General;
- Assist in verifying corrective actions taken by the member state;
- Conduct a follow-up audit if necessary.

It is apparent from the above discussion that the flag state role of a state is an important one carrying with it multifarious responsibilities in respect of the ships possessing its nationality and adherence to the various international instruments applicable to that state under international and domestic law.

Port State Role

At the outset it must be observed that under international law a special kind of enforcement jurisdiction over foreign ships is available to states in their capacities as port states. This is known as port state jurisdiction (PSJ) and is largely exercised through the mechanism of port state control (PSC).

It is to be noted that while the principal characteristics of PSJ have largely evolved through customary international law, there are express provisions in UNCLOS pertaining to the exercise of this jurisdiction in relation to ship-generated marine pollution acts committed by foreign ships, i.e., ships not belonging to the coastal state. Collectively, these are as follows:

(a) Voluntariness—This is an essential element of the PSJ regime. A port state cannot compel a vessel on the high seas or even in its own territorial seas or EEZ to proceed to its ports and face proceedings;
(b) Ports or offshore terminals—The exercise of PSJ is restricted to these areas and does not include the functional internal waters area;
(c) Investigative and adjudicative powers—Jurisdiction can only be asserted by reason of the voluntary presence of a delinquent or suspect vessel in its ports or offshore terminals; the enforcement prerogative, therefore, is primarily investigative and only secondarily adjudicative;
(d) Discharges of pollutants—The enforcement powers are restricted to discharges from ships. These include accidental and intentional discharges of oil, noxious and hazardous substances in bulk or packaged form, sewage and garbage, such as ballast water discharges, tank cleaning operations and discharges or leaks from shipboard machinery spaces;
(e) Act of pollution committed in the high seas or waters beyond national jurisdiction—If followed by voluntary entry of the foreign vessel into the coastal state's port or offshore terminal, PSJ is exercisable;
(f) Applicable international standards established by the competent international organisations (IMO or ILO)—The port state may only enforce standards that are either part of customary international law or set out in maritime conventions such as MARPOL discharge standards or safety standards set out in SOLAS or LOADLINES. Instruments *per a droit* such as resolutions,

guidelines, codes, etc. that are not already incorporated in customary international law are excluded;

(g) Right to enforce—The port state has only a discretionary power to enforce and may decline to do so;

(h) Discharges of pollutants in foreign waters—No investigation may be undertaken except if the port state is so requested by another interested state party to UNCLOS. Even then, the port state must comply "as far as practicable" with a request. A relevant foreign coastal state could also ask for the suspension of such proceedings;

(i) Role of the flag state—It may request the investigation of discharge violations by its vessels on the high seas or foreign waters. It might also decide to pursue legal proceedings in its national courts. The port state must interrupt its own proceedings if a flag state decides to take similar action against its own ship, subject to the safeguards of UNCLOS Article 228;

(j) Penalties—Although UNCLOS specifically refers to monetary penalties, Article 230(2) further suggests, by implication that imprisonment can be ordered as a sanction in the case of "wilful and serious pollution of the territorial sea" (see George C. Kasoulides, *Port State Control and Jurisdiction: Evolution of the Port State Regime*, Dordrecht/Boston/London: Martinus Nijhoff, Ch. 5 pp. 125–126. See also Z. Oya Özçayir, *Port State Control*, London, Singapore: LLP, 2nd Edition, 2004, pp. 74–83).

It is apparent that PSJ can only be asserted over a foreign ship in the circumstances that are congruent with the salient features of this enforcement jurisdiction outlined above.

The practical enforcement method adopted by port states for the application and exercise of PSJ is PSC. In this context it is first to be noted that "control" here does not mean regulation *per se*; rather it means inspection or check as the word "kontrolle" is construed in some European continental languages. There is a significant linguistic nuance which is often not adequately appreciated in the anglophonic PSC jurisdictions. PSC is often referred to as a corrective measure; in other words, its aim is to correct non-compliance of international rules and standards by foreign ships, and is usually attributable to non-effective or under-effective flag state enforcement.

Use of classification societies as recognized organizations (RO) for carrying out convention-mandated statutory surveys and certification on behalf of flag state administrations is now widespread. Even so, there are still many substandard ships plying the world's oceans which do not or are unable to adequately comply with international safety and pollution prevention standards. PSC is viewed as a safety net designed to compensate for the shortcomings of the shipowner, flag state, classification society, and other actors. Under PSJ, states enjoy the prerogative to inspect foreign ships calling at its ports or offshore terminals, but PSC affords and facilitates a coordinated and harmonised system through which PSJ enforcement rights can be exercised in practical terms.

PSC provisions feature in UNCLOS and all the major IMO and ILO conventions. Specifically these are:

- UNCLOS Arts. 218, 226, 230, 231
- SOLAS Chapter I, Part B—Regulation 19—Control
- LOAD LINES—Art. 21—Control
- STCW—Art. X—Control
- ITC—Art. 12
- ILO 147 (Minimum Standards)—Art. 4
- ILO Maritime Labour Convention 2006 — Art. V
- MARPOL—Arts. 4–7

    Annex I: Regulation 11—PSC on Operational Requirements
    Annex II: Regulation 16—Measures of Control by Port State
    Annex III: Regulation 8—PSC on Operational Requirements
    Annex V: Regulation 8—PSC on Operational Requirements
    Annex VI: Regulation 10—PSC on Operational Requirements

- PROCEDURES—Resolution A.787(19) as amended by

    Resolution A.882(21)

PSC was conceived as a complement, not a substitute, to effective enforcement of maritime safety and marine environmental protection standards by flag state administrations. It is to be noted in this context that whereas the recognized organisations perform a delegated flag state function *vis-à-vis* the ship, PSC is a port state prerogative under international law designed to protect port and coastal state interests from the detrimental effects of substandard foreign ships entering the ports or offshore terminals of such states. PSC was originally conceived as an interim measure; however, all indications are that the regime is here to stay. Explicit provisions in a number of specific conventions as mentioned above have institutionalized the PSC regime.

Under the PSC regime, "control" is, in the first instance, limited to inspection of the various certificates which a ship is required to carry under the relevant maritime conventions. Only if there are "clear grounds" for the inspector to believe that the condition of the ship is inconsistent with the relevant certificate, can he then carry out a physical inspection of the ship and its equipment. However, relatively recent amendments to SOLAS, MARPOL and STCW now afford certain extended powers to PSC inspectors.

Under regulation 4 of Chapter XI-I of SOLAS a PSC inspector may check the operational requirements of a foreign ship if there are clear grounds to believe that the master or crew are unfamiliar with essential shipboard procedures relating to ship safety. Chapter XI-I also makes reference to resolution A.742(18), which "acknowledges the need for port States to be able to monitor not only the way in which foreign ships comply with IMO standards" but also to be able to assess "the ability of ships' crews in respect of operational requirements relevant to their duties, especially with regard to passenger ships and ships which may present a special hazard".

Under the 1996 amendments to MARPOL foreign ships may be inspected by PSC officers "to ensure that crews are able to carry out essential shipboard procedures relating to marine pollution prevention." Reference is made to resolution A.742(18) pursuant to which this extension of powers "is seen as an important way of improving the efficiency with which international safety and anti-pollution treaties are implemented".

The 1995 amendments to the STCW Convention in regulation I/4 of its revised Chapter I provides for enhanced procedures in PSC intervention in cases of deficiencies which pose a danger to persons, property or the environment. Such intervention is permissible if certificates are not in order, or if the ship is involved in a collision or grounding, if there is an illegal discharge of substances (causing pollution), or if the ship is maneuvered in an erratic or unsafe manner.

Harmonisation in PSC inspection procedures is achieved through the mechanism of regional Memoranda of Understanding (MOU), the first of which was the Paris MOU established in 1982. Following in its footsteps, a number of other regional MOUs were established. IMO has encouraged the establishment of these regional instruments in the interest of harmonisation and concerted efforts in the implementation of the PSC regime globally. This is borne out by the promulgation of the two IMO Resolutions mentioned above. At present there are nine such arrangements covering virtually all the seas of the world. They are:

- Paris MoU—Europe and the North Atlantic
- Tokyo MoU—Asia and the Pacific
- Acuerdo de Viña del Mar—Latin America
- Caribbean MoU—Caribbean Sea region
- Abuja MoU—West and Central Africa
- Black Sea MoU—Black Sea region
- Mediterranean MoU—Mediterranean Sea region
- Indian Ocean MoU—Indian Ocean region
- Gulf Cooperation Council (GCC) MoU—Arab States of the Gulf.

The MOUs specifically mention the convention instruments that are to be covered by the PSC inspection procedures which include all the ones mentioned above as well as the COLREGS. The MOUs provide for various administrative and operational functions and set quotas for the minimum percentage of vessels calling at ports or offshore terminals of a MOU member to be inspected. It is important to note in the present context that with the exception of one, the MOUs are non-binding instruments *para droit*. They are more like "gentlemen's agreements" reached among government officials of the member states. The exception is the Paris MOU which has been made binding on European Union (EU) states through EU legislation. It is not binding on one non-EU member state of the Paris MOU which is Canada.

The new paradigm is characterized by a wider acceptance and application of the PSC regime as a counterbalance to the indifferent or inadequate efforts of certain shipowners and flag state administrations in fulfilling their obligations under the various convention instruments on maritime safety and marine environmental protection in relation to their ships.

There are several public law implications pertaining to the PSJ and PSC regimes. First, national PSJ is applicable by virtue of the sovereignty of a state when a ship is in its port or offshore terminal. This is simply the jurisdiction of the state to apply its national law. By contrast, under international law, a port state is entitled to apply enforcement jurisdiction in respect of an international maritime convention to which it is a party. As mentioned above, the jurisdiction is applicable even if a foreign ship has committed a pollution violation under an international convention outside the waters of that state on the high seas and has then voluntarily entered a port or offshore installation of that state (UNCLOS Article 218). Such entry under *force majeure* conditions is not to be considered voluntary. In other words, if a ship involuntarily enters a port or offshore jurisdiction under *force majeure* conditions, it is not to be documented by PSC as a deficient or substandard ship in the absence of other independent substantive evidence. However, a port state is obliged to detain the ship until it is seaworthy and therefore fit to proceed to sea, except that it may be permitted to proceed to the nearest appropriate repair yard as provided in UNCLOS Article 219, SOLAS Chapter I, Regulation 19(c) and MARPOL Article 5(2). This co-relationship between the application of PSJ and port state inspection powers under relevant PSC regimes is not always readily appreciated by PSC officials.

There are also civil liability implications relating to unreasonable detentions of foreign ships under PSC regimes. Under SOLAS Regulation 19, MARPOL Article 7 and STCW Article X, ships subjected to undue delay by PSC authorities are entitled to receive compensation. UNCLOS Article 226(b) and (c) and Article 292 provide for prompt release of vessels and crews detained. There are some thirteen cases of prompt release, eight relating to shipping, on record with the International Tribunal for the Law of the Sea (ITLOS) (see Michael White "Prompt Release Cases in ITLOS", in Nidaye and Wolfrum (Eds.) *Law of the Sea, Environmental Law and Settlement of Disputes: Liber Amicorum Judge Thomas A. Mensah* at pp. 1025–1052). There are two other prominent civil liability cases involving PSC. These are: *William Rodman Sellers* v. *Maritime Safety Inspector*, N.Z.C.A. 104/98 (Z. oya Ozcayir, *Port State Control*, London: Informa Publication, pp. 85–86 and 90) and *Budisukma Puncak Sendirian Berhad, Maritime Consortium Management Sendirian Berhar* v. *The Queen in Right of Canada (The Lantau Peak)*.

Coastal State Role

The coastal state role of a state is mainly provided for in UNCLOS. In the domain of IMO conventions, there are few explicit references to the coastal state although by implication, the rights, responsibilities and interests of the coastal state, and by extension its role in terms of maritime governance, are alluded to in some conventions. Altogether, these are the Intervention Convention, the Search and

Rescue Convention and the Nairobi International Convention on Removal of Wrecks as well as SOLAS and COLREGS as explained below. The coastal state role is also alluded to in some non-treaty IMO instruments such as the Guidelines on Places of Refuge and the now mandatory Code on Casualty Investigations.

Under UNCLOS, coastal state jurisdiction is exercisable in the internal waters, territorial sea, and EEZ in respect of maritime safety and marine pollution matters and also marine scientific research including hydrographic surveys. Although not necessarily in relation to commercial ships, it is also exercisable in the continental shelf in respect of sovereign rights over natural resources. As mentioned in a previous chapter, jurisdiction in the territorial sea can be exercised by the coastal state subject to the right of innocent passage of a foreign ship. Ships' routing is one subject matter relating to ships that involves the coastal state role of a state because routing systems apply to one or more of its maritime zones. In this regard, Article 211 of UNCLOS, Chapter V of SOLAS, and by extension Rule 10 of COLREGS dealing with traffic separation schemes are relevant. A state can exercise coastal state jurisdiction on the high seas under the Intervention Convention if, in the event of a pollution casualty, its coast line or related interests are imminently threatened.

It is important to note that, when a ship is in a port or offshore terminal of a state, there is an overlap between port state and coastal state jurisdictions because ports and offshore terminals are located within a maritime zone of that state. Outside ports and offshore terminals, only coastal state jurisdiction applies. When a ship is in a maritime zone of a coastal state or in a port or offshore terminal of that state, dual or concurrent jurisdiction applies to that ship, i.e., both flag state and coastal state jurisdictions or flag state and port state jurisdictions apply. In this context it is further important to note that regardless of a ship's geographical location, flag state jurisdiction can always apply to it. Thus, port and coastal state jurisdictions do not apply to the exclusion of flag state jurisdiction.

Human Factor: The Soft Dimension

The soft dimension of maritime governance variously referred to in shipping jargon as the human factor or human element, involves human beings as these appellations imply. Generally, the term "human element" refers to human involvement in a particular activity. In the present context, the humans are seafarers without whom it is impossible for ships and shipping to operate. In ships, there are two elements that co-exist by necessity to ensure smoothness of shipboard operations including the safety and security of life and property and protection of the marine environment from ship-source pollution. The two elements in question are the technical element and human element which in plain terms stand for the machine and its operator. The faultless interaction between these two elements is vital to the well-being of the ship, its cargo and the persons on board, who are mainly the seafarers. The shipboard human element complements the machinery and *vice versa*.

Traditionally, the man–machine interface in the industrial context has been referred to as the discipline of "ergonomics". However, in the current milieu, this term reflects a wider connotation described as the interaction between the worker and his/her work environment which is intimately connected to the notion of the human element. In the present context, it is the interaction between the seafarer and his/her ship.

In an IMO document published in 1998, the human element is described as "a complex multidimensional issue that affects maritime safety, security and marine environmental protection involving the entire spectrum of human activities performed by ships' crew, shore-based management, regulatory bodies and others". In this discussion, the focus is on the shipboard human element although it is recognised that the shore-based human element is equally important. This recognition is manifested in the introduction of such conceptual entities as the "designated person" and the "company security officer" in the ISM and ISPS Codes respectively.

It is frequently alleged, borne out by statistical data, that maritime casualties are caused primarily by human error. Flowing from that premise is the conclusion that human error is the singular element of the human phenomenon in ships and shipping. In fact, there are multiple dimensions to human involvement as a factor in the equation of maritime safety, security and environmental protection; and there are implications wider than simply the human error attribution to casualties. Thus the notion of what exactly is the human element or human factor suffers from a superficially narrow perception in peoples' minds.

It is submitted that there are essentially two components to the shipboard human factor or the causes of human error. One comprises the level of proficiency and competence of seafarers to carry out their tasks with due regard to maritime safety, security and commercial efficiency and protection of the marine environment. No doubt, the human element is at the very heart of maritime safety, security and marine environmental considerations reflecting a veritable recognition that humans are not infallible despite the availability of advanced technology. Viewed from this perspective, the human element is a contributing phenomenon to endangerment of a ship at sea that could potentially lead to a major disaster. Studies conducted in the 1990s of the last century concluded that some 60–90 % of maritime casualties were attributable to human error.

The other component pertains to the welfare and well-being of the seafarer on which the first component inherently depends. Proficiency and competence can only be achieved through proper maritime education and training (MET). Evidence of proficiency or professional qualifications obtained through prescribed standards of MET is manifested through a globally standardised formal certification system. The second component, i.e., the welfare and well-being of seafarers is achieved through a regime of maritime labour standards both at a national as well as an international level. These components of the human aspect of maritime governance are presented below under the captions of human error, seafarer qualifications and seafarer welfare comprising rights under international maritime labour law.

Human Error

It is perhaps useful to start this discussion with a consideration of the popular perception that human error is the principal cause of casualties at sea. Of course the perception is supported by documented cases of incidents, particularly the sensational ones that have captured public attention in relatively recent times. Shipboard human error is largely precipitated by sub-standard MET and the consequential inadequacy of competence and proficiency of career seafarers. Among other things, the so-called "white list" concept introduced through the 1995 amendments to the STCW Convention seems to be a mechanism that is providing some solution to this problem. Casualty investigation procedures have been formalised through an IMO Code to identify causes of accidents in a more scientific way than before. After a lengthy period of its existence as an instrument *para droit*, it has recently been made mandatory. Port state control measures have been made more rigorous through amendments to the relevant conventions including the STCW and also the regional MOUs mentioned above. All these improvements represent attempts by the international maritime community through the IMO to suppress the possibilities of human error and thereby reduce maritime casualties. It is said that through the instrumentalities of the ISM Code, the ISPS Code and other IMO initiatives such as VIMSAS, etc. mentioned above, the international maritime community has moved away from the hitherto prevalent blame culture into an environment of safety and security culture in dealing with human error, among other things. Despite these commendable attempts, however, human error remains a principal offender in the arena of safe, secure and efficient shipping and marine environmental protection.

Apart from the major disasters resulting in loss of life and property at sea, in recent times pollution incidents of catastrophic proportions alleged to have been caused by human error of ships' crews have prompted a number of states, particularly within the European Union and in North America, to adopt unilateral and regional measures to protect their national interests. One criticism, whether or not it is justified, is that in the process of dealing with the problem, undue effort is being expended by states and organisations on enhancing control measures than on constructive capacity building through standard MET and auxiliary training initiatives.

Seafarer Qualifications

One way to address the shipboard human error problem is through the implementation of a rigorous and globally sound and standardised MET programme in conjunction with a correspondingly appropriate certification regime uniform in scope and application. Together, this would comprise the qualifications of seafarers as professionals and define their competences and proficiencies. Arguably a viable international seafarer qualifications regime is in place through the STCW Convention. Prior to the adoption of this convention in 1978 under IMO auspices, only the so-called traditional maritime states and a handful of others had domestic MET and certification regimes in place. The standards were based on national vocational training systems and requirements of the shipping industry in those countries. To put it mildly, the standards were less than uniform in global terms. The acceptance rate of the STCW Convention when it first came into existence was quite encouraging. The convention was hailed as a significant achievement of the IMO given the hitherto state of disparity and fragmentation internationally.

However, in the years that followed it quickly became apparent that the convention was being implemented by state parties in a disparate manner. Some states applied standards lower than those called for by the convention; others, mainly developed traditional maritime states, thought the convention standards were not high enough to meet their national needs and proceeded to apply their own higher standards. This disparity in the application of the convention eventually led to the international maritime community going back to the drawing board at IMO and embarking on a major revision of the Annex which contained the functional provisions of the instrument. In 1995, at a diplomatic conference amendments were adopted which entered into force in February 1997 through the use of the tacit acceptance procedure. As part of the amendment process, a Code was adopted known as the STCW Code, consisting of a Part A which is mandatory and a Part B which is recommendatory.

Among the important changes made and new provisions that were introduced some reflect more rigorous learning requirements for seafarers seeking STCW certification; others pertain to more onerous responsibilities for administrations of state parties. In essence, maritime administrations are admonished to give full and complete effect to the convention as amended. They must exercise the requisite diligence to ensure that their administrative practices are consistent with the dictates of the convention; at the same time they must keep a watchful eye on the administrative practices of their fellow state parties to determine whether the latter are in compliance with the convention. Unless there is objective evidence of full and complete compliance with the convention, one state party should not recognize the certificates of another for service on board ships flying the flag of the former.

Regulation I/10 of the Annex to the convention governs the particular situation where a state does not issue its own certificates because it lacks the necessary means and resources to deliver MET and examine candidates. It must therefore recognise certificates issued by another state party under the so-called "recognition regime" set out in the above-mentioned regulation. Numerous flag states today are only able to meet the manning requirements of ships under their flags by resorting to the recognition regime. In this regulation there is provision for an endorsement procedure set out in regulation I/2, to which recognising states must adhere. A recognising state must ensure by inspecting the facilities and procedures of a certificate issuing state that the latter is in full compliance with requirements pertaining to standards of competence, the issue and endorsement of certificates and proper maintenance of records, before it recognises the certificate and duly endorses it.

Under the 1995 amendments to the convention, watchkeepers must possess a requisite level of proficiency in English, which by virtue of this and other provisions has by implication become the linguistic medium (lingua franca) of the maritime world. Furthermore, management level officers, namely, masters, chief mates, chief engineers and second engineers (as provided in Section A-I/1 of Chapter 1 of the STCW Code) must have adequate knowledge and understanding of the maritime legislation of the flag state. Recognising flag states must be satisfied that holders of certificates issued by another state party meet these requirements.

In June 2010, another set of amendments to the STCW Convention and its associated Code was adopted at the end of a week-long diplomatic conference held in Manila, Philippines. These major amendments were adopted to ensure the continued relevance of global standards for the training and certification of seafarers in a rapidly changing world. It was a fitting event for the commemoration of 2010 declared as the Year of the Seafarer. Eighty-two State Parties to the STCW Convention signed the Final Act of the Conference. The amendments, known as "The Manila amendments to the STCW Convention and Code" are aimed at bringing the instrument up to date with developments that have taken place in the intervening years since 1978 when the STCW was initially adopted and 1995 when it was further revised and the STCW Code adopted. The amendments entered into force under the tacit acceptance procedure on 1 January 2012. Some of the most important features of the Manila amendments adopted in Manila include:

- Improved measures to prevent fraudulent practices associated with certificates of competency and strengthen the evaluation process (monitoring of Parties' compliance with the Convention);
- Revised requirements on hours of work and rest and new requirements for the prevention of drug and alcohol abuse, as well as updated standards relating to medical fitness standards for seafarers;
- New certification requirements for able seafarers;
- New requirements relating to training in modern technology such as electronic charts and information systems (ECDIS);
- New requirements for marine environment awareness training and training in leadership and teamwork;
- New training and certification requirements for electro-technical officers;
- Updating of competence requirements for personnel serving on board all types of tankers, including new requirements for personnel serving on liquefied gas tankers;
- New requirements for security training, as well as provisions to ensure that seafarers are properly trained to cope if their ship comes under attack by pirates;
- Introduction of modern training methodology including distance learning and web-based learning;
- New training guidance for personnel serving on board ships operating in polar waters; and
- New training guidance for personnel operating Dynamic Positioning Systems.

The full text of the actual amendments to the STCW Convention is contained in Resolution 1 adopted at the Conference, while the amendments to the STCW Code are contained in Resolution 2. The Conference adopted 17 other resolutions dealing with various related issues.

The most contentious issue at the Conference seems to have been the rest period provisions under Section A-VIII/1 (Fitness for duty) of the STCW Code. The compromise text that was finally adopted increases the minimum weekly rest hours for seafarers from 70 to 77, thereby harmonizing the standards with those provided in the International Labour Organization's Maritime Labour Convention of 2006. At the same time, however, the amended text allows owners and operators to retain some flexibility in imposing both daily and weekly exceptions to the minimum rest hour periods in support of short-term operational requirements. A set of requirements for the recording, monitoring, and verification of compliance with minimum rest provisions was added to Section A-VIII/1 to temper this flexibility.

That the STCW Conference was held in the Year of the Seafarer in the capital of the country that supplies 25 % of the world's seafarers was far from serendipitous. It was part of the careful symbolism meant to celebrate the seafarer.

Aside from updating the STCW Convention and Code, the conference in Manila also left another lasting legacy in honour of the seafarer. The Conference unanimously agreed that designating 1 year in remembrance of the seafarer is insufficient. It was decided that the unique contribution made by seafarers from all over the world to international seaborne trade, the world economy and civil society as a whole; the considerable risks seafarers face in the execution of their daily tasks and duties in an often hostile environment; and the deprivations to which seafarers are subject through spending long periods of their professional life at sea away from their families and friends deserve the continued expression of the deep appreciation and gratitude by all. It was therefore resolved that the 25th of June of each year, the anniversary date of the adoption of the Manila amendments, is to be marked as the Day of the Seafarer.

Given the above developments, it can be said that the 1995 amendments as well as the Manila amendments of 2010 reflect the proactive stance adopted by IMO in recent times to enhance the requirements of seafarers and corresponding roles of maritime administrations for furtherance of the human element issue which has surfaced as an area of major concern in the maritime field. However, it must be recognised that aside from deficiencies in adequate training and competence of seafarers there are other human element causes that lead to marine casualties such as collisions, groundings and major oil spills. These are the physical and socio-psychological aspects which comprise the welfare component of the human element.

Seafarer Welfare and Rights

Nobody doubts the fact that safety and security of human lives should take precedence over all other maritime concerns such as safety and security of maritime property and protection of the marine environment. The seafarer's right to life is the same as the universal and fundamental right to life of all humans entrenched in the Universal Declaration of Human Rights and found in various forms in other instruments. For example, in maritime instruments such as UNCLOS and SOLAS, a ship is required to render assistance to a vessel in distress at sea but only if it can do so without endangering the lives of its own crew.

The rights of seafarers, protection of which is an inherent part of seafarer welfare, include the entitlement to enjoy a life on board ship, as close as circumstances allow, to that enjoyed by their counterparts ashore. Apart from these ordinary rights, there are, as well, rights peculiar to the seafaring vocation by reason of such things as isolation, exposure to the elements, mobility of their place of work and shipboard living conditions, etc.

The physical, sociological and psychological well-being of the seafarer is a matter of prime if not paramount importance. But this is not always readily recognised or given practical effect in real terms at the ground level despite the many laudable statements and declarations entrenched in numerous legal instruments, of maritime and non-maritime varieties. Consideration of seafarer welfare is often ignored or simply given lip service by international bodies, national administrations and the shipping industry. Conventions are adopted and national law and policy are put in place but when there is a disaster such as a major oil spill or a security incident, it is the seafarer who is criminalised and who bears the brunt of the consequences because it is politically expedient for national authorities to take that route and ignore the welfare rights of seafarers. Such conduct on the part of those in power and authority can lead to major physical, sociological and psychological damage suffered by seafarers.

Even in ordinary circumstances, that is without the intervention of a disaster or incident, the quality of life on board ships can be sub-standard. Seafarers can be subjected to unreasonable working hours, deprivation of rest, proper rations and water, medical treatment, leave to go ashore in port and the like, despite the existence of revised and new international conventions and flag and port state legislation outlawing such practices. The acceptance rate of ILO instruments has been remarkably low mainly because most of them are archaic. In recent years a number of conventions such as the ILO 147 on Minimum Standards and ILO C180 (Seafarers' Hours of Work and the Manning of Ships Convention, 1996) on Hours and Work and Rest have been revised. As mentioned earlier, the recently adopted Maritime Labour Convention, 2006 (MLC) reached the number of ratifications necessary for it to enter into force in August 2012. The object of this Convention is to replace the old outdated instruments. At any rate, not much can be gained from legal instruments, whether of international or national legislative character unless they are properly implemented and enforced.

Seafarers are also entitled to proper medical treatment if they fall sick but that is only possible if the ship is in port. At sea, other than in passenger ships, there are no medical personnel. The master and deck officers are qualified first aiders but they are neither qualified nor competent to deal with anything beyond minor injuries or ailments. Other rights pertain to hours of work and rest now stipulated in the ILO C 180 Convention and also in the STCW Code Section A-VIII/1 which is mandatory and Title 2, Regulation 2.3 of the MLC. This is a particularly important issue in view of the fact that unlike land-based employment, the ship is a 24-hour, 7 days a week operation and workplace, and the potential for a seafarer to be overworked not only in urgent or emergency situations but under normal circumstances as well, is a serious issue. Lack of adequate rest leads to fatigue which is a principal cause of human error resulting in unsafe operations and accidents. This is a significant aspect of the human element problem.

Among various other rights of seafarers, those pertaining to a reasonable quality of life on board include entitlement to safe and secure living quarters, recreational facilities, privacy of space and time, right to be repatriated when discharged, shipwrecked or otherwise left behind in a foreign port, and above all, shore leave when the ship is in port. The right of the ship-locked seafarer to go ashore has long been recognised in custom and practice and in case law jurisprudence. Although it is not an absolute right, it has been held that "shore leave is necessary for the seaman's mental and physical health". Rutledge J. of the Supreme Court of the United States once held that shore leave was necessary "to make life livable and get work done" and that "shore leave is an elemental necessity in the sailing of ships, a part of the business as old as the art, not merely a personal diversion" (see *Aguilar* v. *Standard Oil Co. of New Jersey* (1943), 143 A.M.C. 451).

However, the customary law does not circumscribe all facets of the issue; it only mandates the master to grant shore leave at his discretion taking account of the exigencies of the ship's employment. It is thus argued that there is no customary law that obliges the port state to allow a seafarer to step ashore; it is a matter of the state's sovereign right and national immigration laws. Notably, the Facilitation Convention, 1965 (FAL) implicitly imposes the obligation on a state parties to the convention to allow seafarers to land ashore when the ship is in a port of such a state by providing that ships' crew members shall not be required to hold visas or have a special permit or pass for shore leave purposes. It is also notable in this context that there is at least one state party to the FAL Convention (United States) which has entered a reservation with respect to this provision, and can therefore rightfully require visas or prevent seafarers from stepping ashore according to its national laws.

Aside from the FAL Convention there is also the ISPS Code in which the importance of shore leave for seafarers is recognised. In paragraph 11 of the Preamble to the Code, a cross-reference is made to the FAL Convention recognising the need for seafarers to go ashore as part of their work pattern. Furthermore, Conference Resolution 11 associated with the ISPS Code, bearing the caption "Human Element Related Aspects and Shore Leave for Seafarers" expressly "[urges] Contracting Governments to take the human element, the need to afford special protection to seafarers and the critical importance of shore leave into account when implementing the provisions of Chapter XI-2 of the Convention and the International Ship and Port Facility Security (ISPS) Code".

It is unfortunate that seafarers who are in the front line of combating maritime terrorism, piracy and other unlawful acts endangering maritime security to protect the ship, its occupants and the cargo on board may be denied the basic amenities and privileges including freedom from forced confinement without cause taken for granted in other sectors of civilized society. This kind of treatment has a major impact on the socio-psychological condition of the seafarer and seriously impinges on the problematic issue of the human element.

The predicament of the seafarer, whether it is due to a pollution disaster or a maritime security incident, must be given due attention by the international maritime community. The need for concerted global action is imperative. When ships collide or run aground or sink, it is seafarers who lose their lives or suffer personal injury. They are the human beings at the centre of the human element issue. The plight of the seafarer cannot be left out of the law and policy equation if the problem of the human element is to be addressed in a meaningful way. Even more importantly, maritime administrators and regulators must not turn a blind eye to seafarer welfare in favour of political expediency. All concerned should pay heed to the physical, social and psychological factors in relation to the seafarer in his work environment; these collectively comprise the human factor.

Chapter 11
Nationality and Registration of Ships: Concept and Practice

The Legal Concepts of Nationality, Registration and Flag

A cardinal principle in international law is that jurisdiction over a vessel on the high seas resides solely with the state to which the vessel belongs. A second principle, which is a corollary of the first, is that all vessels using the high seas must possess a national character. The concept of the flag in maritime law and practice is virtually synonymous with ship registration. Indeed, the expressions "nationality", "flag" and "registration" are often used interchangeably. However, they each have a distinct and essential significance in so far as they all relate to the identification and exercise of jurisdiction over ships. There are legal implications that need to be appreciated in light of these distinctions; and furthermore, the interrelationship between a ship's nationality, registration and ownership needs to be clearly understood because these matters raise some contentious issues and have in certain contexts evoked emotional and sensitive responses.

Nationality

The conceptual theory of ship nationality stems from the functional characteristic of mobility of a ship beyond the jurisdictional limits of a state into the high seas where no jurisdictions would otherwise prevail. As a self-contained communal unit, where people live, work and interact, a ship must, of necessity, be subject to some legal regime at all times. In waters other than the high seas, a ship could well be subject to the laws of a littoral state, at least in some respects. But upon the high seas, without the benefit of flag or nationality, it would, metaphorically speaking, float in a legal vacuum. This is the rationale underlying the legal concept of ship nationality.

A vessel may be considered as possessing the nationality of a state even if it is unregistered and has no documents evidencing that nationality. Thus, the United Kingdom Merchant Shipping Act 1894, prior to the current Merchant Shipping Act

1995, defined a British ship purely in terms of ownership, whether or not it had been registered as the Act required, and the ship was thus entitled to fly the British red ensign. The effect was to make compulsory the registration of all British-owned ships in the register of British ships, provided that the shipowner had its principal place of business in mainland Britain or a British possession or overseas territory. Following the amendment of the 1894 Act in 1988, a ship can assume British character only by means of registration.

In the course of maritime history, a number of so-called "connecting factors" have been put forward as the test of a vessel's nationality. Thus, a statute of George III required every ship to be British-built. The French *Acte de Navigation* of 1793 contained a similar provision in respect of French ships. A British ship also had to be crewed by British nationals until the middle of the nineteenth century. A 1982 report by the UNCTAD Secretariat listed 28 countries at that time which required their vessels to be manned entirely by nationals and a further 24 which stipulated that key personnel, or a specified percentage of the crew, or both, had to be nationals. These factors are much less relevant today.

At any rate, it is the law of the flag state, therefore, that is the operative law on board although the ship may be subject to dual or concurrent jurisdiction when it is within the waters of another state. This "extension of territory" theory, otherwise known as the "floating island doctrine" has been judicially confirmed in a number of cases. In the celebrated *Lotus* case (1927), PCIJ Series A, No. 10 at p.25, the Permanent Court of International Justice held that:

> ...a ship on the high seas is assimilated to the territory of the state the flag of which it flies, for just as in its own territory, that state, exercises its authority upon it, and no other state may do so.

In *R*. v. *Anderson,* (1868), II Cox Crim. Cas. 198, Byles J. referred to a ship being "like a floating island" and Blackburn J. stated the following:

> ... a ship on the high seas, carrying a national flag, is part of the territory of that nation whose flag she carries; and all persons on board her are to be considered as subject to the jurisdiction of the laws of that nation, as much so as if they had been on land within that territory.

In *People* v. *Tyler* (1859), 7 Mich. 160, an American case, Christiancy J. referred to vessels on the high seas as "elongations of the territory of the nation under whose flag they sail". In Article 97 of the United Nations Convention on the Law of the Sea (UNCLOS), it is stated that in the event of a collision or other navigational incident on the high seas, only flag state jurisdiction may prevail over any penal or disciplinary matter.

Under public international law, which is reflected in Article 91 of UNCLOS, states are required to fix conditions for the grant of ships' nationality. This is a codification of age-old state practice. The classic statement of the right of individual states unilaterally to fix the conditions for the grant of nationality to merchant vessels was made by the Permanent Court of Arbitration in 1905 in the following words: "Generally speaking, it belongs to every sovereign to decide to whom he will accord the right to fly his flag and to prescribe the rules governing such grants".

Historically, traditional maritime states such as the United Kingdom, France, the Netherlands and others, sought to limit the categories of ships entitled to fly their flags.

Article 91 provides as a fundamental principle that "there must exist a genuine link between the state and the ship". The doctrine of the genuine link has been imported into the law of ship nationality from the Nottebohm case *Liechtenstein v. Guatemala* (1955), I.C.J. Rep. p. 4, which involved the nationality of an individual. At least in the context of maritime law, it is unclear what constitutes genuine link. For example, does it include political and sociological link? The concept is somewhat elusive. Flag states, in the absence of any definitive jurisprudential elaboration of the term, tend to interpret it in a way that best suits their national needs and interests. An indication of what might constitute genuine link is contained in Article 1 of the United Nations Convention on Conditions for Registration of Ships, 1986 (UNCCROS), where reference is made to the flag state's jurisdiction and control over ships with respect to "administrative, technical, economic and social matters". A similar provision appears in Article 94, paragraph 1 of UNCLOS which refers to "jurisdiction and control in administrative, technical and social matters" of a state over ships flying its flag. This is discussed in more detail below.

What has evolved out of state practice, particularly in relation to the open registry states, is that the nationality of the beneficial owner of a ship is of little, if any, consequence. Those who subscribe to this view would point to the decision of the International Court of Justice in the IMO Advisory Opinion case (*Constitution of the Maritime Safety Committee of the Inter-Governmental Maritime Consultative Organization* (1960), I.C.J. Rep., p. 23.) referred to earlier in Chap. 5. In that case, a number of traditional maritime states challenged the contentions of Liberia and Panama as to their entitlement to membership of the Maritime Safety Committee of the IMO. The Court ruled in favour of Liberia and Panama and held that the entitlement of membership of the Maritime Safety Committee was based on the size of the national tonnage and not on the nationalities of the beneficial owners of ships.

Registration

The term generally used to describe the attribution of national character to a vessel is registration. Every flag state maintains a register in which particulars of ships possessing its nationality are entered. After a ship is properly registered it can then be issued with a wide range of documents evidencing both its nationality and its right to operate.

The registration of ships had its origins in the laws of imperial Rome and was widespread in the City States of medieval Italy. In Britain, the registration system goes back to the seventeenth and eighteenth century Navigation Acts, beginning with a statute of Charles II in 1660. The object was to prevent foreign vessels taking advantage of the commercial privileges enjoyed by vessels flying the British flag; by the late eighteenth century, entitlement to the flag was restricted to ships built within the British dominions.

Whereas nationality is a matter of substantive law, registration is the procedural mechanism through which nationality is conferred. Registration, *per se*, means the entering of a matter in the public records and in the context of ships, is generally—but not always—both a precondition for, and a test of, its nationality. It is the key element both because of the legal consequences and because, historically, registration has attracted important advantages in terms of tax treatment, and because it laid down the degree of flexibility or otherwise permitted to the individual shipowner or operator.

Registration of ships has a twofold function comprising public and private law aspects. The public law function is concerned with administrative matters pertaining to national interests. It concerns the framework of government, the actions of public officials and relations between individuals and the state. It sees the ship in a dynamic sense carrying with it the sovereignty of the state whose flag it flies. It is with these functions that the majority of international maritime conventions are concerned.

The public law functions of registration are to:

- Allocate a vessel to a specific state and make it subject to a single jurisdiction for the purposes, for example, of safety and environmental legislation, crewing and discipline on board;
- Confer nationality and the right to fly the national flag;
- Give rights to diplomatic (and naval) protection and consular assistance by the flag state;
- Give other rights, for example, in regard to access to cargoes or other business activities, such as, resource exploration and exploitation including fishing within the state's maritime zones, and cabotage rights;
- In case of war, determine the application of the rules of war and neutrality to a vessel and engagement of merchant ships for auxiliary services.

In contrast, the private law aspect deals with the relations and interests of, and the settlement of disputes between private entities. It sees the ship as moveable property over which one or more persons may have rights which the law considers worthy of protection.

The private law functions of registration are to:

- Protect the title of the registered owner;
- Protect the title of, and preserve the priorities between, persons holding security interests over the vessel, such as mortgages and hypotheques.

Both the public and private law functions of ship registration have public policy implications. The national interest is obviously a matter of public policy. But there is also an element of public policy involved in the private law function. The mechanism of registration affords to the public, knowledge and notice of who owns, or has a proprietary interest in a ship which is entitled to the privileges of the national flag. These two facets of public policy in the context of ship registration were well articulated by Wood V.C. in the case of *Liverpool Borough Bank* v. *Turner* (1860), 29 L.J. Ch. 827 at p.830. It is noteworthy, however, that the public record only contains information on the registered owner, which in the case of most commercial ships, is a corporation or some other form of business entity. The identity of the beneficial owners is not a matter of public record. The procedural formality requires a certificate of registry to be issued by the flag state, which serves as *prima facie* evidence of registration and nationality of the ship. This certificate is part of the ship's documentation that is kept on board. By analogy to an individual, it is akin to a passport or other evidence of nationality.

Flag

The flag is a symbol; an external manifestation of the ship's nationality. By flying the national flag or ensign the ship provides visible evidence of its nationality. The term "flagging" or "flag" is, however, often loosely used to refer to a ship's nationality, i.e. its state of registration. In recent convention law, as well as in state practice, distinctions have been drawn between "flag state" and "state of registration" which are often unclear and misleading (see e.g. International Convention on Maritime Liens & Mortgages, 1993, Art. 16; UNCCROS Art. 2).

As provided in Article 91 of UNCLOS, "Ships have the nationality of the state whose flag they are entitled to fly". The national flag of the vessel should be flown from the stern whenever the identification of the vessel's national character may be required. This would certainly be the case when sailing through national waters of a foreign state, in ports, roadsteads or through busy waterways and, of course, in circumstances where the national laws of the ship require that the flag be flown. However, outside these cases where the hoisting of the flag is necessary or useful to aid identification, there is no obligation in international law for the vessel's national flag to be flown at all times on the high seas.

The notion of the flag also denotes the assumption of exclusive jurisdiction and control by the flag state over the vessel.

Role and Responsibilities of the Flag State

The duties of the flag state are set out specifically in Article 94 of UNCLOS, paragraph 1 of which provides that "[E]very state shall effectively exercise its jurisdiction and control in administrative, technical and social matters over ships flying its flag". Paragraph 2 requires the flag state to maintain a register of ships flying its flag and assume jurisdiction over each such ship and its master, officers and crew. Paragraphs 3 and 4 require a flag state to take necessary measures for ships flying its flag to ensure safety at sea and set out specific details. These include matters pertaining to construction, equipment, seaworthiness and safe manning of ships, labour conditions, maritime training, seafarers' competence and qualifications, communications, prevention of collisions, surveys and certification of ships, nautical charts and publications and navigational instruments. Paragraph 7 requires a flag state to carry out investigations of casualties and incidents of navigation involving ships flying its flag.

Flag states must ensure compliance of their vessels with international rules and standards, through adoption of necessary implementing legislation and effective enforcement. In particular, flag states must prohibit their vessels from sailing except in accordance with international rules and standards.

Types of Ship Registries

The Traditional Closed Registry System

By conferring nationality on a ship, a flag state acquires certain rights as well as responsibilities over it. For example, it is the responsibility of the flag state to ensure that ships flying its flag comply with international maritime conventions to which the state is a party. It is therefore necessary for them to be subject to exclusive control of the flag state. The term "flag" denotes conferment of nationality on a ship by a state, and flowing from it, the right of the state to exercise exclusive jurisdiction and control over the ship. There are those who believe that in practical terms, this can be best effectuated where the ship owner himself is amenable to the laws and jurisdiction of the flag state. Traditionally, flag states have achieved this by adopting a policy of conferring nationality only on ships owned by nationals of that state. This is the basic premise, on which is founded the closed registry system which most traditional maritime states follow.

There are, of course, varying degrees of "tightness" with respect to closed registries. For example, in the case of a shipowner who is an individual, a tightly closed regime may only consider a natural born citizen as a national. In a less tightly closed jurisdiction, a national may include a domicile; a permanent resident or a subject; who may not necessarily be a citizen. In the case of corporate ship owners, the usual requirement in a closed registry system is that the entity must be a body corporate established under the laws of the flag state and must have its principal place of business in the flag-state. In some cases the law may require that all of the officers as well as shareholders of the corporation be nationals of the flag-state.

In addition, there may be a requirement that all the officers and crew of the ship must be nationals; all certificates and licences held by the personnel must be issued by the national authorities; or that the ship must be built in the flag state and classed only by a nationally recognised classification society. There can thus be a relatively rigid perception of genuine link in the closed registry system in some countries.

Historically, the purpose of requirements that a ship should fly the national flag, and be owned, built and crewed by nationals, or combinations of these requirements, was to ensure a close economic and operational connection between a ship and the state of its registration. In these circumstances, there was little need to examine the extent to which international law required a substantive link between a vessel and the state whose flag it flew. But in the modern context, that time has long gone for most major maritime states. The days when the economic link and the flag link were the same are past and different countries have confronted the change in a variety of ways. Nowadays strict registry requirements are viewed by an increasing number of ship owners and operators as being excessively onerous and detrimental to their economic interests. To escape these strictures, shipowners of some countries tend to flag out to registries which are economically and functionally more attractive or, as many would say, more convenient.

Alternative Registries

Registration is a key element of a particular ship operation because there are certain fiscal and other advantages or disadvantages attached to a particular kind of registration regime and corresponding legal consequences. Historically, there have always been ships which were registered in states other than the state of which the owner was a national, for a variety of good reasons. These often related to securing neutrality, and by extension, the right to continue trading during times of war or conflict.

The more widespread flight from traditional national flags, in such a way and degree as to have an impact on the structure of the international shipping industry, is relatively recent. It probably began in the United States in the 1920s during the years of prohibition. As US-flag ships were required to be dry, i.e. alcohol-free, the only way that US-owned interests could carry alcohol on their passenger liners, was to register them in foreign countries and fly foreign flags.

After the Second World War, in the 1950s, this trend gathered impetus, with the objective more on the avoidance of the high costs associated with trading under the US flag. It also spread as shipowners from other high-cost countries followed the US example. The host countries for these ships came to be known as "flags of convenience" (FOC), "flags of necessity", or "open registries". Their reward was the development of a new area of business activity for their national economies and a new, albeit relatively modest, revenue stream.

While it was relatively rare during the middle of the twentieth century, today this cross-registration is a common feature of modern-day shipping, subject only to a guarantee of the establishment of the shipping company or a representative legal entity in the country of registration. It is no longer—if it ever was—confined to a finite grouping of states commonly thought of as open registries. For example, the United Kingdom mainland registry, which was never considered to be an open registry, has for long permitted the registration of ships owned by US oil majors,

Norwegian bulk and off-shore supply vessel operators, and the businesses of other nationals, through the establishment of a subsidiary company in the UK. The same applies to many other states.

From the shipping company's point of view, the advantages of flagging out or establishing all or part of the shipping operation abroad include:

- Reduction of tax liability in the country in which it is established.
- Lower registration fees.
- Lower crewing costs, since registration in an open register generally means an unrestricted choice of crew in the international market and the opportunity therefore for high-cost country operators to take on lower-cost crews or part-crews.
- Greater flexibility in certain aspects of the corporate structure. In some cases, this may give better access to financial terms or assistance measures which would not otherwise be available. In others, it may provide anonymity, through permitting greater use of bearer shares whereby the identity of the ultimate owner of the ship may be hidden.

Meanwhile, a number of other alternative forms of ship registries have evolved that provide similar benefits as the open registries. There are, nowadays, a range of ship registry options—aside from the conventional or traditional registries—which make it possible for shipowners and operators to obtain the same or similar advantages. Some are the classic FOCs or open registries set up in developing countries. Some have grown up out of registries established, almost by historical accident, in an overseas territory of the state of the owner. These jurisdictions usually provide for some legal mechanism through which a ship can be owned by a local entity. Yet others have been created as "secondary" or "international" registries in individual developed states, with the ships flying the national flag in the same way as those entered in the counterpart conventional registries. There is also the option of bareboat charter registration which allows a bareboat or demise charterer to register the vessel under a flag of its choice.

The Open Registry System

As mentioned earlier, states which permit the registration of ships in their jurisdictions without any or all of the strictures of the closed registry system are frequently referred to as FOC. In recent times, this term has become stigmatised and even the term "open registry" is less in vogue and appears to be replaced by the term "international registry" as in the case of Jamaica. While this expression is also an alternative appellation for the second or secondary registries of traditional flag states as discussed below, it is perhaps quite a reasonable description of the character of an open registry. Proponents of the open registry system, view ship registration more as a service provided for a fee, and less as an assertion of national sovereignty through its fleet of ships.

It is not surprising that the first states to open their registers were those over which the United States had considerable influence. Initially, they were few, the best known being Liberia, Panama and Honduras. Today, some 70 % of the world fleet is flagged with non-traditional registries that are alternatives to the closed registry, a good number of which would fall squarely within the definition of open registry. Among the top 10 registries in the world in terms of fleet size, Panama, Liberia, Marshall Islands, China–Hong Kong, the Bahamas, Singapore, Malta and Cyprus are open registries.

In the beginning, there was considerable concern regarding the growth of open registries, among traditional maritime states which saw their fleets declining as shipowners sought to take advantage of the liberal offers of those registries. Above all, they were of major concern to labour interests, since the use of these new registries inevitably meant a decline in the need for crews from the states whose flags the ships had previously flown.

It is not easy to provide a clear and all-embracing definition of an FOC. The OECD's Maritime Transport Committee in 1958 noted that the laws of such countries "allow – and, indeed, make it easy for – ships owned by foreign nationals or companies to fly these flags. This is in contrast to the practice in the maritime countries (and in many others) where the right to fly the national flag is subject to stringent conditions and involves far-reaching obligations". The typical characteristics of the flag of convenience can be found in the Rochdale Report of 1970 which identifies a number of common features:

- The country of registry allows ownership or control of its merchant vessels or both, by non-citizens;
- Access to the registry is easy. A ship may usually be registered at a consul's office abroad. Equally important, transfer from the registry at the owner's option is not restricted;
- Taxes on the income from the ships are not levied locally or are low. A registry fee and an annual fee, based on tonnage, are normally the only charges made. A guarantee or acceptable understanding regarding future freedom from taxation may also be given;
- The country of registry is a small power with no national requirement under any foreseeable circumstances for the shipping registered, but receipts from very small charges on a large tonnage may produce a substantial effect on its national income and balance of payments;
- Manning of ships by non-nationals is freely permitted;
- The country of registry has neither the power nor the administrative machinery to impose any government or international regulations; nor has the country the wish or the power to control the companies themselves.

In the same way as US shipowners pioneered the open-registry system in the 1930s and after the Second World War, so the harsh commercial climate has since led many shipowners from the traditional maritime states and others to seek to operate under foreign flags which give them possibilities of operating at lower costs. Today, it is not a question of trying to escape from proper safety standards, as we shall see below. It is all to do with competing more effectively by reducing operating costs through, for example, avoiding the necessity to have double crews because of leave requirements and the higher crew costs arising from the employment of seafarers from developed western countries.

Most shipowners, all things being equal, would prefer to keep their ships under the national flag and to crew them with nationals recruited and trained at home, preserving thereby strong national links and company loyalty, not least so that there is a ready supply of professionals for their future shore-based management. But all things are not equal. The stark choice is frequently between flagging out or selling out. For those still committed to retaining and capitalising on the skills they have in an industry they know, there is frequently no practical choice other than to flag out.

Second or Secondary Registries

The early 1980s saw a considerable reduction in some of the high-cost European fleets. The recession hit different countries at different stages, but it became clear to many national shipping industries that greater flexibility was required in the ownership, flagging and crewing of their vessels. Previously, the indicator of the size of a national fleet was essentially the number of ships owned and registered in the flag state in question, supplemented in some cases by the number of flagged-out ships operated under open registries. Later, more open registries began to emerge and it gradually became more common for a proportion of the national fleet to be registered elsewhere. A new dimension was about to be added to counteract the effects of the open registry system on their shipping.

Several traditional maritime states adopted secondary or offshore registries, some of which are also referred to as international registries as mentioned above. Prior to the advent of these registries, traditional maritime states were offering various subsidies and other forms of financial incentives to ship owners. The second or secondary registry system is viewed as a better alternative. These maritime states claim that their international registries afford their ship owners the opportunity to operate within a more favourable economic environment without sacrificing maritime safety by enforcing strict adherence to international regulations. By and large, secondary registries permit, as an economic incentive the hiring of foreign crews at wages lower than those payable to domestic crews.

Faced with heavy losses from its registered fleet (more than 75 % over a 5-year period), Norway was the first country to confront this concern. It did so with a visionary new approach by establishing the Norwegian International Ship Registry (NIS) in 1987. This was intended to offer a quality registry, founded on all the existing international commitments of the Norwegian government and on its reputation as a responsible maritime power, under which certain cost and tax advantages could be obtained. While it was open to non-Norwegian owned and controlled shipping, it was aimed primarily at attracting back to Norway those Norwegian owners who had left the national flag in droves during the previous years. It was extremely successful, turning an outward flow into an equivalent inward flow within a very short space of time. Within 3 years, the national-flag fleet was larger than it had been before the exodus.

The key elements of the NIS are:

- No nationality requirement in respect of crew or equity capital.
- Freedom to negotiate wages and other conditions of employment with any representative union regardless of nationality.
- No requirement for the shipowning company to be incorporated in Norway, provided that an owner's representative and part of the operating functions are located there.
- No taxation of foreign owners.

As of January 2012, the NIS registry ranks at sixteenth place in the world in terms of fleet size in deadweight tonnes.

While the NIS was designed to promote the maritime industries generally within Norway, it did not have the effect of stimulating national seafaring skills. Quite soon after it was launched, it was realised within maritime circles in Norway that the NIS, while helping the overall crew cost position by permitting the employment of low-cost crews from Asia, would inevitably lead in time to acute shortages of Norwegian seafarers. These were important not just to Norwegian shipping company management, but also to other related industries and services ashore, which made up the infrastructure of one of the country's largest economic sectors. With time, this omission has been addressed and, currently, a wage subsidy applies in respect of Norwegian nationals employed on board ships of both the conventional as well as the international registry.

The employment aspect was a key point distinguishing the Norwegian from the Danish International Ship Registry (DIS), which was established 1 year later in 1988 and was aimed directly at boosting the employment of Danish crews. Another important difference was that, although the DIS was also open to foreign shipowning companies, at least 20 % of the foreign company had to be owned by a Danish citizen or company.

Seafarers employed on ships registered on the DIS are exempted from Danish income tax which also covers most of the social security liability. At the same time that the DIS was introduced, the collective agreements, between the Danish shipping companies and seafarers' unions were re-negotiated so as to apply net rather than gross wages. This meant that the benefit was received directly by the employing companies, subject only to the cost of administering the scheme which rests with them.

So popular has been this concept that the Norwegian and Danish models have been followed along similar lines in the Canary Islands (Spain), Germany (although subject to strong domestic criticism by labour interests), Italy, the French territory of the Kerguelen Islands and Madeira (Portugal). There appears to be on-going interest in second registries among several developed as well as developing countries.

Although now a thing of the past, it is interesting that the EU Commission also considered seriously, for about 7 years, proposals to set up a second registry at the EU level—EUROS—which seemed to have the same aims as those at national level. It would not strictly have been a register since it was intended to operate in parallel with registration in individual EU Member States, which would have retained the responsibility for exercising full jurisdiction over their ships from a technical and administrative viewpoint. In the event, the proposals failed to win support for a number of reasons, including lack of agreement on the detailed contents and sensitivity in those Member States which did not wish their national arrangements to be disturbed.

It is sometimes suggested that the United Kingdom also has a secondary registry in the Isle of Man. While it is true that some of the benefits of a second or international registry are available there (and were available before the innovation introduced by Norway), it is not quite the same. For example, since the Isle of Man is not part of the UK but is a self-governing territory, the UK government does not have economic control over the registry and the conditions applicable to its registered ships, as does a government with a full second or international register, although through the oversight of the Secretary of State for Transport, the UK government does have ultimate control over the technical and operating standards. This is evident from the fact that the Isle of Man is not a member of the EU. The red ensign registries of Bermuda, British Virgin Islands (BVI), Cayman Islands and Gibraltar can also be considered as secondary registries of the UK. Although similar to the Isle of Man, they too are beyond the economic control of the UK. At any rate, since the UK has adopted the tonnage tax regime, the benefits derived from the other red ensign flag states are, at least partially, no longer as attractive to British or non-British shipowners in terms of fiscal advantages as in the past.

The same position applies to a number of other registries operated in other territories of European states.

United Nations Convention on Conditions for Registration of Ships, 1986

In addition to the pressures on open registries in terms of standards, during the late 1970s concern also grew strong among other developing countries that the existence of open registries in some way denied them the opportunity to expand their shipping fleets and obtain cargoes. These political pressures gave rise to two studies by the UNCTAD Secretariat, authorised by its Shipping Committee and by the fifth UNCTAD conference in Manila in 1979. The first was on the repercussions of phasing out open registry fleets; the second on the legal mechanisms for regulating the operations of open registry fleets. The UNCTAD Secretariat was perceived at that time to be in favour of phasing out FOC as part of its overall philosophy of redistribution of world shipping for the benefit of developing countries.

There followed a protracted and difficult series of UNCTAD meetings and conference sessions—in all, 23 weeks of meetings spread over 8 years in which the future of the open registry system was put on trial. This led to the adoption of the United Nations Convention on Conditions for Registration of Ships, 1986 (UNCCROS), with the original objective of phasing out FOC finally falling away in favour of a formal agreement on a number of conditions under which a ship should be accepted for registration by a flag state. Essentially it defined, or re-defined, the concept of genuine link in the earlier Conventions on the Law of the Sea and the degree of jurisdiction and control a flag state should have over the ships flying its flag, "with regard to identification and accountability of shipowners and operators, as well as with regard to administrative, technical, economic and social matters".

In the group system that operated then in UNCTAD, the battle was between, on the one hand, the developing countries of the Group of 77 (less Liberia and Panama) and the socialist bloc (Group D), with the support of the international labour interests (through the ITF) and the active assistance of the UNCTAD Secretariat; and, on the other, the OECD maritime nations, supported by the employer interests (through the International Shipping Federation), and Liberia and Panama. Although the Consultative Shipping Group (CSG) states had in 1971 expressed reservations about open registries, by the early 1980s their views had shifted, because of the need for flexibility and because of commercial pressures.

In a reprise of UNCLOS, the text provided that:

- Every state has the right to sail ships flying its flag on the high seas.
- Ships have the nationality of the state whose flag they are entitled to fly and shall sail under the flag of one state only, an exception being made for ships operated under a bareboat charter registration arrangement.

It also provided that a flag state shall:

- Have an effective maritime administration, including proper ship registration machinery and enforcement arrangements.
- Fix the conditions for the grant of nationality to ships, for the registration of ships in its territory and for the right to fly its flag.
- Ensure that ships on its register comply with applicable international standards in relation to safety, pollution control, surveys and competence of officers and crew.
- Ensure that those responsible for the management and operation of its registered ships are readily identifiable and accountable.

The most contentious issues in the negotiations were:

- *Ownership and manning criteria.* There were long debates on the degree to which registered ships should be either owned and crewed in the flag state. Those countries that were hostile to open registry operations sought tight nationality requirements in regard to both. Those wishing to maintain the option of registering away from the country of ownership argued for greater flexibility and for total discretion to remain with the flag state. Under the convention, each contracting party would decide to apply either an ownership or a crew-nationality criterion. States could, of course, apply both. Thus appropriate provisions could be made for participation by flag state interests in the *owner-ship* of registered ships to include the level of that participation and be sufficient to enable the flag state to exercise jurisdiction and control. Alternatively, a flag state would have to observe the principle in regard to *manning* that a satisfactory part of the complement consisting of officers and ratings of its registered ships would be nationals or residents, either on a ship, company or fleet basis. The convention explicitly provided for persons of other nationalities to serve on board their registered ships and called for training of flag state nationals to be promoted.

• *Management.* In addition, there was much controversy over the accountability of the shipowner or his representative in the flag state and the financial guarantees that should attach to an operation clearly not owned in the flag state. The final text required the flag state to ensure that the company owning or operating the registered ship was either established or had its principal place of business in its territory, or at least had a representative person or company there, who could be held to account legally for the owner's responsibilities, including any financial obligations.

The convention was designed to enter into force upon 40 states controlling 25 % of world tonnage at the time of the Convention ratifying or acceding to it. Unfortunately, like most UNCTAD Conventions, this Convention did not attract much support from the world shipping community. With only 14 ratifications, the convention is not likely to ever enter into force.

Its importance lies, however, in the changing atmosphere it engendered during the period of its development and the long and difficult negotiations; particularly in the fact that, subject to conditions, the principle of open registry has now been firmly established. This has opened the way to flag flexibility in pursuit of cost-saving, an economic necessity in most of the traditional maritime states and increasingly elsewhere. Among other things, UNCCROS also provides for the registration of bareboat chartered-in vessels subject to conditions contained in the convention. It provides for the promotion of joint ventures for the development of national shipping industries; and, there are provisions relating to the protection of labour supplying countries. Furthermore, it has engendered two other ship registra-tion characteristics that are currently in vogue. Registries based on these concepts are viable and functional alternatives to the totally closed and open varieties.

The Hybrid Registry

The emerging hybrid registry arguably provides the best of both worlds. The impetus for it clearly lies in the provisions of UNCCROS. The Convention, in attempting to articulate the meaning of genuine link in definitive terms, addresses some aspects of the requirements. Without dictating any specific qualifications for ownership, the Convention requires that the laws of the flag state pertaining to qualifications be sufficient to permit it to exercise effective jurisdiction and control over its ships. As indicated above, the Convention also permits partial manning of ships by non-nationals, but their level of competence and conditions of employment must be in conformity with applicable international rules and standards.

It is worth reiterating as well, in this context, that the Convention requires a corporate shipowner to be established within the territory of the state of registration and have its principal place of business located there. Where such is not the case, there must be a representative or management person, natural or juridical, who or which, must be a national of the flag state and must be available to meet all legal, financial and other obligations of the ship owner. Several registries operating today that are by certain imprecise definitions identified as "open", largely fit the above description of what may be termed the typical hybrid system. Some of these registries operate in a highly responsible manner and have strictures pertaining to maritime safety and pollution control standards that are characteristic of, and sometimes higher than, the standards of many closed registry flag states.

Bareboat Charter Registration

Among various flagging options, bareboat charter registration is becoming increasingly popular. In essence, it is a temporary change of flag for the duration of the charter. Bareboat chartering involves two parties, the owner and the charterer; and two states, the state of registration of the owner and the flag state of the charterer. The involvement of two registries in the context of bareboat charters has virtually created a regime of dual or parallel registration. It is to be noted in this context that although these two terms are used widely, they are misleading (see Frank Wiswall (ed.) *Bareboat Charter Registration, Legal Issues and Commercial Benefits*, International Chamber of Commerce, 1988; and *infra*, at p. 33). Registration, in law, is *prima facie* evidence of nationality; and dual flagging; i.e., dual nationality is prohibited by UNCLOS Art. 92.

The system provides considerable advantages to the parties involved. The owner earns charter revenue without having to operate a ship. The charterer acquires a ship without having to purchase one and enjoys the benefits offered by a flagging-in state. The flagging-in state enjoys economic gains from more tonnage added to its national fleet and, possibly, more employment for its seafarers. In this arrangement, as will be seen later, there must be compatibility between the legal regimes of the flagging-out and the flagging-in states. The state of registration of the owner must ensure that proprietary interests in the ship including those of purchasers, mortgagees and other creditors are adequately protected. At present, there is no uniform international regime governing bareboat charter registrations. The concept, however, is recognised and defined in UNCCROS, which makes a distinction between a state of registration and a flag state, i.e., the flagging-out and the flagging-in states, respectively. The Convention also provides some procedural guidance.

Among the states, which have bareboat charter registration regimes allowing flagging-in, flagging-out or both, the following are included; namely, Antigua and Barbuda, Australia, the Bahamas, Cayman Islands, Cyprus, France, Germany, Ghana, Guyana, Isle of Man, Italy, Jamaica, Latvia, Liberia, Malta, Mexico, Panama, Poland, the Philippines, St. Vincent and the Grenadines, Spain, Sri Lanka, Trinidad and Tobago, United Kingdom and Vanuatu. Some states such as Australia, Germany and Italy permit both bareboating-in as well as bareboating-out. Some states such as Trinidad and Tobago, Guyana and Latvia provide for bareboating-in, but the legislation in each of these cases is silent with regard to bareboating-out. In the Ghanaian legislation there is express prohibition against any kind of flagging-out. Some states such as Australia consider bareboat charter registration as a completely new registration and require cancellation of the registration in the flagging-out state even if it is temporary.

Most states allow the flagging-out registration to remain open in respect of proprietary interests. Some flagging-in states require such interests to be recorded in their registers. Recording should not be construed as registration; otherwise legal problems will inevitably arise by way of conflicts regarding the disposition of proprietary interests if the law of the flagging-out state requires that either the mortgages, hypotheques or charges be discharged and satisfied, or that they remain in the registry. Such is the case with Italy, which like many other civil law jurisdictions, e.g., Spain, has a divided system of registration in the domestic regime. There is a maritime or navigation register through which the public law functions are executed. In the event of a bareboating-out, this register, is temporarily closed, but the commercial register through which the private law functions are executed, is kept open in respect of proprietary interests.

For bareboating-in to Panama, the consent of the flagging-out state is required, but there is no requirement to show that the old registration is suspended or cancelled. In the case of Liberia, proof of suspension of the previous registry is required in a similar bareboating-in situation. Where a Liberian ship is bareboated-out, its permanent certificate with restrictive endorsements is granted instead. Cyprus recognises dual or parallel registration but requires proof that the corresponding state allows similar registration. Mexico permits flagging-in of ships chartered to Mexican nationals, through a special registry, provided ownership of the ship is transferred to the charterer before the charter period expires. No formal consent of the same practice is followed in Argentina in respect of ships bareboated-in.

Flagging Options

In today's scenario, various flagging options are available to potential shipowners who wish to operate a profitable business without cutting corners on safety and pollution prevention standards. There are flag states that have the same objectives. They operate responsible registries and are able to offer attractive incentives to shipowners without sacrificing maritime safety and environmental protection standards. Some of these incentives are described below:

Ships Under Construction

Common law jurisdictions which have opted to follow the United Kingdom do not provide for registration of ships under construction. The underlying rationale is that a craft or structure of any description whatsoever cannot be afforded the privileges of registration until and unless it is a ship by definition. There is thus the element of doubt as to when a ship under construction becomes a ship. Furthermore, there is the complex question of who is the owner of the heap of steel at any given time from the moment construction commences. The passing of property from the builder to the party who has ordered the construction depends on the terms of the particular ship building contract.

However, until the craft or structure in question is a ship by definition, it is nevertheless property, and as such, would possess the normal legal attributes of property. For example, it could stand as security for a loan and the lender would have certain rights over it. However, if the security for the loan is in the form of a mortgage, it would only enjoy the status of an equitable mortgage. In contrast, a ship's mortgage would enjoy the status of a legal mortgage and consequently, would rank higher in priority in the event of contesting claims against the *res*. It is mainly due to the above mentioned reasons that the United Kingdom has up to now declined to register ships under construction.

It is notable that a number of common law countries do provide for registration of ships under construction. Some of these countries, for example Trinidad and Tobago, have the provision in the legislation but have not actually implemented it. A number of other common law Caribbean jurisdictions are in the same position. These countries have in recent times enacted their shipping legislation based on the IMO-inspired Model Maritime Code which contains provision for registration of ships under construction. But none of these countries, it would appear, have actually utilised the provision to any benefit for registration of ships under construction. There are several European jurisdictions that provide for such a regime. Germany and the Scandinavian countries are examples.

From the perspective of aspiring open registry states, this is yet another avenue which can be explored in terms of marketing the registry and thereby attracting prospective foreign as well as domestic tonnage. The legal implications referred to earlier in the discussion regarding the United Kingdom rationale can be dealt with by learning from the practices and procedures of those jurisdictions that do have such a regime. It is evident that there is growing interest with regard to registering ships under construction among prospective shipowners seeking international registries. The Cayman Islands after receiving inquiries relating to registration of ships under construction amended its legislation to afford this facility to prospective shipowners. The Isle of Man and Gibraltar are British registries with a common law legal system that have also adopted this route. It is apparent that this is a viable avenue for potential growth of responsible registries.

Provisional Registration

Many countries provide for the issue of a provisional certificate of registry in certain circumstances. Usually such a certificate is valid for 6 months. These provisions in shipping legislation of common law jurisdictions typically follow the corresponding provision in the United Kingdom Merchant Shipping Act 1894. The rationale for continuing to provide for this regime is questionable in this day and age, particularly in the context of open registries where ships hardly ever touch their port of registry, and where the documentary procedure for change of flag is carried out, at least partly, by electronic communication. The United Kingdom has decided that the provisional registration regime should, on balance, remain as it still serves some useful purpose. Other British registries, including those that are open, have followed suit. It has been the experience with Cayman Islands, that the device of provisional registration is more functional where a Consul is available and a routine for such registration has been well established. In countries such as Greece, where a significant amount of flag change activity takes place, and where Consuls are readily available, the provisional registration device appears to be quite popular.

Having gone through this debate one is then confronted with the question as to whether a mortgage can be registered against a provisionally registered ship. Thus far, the United Kingdom has not permitted such registration. Again, this is a matter which currently appears to be under consideration by the policy makers of that jurisdiction. It is notable that Gibraltar which is a British registry provides for the registration of mortgages against provisionally registered ships. The Cayman Islands which is another such registry, has amended its legislation to allow for the same.

In commercial sales and purchases of ships, more often than not, mortgage financing is at the heart of the transaction. It is highly unlikely that a commercial mortgage lender will part with his money unless his security is protected by registration. This is evidently always the case in some civil law jurisdictions where a ship mortgage can only be created through registration. There is no concept of an equitable mortgage. It would seem, therefore, that in those civil law jurisdictions ships' mortgages must of necessity be registered regardless of whether or not the ship's registration is provisional or permanent. In the common law system, of course, an equitable mortgage can subsist against a ship if it is only provisionally registered. Such is the case under the law of the United Kingdom. However, some registries seeking enhanced mortgagee protection would seriously consider providing for mortgage registration in respect of a provisionally registered ship.

Priority of Mortgages

Under English law, mortgages rank third in priority after maritime liens and possessory liens and ahead of statutory rights *in rem*, otherwise known as statutory liens. Several countries have adopted the regime of the International Convention on Maritime Liens and Mortgages, 1993 even if they are not parties to that convention. The convention regime, it is generally held, is closely aligned to the European continental position which is a compromise between the English and American extremes. On the question of priority ranking, the convention is not too different from the English regime. Notably, in both instances, mortgagees rank fairly low; lower than, for example, crews' wages, salvage claims, collision claims (all of which are maritime liens by definition). As well, mortgagees rank behind shipyards which hold possessory liens or rights of retention.

This order of priority ranking does not find favour with ship financiers. Along with other provisions protecting mortgagee interests, consideration may be given to granting mortgagees a higher ranking. From the perspective of an international registry, this could be quite groundbreaking and is likely to attract ship financing interests and boost the promotion of the "one stop shop" concept.

Labour Issues and the ITF

Since the late 1940s, the international seafaring unions and their associated transport unions have carried out a particular sectoral campaign against FOCs. The basis was that those registries merely offered owners a chance to escape their taxation, safety and other obligations in their home country, including in particular, obligations towards trade unions. The test has been whether the ownership and registration are both within the same country. If not, the ship is deemed to be an FOC ship. For other purposes, in the past, the ITF has also taken action against "crews of convenience", where the nationality of the crew and the ownership were different.

The designation of which countries are FOCs is rather subjective. The current list, as determined by the ITF Fair Practices Committee, includes Antigua and Barbuda, Bahamas, Barbados, Belize, Bermuda (UK), Bolivia, Cambodia, Cayman Islands, Comoros, Cyprus, Equatorial Guinea, Faroe Islands (FAS), French International Ship Register (FIS), German International Ship Register (GIS), Georgia,

Gibraltar (UK), Honduras, Jamaica, Lebanon, Liberia, Malta, Marshall Islands (USA), Mauritius, Moldova, Mongolia, Myanmar (previously known as Burma), Netherlands Antilles, North Korea, Panama, Sao Tome and Príncipe, St Vincent, Sri Lanka, Tonga and Vanuatu.

The ITF also lists certain secondary registries as FOCs, namely the secondary registry of Denmark, the Isle of Man, Kerguelen Islands, Luxembourg (for Belgian ships), Madeira and the NIS of Norway. Their status for ITF purposes depends on whether ownership is resident in the flag state and whether there are employment agreements in force which are acceptable to the flag state's unions. The determination, as suggested above, is subjective and, in some cases, anomalous since flag states such as the Cayman Islands and Bermuda do not have national labour unions. In the cases of such countries, the test is whether there are in place ITF approved employment contracts in respect of seafarers. Another anomaly is the test of a corporate or other business entity's residence or domicile. In the case of the United Kingdom, for example, the requirement of "principal place of business" of a corporate entity is satisfied if the holders of a majority interest in the ship are resident in the flag state, or in the alternative, a representative person, is resident there. Some flag states, such as the Cayman Islands, only require a place of business to be situated in the flag state. The term "place of business" is statutorily defined as the place where the directors meet regularly.

The motivation of the ITF campaign, which is pursued through boycott and other practical actions directed at individual ships, is overtly to raise the standards and employment conditions on the ships in question. Much publicity can result from its actions in cases where there is evident exploitation; here, ITF action clearly can play a part, for example, in drawing attention to the plight of a crew who may not have been paid or where the on-board conditions are dire. In such cases, there may be sympathy with the campaign's objectives. However, the ITF also threatens and takes action against ships which are not open to challenge on grounds of inadequate standards. Its objective here is more questionable, since the immediate aim is to persuade the shipowner to sign an agreement to enter into a new employment contract with his existing crew on standard terms laid down unilaterally by the ITF. The intention of the ITF is to ensure that the total crew cost arising under such contracts matches a level which it determines is appropriate; this clearly leaves some scope for negotiation in individual cases. The owner is also required to make payments into the so-called ITF Welfare Fund on behalf of the crew members in question. In return, he receives a "blue ticket" which should place him free from further action by the ITF and its affiliated seafaring and dock-worker unions.

While the concern of the ITF on standards may in some cases be commendable, to the extent that it goes beyond the calling of the relevant flag or port state authorities, it effectively takes the law into the hands of an association with its own vested interests and is therefore questionable. The same can be said of the ITF's actions on crew costs, which results in many shipping companies—including those with respectable employment and safety records—being pressurised into agreeing to an ITF agreement in order to avoid the massive commercial penalties that build up as a result of having their ship kept idle for an indefinite period. These actions have caused shipowner interests to call for stronger legal remedies against boycott or secondary picketing action in the main trading countries throughout the world and the practical capability of the ITF to take action in some of these is now much reduced.

The ITF undeniably represents the interests of transport workers world wide with members in some 150 countries. However, the impression given is that it is pursuing a policy which is fundamentally aimed at raising the costs of employing lower-cost crews to the point that their jobs must be put at risk, the closer their costs come to those of the higher-cost crews that they have displaced. It seems to be a question of short-term gain for the crews and ITF affiliates from the low-cost countries concerned, but potentially long-term loss.

The Case for and Against Open Registries

Without going into a review of the long and protracted evolution of the open registry system, suffice it to say that the system - whether it is referred to as flag of convenience or by some other appellation is here to stay. This is undoubtedly one of the most topical issues in contemporary shipping. With the changing economic environment in world shipping the maritime aspirations of states which were hitherto considered non-maritime in the traditional sense are increasingly evident. The former Secretary General of the IMO has stated that international shipping is now virtually in the hands of the developing world and that the process is irreversible (Speech by William A. O'Neil at Seatrade Awards Ceremony Dinner reported in *Seatrade Review*, July/August, 1999 at pp. 4–6). Needless to say, this dramatic change in the very constitution of international shipping has largely been caused by the rise of the open registry system. On this premise a central question is whether it is necessary to compromise safety standards in order to realise the most alluring aspect of the open registry system, namely, the financial advantages. Perhaps the question ought to be characterised in a somewhat different way. Can the interested parties afford to compromise standards? This is a provocative inquiry; more than simply thought-provoking.

The original *raison d'être* for the closed registry system, at least in Great Britain, was to reserve British seaborne trade for the benefit of British shipowners. The underlying rationale today might be characterised in terms of the flag state's obligation and responsibility under international law to regulate its ships. As mentioned earlier, this may be best effectuated where the shipowner is amenable to the laws of the flag state. Traditionally, this has been achieved by conferring nationality only on ships owned by nationals of that state. The closed registry system with its attendant strictures are viewed by many shipowners as being excessively onerous and an impediment to their economic objectives. The open registry alternative has thus gained immense popularity in recent times.

Proponents of the open registry system, view ship registration as a service-oriented activity provided for a fee. This is in sharp contrast with the traditional view of ship registration; namely, the flag state's assertion of national sovereignty over its ships. Open registries have been loosely described as "[N]ational flags of those states with whom shipowners register their vessels in order to avoid, firstly, the fiscal obligations, and secondly, the conditions and terms of employment or factors of production that would have been applicable if their tonnage was entered in the register of their own countries" (see B. Metaxas, "Some Thoughts on Flags of Convenience", *Maritime Studies and Management*, 1974, Vol II at p. 165).

In this context it is noteworthy that some open registries have adopted certain strictures such as age limits on vessels; requirement for surveys as a pre-condition for the issue of a permanent certificate of registry, and enforcement of compliance with international maritime safety standards. The principal criticism levelled against open registries is that they harbour substandard ships. This is borne out by statistical and empirical data on maritime casualties. It is well known, however, that such data do not always reflect the complete picture.

The substandardness of a ship is not only characterised by its unsafe physical condition, but also by the want of skill and competence on the part of the officers and crew or by their unsafe, irresponsible and imprudent conduct. The lack of communication between officers and crew due to linguistic or other reasons is another factor at play, which is often attributed to the practice of hiring cheap and inadequately trained labour.

On the one hand there are the allegations of substandard ships and exploitation of cheap labour; on the other hand there are the considerations of economic benefits of shipowners and the maritime aspirations of developing countries offering FOC. The central question is—should the economic considerations prevail untrammelled at the expense of maritime safety and an acceptable standard of labour conditions?

Much has been said about the need for uniform safety and other standards in international shipping. From an international public policy perspective, no one can deny or dispute that the highest standards obtainable should be imposed on ships to achieve this objective. As demonstrated elsewhere in this book, numerous international conventions and other instruments have been created under the auspices of the IMO, the ILO and UNCTAD. By and large, the majority of states with maritime interests have embraced these conventions; albeit that implementation and enforcement of the standards has been lacking, which is the principal criticism levelled against the open registry states. Rather than viewing the issue in philosophical terms, i.e., reiterating the undeniably lofty ideals, it is suggested that the issue be approached from a more pragmatic perspective. Hence the question—can open registry states afford to compromise standards? Clearly not.

Needless to say, interests of all these entities are intertwined in several ways. While there are sociological, political and other implications involved, it is apparent that the underlying interest common to all of these entities is economic gain in some form or another. For the purposes of this discussion it is sufficient to examine the question of benefits and detriments from the vantage points of the flag state and the shipowner.

An uninformed shipowner who simply wishes to increase his profits without due regard to other impacting factors, would attempt to seek out a flag state which imposes little or no impediments to his operations. In other words, he would attempt to operate his ship with unbridled freedom. Even if he succeeds in finding such a flag state, which he no doubt would; in the worst case scenario he may not be able to obtain any mortgage financing for the acquisition of his ship. Even if he succeeds on that count, and is also able to find cheap, albeit inadequately trained crew, he may still not be able to obtain insurance cover for his ship or for third party liabilities. He might even find it difficult, if not possible to obtain cargo bookings.

In a somewhat better scenario, the shipowner may have successfully acquired a vessel, although it may be considered unseaworthy by any standards, and have it registered in a flag state which is reasonably relaxed in terms of enforcement of standards. The ship is not fully in compliance with all of the safety standards required under international law, but nevertheless, has been able to acquire cargo as well as insurance coverage. The officers and crew come from different linguistic backgrounds but they are affordable. The flag state has granted exemption certificates and dispensations relating to manning, certification, safety equipment *etc.*, on a virtually perpetual basis. No proper surveys have been conducted, but classification society surveyors have issued all kinds of certificates on behalf of the flag state. The society has also issued documentation to the effect that the vessel is seaworthy and has been maintained in class.

Under this scenario, the ship may be subjected to various pitfalls which have serious legal implications both in regulatory terms as well as from the point of view of civil liability. For example, the ship may be involved in a casualty such as a collision, grounding, or an oil spill. It may be detained under some port state control regime. It may be blacklisted by the ITF and boycotted by stevedores in a port. It may even be refused entry into a port, having appeared on some computerised list of substandard ships. All of these eventualities may spell financial disaster for the shipowner who initially may have thought that the first rule in doing profitable business in the shipping field, is to register your ship in a completely relaxed registry. The obvious moral of this hypothetical scenario is "short cuts in standards don't pay".

It is enlightening to view this issue from the vantage point of a flag state aspiring to increase its tonnage. In the first instance, such a flag state might lower its standards to attract more tonnage. But it may be faced with an exodus from its registry if the flag acquires a bad reputation. The ill repute of the flag may well be triggered by a major maritime disaster or a series of such incidents. This would obviously mean less revenues for the flag state. The question of competitiveness therefore does not necessarily rest on how relaxed the standards are of a flag state, as many would fallaciously believe. Reputation and competitiveness do not lie at opposite ends of the spectrum. To remain competitive, reputation has to be maintained. This is true for both the shipowner and the flag state.

At the risk of being provocative, one might even suggest that substandard regulatory action by a flag state may well expose it to civil liability. In recent times, classification societies, for example, have been sued for negligence. Government authorities have not escaped civil liability for such things as negligence in charting and misplacement of aids to navigation. It is not beyond the realm of possibilities that government authorities may be faced with civil liability actions in appropriate cases. For example, a vessel detained under a port state control regime may well consider legal action against its own flag state which had issued it with a particular certificate. A shipowner who is deprived of indemnification by his insurer on the grounds of breach of the statutory implied warranty of seaworthiness may also have a similar cause of action against the flag state of the ship.

In summary it can be said that compromising of standards is not something which is necessary to achieve fiscal success, whether it is from the perspective of the shipowner or the flag state. Indeed, neither of these two entities can afford to compromise any maritime standards if it wishes to stay afloat as a viable, economic, going concern. The competitiveness of a flag depends to a significant extent on its standards, which in turn enhances or recedes its reputation, as the case may be.

The Way Forward

It is evident that views are split on the concepts and value of registration and flag. The debates may well continue for some years ahead. While this can be an issue which evokes strong emotions, at the end of the day it should be a purely practical and administrative matter.

There is no argument that where a ship is registered is important in terms of the application of international technical and other standards and of law and order, though equally, most would agree that port state control is a necessary complement to the regulatory functions of the flag state. Registration or flag is also important in connection with defence and security responsibilities since, in some countries, usually only registered assets can be requisitioned in time of need.

The key question is whether registration has a practical role to play in the commercial and operational aspects of shipping. Many consider, in the light not just of the internationalisation of the shipping industry but of the globalisation of the world economy and trading system as a whole, that registration as evidenced by the flag is just one among many essential elements which make up the particular business venture. To them, the important economic unit is the company, whose ships are merely trading entities. It is the shipping company or shipowner, not the ship, which is the focus for employment and creation or loss of jobs. In other words, it is the economic link rather than the flag link which is the crucial factor. On the other hand, a number of governments and other institutions still hold on to the flag criterion as in some way closely linked to or indicative of the ship's contribution to the economy or wider national interest.

It is certainly not realistic to try to pigeon-hole shipping operations or the ships themselves into a national or even regional context, except in very specific instances. As well as trading between two or more countries, in theory ships may well be built, owned, financed, registered, leased, commercially managed, technically managed, crewed, chartered, insured, maintained and more, all in different countries. The important point is that, at each level, the appropriate responsibilities should be properly fulfilled in commercial and regulatory terms. That is what makes shipping at once complex and fascinating.

Chapter 12
Maritime Safety Standards: Compliance and Enforcement

Maritime Safety

Ever since the era of iron men manning wooden ships, the sea and the elements have relentlessly challenged the undaunted spirit of seafarers. Mariners, shipowners, governments and others in the maritime world have been concerned for years about the safety of ships, their crews, cargo and passengers. Maritime safety has never ceased to be a matter of grave concern for the world community at large. Indeed, the original IMO motto or abbreviated mission statement of "safer ships and cleaner seas" continues to be the cornerstone of maritime activities. In the modern era, concern for safety was brought to the forefront with the sinking of the *Titanic*, and in recent times it has been driven home time and again by disasters such as the capsizing of the roll on-roll off ferry *Herald of Free Enterprise* off Zeebrugge, the sinkings of the *Donna Paz* in The Philippines, and the *Estonia* in the Baltic Sea. While the rate of shipping casualties fell steadily during the early 1980s and the amount of pollution dropped by as much as 60 %, the late 1980s and early 1990s saw a sharp and dramatic reversal which rekindled global concern in both the public and private sectors over maritime safety and pollution of the seas. The following are some of the major maritime disasters involving both safety and pollution of the seas during this time:

– The grounding of the tanker *Exxon Valdez* in Alaskan waters giving rise to heavy pollution in an ecologically sensitive area.
– The fire on board the *Scandinavian Star* off Norway with loss of life and severe damage to the vessel.
– The *Aegean Sea* smashing onto the rocks while manoeuvring to enter port off the northwest tip of Spain with consequential heavy pollution from her cargo of oil.
– The grounding and break-up of the tanker *Braer* on the craggy Shetlands coast following loss of power; remarkably, the storms and hurricane force winds which persisted for the following week cleaned the sea and beaches from heavy pollution by the cargo of light crude oil much better than any chemical dispersant could have done.

P.K. Mukherjee and M. Brownrigg, *Farthing on International Shipping*,
WMU Studies in Maritime Affairs, Vol. 1, DOI 10.1007/978-3-642-34598-2_12,
© Springer-Verlag Berlin Heidelberg 2013

– The collision involving the tanker *Maersk Navigator* in the Malacca Straits.
– The loss of the roll-on/roll-off ferry *Estonia* on a stormy night whilst on passage from Finland to Sweden in the Baltic Sea with the loss of virtually all passengers and crew.
– The grounding of the tanker *Sea Empress* when seeking to enter Milford Haven. While she was eventually refloated, it was a lengthy process and there was considerable pollution of local beaches.

In the background of these more recent casualties was the loss without trace until recently of the large bulk carrier *Derbyshire* in the Pacific Ocean. Although, generally speaking, there has been considerable improvement with regard to maritime safety incidents, the losses, especially of lives, remain unacceptably high despite the fact that the number of fatalities compared with, for example, road accidents, is relatively small. Nonetheless, the incidents referred to above have led to government inquiries, to private sector concerns and to considerable activity at the international level through the IMO.

The issue of marine environmental protection is often considered to be a part of maritime safety. Indeed there are close connections between the two phenomena. However, in this chapter it is maritime safety that is addressed primarily. Maritime safety comprises several aspects of which four are conspicuous. The first is ship safety; then there is navigational safety and cargo safety. Finally, there is personal and occupational safety. All of these are equally important in the overall legal and operational framework of maritime safety. Two other issues are an integral part of maritime safety and are intimately connected to the above-mentioned aspects. These are seaworthiness of the ship and the professional or vocational competence of the crew. Much of the law of maritime safety is regulatory in scope but there are also private law elements pertaining to liability for damage and injury and the attendant remedy, primarily that of compensation or damages.

Ship Safety

Ship safety is concerned with how safe a ship is as a waterborne object that houses human beings and property including crew, passengers and cargo. In particular, sinkings of ro–ro passenger ferries are of grave concern. In the wake of disasters such as the *Herald of Free Enterprise*, the *Estonia* and the *Donna Paz*, regulations under the International Conventions for the Safety of Life At Sea (SOLAS) pertaining to damage and intact stability have been reinforced and a safety management regime has been introduced through the International Safety Management (ISM) Code in Chapter IX of SOLAS which imposes on shipowners and flag states added responsibility and aims to promote safety culture in the shipping industry.

Ship safety embraces the physical concepts of structural soundness and watertight integrity of a ship and includes considerations of statical and dynamical stability, damage stability, stresses and strains as well as safety and radio communications equipment necessary for the safe preservation of the ship and its constituents. The concerns associated with ship safety are primarily of a technical nature. The standards for construction, safe operation and maintenance are contained in the rules of classification societies setting out scantlings and in the technical safety conventions of the International Maritime Organization (IMO). The principal convention in this regard is SOLAS and its associated treaty instruments. SOLAS 1974 is the principal IMO Convention in the field of ship safety. The Convention proper consists of nine Articles. Its Annex consists of 12 chapters which contain the applicable regulations pertaining to virtually all facets of maritime safety. The chapters contain, *inter alia*, detailed provisions regarding surveys and certification systems for passenger and cargo ships. Survey and certification systems under SOLAS, International Convention for the Prevention of Pollution from Ships (MARPOL) and International Convention on Load Lines, 1966 (LOADLINES) have now been integrated by means of a "Harmonized System of Surveys and Certification" (HSSC). Other subject matters in SOLAS include safety construction, life saving appliances, radio communications, safety of navigation, carriage of cargoes including dangerous goods, nuclear ships, safe management of ships and shipping operations, safety of bulk carriers and high speed craft and maritime security. The SOLAS body of numerous instruments includes mandatory Codes such as the International Maritime Dangerous Goods (IMDG), Gas Carrier, Liquid Natural Gas (LNG) Carrier and Bulk Chemical Codes, as well as the Casualty Investigation Code which became mandatory recently. There also *para droit* (soft law) instruments comprising Guidelines, Recommendations, Resolutions and the like, that are not mandatory. Other conventions such as Search and Rescue (SAR), International Convention on Tonnage Measurement of Ships, 1969 (TONNAGE) and MARPOL are also important with regard to particular aspects of ship safety.

Loadlines

Equally important is the LOADLINE Convention which sets the maximum levels to which a ship can be loaded so that safe freeboard is maintained under varying conditions of water density and seasonal and geoclimatic considerations. The subject of freeboard is an integral part of the maritime safety regime which straddles both ship safety as well as navigational safety and is governed by the 1966 Loadline Convention. This Convention also enjoys widespread universality. As freeboard relates to the watertight integrity of the ship, as well as its ability to float safely, there are provisions in the Convention relating to the carriage of deck cargo, and to special loadlines for timber deck cargo. The Convention makes each state party responsible for ensuring compliance with the convention by ships flying its flag. In practice, however, loadlines are assigned by classification societies, which are private organizations, although a flag-state may have its own classification authority within its maritime infrastructure.

Seaworthiness

Seaworthiness is an integral part of ship safety and has both public as well as a private law implications. A vessel is considered to be seaworthy when it has "...that degree of fitness which an ordinary, careful and prudent owner would require his vessel to have at the commencement of her voyage, having regard to all the probable circumstances of it" (*McFadden* v. *Blue Star Line* [1905], 1 K.B. 697 at p. 706). While this judicial definition emanates from a private law court decision involving carriage of goods by sea, it is one that is equally applicable to seaworthiness in public law. In the definition, fitness necessarily includes safety, and safety in its expanded connotation extends to adequacy of safety construction, safety equipment, safe manning, adequate freeboard (not to be overloaded) and compliance with other safety requirements and safety procedures. The standard for determining whether or not a vessel is seaworthy is an objective one. This determination can be made with a reasonable degree of certainty arguably at the commencement of a voyage only; it is virtually impossible to guarantee that the ship will be maintained in a seaworthy condition during the voyage given the vessel's exposure to the elements and the ensuing consequences which may lie beyond the control of its owners and the crew.

Seaworthiness in terms of regulatory law is usually referred to as statutory seaworthiness. It is a matter of public policy that a ship should not be allowed to sail from a port unless it is seaworthy, and to that end, any member of the public has the right to lay an information to the relevant authorities to prevent an unseaworthy ship from sailing. Deficiency in safe manning or in safety equipment can render a ship unseaworthy. In many jurisdictions, sending or taking an unseaworthy ship to sea is an offence, and an unseaworthy ship is liable to be detained by the maritime authorities in a port until it is seaworthy. It is important to note that an obligation on the part of the shipowner to comply with seaworthiness requirements is statutorily implied in crew employment contracts.

In the current United Kingdom legislation, in addition to unseaworthy ships there is the notion of unsafe ships. The distinction is often inconsequential in practical terms but on close examination it is apparent that even if a ship is technically unseaworthy it is not necessarily unsafe but an unsafe ship is at the same time also unseaworthy. The term "dangerously unsafe" has now entered the vocabulary of maritime legislation in the United Kingdom and elsewhere. It was introduced in the legislation following the official enquiry on the *Herald of Free Enterprise* disaster. The term "dangerously unsafe" is somewhat superfluous. As remarked by an eminent author, "unseaworthiness" in itself requires consideration of the dangers of the ship in the context of its use at sea, and must necessarily involve "serious danger to human life". The concept in this form has been around at least for the past century with the need for interpretation (Robert Grime, *Shipping Law*, Second Edition, London: Sweet & Maxwell, 1991, at p. 43). It is notable that other English common law jurisdictions have not considered it necessary to introduce the term "dangerously unsafe" in their maritime legislation.

The notion of seaworthiness as a maritime safety issue is prominent in the sphere of commercial maritime law. It pertains largely to commercial maritime law, mainly with regard to marine insurance contracts where seaworthiness is a warranty the breach of which by the assured can deprive him of indemnification; and in carriage contracts evidenced by bills of lading, or in charterparties where specific obligations are imposed on the carrier to exercise due diligence to provide a seaworthy ship at the commencement of the voyage. The international conventions dealing with carriage of goods by sea, i.e., the Hague Rules, Hague-Visby Rules and Hamburg Rules all provide for seaworthiness as well as cargoworthiness requirements. The requirements are reflected in national legislation giving effect to the particular convention applicable in that jurisdiction.

The obligation of seaworthiness is not only found in contracts of affreightment, i.e. carriage contracts contained in charterparties and those evidenced by bills of lading, but also in marine insurance contracts. In carriage contracts, typically the obligation is for the carrier to exercise due diligence to make the ship seaworthy before and at the commencement of the voyage. In charterparties there is an implied warranty of seaworthiness on the part of the shipowner; even then, charterparties often contain an express term that the ship is "tight staunch and strong and in every way fitted for the voyage". A warranty of seaworthiness is also implied in every marine insurance contract. A breach of the warranty by the assured can result in the insurer lawfully refusing to indemnify the assured in the event of a loss. Indeed, in voyage policies, the application of the implied warranty is quite rigorous. The shipowner warrants absolutely that the ship is not only seaworthy at the commencement of a voyage but at every stage of the voyage as well. By contrast, in time policies the implied warranty of seaworthiness normally does not apply at any particular stage of the adventure (U.K. Marine Insurance Act 1906, s.39).

Navigational Safety

Navigational safety has to do with the safety of the ship as a manoeverable floating object including the safety of humans and property on board. This obviously entails rules of navigation as well as navigational equipment. Some of the rules and standards of safety of navigation are contained in Chapter V of the SOLAS Convention which has recently undergone extensive revision; others are contained in the Collision Regulations (COLREGS). Chapter V of SOLAS addresses such issues as navigational and meteorological warnings, search and rescue services and life-saving signals, hydrographic services including nautical charting and publications, ships' routeing, reporting systems, vessel traffic services, external aids to navigation, shipboard navigational equipment, voyage data recorders, automatic identification systems (AIS), international code of signals, navigation bridge visibility, pilot transfer arrangements, steering gear, danger and distress messages, distress signals and avoidance of dangerous situations at sea.

Collisions

The COLREGS are the most universally accepted maritime rules. Apart from being regulatory law, as the name implies, the rules frequently have important implications for the judicial resolution of civil liabilities in marine collision cases. The law of marine collisions is probably the best example of the interface between public and private law within the sphere of maritime safety. The regulatory law of marine collisions is contained in the COLREGS Convention. This Convention enjoys one of the highest rates of ratification or accession among all maritime safety conventions so much so that it is arguably a part of customary international law and is incorporated in national legislation virtually in all maritime states. The COLREGS are entirely regulatory in scope, and therefore, in corresponding national legislation violations of the regulations are offences for which there are regulatory sanctions. For example, in the case of *The V.F. Tiger* [1982] 2 Lloyd's Rep. 564, the vessel in question was held to be in violation of Rule 10(c) of the COLREGS which prohibited vessels from crossing traffic lanes otherwise than at right angles. In this case there was no civil liability element involved. The main issue was whether the master could be convicted for failing to observe the rule. The court held that there was no wilful default on the part of the master because he had no actual knowledge of the violation; nor had he been deliberately negligent.

Collision liability in civil or private law terms is governed by the principles of the law of torts. Liability is based on fault, and in particular, the notion of contributory negligence is important in collision liability cases. The international law of collision liability is contained in the International Convention for the Unification of Certain Rules with Respect to Collision Between Vessels, 1910 (Collision Liability Convention) to which most maritime states are parties. An important feature of the Convention is the express abolition through Article 6, of the hitherto statutory presumption of fault under which a ship in contravention of the COLREGS was presumed to be at fault. Among other things, the Convention sets out in Article 4, the rule of proportionality in collision liability. Pursuant to Article 4, in a collision between two or more vessels, liability is apportioned according to the degree of fault of each vessel. Where the degree of fault of each vessel cannot be determined, liability is apportioned equally, and where the collision is accidental or due to *force majeure*, the loss lies where it falls. If a collision is caused by the fault of only one ship, then that ship only is liable to make good the damages.

Most importantly, the COLREGS are applied to determine negligence and the degree of fault of each ship involved in a collision. Thus in practice, the COLREGS not only serve as a regulatory mechanism but also as a convenient tool for the determination of the degree of fault and the consequent proportion of liability in accordance with the Collision Liability Convention or the tort law prevailing in the jurisdiction. In a collision, out of the same factual situation there can arise both a regulatory or criminal case as well as a civil liability case. This was demonstrated in the Canadian case *The Hermes* [1969], 1 Ll.L.R. 425 (Can. Exchq. Ct.). The collision between the *m.v. Transatlantic* and the *m.v. Hermes* in the navigation channel of Lac St. Pierre in the St. Lawrence River resulted in the loss of several lives. Civil and criminal actions ensued.

Personal and Occupational Safety of Crew

Occupational safety concerns the safety of seafarers serving on board ships. The safe working conditions of the seafarer are of primary importance. Safety, in this context, extends to the seafarer's welfare and well-being on board in potentially hostile maritime conditions at sea. Much depends on how well the seafarer is trained to cope with these conditions and carry out his tasks safely and efficiently. The rules and standards relating to occupational safety are contained largely in a host of conventions and treaty instruments of the International Labour Organization (ILO), in particular, ILO Convention 147 on Minimum Standards, as well as the STCW Convention and parts of SOLAS. Most recently, as mentioned earlier in this book, the very comprehensive and consolidated Maritime Labour Convention was adopted under the auspices of the ILO in 2006 and will enter into force in August 2013. It addresses many of these aspects, including issues such as fatigue and adequate hours of rest.

Standards relating to the personal safety of passengers are covered under SOLAS through the safety equipment requirements.

Occupational safety covers a host of subject matter ranging from living and working conditions on board the ship to social welfare issues such as medical treatment, victualling, hours of work and rest, fatigue, overtime work, shore leave, discipline, *etc.* which are usually related to the rights and entitlements of seafarers and their corresponding duties and obligation under their employment contract or statute. As a ship is a floating, self-contained communal unit, all of these issues are connected to the safe operation of the ship. There are extended and interrelated implications involving competence and adequacy of performance of a seafarer, and eventually, the safe existence of the shipboard community and the cargo and other property carried on board.

Professional and Vocational Competence and the Human Element

At the centre of navigation, regardless of the availability of technology, state of the art or otherwise, lies the human factor which has been discussed in detail earlier. The so-called "human element" in shipping is a major consideration embracing all facets and activities that have the potential for endangering a vessel at sea or spelling disaster. In a 1995 document submitted by the Government of the United States to the International Maritime Organization (IMO), it was stated that analyses of marine casualties occurring over a 30-year period indicated human error to be the cause in 65–80 % of marine casualties. An earlier study done in 1991 in the United Kingdom revealed that over 90 % of collisions and groundings and over 75 % of fires and explosions were attributable to the human element in some form.

Standards of Training, Certification and Watchkeeping

Although this topic has been addressed in detail in Chap. 10, some aspects of it are worth reiterating in the context of this chapter. It has long been recognised by the international maritime community that the problem of human error can be resolved to a large extent by establishing an international standard of maritime training and education (MET) coupled with a compatible regime of certification, that is of sound professional content and uniform in scope and application. The first such attempt crystallised into the adoption by the IMO of the International Convention on Standards of Training, Certification and Watchkeeping (STCW) in 1978. The global regime for seafarers' qualifications continues to be governed by this Convention which has undergone substantial changes in the recent past. Initially, it was hailed as a major accomplishment, which no doubt it was in 1978, when at the international level there was disparity and fragmentation at best. It was primarily the traditional maritime states and a few aspiring others that had MET and certification regimes in place. The standards were based on national vocational training systems and requirements of the shipping industry in those countries.

However, it soon became painfully apparent that state parties were not implementing the convention uniformly. Some were applying standards that were far from what was required to give full and complete effect to the convention. There were inherent weaknesses in the convention that gradually became apparent during and after the period of transition from the old national regimes to the new international one. At a diplomatic conference held in 1995, amendments to the STCW convention were adopted to address these concerns and shortcomings. Through application of the tacit amendment procedure provided for in the convention, the amendments entered into force on 1 February 1997.

The amendments introduced several new and important elements into the MET and certification regime of STCW 1978. Some of these translate into quite onerous learning requirements for seafarers seeking to qualify under the convention. In their turn, the Maritime Administrations of state parties were charged with the obligation and responsibility of giving full and complete effect to the amended convention; and to that end, it was incumbent upon them to be increasingly mindful and vigilant of their own administrative practices and the interests of their respective constituencies, the MET institutions and the seafarers concerned. One of the important changes was to give the IMO authority for the first time to judge whether the training, qualification and certification given to seafarers by a state party to the

Convention matched up to required STCW standards. This innovative measure gives transparency to the training and certification resources provided by a Maritime Administration and ensures that standards of competency do not vary widely from one state party to another and that certificates issued by each state party are authentic and reliable. Further amendments were adopted at a conference held in Manila in 2010 which recently entered into force.

The STCW package consists of the following components, namely, the text of the 1978 Convention, the Final Act of the 1995 Conference, Attachment 1 to the Final Act which contains Resolution 1 adopting the amendments, the Annex containing the Regulations housed in Chapters I to VIII, Attachment 2 containing Resolution 2 adopting the Seafarers' Training, Certification and Watchkeeping Code (STCW Code) and Attachment 3 containing Resolutions 3–14 and the Final Act of the 2010 Conference. This complex body of instruments governs the international regime for seafarer training and qualifications.

Cargo Safety

Cargo safety deals with changes in the safety condition of a ship attributable to cargo of different characteristics such as dangerous goods, oil, ore, grain or other bulk cargo, *etc.* The rules and standards are governed by relevant chapters of SOLAS as well as the various Codes. Cargoes carried in bulk affect the stability of the ship. If they are ore-concentrates, they tend to make the ship stiff and prone to sinking very quickly, in the event of seawater entering the holds through a hole in the hull. Other bulk cargoes have certain inherent characteristics which can make a ship unstable. If grain becomes wet, it rapidly ferments, and increases in weight causing instability. Also, bulk grain is prone to free surface effect which can cause serious stability problems. Bulk coal without proper ventilation is liable to create an inflammable gas which may ignite or cause an explosion. Bulk carriers have the worst record in terms of maritime casualties. There are also cargoes that are classed as dangerous goods whether they are carried in bulk or in packaged form. The marking, packaging, loading, stowage, carriage and discharge of such cargo is regulated by SOLAS instruments, the Carriage of Dangerous Goods Regulations and the International Maritime Dangerous Goods (IMDG) Code.

Liability Pertaining to Maritime Safety

Public and Private Law

Public law is the law which governs matters related to the public interest. In broad terms it concerns the legal relationship between public authorities including governments and the public. Within the national domain, public law includes constitutional law, criminal law, regulatory law, and administrative law. In federal political systems public law governs the interrelationships between political units such as provinces or states within the sovereign state and also between such a political unit and the sovereign state itself. In the international sphere, there is public international law which governs the relationships between sovereign states as well as between states and international organizations and bodies. There is also international regulatory law which predominates the international law relating to maritime safety. Thus the laws pertaining to safety conventions such as SOLAS, MARPOL, LOADLINE including laws pertaining to ship registration, flag, port and coastal state rights and responsibilities, *etc.* fall within public maritime law much of which is regulatory in scope.

By contrast, private law is the law that governs private interests. It concerns the legal relationships between private entities such as individuals, corporations and other kinds of entities that possess legal personality in one way or another. Perhaps the best example in the maritime context is the ship, which, in certain jurisdictions has a legal personality independent of its owner. Thus, private law deals with rights and liabilities of private entities *vis a vis* each other. It also governs rights and liabilities between such entities and governments or other public authorities where the subject matter of a dispute is of a private nature. In such cases the government or public authority in question wears a "private hat" and is treated by the law as a private entity for that specific purpose. Private law comprises the laws of torts, property and contract and their constituent elements such as commercial law, estate law, corporate law, etc. In the maritime field the laws of ship sales and purchases, maritime mortgages, maritime liens, arrest of ships, collision, salvage, towage, carriage of goods, marine insurance, general average, *etc.* all fall within the rubric of private law.

The Concept of Liability

Liability is essentially a qualitative concept. It is best described as the quality or standard of conduct or behaviour that makes an action or omission wrongful in the eyes of the law and for which the law provides a sanction. In some jurisdictions, by virtue of linguistic nuance, it may appear that the term responsibility is used as a synonym for liability. In terms of English law and the English language, the subtlety is, perhaps, best expressed by the statement that liability connotes legal responsibility; i.e., responsibility the exaction of which is legally enforceable and failure of which attracts legal sanction. Liability can arise in both public as well as private law although in the context of a crime it is common to use the term "guilt" which connotes criminal liability. The corresponding term in private law is "fault" in conjunction with which the terms "liability" or "civil liability" are used exclusively.

Liability for Maritime Safety in Public Law

In public law there is criminal liability arising from the commission of a crime. In the maritime field, piracy, hijacking, forgery of certificates, fraudulent cargo transactions, *etc*. are criminal offences. As well, there can be penal liability arising out of the commission of a regulatory maritime offence such as violation of a maritime safety regulation in relation to SOLAS, LOADLINE or the COLREGS. Numerous examples of such offences can be found in national maritime legislation.

Sanctions in public law are quite different from those in private law. Public law sanctions include incarceration, monetary penalties, i.e., fines, prohibition and detention orders, and even such things as community service, although it is rare in the maritime field. The severity of a sanction depends on whether the offence is characterised as a criminal offence requiring proof of *mens rea* or a regulatory strict liability offence requiring only proof of *actus reus*, or a regulatory "halfway house" offence which, in the first instance, is treated as strict liability but the accused is afforded the defence of due diligence. Most maritime safety and marine environ-mental offences are so characterized. This is evident from the way an offence is articulated in national legislation. The halfway house approach in relation to maritime safety offences has proven to be functional and effective.

The principal object of public law sanctions is to punish the perpetrator who is found to be guilty. Such sanctions are also meant to serve as deterrents. The accused found guilty is held up as an example to the rest of society so that would-be perpetrators will be deterred from committing such an offence. The lower the sanction the less is its deterrent effect. The law of maritime safety is largely regulatory law. It is international in scope and is established through conventions generated mainly by the IMO and some by the ILO. The regulatory conventions set out what acts or omissions constitute violations, but they do not create offences. Convention violations need to be transformed into offences in domestic legislation that are punishable through appropriate sanctions prescribed also in the legislation. The only sanction that is expressly provided for in conventions is detention of ships that are unseaworthy or otherwise deficient in terms of maritime safety. Detention is an administrative sanction which usually does not require resort to any judicial process.

Regulatory sanctions for maritime safety offences are normally in the form of fines or monetary penalties. The seriousness of the offence and the degree of liability should dictate the quantum of fines, and there should be some degree of regional harmonization in this regard, otherwise unscrupulous ships will seek out ports and jurisdictions that are relatively lenient. The commission of what is, in the first instance, a regulatory offence may have such serious consequences that the offence may well take the shape of a criminal offence, and the attendant penal sanction will have to be commensurate with the offence. In other words, the punishment must fit the crime. Thus a failure to proceed at a safe speed in fog may well lead to a collision or grounding resulting in personal injury or death in which case the offence may be one of criminal negligence or manslaughter and the sanction may be incarceration.

Liability for Maritime Safety in Private Law

Liability in private law is generally referred to as civil liability. It arises out of tortious acts, breach of contract, unlawful conversion of property, failure to deliver property and the like. In private maritime law related to maritime safety, there are several acts or omissions that can give rise to civil liability. A collision, for example is a maritime tort; so is damage caused by fire or explosion on board a ship attributable to human error or negligence. Death or personal injury suffered by a passenger, crewmember or shore worker on board also falls under the rubric of maritime tort. Sinkings, strandings, groundings are all maritime torts. Salvage is a maritime saving act which involves maritime safety. It can be contractual or quasi-contractual in character. Towage is another contractual arrangement with maritime safety implications.

Civil liability is usually based on the notion of fault. In most cases related to maritime safety, the fault is in the form of the tort of negligence. A tort is defined as a civil wrong. In several civil law jurisdictions tort is referred to as "delict". There can be no liability for collision damage or a grounding of a ship, or the death or personal injury of an individual on board unless the plaintiff or claimant can prove that the defendant, usually the shipowner, charterer or operator, was at fault. However, there is also the notion of strict or absolute liability in maritime safety under which, the plaintiff need not prove fault but must only show that he suffered the damage or injury. The distinction between strict and absolute liability is that in the former certain defences are available to the defendant by virtue of which he may be exonerated from liability. In an absolute liability regime no such defences are available. For example, Article II, paragraph 1 of the Convention on the Liability of Nuclear Ships, 1962 provides for absolute liability of the operator of a nuclear ship where it is proved that the damage in question was caused by a nuclear incident. The rationale for imposing strict or absolute liability is that the law makes it less onerous for a victim of damage resulting from an ultra hazardous activity carried out by the defendant, to obtain an appropriate remedy. The classic case in English law, considered to be the progenitor of the doctrine of strict liability in torts is *Rylands* v. *Fletcher* (1868), L.R. 3 H.L. 330.

Private law sanctions are known as remedies. There are different kinds of remedies available depending on the nature of the dispute and the wrongful act, the extent of the loss, damage or injury and the subject matter involved. The principle is to put the successful plaintiff in the same position as he would have been had the wrongful act not occurred. The principal remedy in private law is damages or compensation. It is notable that while liability is a qualitative concept, compensation is a quantitative concept because it has to do quantum. Another important remedy in private law is specific performance which is usually available for breach of contract in certain cases. It is an extraordinary remedy granted only in extraordinary circumstances dictated by fairness and practical possibility. There are also other civil liability remedies such as restitution, rescission, restoration, *etc*. These are granted in appropriate cases depending on whether the action was framed in tort or contract.

Damages in private law and monetary penalties or fines in public law both involve money. The crucial distinction between the two is that in public law the monies end up in government coffers in much the same way as fees and dues payable to governments or other public authorities and agencies. Damages, on the other hand, are payable to the successful plaintiff in a civil action. It is recompense for the wrong suffered. Even if punitive damages are payable, they are payable to the plaintiff alone.

Liability Interfaces in Selected Maritime Safety Issues

There are certain subject matters pertaining to maritime safety that are hybrid in scope, in that, they are not identifiable simply as public or private. The subject of maritime labour is a case in point. A relationship of employment between employer and employee or master and servant is at once a contractual relationship that falls under private law and at the same time is a concern of public policy governed by statutory provisions and an administrative and regulatory law regime. Ship registration is also a hybrid area of law. It provides at once evidence of proprietary interests such as ownership and mortgages which are private law matters, as well as evidence of the right to fly the flag of the state where the ship is registered which a public law matter (*Liverpool Borough Bank* v. *Turner* (1860), 29 L.J. Ch. at p. 830). Both involve maritime safety in different ways. The liability regimes are different and so are the attendant sanctions.

In relation to other maritime safety issues, the public and private law aspects of the same matter interface each other. In other words, the same factual situation comprising an event, casualty, breach or dispute, as the case may be, can give rise to public as well as private law implications. Needless to say, the treatment of public and private law aspects including the respective sanctions are different. Some of these maritime safety issues are discussed below.

Death and Personal Injury

Cases of death and personal injury on board may arise from collision, grounding, sinking or fire or explosion on board. These are undoubtedly the most serious of maritime safety cases and almost always result in both public and private law proceedings. The *Herald of Free Enterprise* and *Estonia* sinkings are cases in point. Very often the civil liability actions take longer to be resolved, particularly if there are multiple claimants. Ferry or passenger ship sinkings typically involve numerous claimants. The Athens Convention Relating to the Carriage of Passengers and Their Luggage by Sea, 1974 (PAL) or one of the global limitation conventions may come into play depending on whether the flag state or the forum state is a party to the relevant convention.

The public law proceedings may be in terms of regulatory or criminal law or both. The civil law proceedings would be mainly in tort, although there may, in addition, be some contractual element involved emanating from the employment contract in the case of a crew member. As well, there may be statutory provisions relating to liability and compensation that may come into play in a particular situation. This is invariably the case in the English common law jurisdictions where the maritime legislation contains express provisions relating to the responsibilities of employers of seafarers. Thus there is the application of maritime labour law which is of hybrid character as indicated earlier.

Personal injury may arise out of an accident that is fortuitous or attributable to a condition on board that is harmful or injurious. In one case, a seaman suffered a serious case of scald when he turned on the shower and stood below it. The investigation revealed that the hot water in the showers was always at a very high temperature and seafarers simply took personal precautionary measures to avoid being directly exposed to it which the plaintiff in this case did not take. In another case, a seafarer successfully sued the owners after contracting a chronic respiratory disease which was attributable to the faulty ventilation system on board through which exhaust gases flowed into the accommodation.

The employer who may be liable at law is not necessarily the shipowner. He may be a charterer, operator or even a recruiting agent. Where the shipowner is potentially liable, the role of the Protection and Indemnity Club (P&I Club) is crucial. It is the third party liability cover provided by the P&I Club that pays for the compensation for which the shipowner is liable. Where the party liable is not a shipowner, the third party liability insurer, if any, will provide the indemnification.

The defendant may successfully invoke limitation of liability under the relevant convention law if the convention in question is applicable, or under national legislation; in both cases subject to the rules relating to conduct barring limitation. Another important issue is vicarious liability. Again, subject to the conduct barring limitation provisions, where a crew member is found to be at fault in relation to the death or injury of a person, the employer may be held vicariously liable in a civil action. A Canadian case in point is *The Ogopogo* (1972), 22 D.L.R. (3d) 545, although on the facts of that case the owner of the vessel was held not liable and the persons in question to whom fault was attributable were not employees but invitees of the owner. In a criminal action, liability is normally personal and not vicarious. Indeed the principle applies in reverse in the case of an entity with independent legal personality. For example, if a ship owning company is found to be guilty of a crime which resulted in death or personal injury of a crew member or passenger, it is possible that a Director of the company will be held criminally liable if the offence is directly linked to the Director's actions or lack thereof. In a case involving an environmental offence in the United States, an ISM designated person of the ship owning company was charged with the offence.

Casualty Investigations

An eventuality in connection with a ship arising out of an unsafe condition whether accidental, fortuitous or attributable to human error is a maritime casualty where loss of life or injury has been sustained or there has been damage to property or the environment. "Maritime casualty" is defined in the IMO Code for the Investigation of Marine Casualties and Incidents (IMO Code). According to this Code maritime casualties are categorised as "very serious" or "serious".

In many jurisdictions there is a two-stage process to casualty investigation; first a preliminary inquiry, and then if the situation warrants, a formal investigation. The preliminary inquiry is usually done at an administrative level. The body conducting the formal investigation and the procedure involved may be administrative or judicial. In all cases it is a fact-finding mission. Decisions are not rendered but recommendations may be made depending on the nature of the casualty and the level of the investigation.

A casualty investigation may well lead to civil or criminal judicial proceedings or both. Or, the recommendations, if any, of the investigative body may be implemented through administrative decision. Where judicial proceedings are initiated a question arises as to whether the findings of fact of the investigative body are admissible as evidence. In this regard different jurisdictions have different rules. In some jurisdictions such as Canada and the United Kingdom the evidentiary value of the findings is zero but they can be used as a tool for cross-examining witnesses. In others, such as Italy and The Netherlands, such findings are acceptable as *prima facie* evidence (*Guidelines for Maritime Legislation*, Bangkok: ESCAP Publications, Vol. I Third Edition, 1991, at p. 191).

It is apparent from the foregoing discussion that liability issues relating to maritime safety are numerous indeed. There are many dimensions to the issues but the principles involved transcend national and regional boundaries because the concerns are global in character. There are several aspects to maritime safety itself, and the liability issues range from public law, both regulatory and criminal, to private law. In many cases, as demonstrated in this chapter, the public and private law aspects interface with each other in the context of a given set of facts such as in collision cases. In other words, the same factual situation gives rise to both public as well as private law issues. In other instances such as seaworthiness, the facts dictate whether the issue is one of public or of private law. Policies, practices and procedures pertaining to liability issues in the field of maritime safety are often different in different jurisdictions. Needless to say, harmonization in these matters is desirable, particularly on a regional basis, but whether or not that is achievable remains to be seen. Within the European Union, concerted efforts to this end are being made, and it is hoped that this region imbued with many similarities in terms of local maritime culture among the countries can serve as a model of harmonization with regard to maritime safety matters.

Safety Management

The International Safety Management (ISM) Code came about as a consequence of the sinking of the British flag cross-channel ferry *Herald of Free Enterprise* with the loss of 193 human lives. The Code was initially a set of Guidelines but was made mandatory through its incorporation into Chapter IX of SOLAS. The regime as it exists thus consists of the regulations in Chapter IX, which are six in number, and the Code itself which is a self-contained document. The Code consists of 13 Sections. Associated with the Code are "Guidelines on Implementation of the ISM Code by Administrations" (Guidelines). This document is very important for Maritime Administrations of state parties to the Convention, but it must be borne in mind that they are Guidelines only, and therefore not binding. The Guidelines have two Appendices. Appendix 1 sets out "Standards on ISM Code Certification Arrangements" and Appendix 2 contains the standard forms for the various documents and certificates required under the Code. The application of the ISM Code must involve consideration of the whole package described above.

Regulations 1 and 2 of Chapter IX contain, respectively, the Definitions and Application clauses. The ISM Code is defined; as well, various specialized types of ships in respect of which the Code is applicable are defined. The term "company" is a defined term. It does not simply bear its ordinary meaning as a body corporate, but is to be construed as the shipowner in its various forms including any organization or person who assumes operational responsibility for the ship, and has agreed to take over all of those imposed by the Code. Such an organization or person could include a manager or bareboat charterer of the ship. The word "company" is virtually a substitute for "shipowner" as the latter term is used in other maritime conventions. The Application clause provides that the Code applies to all commercial vessels of specified descriptions but, in line with all other IMO Conventions, does not apply to government-operated non-commercial vessels. The dates of application in this clause are now of little significance as they are independent of construction dates and all the application dates are now past. Thus the Code is presently applicable to all commercial vessels.

Regulation 3 is the most important as it provides the fundamental statement of law that company and ship must comply with the Code. This regulation also requires a ship to be operated by a company holding a Document of Compliance (DOC). This is a document, which pursuant to regulation 4, is to be issued by the flag state Administration or a recognized organization, usually a classification society, to a company that is in compliance with the Code. Under this regulation the flag state Administration or a recognized organization is to issue a Safety Management Certificate (SMC) to every ship complying with the Code after verifying that the company and the shipboard management operate according to the so-called "safety management system" (SMS). Regulation 5 provides that the SMS is to be maintained according to the Code requirements and regulation 6 provides for periodic verification of proper functioning of the SMS.

The first Section of the ISM Code is the Preamble which contains a statement of its purpose, which is "to provide an international standard for the safe management and operation of ships and for pollution prevention". It is thus clear that the Code does not simply address safety but also environmental protection, which until recently, were the dual objectives of the IMO's mandate. It is also apparent from the first preambular clause that the ISM Code is essentially a standard-setting instrument. The Code is expressed in broad terms to facilitate wide spread application. The basic philosophy of the Code is expressed in the sentiment that good safety management begins with commitment from the top but the commitment must filter through to all levels for it to succeed. Section 2 sets out the definitions, objectives, and application of the Code, and the functional requirements of the SMS.

The word "audit" is very familiar to those involved in ISM matters. It means systematic verification of compliance with mandatory requirements. The significance of audit is mainly in relation to the role and responsibilities of the flag state Administration under the ISM package. The Administration is responsible for issuing the DOC and SMC, and for the periodic verification of proper functioning of the SMS.

Clearly, the primary object of the Code is to exact adequate safety management responsibility from the Company both in terms of its shore-based and shipboard operations. This hallmark of the Code is patently visible in the creation of the entity known as the designated person (DP) and the specification of his responsibilities. The functions are to ensure the safe operation of each ship and provide a link between ship and shore management at the highest level. The responsibilities include monitoring of the safety and pollution prevention aspects of the operation of each ship and ensuring the application of adequate resources and shore-based support. The DP could be a superintendent or operations manager of the Company; or the Company could engage a firm to carry out the functions and discharge the responsibilities.

The DP could be considered an *alter ego* of the Company for purposes of determining whether due diligence was exercised as required under rules relating to carriage of goods by sea. His conduct could be decisive of whether the shipowner's claim to limitation could be barred. The DP is also potentially at risk for criminal liability. *The Freja Jutlandic* is a case in point where U.S. federal prosecutors commenced criminal prosecution actions against, *inter alia*, the DP of a ship owned and operated by a Danish company in connection with oily water discharges from the ship and alleged falsifications of log books. The case is discussed in one of the few books available on the ISM Code (Philip Anderson, *et al., Cracking the Code*, London: Nautical Institute, pp. 133–134). While the creation of the DP in the ISM Code was envisaged as a regulatory device to exact Company responsibility for affirmative action regarding safety management, it seems to have generated some negative unintended outfalls and its effectiveness has been questioned. Three classification societies, ABS, DNV and LR have reportedly stated that the Code is ineffective (Fairplay, June 14, 2001 at p. 12).

The distinctive feature of the Guidelines is that it is directed to Maritime Administrations as distinguished from the Code itself which is primarily directed to the Company. As such, the Code and the Guidelines complement each other and both flow from the Regulations in Chapter IX.

Apart from the Introduction, in which there appears a brief statement on the mandatory nature of the Code and the verification and certification responsibilities of the Administration, the Guidelines consist of four sections addressing respectively, the scope and application of the Guidelines, verification of Code compliance, issuance and validity of the DOC and SMC, and the certification process. Appendix 1 to the Guidelines speaks to certification arrangement standards and Appendix 2 provides the standard forms of the DOC and SMC including their interim versions. It is apparent that considerable stress is laid on the ability of the SMS to meet the general safety management objectives identified in the Code. The issue and renewal at 5-yearly intervals of the DOC and SMC is subject to initial and annual verification of proper establishment and effective functioning of the SMS.

Maritime Safety in the Current Milieu

The Private Sector Perspective

The shipping industry does not seek to excuse or condone low standards or sloppy practices ashore or afloat. But through its various associations and bodies it endeavours to explain that losses and casualties are the exception rather than the norm and that millions of miles are steamed each year without loss of lives, cargo or other incident; and that cargoes normally arrive intact and on time. Equally, the industry has sought to underline the relationship between revenue (freight rates) and the ability to maintain a vessel to the highest standard; and the fact that an old vessel is not necessarily a bad vessel let alone that creature so beloved by the media, "a rust bucket". Quite obviously the older the vessel the more has to be spent on maintenance. If freights, as has so often been the case, do no more than cover day-to-day running costs, then the temptation to cut back on maintenance is obvious. Nonetheless, there exists a real determination to eliminate sub-standard ships; to reduce casualties and to prevent loss of life, injury, damage to the environment and property; and to promote safe and efficient maritime transport on the basis of the following principles.

Prevention Rather than Overkill

Regulatory overkill is due, almost invariably, to over-reaction to major accidents. The investigation of a serious casualty seems often to end up with a string of proposals to ensure that every lesson, real or imagined, is addressed. That is not necessarily helpful. Often, recommendations are little more than knee-jerk reactions and have minimum effect on future levels of safety and the prevention of pollution. Even when addressed to the central cause of the accidents, the remedy can sometimes be disproportionate to the risk or excessive in relation to what can be achieved. The cost to the industry of frequent changes, especially if applied retrospectively, is not just financial. It engenders an undesirable scepticism about the whole regulation-making process.

A regulatory regime based on a careful analysis of all the risks is all important and gives confidence that matters will be carried through to effective implementation. It will not of course eliminate all accidents because ships are operated by human beings with all their failings. But it will reduce the risk of matters going seriously wrong.

Non-discrimination on the Basis of Age

An old ship is not necessarily a bad ship; equally, a new ship is not necessarily a good one. Everything else being equal the condition of a ship and her maintenance is all important. There are times, however, when other factors need to be considered; but these should be the exception rather than the rule. Examples are bad design or imperfect construction or when contemporary standards have overtaken past practice so that the resultant gap in safety levels is too wide.

A Fully International Approach

A national or regional approach, as has frequently been said, can only lead to clashes—an unworkable situation for shipping—and regulatory chaos. Unfortunately every incident, particularly if it involves loss of passengers' lives, leads to pressure on politicians to see that something is done. This inevitably finds expression in unilateral action (for example, by the US after the *Exxon Valdez*, the UK after the *Herald of Free Enterprise* and by North European nations after the *Estonia*). It can also result in threats of unilateral action, for example, by the European Commission or other regional groupings as a result of incidents which directly affect them or their interests.

The Sharing of Risks and Liabilities

Sharing of risks and liabilities must be on an equitable and internationally agreed basis. Whilst the main responsibility for safety, the maintenance of vessels, and where necessary, improvement of standards, lies on shipowners, operators and managers, other parties in maritime ventures have an important role to play. For instance, classification societies, shipbuilders and repairers, manning agents and equipment manufacturers all have an influence on design, construction and operation. Their decisions can significantly affect safety and the well-being of the vessel. Damage to vessels can also be caused by incorrect use of modern loading and discharging equipment. This must be recognised by ports and terminals. Charterers and cargo interests also have a role to play recognising that all voyages are, and should be seen as, joint ventures for the parties involved.

Classification Societies through IACS

Classification societies are a basic and vital part of the fabric of the industry. In them rests the technical knowledge and expertise for carrying out the classification, and maintenance in class, of vessels entered with them. In them and through their boards of shipowners is vested the accumulated wisdom and experience of the industry. The unacceptably high rate of ship casualties in recent years and loss of lives, means that the classification societies have come in for a barrage of criticism, some justified, some not. One particular area of criticism has been that competition leads to "class hopping" and the readiness of one society to have vessels entered with it previously denied class by another. Both in this respect and generally the societies have taken positive initiatives to improve their standards in particular by giving IACS a strong, co-ordinating and policing role in their affairs. IACS now acts as a well-drilled force not only in matters of ethics and policy but also in committing its members to the highest professional and technical standards. There is little doubt that the classification societies both through IACS and of their own volition have, despite difficulties, achieved a much greater degree of cohesion in recent years.

Underwriters and the Insurance Industry Generally

The insurance industry has over the years been badly hit in the marine and offshore sectors, quite aside from hurricanes and other disasters. This has made them extremely sensitive to standards and the record of owners. It has also resulted in their taking steps to tighten up the terms of cover (through amendments to the so-called Hull Clauses) and to invite the Salvage Association surveyors to undertake special and additional surveys. These steps have come in for some criticism from shipowners because they felt they had not been sufficiently consulted and because of the additional surveys and inspections in an already overburdened industry. It has also been pointed out to underwriters that they were undermining the role of classification societies, bodies they themselves established during the previous century for the precise purpose of assuring themselves that they were underwriting a good risk.

P&I Clubs

The Clubs are another very important part of the overall framework of insurance. They obviously have a keen interest in safety, the avoidance of damage and pollution. They have assessed that 60 % or more of claims arise from human error, a statistic not lost on shipowners. The important thing is that the Clubs, shipowners and others all work together towards the same goal.

Cargo Interests

Cargo owners, charterers, shippers and receivers are all part and parcel of maritime ventures (or adventures) as has already been said. Too often cargo interests show little readiness to participate in shipping industry affairs. This gives the impression that they are only concerned when cargo is lost or damaged; and even then, not always. The fact that, at the end of the day, insurance will pay is often all what they perceive. The appearance, coupled with competitive factors, is thus that their only interest is in getting their goods or cargo carried at the lowest possible rate of freight. This has led to the phrase "sub-standard charterers", namely, those who drive the hardest bargain on rates and are not too fussy about the quality of the vessel. On the other hand some big charterers, principally but by no means exclusively the oil majors, are extremely strict about the vessel they are negotiating to charter and insist on establishing her quality by independent inspection or in other ways. At the same time they understandably drive the best bargain they can on rates. While many charterers say that they are prepared to pay a premium rate for good quality tonnage the reality, certainly in the eyes of the shipowners, is often to the contrary.

There is room for greater dialogue between cargo interests in the bulk trades (as has happened in the liner trades) on general issues which affect shipping as well as full co-operation when it comes to questions of detail about the condition of the cargo, loading, stowage, receiving and discharge especially when these relate to matters of safety.

Ports and Terminals

Practices in ports and terminals do not generally impinge much on the safety of a ship itself although they may sometimes pose risks to seafarers. The loading and unloading of solid bulk cargoes is, however, an exception. But there has, in recent years, been a recognition of the danger for the structural integrity of a vessel from modern fast loading and discharging practices. Unlike years ago when virtually all cargoes were loaded by hand in sack or parcel loads, today coal, iron ore, grain, phosphates, rock and the like are loaded mechanically from shutes at very fast speeds. This can place the vessel under tremendous stresses and strains.

Unloading of bulk carriers, furthermore, is frequently done by very large and weighty mechanical grabs. Even bulldozers are used in the huge cathedral-size holds. If unskilfully or carelessly used, significant damage to the ship's structure can result. Accordingly, there must be full co-ordination and co-operation between the vessel and the shore gangs. Similar considerations apply to all types of vessels where modern loading and discharging techniques are used. This has resulted in various private sector initiatives in order to ensure that loading and discharging operations are carried out with mutual understanding between ship and shore and that terminal operators fully understand the safety implications for vessels if they are subjected to excessive stresses and bending moments. An example of this is the November 1994 incident of the 145,033 DWT Cypriot bulk carrier *Trade Daring* which literally broke its back during loading in the Brazilian port of Ponta da Madeira.

Crew Quality and Training

Modern ships are large and complex with an increasing amount of sophisticated equipment. The quality of crew has accordingly to be much higher than hitherto especially when their numbers are constantly being pared down. Thus recruitment, initial training and constant retraining must have the highest priority. This is all the more difficult in an age when the call of the sea, certainly in the traditional fleets, means that there no longer exists a pool of officers and trained seafarers from the principal maritime states. The result is that vessels are increasingly crewed by non-nationals, even among the officers, with a danger of communication problems. The IMO addresses this issue through measures under the STCW Convention within the scope of its technical cooperation role. Whilst the call of the sea may not be heard as clearly as hitherto (and there is today much less of a need to go to sea to earn a wage), the opportunities are there for those who wish to have early responsibility for increasingly valuable and complex equipment.

The Governmental Dimension

The Role of the IMO

As is obvious, governments through the IMO have   pivotal role in all matters pertaining to safety and the avoidance of pollution from sea-going craft. But, being an inter-governmental body comprising 170 member states and 3 associate members, it inevitably moves at a fairly slow pace, although much has been done in recent years to quicken the decision-making process. Procedures and working arrangements have been streamlined but, most importantly, the technical requirements of some of the major Conventions (SOLAS, MARPOL, COLREGS and STCW) can now be changed by the so-called tacit amendment procedure. Unlike the explicit procedure, where parties to a convention had formally to ratify amendments, under the tacit procedure, they become international law by a vote in the Maritime Safety Committee or the Marine Environment Protection Committee. If greater speed is required, an amendment in 1994 to SOLAS permits, in exceptional circumstances, the convening of a Conference of Contracting Governments to reduce the period from 12 to 6 months for an amendment to the technical chapters to the convention to come into effect.

This ability to change regulations quickly, and with minimum formality, has proved to be very useful. But it is two-edged. Despite a general commitment to proceed only on the basis of compelling need, the tacit amendment procedure has encouraged the making of an avalanche of new regulations so that the shipping industry finds it increasingly difficult to keep up with the changes. More seriously, very little account is taken of the costs involved. These can be considerable, especially if new standards are applied retrospectively to existing ships; a new and novel trend. In an attempt to reduce the rate at which amendments to SOLAS have been adopted, it has been agreed that amendments will only be made once every 4 years, except in special circumstances. This, however, is only partially helpful, since the setting of standards at the IMO is only one element of the action required. The other key to success lies in full, timely and accurate implementation of standards enshrined in the various treaty instruments agreed at the IMO by member states; and for the IMO to address issues as they arise in an authoritative yet sensitive manner since none of them are easily resolved.

The IMO is often pilloried following major incidents for having failed to be a law enforcer. The IMO lacks teeth mainly because enforcement of conventions is not within its mandate. That is the province of each state party to an IMO Convention. At any rate, there are practical difficulties and costs that would be involved in the recruitment and maintenance of an international cadre of surveyors to enforce the conventions. In recent times, however, the IMO has been assuming quite a proactive role, not only in terms of the treaty instruments it is generating but also their effective implementation. The ISM Code and STCW 1995 are prime examples of treaty instruments with more teeth than would have been expected in earlier times. The ISM Code imposes requirements directly on owners and operators of ships and STCW 1995 breaks new ground by giving IMO the authority to scrutinise the performance of a Maritime Administration in meeting its commitments under the convention. We may well see more of this in the future. The IMO should have a more unifying role and its powers should be extended to make state parties to conventions and other entities in shipping more accountable in terms of enforcement of the conventions. The need for this is borne out in an OECD report which found that:

> . . . different bodies in charge of ensuring and/or monitoring compliance (Flag State and Port State authorities, classification societies, chartering or marine insurance interests and the maritime labour unions) vary in the degree of diligence they apply when conducting such activities and when following up any non-observance of internationally agreed rules and regulations as regards safety and the protection of the marine environment. (See Foreword to "Competitive Advantages Obtained by Some Shipowners as a Result of Non-Observance of Applicable International Rules and Standards", Paris 1996, OCDE/GD(96)4.)

Over the years, the IMO has addressed several issues relating to tanker safety and pollution prevention. Cargo liners and container ships have not been the focus of specific attention although inevitably they have been the subject of numerous general rules affecting design, construction, stability, collision avoidance, navigation, *etc*. The IMO has also concentrated on issues relating to the safety of ro–ro ferries and bulk carriers as the direct result of some relatively recent casualties. The causes of some of these have remained unexplained. For ferries, the issues were complex and commercially sensitive since the whole principle of "drive on/drive off" through open car/lorry decks was at stake. They were eventually resolved after long and difficult negotiations resulting in five Resolutions at the 19th Assembly amending SOLAS and covering the following:

- A safety culture in and around passenger ships.
- The strength of locking devices and the security of "shell" doors, which of course includes bow doors.
- Surveys and inspections.
- Navigational guidance and information systems.
- Decision support systems for Masters in emergency situations.

Since the *Estonia* casualty was the prime motivation for these measures, it is significant that political forces in Northern Europe have led to further measures under the so-called Stockholm Agreement whereby ro–ro passenger ships on scheduled voyages in NW Europe and the Baltic Sea have to be capable of remaining afloat after flooding of the car deck. It may be that such regional extensions of IMO decisions are undesirable in policy terms while they are understandable from the public and political standpoints. It is thus a significant observation that as of 1 March 2005, the floatability and stability measures of the Stockholm Agreement have been made mandatory through EU legislation in respect of all EU passenger vessels and all non-EU passenger vessels trading in European waters. Although the IMO was faced at the same time with both ro–ro ferry and bulk carrier safety issues, it gave priority to the former. Nevertheless, in relation to bulk carriers, the following improvements have been brought about through recent amendments to SOLAS.

- Damage stability requirements are effective with particular reference to "high density" solid bulk cargoes (essentially iron ore).
- Structural strength requirements, through new rules, with specific reference to "high density" cargoes, entered into force on 1 April, 2006.
- Regulations relating to enhanced surveys have been introduced which include surveys of hold structures.
- Special endorsement of safety construction certificates.
- Loading computers are compulsory for all bulk carriers.

In all this work, the IMO has placed heavy reliance on the expert advice of the classification societies through IACS and other private sector shipowners organisations. But this is by no means the only safety work undertaken by the

IMO. Other extremely important initiatives, some of which have already been mentioned, include the following:

- STCW 1995 which provides a comprehensive package of interrelated measures addressing the inadequacies of the original convention and seeking to improve the competence of seafarers world wide. The amendments place new responsibilities on shipping companies; establish new and uniform standards of competence; and incorporate measures designed to ensure that governments implement the requirements properly. These amendments entered into force on 1 February 1997. Further improvements have been brought about through the Manila Amendments of 2010 which are now in force as mentioned earlier.
- A more critical approach to the so-called "grandfather clause" which excepted existing ships from new structural requirements. Notably, "grandfathering" is no longer applicable with respect to damage stability requirements for passenger ships.
- Work programmes designed to ensure that Maritime Administrations fully and properly discharge their obligations under the IMO conventions to which they are parties. These include such devices as the flag state implementation initiative and the IMO member state audit scheme particularly directed towards flag states that are deficient in terms of enforcement of standards on ships flying their flags.

There is little doubt that port state control has made a significant contribution to the eradication of sub-standard ships and to safety in general. However, care has to be taken in its implementation so as to ensure that inspections go to the root of safety and are not concerned with purely technical and often minor infringements; that there is a reasonable degree of uniformity of application between different ports and regions; and that those responsible for inspections are properly trained, fully qualified and experienced. It quite simply enables port state inspectors to check whether a ship complies with convention requirements, in the first instance, by inspecting all documentation, and then, by physically inspecting the ship if there are clear grounds to believe that such inspection is necessary. If deficiencies are found, the vessel may be detained for necessary repairs. These powers, whilst justified in pursuit of safety and the protection of the environment from pollution, must be viewed as ancillary to those of flag states. The primary responsibility for a ship's compliance with conventions still rests with the flag state.

Facts of Life in the Maritime World

As already stated, each incident produces ideas for instant solutions, often from those who simply do not understand ships and the sea. It is appropriate, therefore, to re-emphasise certain facts of the maritime world:

- Despite the very best and continuing efforts of many ashore and afloat, by governments, classification societies and others, accidents will continue. It would be unrealistic to believe otherwise. This must not, however, discourage anyone from trying their utmost to minimise the possibility.

- Open registries, FOCs or flags of necessity, whatever they might be called, are facts of life brought about by commercial realities and are here to stay. Indeed, their place in the shipping world was accepted by governments internationally at the time of the Ship Registration Conference of UNCTAD in 1986.
- Mixed crews are not a new phenomenon. They have been part of the shipping scene for a century or more, although perhaps today they are more mixed than ever before. They are also a fall-out from trading conditions and other changes in shipping world wide. Their existence underscores, however, the need for more attention to be paid to communication skills, not only in passenger ships, but generally. They are also here to stay.
- Some 75 % of the world, as has been previously stressed, is covered by the oceans and over 80 % of world trade is carried in whole or in part by sea. Incidents are the exception and not the norm. Shipping remains, as it has always been, the handmaiden of world trade.

Conclusion

There are many dimensions to maritime safety some of which are co-related to protection of the marine environment which today is a major concern. The legal and practical principles involved transcend national and regional boundaries because the concerns are global in character. The issues range from public law, both regulatory and criminal, to private law, and in many cases, with several interfaces. Much can be learned from the experiences of disasters such as the *Herald of Free Enterprise, Doña Paz, Haven, Estonia* and the *Scandinavian Star*. Research in relevant areas of maritime safety will inure to the benefit of the maritime world at large. If shipping is to prosper, due attention must be paid by all parties involved to the subject of maritime safety which is invariably a matter of paramount concern.

Chapter 13
Maritime Security: Legal Framework in International Law

Introduction

Over the past few decades maritime security has emerged as an issue of serious concern and in recent years has been pushed forward into the forefront of IMO's agenda. The current activity in this field largely stems from the recent upsurge in piracy incidents in the Horn of Africa and the tragic events which took place in New York City on 11 September 2001. However, maritime insecurity as a real and significant threat in the current milieu was triggered as early as 1985 by the *Achille Lauro* incident occurring in the Mediterranean Sea. That unfortunate event led to the adoption in 1988 of the Convention for the Suppression of Unlawful Acts Against the Safety of Maritime Navigation (SUA). Other incidents have occurred subsequently which may be termed acts of terrorism in line with the contemporary perception of that phenomenon. Some of these are mentioned later in this chapter. There has also been a significant increase in other types of violent criminal acts at sea, which are generally referred to as piracy, although the term does not always necessarily reflect an accurate description of the atrocity committed and is often a misnomer in terms of international law. Whatever rhetorical and other implications may result from the spurious use of the terms mentioned above, it is imperative that a realistic re-examination of the international regime of maritime security be carried out urgently, and that due heed be paid to the plight of those, including seafarers, who are directly involved in the movement of goods by sea.

As outlined above, there are essentially three facets to the problem of maritime security. These are high seas piracy, piracy-like acts committed within coastal zone waters and maritime terrorism. Piracy is the original seaborne criminal offence. It has for centuries been outlawed under international as well as national law. The present public international law governing piracy, which is largely a codification of the customary law in this field, is to be found in a number of provisions within the high seas regime of the United Nations Convention on the Law of the Sea (UNCLOS), 1982. Traditionally, under the admiralty jurisdiction a pirate could be tried in the courts of England regardless of where the act of piracy was committed so long as the perpetrator was apprehended and brought before the court. Arguably, there is no specific international regime in place as yet designed exclusively to deal with the menace of piracy-like acts committed in waters within the jurisdictions of coastal states, in this chapter referred to as "coastal zone piracy". However, the 2005 Protocol to the SUA Convention may to some extent be a useful device in this regard although it essentially has an anti-terrorism orientation. In the realm of maritime terrorism, following the so-called "9/11" disaster, the United States strengthened its regulatory maritime security regime through the Maritime Transportation Security Act (MTSA), 2002. Largely influenced by that development, the IMO embarked in parallel on a speedy amendment of the International Convention for the Safety of Life at Sea (SOLAS), 1974 through the tacit acceptance process and adopted the International Ship and Port Facility Security (ISPS) Code as an extension of an additional chapter in the Annex to the Convention. The Code became effective on 1 July 2004 and its implementation and enforcement is understandably high on the maritime agendas of state parties to SOLAS.

Maritime Security

It can be said that "maritime security" measures are those deployed by maritime administrations, shipowners, ship operators and managers, port facilities and offshore installation administrations, and other maritime organizations for *protection against unlawful acts such as piracy, armed robbery, terrorism, and maritime violence*. By contrast, "maritime safety" measures refer to those instituted by maritime administrations, shipowners, ship operators and managers, port facilities and offshore installation administrations, and other maritime organizations to *prevent or minimize the occurrence of accidents at sea that may be caused by substandard ships, unqualified crew, or operator error*. While "safety" and "security" can be used synonymously or interchangeably in several situations, the distinction as is apparent in the above descriptions is crucial in the context of shipping because each term connotes protection against different categories of threat to life and property at sea and is conspicuously so depicted in chapters IX and XI of the SOLAS Convention. One threat involves accidents caused by unsafe ships and unsafe ship operations while the other involves crimes perpetrated by humans against the ship's crew, passengers or cargo, or the ship itself. It is also to be noted that the distinction between these two types of threats is apparent in the respective themes of SOLAS and SUA. The former is primarily concerned with maritime safety, while the latter relates to maritime security.

It is important to appreciate the substantive distinction between safety and security which is not much of a problem when the terms are used in the English language as illustrated above. However, in certain languages the word "security" (spelt appropriately) bears the connotation of both security and safety causing apparent confusion in terminology. Examples are French and Spanish both of which are official languages of IMO. Prior to 2002, the same word, *seguridad maritima*, stood interchangeably for both maritime safety and maritime security in IMO documents in the Spanish language. In French, the word used was *sécurité maritime*. The same linguistic situation arises in several non-official IMO languages. The ambiguity was resolved in 2002 when the ISPS Code was adopted. At the diplomatic negotiations Hispanophone delegations retained *seguridad marítima* to mean maritime safety and designated *protección marítima* to mean maritime security. The Francophones decided to employ the term *sécurité maritime* for maritime safety and *sûreté maritime* for maritime security.

The discussion on maritime security in this chapter focuses on threats that frequently lead to serious human injury or death. These are generally exemplified by acts of terrorism, high seas and coastal zone piracy, armed robbery against ships, and other acts of maritime violence. It is recognized, however, that there are equally repugnant sea crimes such as smuggling, narcotics trafficking, gunrunning, stowaways, and human smuggling which present serious maritime security threats.

Piracy

Piracy in all its facets is as old as seafaring and seafaring itself as a profession is arguably as old as human civilisation given that the use of floating logs as a means of waterborne transportation predates the invention of the cart and wheel. Piracy has been a maritime menace since time immemorial characterized by deliberate and unscrupulous violence as its hallmark. In recent times waterways such as the Straits of Malacca have been highly vulnerable to the despicable activities of marauders who have carved out natural habitats for themselves in these and other waters.

Most recently, seafarers and ships have been the target of vicious criminal activity particularly in the waters off Somalia and across the Indian Ocean—one of the key arteries of world trade—and also in West Africa (where the incidents are to date more akin to armed robbery—see following section). In recent years, several hundred seafarers have been held hostage onshore in Somalia in terrifying conditions, some for very long periods and most being released eventually following negotiations to achieve their freedom and the payment of ransoms. Sadly, at the time of writing, over 50 seafarers still remain in captivity—with all the pain and anguish that brings to them and their families.

The notion of piracy at international law suffers from confusion and ambiguity in the current maritime milieu because of its two characteristic dimensions, the nature of the act that attracts the appellation and the location of its commitment. Superimposed on this international perspective of piracy is the manner in which piracy is treated as a criminal offence under national law. Needless to say, there is little uniformity in the different ways domestic jurisdictions deal with piracy. In colonial times, insurgencies committed in some of the islands of the East Indies were considered as piratical acts.

The definition of piracy in international law as it appears in Article 101 of UNCLOS is conspicuously restrictive in terms of the constitutive elements of the act and the zonal location of its commission. With regard to the first dimension, there is the limitation of the two-ship requirement. As well, the act must have been committed for private ends by crew or passengers of a private ship. The restrictions would preclude as piracy acts of terrorism such as hijacking that are politically motivated and ones where the perpetrator is on board the victim ship and there is no second ship involved, as was the case in the *Achille Lauro* incident. Notably, there is no definition of a private ship; but a reading of Article 102 would impliedly indicate by interpretation in reverse that a private ship is one that is not a warship or government ship. However, that in turn begs a definition for the term "government ship".

The other limitation is that the act will not be considered piracy in terms of international law unless it is committed on the high seas. The rationale, of course, is that piracy being a universal crime *jure gentium* any state should be able to take action against it. Regulation and enforcement of piracy should not be the exclusive province of the flag state of the pirate ship or the victim ship. The right of any state to take action against piracy is considered a peremptory norm of international law, but if the right extends to waters landward of the high seas or arguably the EEZ, it is an impingement on the sovereignty and jurisdiction of the coastal state. The status of piracy as a high seas crime would not perhaps have been so problematic had the outer limit of the territorial sea not been extended to 12 nautical miles and had there been no exclusive economic zone; in other words, the high seas would have started unequivocally seaward from the outer limit of the territorial sea. The present regimes are products of the redefinition of maritime zones by UNCLOS. The anomaly in the existing state of affairs, save for the current crisis off the coast of Somalia, is that many piratical acts, i.e., acts that would have qualified as piracy had they been committed on the high seas, occur today in waters where only the littoral state can exercise jurisdiction under international law.

Off the Somali coast, piracy takes a particular form—the hijacking of vessels and kidnapping of crew for ransom. In recent times, those waters have become exceptionally notorious and ships continue to be warned to keep as far away from the Somali coast as possible if they are to avoid being hijacked and victimised by one of the pirate groups in that region. Hijacked ships invariably stay in captivity for an average of 4–5 months and are released only after the payment of millions of US dollars in ransom.

Armed Robbery Against Ships

Since IMO is a specialized agency of the United Nations, it would be inappropriate for any IMO instrument to deviate from the definition of piracy as it appears in UNCLOS. Yet, consistent with its mandate in respect of international maritime safety and environmental protection, IMO does have responsibility for facilitating the development of regimes for combating criminal activities that would otherwise have qualified as piracy had the UNCLOS definition not been restrictive. The tentative solution was the articulation of the term "armed robbery against ships" defined by IMO as "any unlawful act of violence or detention or any act of depredation, threat thereof, other than an act of 'piracy,' directed against a ship or against persons or property on board such ships, within a state's jurisdiction over such offences". It was adopted to accommodate those criminal acts that bear the characteristics of piracy *per se* but fall outside the scope of the restrictive definition of piracy under UNCLOS.

Thus, under the caption "armed robbery against ships" there is a broader spectrum of criminal acts. At one end of the spectrum there are attacks that are akin to muggings committed at sea. They are opportunistic in character often perpetrated by unemployed fishermen. These attacks are usually brief and swift and the goods targeted are the ship's safe, cash, personal valuables, coils of rope, cans of paint; mainly articles that can be easily carried away and sold conveniently. At the other end of the spectrum there are attacks that are pre-meditated, highly sophisticated, and extremely violent. These take weeks or months of planning by well-organized crime syndicates. They usually target the ship lock, stock and barrel, including cargo, stores, bunkers and personal possessions of the ship's inhabitants. The operation usually involves hijacking of the ship following which it is often renamed, re-crewed, and used for trading. Needless to say, the stolen cargo is sold to unscrupulous black market buyers and the ship may then continue trading in that market. Such activity is only possible where the perpetrators are well versed in the technical and commercial operations of ships. These are the typical "phantom ships" which assume fictitious identities and blend into the seascape of normal shipping operations often with success. A phantom ship continues a criminal existence that typically involves the perpetrator entering into carriage contracts with unsuspecting cargo owners and then stealing, diverting, and selling the cargoes. This cycle is repeated as many times as can be sustained without being apprehended by the law. As a result, enormous financial losses are suffered by ship owners, cargo owners, and marine insurers. Furthermore, the crew of a hijacked ship is frequently exposed to traumatic conditions, extreme physical discomfort, serious personal injury and even death in some instances.

Unlawful Acts

The *Achille Lauro* incident in 1986 was a rude awakening for the world maritime community. It suddenly drove home to governments and the shipping industry the woeful inadequacy of the international regime of piracy. Under the auspices of the IMO a new international instrument was adopted; the Convention for the Suppression of Unlawful Acts Against the Safety of Maritime Navigation, 1988 otherwise referred to as the SUA Convention. In retrospect it can perhaps be said that it did not go much beyond the level of a cautious, preliminary attempt to deal with incidents exemplified by the *Achille Lauro* and acts of maritime violence committed in waters that are not necessarily high seas. While it imported the all-embracing term "unlawful acts" the convention also had its own limitations. The most significant drawback is that it is applicable only to unlawful acts that endanger the safety of maritime navigation. However, it was the first IMO convention that created substantive maritime criminal offences but left it to state parties to prescribe sanctions. This, as may be expected, has resulted in a serious lack of uniformity in the overall international effectuation of the regime.

Following the disaster of 11 September 2001, the SUA Convention was brought back to the drawing board at IMO for major revision. A new Protocol was adopted in 2005 which introduced a number of far-reaching provisions in an attempt to make the regime more stringent and comprehensive. More criminal offences have been added focusing on maritime terrorism together with their associated or ancillary offences. There are cross-references to other terrorism-related treaties. The most significant additions are the new detailed provisions dealing with boarding of suspect ships by authorized officials of third party states.

A serious question that provokes curiosity is the lack of linkage between the criminal law regime of the SUA Convention and the regulatory package of SOLAS Chapter XI combined with the ISPS Code. While the adoption and entry into force of the ISPS Code moved at full speed ahead pushed unabashedly by a few major IMO member states, the revision of the SUA progressed at a relatively slower pace. There are no cross-references between the two instruments and no recognition of a common platform even though both supposedly deal with maritime security. The ISPS Code is simply a preventative tool, the productive utility of which remains to be seen. Some view it as nothing more than economic convenience inuring to the benefit of states that are relatively more vulnerable to terrorism at the expense of others whose exposures to such threats may be little or nil. As regards SUA 2005, as it is now called, there are several substantive problem areas which need careful reviewing. The regime, it is submitted, is still incomplete as it does not properly address the lingering problem of coastal zone piracy.

Terrorism

The maritime version of terrorism is distinguishable from piracy and armed robbery against ships in terms of their respective motives. Maritime terrorism like terrorism in general is politically motivated. The core object of the perpetrators is to establish political power and dominance through violence and intimidation. By contrast, the motivation behind acts of piracy and armed robbery is largely private financial gain, although in certain instances the monetary gains of the perpetrators are used for overtly or directly financing operations that perpetuate terrorism of sorts. It is sometimes said that the object of terrorism is to influence the political conduct of adversaries through threats and violent attacks on calculated targets. Acts of terrorism are characterised by symbolic rather than material significance, and their object and motivation are thus clearly different from those of piracy and armed robbery. The numerous cases of maritime terror such as the 1970 explosion claimed by Al-Fatah and the Popular Front for the Liberation of Palestine (PFLP) that killed 19 and injured 36 in an Israeli port, the 1971 explosion of a bomb by a Mozambican terror group that killed 23 crew members on board a Portuguese cargo ship, and the 1988 Abu Nidal attack against the Greek passenger ferry *City of Poros* that resulted in 9 persons being killed and 80 being injured are all different from cases of piracy and armed robbery against ships.

The literal meaning of "terror" from which the word "terrorism" is derived is fear. All the incidents referred to above were designed to elicit fear and horror. Piracy and armed robbery, in contradistinction, are motivated by private pecuniary benefit. The intention of these acts is to plunder (*animo furandi*) for the sake of gain (*lucri causa*). Acts of terrorism, on the other hand, are carried out to draw attention and publicity through exploitation of public sentiment fuelled by sensational media exposures.

The *Santa Maria* incident of 1961 is generally considered to be the first case of maritime terrorism in the modern era. In this case, one Captain Henrique Galvao together with 23 of his men took control of the Portuguese luxury liner *Santa Maria* in the Caribbean Sea. At the time the ship was carrying some 600 passengers and 350 crew members. Captain Galvao captured the ship in the name of General Humberto Delgado, who had been elected President of the Portuguese Republic. Notably, the incumbent Salazar government had declared the results of the election to be invalid. While the incident did not trigger the creation of any international treaty instrument, it generated some debate within the global maritime community regarding distinctions between acts of piracy, insurrection, rebellion and terrorism. Soon after news of the hijacking spread across the globe and was confirmed, the Salazar government, the ship owner, and several states labeled it as an act of piracy. Delgado's government exerted great effort to convince the international community that the act was not piracy, but an "appropriation of Portuguese transport by Portuguese for Portuguese political objectives." There was a possibility that had Galvao's actions been labeled piracy *jure gentium*, he would be branded *hostis humani generis* which would then give any state the jurisdiction to seize the *Santa Maria* on the high seas. Galvao's actions eventually became widely recognized as an act of protest against the Iberian dictatorship rather than as piracy. At the end of the 12-day dramatic event Galvao was offered political asylum in Brazil.

In relatively recent times, the *Achille Lauro* hijacking is a landmark incident which led to the adoption of the IMO instrument the Suppression of Unlawful Acts Convention of 1988 (SUA) referred to above. The atrocious brutality with which the act of terrorism was executed shocked the international community into taking concerted action. Briefly stated, the facts of the case are as follows:

On October 7, 1985, four Palestinian gunmen hijacked the Italian cruise ship *Achille Lauro* while the vessel was traversing the eastern part of the Mediterranean Sea with 400 people on board. While they were engaged in negotiations, the gunmen shot an elderly Jewish-American paraplegic passenger and then threw him overboard in his wheelchair. Similar to the *Santa Maria* case, debate and controversy followed the incident with regard to the motives of the perpetrators and whether the heinous act was piracy or terrorism. Notably, in this case, just like in the *Santa Maria* incident, there was no "pirate vessel". The perpetrators were in the guise of *bona fide* fare-paying passengers at the time they hijacked the vessel. Eventually, the *Achille Lauro* sailed to Egypt and the terrorists were put on board an

Egyptian aircraft which subsequently was forced to land in Italy as a result of intervention actuated by United States Air Force planes. The government of the United States demanded custody of the terrorists during the complex and protracted negotiations that ensued but it was denied by the Egyptian authorities. To make matters worse from the American perspective, the terrorists eventually escaped to Yugoslavia. As mentioned above, this tragic occurrence prompted the articulation and adoption of the SUA Convention, which incidentally, contains detailed extradition provisions.

Maritime terrorism has continued to cause death and destruction since the *Achille Lauro* incident. In 2000, the bomb explosion on the ro–ro ferry *Our Lady of Mediatrix* in Panguil Bay, Philippines resulted in some 50 people being injured and 40 others losing their lives. In that same year the United States warship *Cole* was bombed by terrorists, which caused the death of 19 people and wounded 37 others. One person, a member of the ship's crew, died when the oil tanker *Limburg* was bombed in the Gulf of Aden in October 2002. The attack also resulted in 90,000 barrels of oil being spilt. Of course, the oil spill itself was not of any major proportion, but it sparked fears of environmental terrorism and ships being used as instruments of terror with or without the environmental factor. Undoubtedly, a successful act of maritime terrorism cannot only cost human lives and result in personal injuries, but also dangerously affect the marine environment and impede trade and commerce in a serious way.

Maritime Violence

The use of the term "maritime violence" is relatively new. An elaborate definition of the term is provided in a so-called model national law devised by a Joint International Working Group on Uniformity of Law Concerning Acts of Piracy and Maritime Violence spearheaded by the Comite Maritime International (CMI). It has resulted from a perceived need to highlight certain commonalities among maritime criminal offences including piracy, armed robbery against ships, terrorism, *etc*. It appears for want of a more precise term and to deliberately cast the definitional net wider to encapsulate sundry violent maritime offences, the IMO, through the SUA Convention, coined another term, i.e., "unlawful acts" at sea.

The maritime community at large and the shipping industry in particular have been subjected to micro-surgical debate over whether a certain "unlawful act" constitutes piracy or terrorism, or armed robbery against ships. Legal technicalities, particularly where different jurisdictions have been involved because different segments of the same crime were committed in different locales, have helped pirates, armed robbers, and hijackers to escape prosecution. The reality is that the victim of a crime, whether he/she is a passenger, ship owner, cargo owner, crew, or bystander, is hardly concerned with legal niceties of zonal or jurisdictional consequence, or whether the crime was perpetrated for the sake of any pecuniary gain or a political cause. Victims are concerned with loss of life, personal injury and loss of or damage to property.

As indicated above, the CMI has embarked on a useful exercise, namely, the drafting of a model national law on piracy. The object is to sensitise states to the fact that piratical acts or acts of maritime violence are, in the first instance, a national problem for individual states. By and large, the majority of these unlawful acts occur in waters within national jurisdictions and is therefore a matter for domestic law. The development of national legislation by use of a model law fosters uniformity and assists in the national law-making process. The CMI initiative can thus be instrumental in promoting systematic uniformity in the development of national legislation on the subject. In case there are any misconceptions about the so-called model law, it should be pointed out that it is not exactly drafted legislation, but is a framework of principles based on which domestic legislation can be articulated in a meaningful way. The model law identifies piracy and maritime violence as two separate criminal offences. It defines piracy in both treaty i.e. UNCLOS, as well as non-treaty terms. Through this initiative the intention of the CMI is to continue exploring the question of adequacy of the present international regime to deal with criminal acts committed on and against merchant ships, in particular, container ships, tankers and passenger vessels.

It is abundantly clear that separation of piracy and other maritime criminal offences in legal terms is of little or no benefit to ships which end up as victims of these heinous crimes. Violent attacks, whether they are called piracy (rightly or wrongly) are being carried out regularly and systematically in certain waterways of the world that have gained negative notoriety in this regard. Merchant ships are highly vulnerable to being hijacked and used for financial and material gains, or being used as vehicles for carrying out acts of terrorism. If a rational and meaningful solution is to be reached it must be approached through the articulation of a well-thought out integrated legal regime. With proper enforcement through interstate cooperation, it may well be possible to combat the maritime menace of crime at sea whether it is piracy, unlawful act or maritime violence or howsoever characterised otherwise.

International Legal Instruments and Current Developments

In temporal order, piracy has historically been the oldest threat to maritime security if one can characterize the statement in those terms. Of course, the distinction between high seas piracy and what is being referred to as coastal zone piracy, is one of relatively recent vintage. Be that as it may, the codification of the customary international regime of high seas piracy is reflected in UNCLOS. The provisions are contained in Articles 100–107 of that convention. Many are of the view that these provisions need to be revised in light of the current frequency of coastal zone piracy and the dislocation of the legal definition of piracy due to significant changes in the configurations of maritime zones under UNCLOS. Under UNCLOS, the high seas have shrunk in area and, therefore, acts committed in certain waters that were previously part of the high seas are no longer high seas crimes because those waters now fall under the jurisdictions of coastal states. Given the geographical locations of most present day piratical acts the adequacy of the present regimes is seriously questionable.

While the problem is acknowledged by the international maritime community at large, it is also recognized that altering UNCLOS may not be the best solution. The rights of ships of all states to intervene in the event of high seas piracy must be retained. The problem of coastal zone piracy must be addressed without disturbing the UNCLOS regime. At any rate, any attempt to revise UNCLOS will be an inordinately long and arduous exercise simply in view of past experience with that convention. It took some 12 years for UNCLOS to be adopted and then another 12 for it to enter into force.

Another international legal instrument that features prominently in the domain of maritime security is the SUA Convention. The limitations of the piracy provisions under UNCLOS and the hijacking of the *Achille Lauro* stirred IMO into coining the concept of "unlawful acts against maritime navigation." This phraseology was intended not only to deal with the issue of geographical jurisdiction but also embrace criminal acts that did not fall within the UNCLOS definition of piracy. In the aftermath of the "9-11" disaster, the international community recognized that the 1988 version of the SUA Convention was inadequate to deal with all varieties of violent maritime acts that fell within contemplation. The revision of SUA was then put on the agenda of the IMO Legal Committee with the aim of making the convention more sound and effective in substantive terms and also wider in scope. In functional terms this objective was manifested mainly in the expansion of the Article 3 offences in the convention to accommodate a broader range of "unlawful acts". The coverage, it was envisaged, would extend to such atrocious and vile acts of crime as were exemplified by the 11 September event. The scope of application of the convention was enlarged to cover domestic and cabotage trade. As well, the provisions relating to jurisdiction and extradition were strengthened and made wider in scope. As an example, under the new draft the so-called political offence exception is no longer a valid ground for denying extradition under the convention.

The Model National Law initiated by the CMI has already been mentioned. Although the model is intended to be used to articulate and consolidate domestic legislation, the way it is designed, it serves to complement the piracy provisions of UNCLOS as well as the offences of the SUA Convention. One remarkable attribute of the Model National Law is that the definition of piracy in it accommodates the offence in virtually all its possible forms including those prevailing in international law as well as in the laws of various municipal jurisdictions. As well, the definition of maritime violence has been articulated in such a way that it is not as restrictive as in the SUA Convention; nor does it have the limitations of the definition of piracy in UNCLOS. Thus, the generalized definition of maritime violence in the Model National Law tempered by adaptations of relevant provisions from existing international instruments, allows the model law to accommodate a wider range of offences. It is flexible enough to challenge individual states to modify and tailor the model to meet their special needs in terms of definitional and jurisdictional issues, at the same time taking cognizance of the fact that there is a global maritime menace that needs to be dealt with through concerted action.

Finally, there is the so-called ISPS package which is an integral part of the SOLAS scheme of maritime safety. Following the 9-11 disaster, the international maritime community adopted amendments to Chapters V and XI of the SOLAS Convention and created a new instrument known as the International Ship and Port Facility Security Code (ISPS Code). Chapter V which addresses the subject of safety of navigation has been amended to include requirements such as the automatic identification system (AIS) and the ship identification number (SIN). The old Chapter XI has been re-named Chapter XI-1 with the title "Special Measures to Enhance Maritime Safety" and a new Chapter XI-2 has been created bearing the title "Special Measures to Enhance Maritime Security" through which the ISPS Code has been adopted as an associated instrument. Part A of the ISPS Code is mandatory while Part B is recommendatory. The object and purpose of the Code is to assemble "an international framework involving co-operation between Contracting Governments, Government agencies, local administrations and the shipping and port industries to detect/assess security threats and take preventive measures against security incidents affecting ships or port facilities used in international trade". The Code aims to achieve this objective by establishing "the respective roles and responsibilities of all parties concerned, at the national and international level, for ensuring maritime security".

In the past, IMO instruments had not addressed any issues relating to ports. The ISPS Code marks a departure from that norm. It is to be noted, however, that the Code only purports to regulate security from seawards to the ship-port interface. Landward of that interface the jurisdiction and responsibility is that of the shore-based port authority and related enforcement authorities. One notable observation with regard to the ISPS Code is that unlike, for example, the ISM Code, it did not go through a period of gestation as an instrument *para droit*. From its inception it was intended to be an integral part of SOLAS and was made partly mandatory. The Code became fully effective internationally by July 2004. The ISPS Code has also re-demonstrated the recent trend of enhanced enforcement capability of IMO instruments. The Code has imposed direct responsibilities on companies, i.e., owners and operators of ships. In that respect, both the ISPS and ISM Codes of SOLAS are "self-executing" or "directly applicable" instruments in terms of international treaty law. The significance, of course, is that in states where the monistic system of treaty implementation is applicable under their constitutional laws, these Codes immediately become part of the law of the land upon their ratification or accession by the states in question.

Problem Areas

With regard to the international regime of maritime security and the global communities strive to gain uniformity there are still a number of problem areas that need to be revisited. While disturbing the piracy regime of UNCLOS is not being advocated, it must be observed that under Article 101 of that convention only if the following elements are present an act will qualify as piracy under international law. There must be: (1) an illegal act of violence; (2) motivated by private gain; (3) committed by persons on board a private ship; (4) directed against another vessel, or the persons and property on board; and (5) committed on the high seas or outside the jurisdiction of any State. But for the recent surge of piracy off the coast of Somalia, these requirements have proven to be anachronistic in a world of reduced ship manning and cheap high speed rubber boats, and where the high seas have shrunk and coastal maritime zones and related jurisdictions are now extended to 200 nautical miles from territorial sea baselines which themselves are further away from land than was the case in the past.

One of the most problematic elements of the UNCLOS definition of piracy is that the act in question must be committed on the high seas or outside the jurisdiction of any state. If piracy can only be a high seas crime under international law, then most acts that would otherwise be considered piratical would fall outside the scope of that definition and would only be subject to the national law of the coastal state in whose maritime zone the act was committed. Prior to the prevailing maritime zones under UNCLOS, such an act motivated by private gain committed by the crew of a private vessel against persons belonging to another private vessel would have constituted an act of piracy if the act occurred just beyond the three nautical mile limit from the territorial seas baseline. At the present time, however, the same act committed in the same geographical location as described above, or perhaps even as afar from shore as 200 nautical miles, would not be an act of piracy. Whether a violent unlawful act meeting the requirements of Article 101 qualifies as piracy if it occurs beyond the outer limit of the EEZ, or whether to so qualify it is sufficient for the act to be committed only beyond the territorial sea, is not entirely clear. Much depends on how Articles 58 and 101 are construed together. A great number of piracy-like incidents are reported to occur in either the EEZ or the territorial seas of states. Reports in fact indicate that numerous attacks take place against ships tied up alongside a pier or while at anchor.

The requirement in the Article 101 definition for an act to be motivated by private gain is also problematic because defining private ends is quite a Herculean task. A slew of questions arises immediately. Is "private" to be construed synonymously as "personal"; in other words, not "collective"? Is it "private" as distinguished from "public", or "political", or "religious", or for that matter, is it any cause or end that, strictly speaking, is not "private"? The definition of the relevant end is not simply a matter of judicial construction to be undertaken by resorting to the rules of treaty interpretation. There are serious issues at stake for the individual victim, the state of his/her nationality, the flag state of the victim ship, commercial

interests suffering damage, perhaps a coastal state. The perspective of the perpetrator as well is important, as to whether his intention was or was not to achieve a
private end. A review of the proceedings and *travaux préparatoires* of the Harvard
Research Group of the early 1900s, and the deliberations of the International Law
Commission drafting the 1958 Geneva Convention reveal that the "private end"
requirement was deliberately inserted by the drafters of the relevant treaty
provisions in their attempt to codify the international law of piracy. Apparently it
was done to make a conscious distinction between "private ends" and "public" or
"political" ends. The object and purpose of the exercise was to exclude from the
definition, acts of insurgencies against foreign governments and ships acting under
public authority, and thereby also excluding them from the application of universal
jurisdiction. Some scholars have thus concluded that the acts committed against the
Achille Lauro could be assimilated to piracy as defined in UNCLOS [see Samuel
P. Menefee, "The Achille Lauro and Similar Incidents as Piracy: Two Arguments",
in Eric Ellen (ed.), *Piracy at Sea*, 1989 at p. 179. See also, Malvina Halberstam,
"Terrorism on the High Seas: The Achille Lauro, Piracy and the IMO Convention
on Maritime Safety", 82 Am. J. Int'l. L. 269, 285 (1998)].

There are those who suggest that the SUA Convention can fill the *lacunae*
inherent in UNCLOS Article 101 by subsuming piracy, high seas or otherwise,
under it as an "unlawful act" without regard to the place of commission of the
piratical act. The point is, of course, that SUA, which, as mentioned earlier, was
adopted by IMO as a direct result of the *Achille Lauro* incident, is generally
considered to be the convention designed to suppress maritime terrorism. But
there is no convention definition of maritime terrorism or terrorism, for that matter;
instead there is a list of offences designated as unlawful acts, albeit maritime acts
connected to activities involving the sea. The Convention does attempt to overcome
some of the hurdles of the Article 101 impediments of UNCLOS. For example,
there is no two-ship requirement, no geographical restriction, and no motive
specified in the Convention. Nevertheless, SUA is still relatively inadequate
because not all criminal offences relating to maritime security are addressed.
Theft and armed robbery are two glaring omissions.

Perhaps the most striking and conspicuous anomaly in SUA is that for an act to
be "unlawful" under the Convention it must "endanger the safety of maritime
navigation." In other words a criminal act that does not jeopardize navigational
safety is not an unlawful act under the convention and therefore cannot be
prosecuted. This is a major deficiency of the Convention. No reasonable "maritime"
person will disagree that unlawful acts against ships regardless of whether or not
safety of navigation is at risk should be covered by an international convention
regime; not just instances where an attack exposes the ship to a risk of collision,
grounding or the like. Furthermore, acts endangering port security should also be
articulated as maritime criminal offences although this may just as well be
addressed through land-based criminal law.

In the domestic legislation of the United Kingdom and some other British
jurisdictions, hijacking is specified as an offence. Incidentally, in the United
Kingdom, aviation security and maritime security are addressed together in one

piece of legislation known as the Aviation and Maritime Security Act (AMSA), 1990 which, *inter alia*, gives effect to the SUA Convention.

In the 2005 Protocol of SUA, Article 3 has been expanded to include seven new categories of offences. It is noteworthy that none of these offences are predicated on the unlawful act being a threat to the safety of maritime navigation. The SUA Convention bears the distinction of being the first instance of actually creating offences in the sphere of international maritime conventions. Unfortunately, it stops short of recommending sanctions. From the perspective of uniformity in international maritime law this is a perceived problem as different countries have different kinds of sanctions even though these offences are typically considered to be capital offences. Due cognizance must be taken of the fact that in some jurisdictions these offences could carry the death penalty, while in others, life imprisonment could be the maximum penalty that could be imposed.

As far as the ISPS Code is concerned, there are a number of issues that need further consideration. First, its lack of compatibility with SUA does not seem to have attracted any meaningful discussion. The ISPS Code is procedural and should therefore be related to its substantive counterpart which should be found in the SUA Convention. It is arguable that it is misplaced in SOLAS simply because it relates to security which is quite different from the notion of maritime safety as the latter concept has been envisaged since the inception of the Convention. While it is recognized that preservation of life is the common denominator, traditional maritime safety does not contemplate risk to safety of life at sea emanating from intentional human intervention, whereas maritime security does. That is not to categorically say that the ISPS Code could not belong to the SOLAS regime. In order to effectuate that, however, the object and purpose of the SOLAS would need to be restated and the link with the SUA would have to be established. In other words, the ISPS Code could derive its legitimacy as an international legal instrument from both those conventions.

Last, but not least, once the component elements of the international legal framework are adjusted and put in order, UNCLOS as the constitution of the world's oceans would need to be amended to accommodate it as a fundamental precept, perhaps even as a peremptory norm of international law otherwise referred to as *jus cogens*, the various unlawful acts and their technical and procedural elements.

Conclusion

With rapid changes taking place in the international regime for maritime security including several new initiatives, the legal framework both in terms of public international law as well as regulatory and criminal law warrants careful review and discussion. It is recognized that the international community particularly under the aegis of the IMO, is continuing its deliberations to adequately and effectively address the concerns of maritime security. As well, some initiatives in non-governmental spheres are unfolding. It is also desirable that at the level of the United Nations, the constitution of the oceans, namely the Law of the Sea Convention, be revisited in order to provide a sound legal umbrella under which the specific regimes, both regulatory and those pertaining to criminal law, can operate in a satisfactory manner, having regard to the position of the seafarer in relation to his work environment on the ship. There is no doubt that maritime security is a crucial element of sound ocean governance and is an issue that is going to dominate the agendas of various maritime fora for some time to come.

Chapter 14
Protection of the Marine Environment

Introduction

The marine environment is vulnerable to different kinds of pollution emanating from various sources as depicted in Fig. 14.1. It is well-known that land-based sources of pollution are the most damaging to the marine environment both in terms of quantity as well as severity. There is also pollution coming from the seabed itself incidental to oil exploration and exploitation activities. Air-borne pollution resulting from land-based carbon dioxide (CO_2) emissions entering the sea in the form of acid rain is another source. Finally there is ship-source marine pollution, the harmful effects of which are relatively less whether they enter the sea directly from the ship or through the atmosphere as air pollution in the form of NO_x or SO_x. Be that as it may, this chapter is mainly concerned with ship-generated pollution and the focus is largely on oil pollution. The pollution types and their sources are best explained graphically and diagrammatically. The marine pollution continuum diagram and the marine pollution spectrum chart (Fig. 14.2) depict not only the philosophy of combating marine pollution but also the international convention regimes designed and articulated to address the pertinent issues respecting ship-generated marine pollution.

The Regime of Ship-Source Oil Pollution in Public Law

Legal Framework Under UNCLOS

The caption "Protection and Preservation of the Marine Environment" is a comprehensive and appropriate description of the regime of marine pollution as it pertains to public international law. The legal framework is found in Part XII of UNCLOS. Prior to the advent of UNCLOS there was no finite and systematic body of customary law on the subject of marine pollution. Part XII consists of Articles

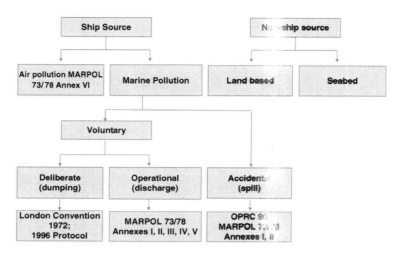

Fig. 14.1 Sources of marine pollution

192–237 arranged under 11 Sections. The discussion in this chapter is confined to ship source oil pollution and associated matters. In the first part of the text those salient provisions will be highlighted which provide the blueprint for various detailed preventive and remedial conventions. Most of these have been generated by IMO but there are also others which are independent of the IMO family of instruments but are closely correlated through UNCLOS Part XII. Even at the risk of reiteration it is perhaps useful to recall that UNCLOS being the global framework convention for all matters maritime is often referred to as the constitution of the seas.

In Section 1, Articles 192 and 193 set out the fundamental principles that states are obliged to protect and preserve the marine environment. Under Article 194, states must take measures to prevent, reduce and control marine pollution from any source, and ensure that pollution does not spread beyond the areas of national jurisdiction. The measures must be designed to minimize, *inter alia*, ship source pollution and must extend to preventing accidents, dealing with emergencies, ensuring maritime safety and regulating intentional and unintentional discharges. Article 195 prohibits the transfer of pollution from one sea area to another or the transformation of pollution from one form to another. Article 196 requires states to take preventive and remedial action against the transportation of harmful alien species.

Pursuant to Section 2 of Part XII states are required to co-operate on a global and regional basis for the purpose of developing international rules and standards. States are required to promptly notify each other when danger of pollution is imminent. Article 199 requires states to develop contingency plans for responding to pollution incidents. This article represents the blueprint for the Oil Pollution Preparedness and Response (OPRC) Convention of 1990.

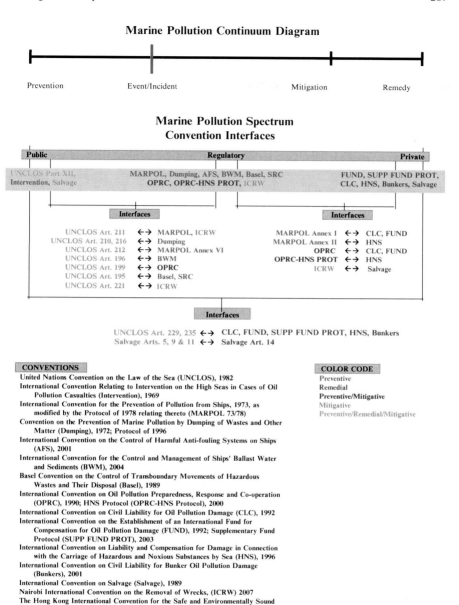

Fig. 14.2 Marine pollution continuum diagram and marine pollution spectrum chart

Section 5 contains the prescriptions for establishing international rules and domestic legislation by States for the purpose of preventing, reducing and controlling marine pollution. This Section is important in terms of the setting of certain basic principles. Of particular significance are Articles 210, 211 and 212. They consist of provisions dealing with ship-source pollution issues that are germane to the analytical treatment of the regulatory law on the subject. Article 210 bears the caption "pollution by dumping". It serves as the blueprint for the more particularized instrument generally known as the London Dumping Convention. This Article provides that states must make laws and take other related measures to minimize and control the dumping of wastes at sea. It prescribes a regime under which dumping activities can only be carried out subject to permission given by the competent authorities of a state.

Article 211 contains a detailed blueprint pertaining exclusively to regulation of ship-source marine pollution. In that regard it is perhaps the most important provision setting the basic principles for the control of operational discharges from ships. There are seven paragraphs in Article 211. The first paragraph provides that states must establish international rules and standards for the prevention, reduction and control of ship-generated pollution and to achieve that, design routing systems to prevent accidents if it is appropriate to do so. States are required to do so under the auspices of the competent international organization or through diplomatic conference. While it is not expressly so stated, the relevant body in this context is IMO. The measures adopted are in contemplation of preventing pollution damage to a coastal state and its related interests. Pursuant to paragraph 2, flag states are required to generate domestic legislation reflecting those rules and standards to be applicable to their ships. Undoubtedly, these provisions represent the legal foundation for the MARPOL Convention.

Paragraph 3 of Article 211 recognizes the coastal state's right to impose regulatory requirements regarding ship-source pollution on foreign ships. The requirements must be given due publicity and must be communicated to IMO, the competent international organization. States are expected to harmonize their policies and enter into co-operative arrangements with each other. Without prejudice to the right of innocent passage provided under UNCLOS, ships navigating in the territorial seas of states participating in such co-operative arrangements must furnish such information as may be demanded of them. In paragraphs 4 and 5, the sovereignty of a coastal state in its territorial seas and its enforcement rights in the exclusive economic zone regarding marine pollution are expressly recognized.

Paragraph 6 of Article 211 is concerned entirely with the notion of the "special area". This paragraph provides the blueprint for that regime elaborated in the MARPOL Convention although there is a subtle distinction between the respective regimes in the two instruments. Sub-paragraph (a) of paragraph 6 provides that if within the exclusive economic zone of a coastal state, special mandatory measures are needed for the prevention of ship-source pollution, then subject to a determination by the IMO, special legislative measures may be adopted in respect of these special areas. Any such special legislation, however, cannot require foreign vessels to comply with design, construction, manning or equipment standards other than those established internationally through relevant instruments of the competent international organization. Article 212 deals with pollution from and through the atmosphere. It basically provides the blueprint for the regime now contained in Annex VI of MARPOL with regard to ship-source air pollution.

In Section 6 there are ten Articles. The principal area of focus of this Section is enforcement of laws relating to pollution emanating from various sources. Enforcement from the perspectives of the flag state, the port state and the coastal state are addressed. Article 216 speaks to pollution by dumping and requires laws and regulations on the subject to be enforced by coastal states and flag states. Article 217 contains detailed provisions dealing with flag state enforcement of pollution laws. Under paragraph 2 of this Article, flag states are required to prevent defaulting vessels from sailing until they are fit to proceed to sea in compliance with the relevant rules and standards, including those concerning design, construction, manning and equipment. Paragraph 3 requires states to ensure that a proper and effective certification regime is put into place pursuant to the relevant international rules and standards, and that vessels are periodically inspected to verify that the actual physical condition of a ship is in conformity with what is stated in a particular certificate. Under paragraph 4, flags states enjoy a prerogative but also have an obligation to investigate violations of rules and standards by their ships. Where appropriate, they may commence proceedings against violating ships regardless of the location of the violation or where the pollution has been observed. Paragraphs 5–7 provide for the carrying out of investigations and institution of proceedings. Once satisfactory and sufficient evidence is collected, flag states are required to commence proceedings expeditiously. Paragraph 8 provides that penalties must be severe enough to discourage violations regardless of where they occur. It is apparent that the object of this provision is to discourage the institution of nominal penalties by flag state laws.

Article 218 deals specifically with enforcement by port states. This Article is unique in UNCLOS for a number of reasons, not the least of which is the establishment in UNCLOS of the topical notion of what has come to be known as port state control (PSC). It is notable that in UNCLOS, the regime of PSC is addressed only in respect of marine pollution. By contrast, this regime is provided for in express terms in regulatory conventions dealing specifically with maritime safety and seafarers' matters. As such PSC forms an integral part of those conventions. Be that as it may, UNCLOS being the constitution of the oceans, it can be said that PSC provisions entrenched in Article 218 represents a codification of the legal concept of port state jurisdiction (PSJ) in international maritime law at least with respect to marine pollution. The central core of this jurisdiction is that it is exercisable only when a ship is voluntarily in a port or offshore terminal of a state. Furthermore, PSJ allows the port state to enforce international rules and standards established through the instrumentality of a competent international organization against a violating ship voluntarily visiting a port or offshore terminal of that state even if the location of the violation falls outside that state's maritime zones. Where, however, a discharge violation occurs in waters under the jurisdiction of another state, the port state is precluded from bringing proceedings against an offending ship unless the other state or the ship's flag state so requests; or unless the violation causes pollution in waters of the state instituting the proceedings.

Under Article 219 a foreign vessel can be detained if it has committed a violation which has rendered it unseaworthy; and as a result, it is a marine environmental threat. The Article contemplates relevant administrative measures to be taken and release from detention is only permissible if the vessel proceeds to the nearest repair yard.

Article 220 deals with enforcement by states in their capacity as coastal states. Whereas enforcement by flag and port states is also covered in more detail by other treaty instruments, such as MARPOL, enforcement by coastal states is only addressed in UNCLOS. This is a unique feature of this Article the substance of which is in many respects similar to the regime in the previous Article. First, the coastal state may institute proceedings for a violation committed in waters under its jurisdiction if the offending foreign vessel is voluntarily within its port or offshore terminal. Second, where there are clear grounds for believing that a vessel during its passage through the territorial seas of the coastal state has committed a violation, then the coastal state is empowered to carry out a physical inspection of the vessel. However, if there are similar clear grounds in respect of a violation in the exclusive economic zone or territorial seas of the coastal state by a vessel navigating such zone, then that state can require the vessel to provide information regarding its identity and port of registry, its last and next port of call and any other relevant information. If, in such a case, there is a substantial discharge resulting in or threatening a significant amount of pollution, the coastal state may undertake physical inspection of the vessel if the vessel refuses to give the requested information or if the information is not consistent with the evident factual situation. In a similar navigational situation, if a violation is committed which results in a discharge causing major environmental damage or threat of such damage to the coastline or related interests of the coastal state, or to its resources in the territorial sea or exclusive economic zone, the coastal state can institute proceedings and detain the ship. However, in such case the threshold of evidence provided for is different; it must be clear and objective.

Under Article 221 coastal states are entitled to take measures to protect their coastline and related interests such as fisheries resources from pollution threats resulting from a maritime casualty. They could include enforcement measures which may be taken under convention law as well as customary law. It would appear that the provision tacitly assumes the existence of the Intervention Convention. States can take these measures beyond their territorial seas. In appropriate circumstances that would include the high seas. There is a definition of the term "maritime casualty" in this Article which includes collisions and strandings. Article 222 provides for enforcement relating to air pollution. This is characterized as "pollution from and through the atmosphere" generated by ships and aircraft. The Article is directed to both coastal as well as flag states and evidently provides the blueprint for Annex VI of MARPOL.

Section 7 provides for safeguards against excessive use of enforcement powers or abusive actions of states. Safeguards are important measures from the viewpoint of the ship against which enforcement actions are contemplated. The measures are directed towards coastal and port states. Article 226 is an elaboration of the procedures to be followed in the course of investigation of foreign vessels by port states and coastal states. A vessel must not be delayed beyond the time that is necessary for inspection and the physical inspection must, in the first instance, be limited to an examination of the documentation which the ship is required to carry under the relevant international law. If there are clear grounds for belief that the physical condition of the vessel is not consistent with what the documentation purports to state or there is inadequate information, then only can further physical inspection be carried out. It is the flag state's prerogative to take measures under its laws including institution of proceedings and imposition of penalties against its ships in the event of a pollution violation. This is confirmed by Article 228. A coastal or port state that has commenced proceedings in respect of a violation committed beyond its territorial seas by a foreign vessel must suspend such action if within 6 months the flag state of the vessel also institutes proceedings.

Article 230 is of particular importance; adherence to it is often lacking by over-enthusiastic coastal and port states. With respect to sanctions, if a foreign vessel commits a violation beyond the territorial seas, only monetary penalties are permitted. The same rule applies within territorial seas except for cases of willful and serious acts of pollution. In any proceedings, judicial or administrative, the recognized rights of the accused must be respected. Under Article 231, whenever any enforcement measures are taken by a coastal state against foreign vessels the flag state and any other affected state must be promptly notified. Article 232 provides that a state which takes unlawful or unreasonably excessive measures is liable for any loss or damage that may result, and legal recourse must be provided in its courts for actions in relation to such loss or damage.

Section 9 contains a single Article which restates the responsibility of each state to fulfill its international obligations regarding protection and preservation of the marine environment. Under this Article states are also required to ensure the provision of adequate compensation under their laws. States must co-operate in the implementation and further development of international law on liability and compensation for pollution damage and consider such mechanisms as compulsory insurance and compensation funds. This Article provides, through the vehicle of a public international law convention, the framework and principle for the institution and enhancement of an appropriate private law regime to address pollution damage.

The Intervention Convention

In the field of marine pollution, apart from UNCLOS there is one other public international law convention. It is the International Convention Relating to Intervention on the High Seas in Cases of Oil Pollution, 1969, generally referred to as the Intervention Convention in short. This Convention was one of two adopted at the diplomatic conference held in Brussels in the wake of the *Torrey Canyon* disaster. The international maritime community at the time felt the need for a public international law as well as an international private law convention to cover the two dimensions of ship-generated oil pollution damage. The corresponding private law convention was the Civil Liability Convention, 1969 (CLC 1969). At the time the only other international convention dealing with oil pollution was the 1954 Oil Pollution Prevention Convention which was a regulatory convention. The two 1969 conventions emerging from the deliberations at Brussels marked the beginning of a new generation of marine pollution conventions. One of them dealt with public international law and the other with the private law implications of liability for an oil spill unprecedented together with a compensation regime for its victims.

The adoption of the Intervention Convention was at once a landmark event and groundbreaking in maritime history. For the first time the unbridled pre-eminence of the flag state over its ships on the high seas was put under a severe constraint. The convention conferred on the coastal state the right to intervene on the high seas in cases of imminent threat of oil pollution damage to the coast or related interests. The impetus for the creation of an international regime through this convention came from the unilateral actions taken by the British Government in reaction to the damage caused by the incident to its national interests. Ironically, the action taken by the British Government of sinking the polluting ship by bombing it was contrary to existing international law. At the time of the incident the ship was located beyond 3 nautical miles from the British coast, that is, it was on the high seas. The United Kingdom had not yet instituted the emerging international regime of a 12 nautical mile territorial sea.

In the face of widespread criticism at home and abroad, the British Government referred the matter to what was then the Intergovernmental Maritime Consultative Organization known by the acronym IMCO. The Legal Committee of IMCO (now IMO) was established in response to the *Torrey Canyon* disaster. Its task at the time was to clarify and specify through the relevant legal process, the rights and responsibilities of coastal states in such circumstances. The Legal Committee recommended that a diplomatic conference be convened to, *inter alia*, define the rights of coastal states in the event of an oil spill threatening pollution damage to their coasts and related interests.

The Intervention Convention which eventually came into force in 1975 after the required number of ratifications were deposited gives to coastal states the right to intervene when there is an actual or threatened incident of pollution giving rise to grave and imminent danger to the coastline or its related interests. Under Article 1 (1), the right of intervention may be exercised on the high seas and any measure deemed suitable in the circumstances may be taken by the coastal state to prevent, mitigate or eliminate the grave and imminent danger.

The definition of "related interests" contained in Article II (4) encompasses interests of the coastal state directly affected or threatened by a maritime casualty. The term "maritime casualty" is defined in Article II(1) to include marine collisions, strandings and other such incidents of navigation, or other occurrences resulting in actual or threatened damage to a ship or its cargo. Examples of related interests are maritime activities in coastal, port or estuarine areas including fisheries activities that are necessary for persons involved in those activities to maintain their livelihoods. Other examples are tourist attractions in the affected areas, the health of the population in the coastal zone and the well-being of the affected areas in general including the conservation of living resources.

Under Article III of this Convention, the coastal state is required to consult with other states affected by the casualty, before taking any intervention action. In particular the flag state of the polluting vessel must be consulted. The coastal state must also consult with independent experts. They must be selected from a list of names established and maintained by the IMO pursuant to Article IV. A coastal state can only preclude such consultation in a case of extreme urgency where immediate action needs to be taken. Member states of IMO and state parties to the Intervention Convention may nominate persons to the list of experts referred to in Article IV who are entitled to payment for their services. The coastal state must notify any person or corporate entity whose interests may be affected by its actions and take into account their views if they are made known. The coastal state must use its best endeavors to avoid risk to human life and it must provide assistance to people in distress. In appropriate cases, the coastal state must facilitate the repatriation of crew members of the ship concerned.

Article V requires the intervention measures to be proportionate to the actual or threatened damage. The measures must be restricted to what is reasonably neces-sary to achieve the end objective and the actions undertaken must be discontinued upon those objectives being reached. Unnecessary interference with the rights and interests of others is prohibited. Under Article VI, if the intervention action results in damage to others, the coastal state is obligated to pay compensation to them.

The rights, duties, privileges or immunities enjoyed by any person and any remedy otherwise applicable are preserved under Article VII. Pursuant to Article VIII, if there are disputes between parties to the Convention regarding any matter under the Convention every effort must first be expended to settle by negotiation, failing which, the parties must attempt conciliation. If that does not succeed, then the dispute must be submitted to arbitration. The procedures for conciliation and arbitration are set out in Chapters I and II, respectively, of the Annex to the Convention.

In summary, the foregoing are the substantive provisions of the Convention of 1969. In 1973, a Protocol to the Convention was adopted to include pollution or threat of pollution from substances other than oil. A list of such substances in contained in the Annex to the Protocol. The list has been updated subsequently through a Supplement to the Annex adopted in 1996.

Regulatory International Law Framework

As shown in the spectrum diagram above, there are a number international conventions dealing with marine pollution that are regulatory in scope. The most important of these is MARPOL 73/78. The OPRC Convention is also important. Both these conventions are examined below in some detail.

Overview of MARPOL 73/78

The MARPOL Convention was adopted in 1973. It was intended to replace the earlier International Convention for the Prevention of Pollution from Oil (OILPOL) of 1954 which addressed only oil as a ship-source pollutant. MARPOL, at its very inception was far more comprehensive in scope. It dealt with five types of pollutants through its five original Annexes. In 1996, a Sixth Annex was added to cover ship-source pollution entering the sea from the air and through the atmosphere. Thus at present there are six Annexes to the Convention that regulate six different types of ship-source pollutants. They are the following:

Annex I—Oil;
Annex II—Noxious Liquid Substances;
Annex III—Packaged Harmful Substances;
Annex IV—Sewage;
Annex V—Garbage; and
Annex VI—Air Pollution

The MARPOL Convention is the instrument that regulates ship source pollution from operational discharges. Furthermore, it deals exclusively with preventive measures as can be gleaned from its title—International Convention for Preventing Pollution from Ships. By comparison, the OPRC Convention is regulatory as well, but it embodies preventive, mitigative as well as remedial elements. The CLC and Fund Convention, on the other hand, are exclusively remedial in scope as explained through the continuum chart and the spectrum diagram (Fig. 14.2). Although MARPOL is directed primarily to regulating operational discharges, there are several provisions that deal with design and construction of tankers and address such matters as damage control and subdivision and stability pertaining to accidental spills of oils and chemicals. These are, of course, strictly speaking, non-operational matters, but nevertheless they fall within the scope of the object and purpose of the convention, namely, to prevent ship-generated pollution.

As mentioned above, marine pollution emanates mainly from land based sources such as industrial by-products, pesticides and herbicides and other effluents resulting largely from daily urban activities. Even so, considerable pollution is generated by ships, and in terms of quantity entering the oceans, oil undoubtedly remains the most important pollutant.

It is also mentioned above that the 1954 OILPOL Convention dealt only with oil as is evident from its title. But it is significant that much of it has been drawn into Annex I of MARPOL. Of course, the regulatory regime is not static and amendments continue to be adopted as and when updating becomes necessary.

The MARPOL Convention of 1973 went through a major revision through its 1978 Protocol. The Protocol adopted was the result of the deliberations of the Tanker Safety and Pollution Prevention (TSPP) Conference of 1978 which took place in the wake of the *Amoco Cadiz* disaster. The provisions of the Protocol were merged with the original text and the Convention thenceforth came to be known as the MARPOL 73/78 Convention. It is now simply referred to as "MARPOL". The main body of the Convention as it stands now consists of 20 Articles. It contains the basic principles and the contractual elements of the Convention. There are two Protocols to the main body of the Convention. Protocol I contains provisions concerning procedures to be adopted for reporting incidents involving harmful substances pursuant to Article 8 of the Convention. Protocol II provides the arbitration procedures applicable to disputes between state parties which are to be settled in accordance with Article 10 of the Convention.

The following is a list of some of the important articles in the Convention proper:

Article 2 – Definitions
(2) Harmful Substances:

   (i) Human health
   (ii) Living resources and marine life
   (iii) Interference with other legitimate sea uses.

(3) Discharge: Release of effluent from ship howsoever caused—escape, disposal, spilling, leaking, pumping, emitting or emptying.

Note: does not include:

   (i) "dumping" within the meaning of the London Convention
   (ii) Release of harmful substances form offshore exploration
   (iii) Legitimate MSR for pollution abatement.

(4) Ship—includes fixed or floating platform

Article 4 – Violation: Flag State jurisdiction regardless of place of violation. Coastal State has jurisdiction—if violation occurs within jurisdiction.

Article 12 – Casualty Investigation—Where there is a major deleterious effect on the marine environment. Obligation similar to SOLAS, Ch. 1 Part C. Reg. 21.

Article 15 – Entry into force: Compulsory Annexes—12 months following date on which 15 States comprising 50 % of world tonnage became parties.

Article 16 – Amendments.

Paragraph (2)(d)—adoption by 2/3rds majority of Parties present and voting.

Paragraph (2)(f)—acceptance

   (i) Convention Article—date on which 2/3rds of Parties comprising at least 50 % of GT of world fleet.
   (ii) Annex—either by the "2/3rds – 50%" rule as above or by tacit acceptance on date determined at time of adoption (not less then 10 months) unless objection by not less 1/3rd Parties or by Parties whose combined fleets comprise not less then 50 % of GT of world fleet.
   (iii) Appendix to Annex—only tacit procedure.
   (iv) Protocol I—same procedure as for Annexes.
   (v) Protocol II—same procedure as for Convention Article.

Paragraph (2)(g)—entry into force of amendment 6 months following acceptance in each case; not applicable to Parties who have expressly declined to accept or have declared that their express approval is required.

The substance of the Convention is essentially the regulatory law. This is contained in the Annexes which consist of Regulations. Annexes I and II are compulsory. For a state to be a party to MARPOL if must ratify or accede to those two Annexes. The remaining Annexes are optional but state parties are encouraged to subscribe to all of them for the sake of harmonious and globally consistent application of the convention. The remaining Annexes also make the convention comprehensive and complete. These are added reasons for states to consider acceding to or accepting all the Annexes. The salient features of the MARPOL Annexes are summarized below.

IMO publishes up to date Consolidated Editions of the MARPOL Convention, from time to time. These, of course, are supplemented by amendments, if any, that are adopted in the interim periods between these editions. The Consolidated Editions contain a unique feature, namely, the so-called "Unified Interpretations" which appear at the end of each of the respective texts of Annexes I, II and III and VI. These are not, in strict terms, part of the Convention. However, they contain valuable explanatory elaborations of the highly technical regulations. If used selectively and judiciously, these detailed supplementary texts can be very useful in the drafting of domestic legislation aimed at implementing the MARPOL Convention. They are of great practical utility for professional users of the convention such as surveyors, inspectors, maritime administrators and shipboard personnel. As well, the unified interpretations serve as an interpretive tool for tribunals charged with the task of applying relevant provisions of the Convention, whether in the context of passing judgment regarding a casualty or in the event of litigation of a dispute.

Common Features of the Annexes

For the purposes of setting discharge standards, the concept of special areas is a significant feature of MARPOL. As mentioned in the discussion above on UNCLOS, the notion of special areas is also addressed in that convention, but there are differences between the two respective concepts in the two conventions. Under MARPOL, discharges are totally prohibited in special areas under Annexes I, II and V. There is no mention of special areas in the other Annexes because of the particular characteristics of the pollutants and the ways in which they are regulated under those Annexes. The generic definition of "special area" is:

> ... a sea area where for recognized technical reasons in relation to its oceanographic and ecological condition and to the particular character of its traffic the adoption of special mandatory methods for the prevention of sea pollution is required. [**Note:** See Annex I Regulation 1 (11) and Annex V Regulation 1 (3)]

The special areas under the convention are the Mediterranean Sea area, the Baltic Sea area, the Black Sea area, the Red Sea area, the Gulfs area, the Gulf of Aden area, the Antarctic area, The North Sea area, the North-West European waters and the Wider Caribbean Region. They are identified by reference to geographical co-ordinates or other descriptive features circumscribing their respective perimeters. Not all the above-mentioned areas are included in each Annex. With respect to Annex I, the North Sea area and the Wider Caribbean Region are not special areas. The only special areas under Annex II were the Baltic Sea, and Black Sea and the Antarctic. But now all seas are special areas (see p.281). Under Annex V all except the Gulf of Aden area and the North-West European waters are special areas. Annex VI contains something akin to a special area known as "special emission control area" (SECA). At present there are two designated SECAs, namely, the Baltic Sea and the North Sea.

Since all discharges are prohibited in special areas, vessels are required to contain their respective wastes on board and discharge them to shore based reception facilities. Complementary to this requirement, state parties are required to provide adequate reception facilities at locations ashore designated by them. It is recognized that providing waste reception facilities is a costly affair, especially so for the developing countries. Over the years since MARPOL was adopted in 1973, this has been an issue for discussion within and outside of the IMO regarding how such facilities are to be financed. The financial implications of this important preventive prescription in the Convention can be considerably burdensome for some countries, but equally, without adequate reception facilities a major objective of the convention will remain unfulfilled. Compliance with the discharge standards under all Annexes may be excepted if the non-compliance is necessary for saving life at sea or for securing the safety of the ship.

Annexes I, II, IV and VI contain another important preventive feature. These are the provisions requiring vessels to be properly surveyed and accordingly certificated. These provisions have been now harmonized with corresponding requirements under the SOLAS and LOADLINE Conventions. The relevant certificates are the International Oil Pollution Prevention (IOPP) Certificate under Annex I, the International Pollution Certificate for the Carriage of Noxious Liquid Substance in Bulk, otherwise referred to as the NLS Certificate under Annex II, the International Sewage Pollution Certificate under Annex IV and the International Air Pollution Prevention (IAPP) Certificate under Annex VI. Record Books are required to be maintained under Annexes I, II and V known respectively as the Oil Record Book, the Cargo Record Book and the Garbage Record Book. Under Annex V there is also a requirement for each vessel to have a Garbage Management Plan. The Convention requires member states to treat violations of the Convention as offences and provide for appropriate sanctions.

A significant feature of MARPOL is the "tacit acceptance" procedure for amending the Convention found in Article 16. This methodology provides that following the adoption of an amendment, it is deemed to be accepted if no objections from a specified number of member states are received by IMO within a pre-established period of time allocated for the purpose. Once it is accepted, the amendment enters into force on a date fixed by the relevant IMO Committee. It cannot enter into force if it is rejected by one-third or more of the state parties whose combined merchant fleets represent at least 50 % of global gross tonnage.

When a foreign ship is in a port or off shore terminal of a state party to the Convention, that state can exercise port state jurisdiction over that ship and exercise port state control. The general requirements are provided for in Article 5 of the Convention and the detailed control procedures in relation to operational requirement are set out in the respective Annexes. For Annex I the relevant provision is Regulation 8A, for Annex II it is Regulation 15, for Annexes III and V, the provision resides in the respective Regulation 8 of each of those Annexes, and in Annex VI it is Regulation 10. A detailed depiction of all the Annexes of the Convention, even in summary form, would be somewhat disproportionate given the generality of scope of this Chapter and the book as a whole. However, it is considered expedient and useful to provide some description of the salient features of Annex I given that oil is the most common ship-generated pollutant of all. Also, some of the important changes need to be pointed out in view of the fact that a revised new version of this Annex was adopted on 15 October 2004 and entered into force on 1 January 2007.

Originally, there were 26 Regulations in Annex I. At present the total number is 39 including new Regulations adopted over the years. It is notable that the present Annex I reflects recent changes in form but not in substance. As such, provisions have been mixed and matched with new numberings but without any substantive alterations of the regulatory requirements or standards. The Regulations are grouped under seven chapters. The first Chapter contains general provisions. Chapter 2 deals with procedures pertaining to surveys and certification. Chapter 3 prescribes the requirements for control of pollution from machinery spaces of all ships. Requirements for control of pollution from the cargo areas of oil tankers are contained in Chapter 4. Chapter 5 consists of only one Regulation prescribing requirements for the carriage on board of a shipboard oil pollution emergency plan (SOPEP). In Chapter 6 there are requirements for reception facilities, and in Chapter 7 there is a single Regulation prescribing special requirements for fixed or floating platforms.

In the aftermath of the infamous *Erika* oil spill, decisions were made by the Marine Environment Protection Committee (MEPC) at its 45th and 46th sessions, to expedite the phasing out of single hull tankers and bring the double hull requirements into effect sooner than originally contemplated. Considerable pressure was exerted on the IMO by the member states of the EU to that effect. Eventually, the final phasing-out date for Category 1 tankers was brought forward from 2007 to 2005, and the final phasing-out date for Category 2 and 3 tankers, from 2015 to 2010 (the categorization of tankers is contained in the Regulations).

The incorporation of the double hull requirement in MARPOL generated extensive debate within IMO. Its supporters pointed to the Oil Pollution Act, 1990 (OPA 90) of the United States to advance their position. It is notable in this context that other technologies are available that are equally if not more effective such as the Coulombi-Egg design. However, the predominant view appears to be that the double hull alternative is the most feasible technologically as well as financially.

A synopsis of the important Regulations of Annex I is set out below; on a selective basis some are expanded.

Regulation 1. Definitions

1. "Oil" means petroleum in any form including, *inter alia*, refined products but not petrochemicals under Annex II and includes substances listed in Appendix I.
5. "Oil tanker" means a ship constructed or adapted primarily to carry oil in bulk in cargo spaces; includes combination carrier, NLS tanker and gas carrier if carrying cargo or part cargo of oil in bulk.
10. "Nearest Land" – territorial sea baselines except for North East Australia identified by geographical coordinates.
11. "Special Area" – four factors taken into consideration, i.e. technical reasons, oceanographic condition, ecological condition and traffic density/character.

    Note: As per Paragraphs 11.1–11.9, Annex I special areas are: Mediterranean Sea area, Baltic Sea area, Black Sea area, Red Sea area, Gulfs area, Gulf of Aden area, Antarctic area, North West European waters and Oman area of the Arabian Sea.
17. "Clean ballast" – no visible sheen

    – 15 p.p.m. reading if discharged through ODMACS even if there is sheen.

18. "Segregated ballast"—ballast water in tank permanently allocated for that purpose and completely separated from cargo oil and oil fuel system.

Regulation 3. Exemptions and waivers

1. Exemptions—hydrofoil, air-cushion vehicle, near-surface craft, submarine craft.
4. Waivers—oil tankers exclusively on voyages up to 72 h and within 50 nm from nearest land within a State Party in respect of Regulations 29 (Slop tanks), 31 (ODMACS) and 32 (Oil/Water interface detector).

Regulation 4. Exceptions

– Granted in respect of Regulations 15 and 34 (Control of discharge of oil from all ships and oil tankers, respectively)
– For safety of ship or life at sea, discharge resulting from damage to ship or equipment, and discharge for combating specific pollution incidents

Regulation 6. Surveys and certification

– Oil tanker 150 GT and above and other ship 400 GT and above: initial, renewal, intermediate, annual and additional surveys
– Surveys may be delegated to recognised organizations

Regulations 7–10. IOPP Certificate

– Issue, endorsement, form, duration and validity

Regulation 11. PSC on operational requirements

Regulation 12. Oil residues (sludge) from machinery spaces
– All ships of 400 GT and above

Regulation 14. Oil filtering equipment
– For machinery spaces of all ships from 400 to less than 10,000 GT

Regulation 15. Standards for operational discharges from machinery spaces of all ships
A (outside special areas) and B (in special areas) for ships 400 GT and above

- *En route*;
- Oil filtering equipment
- Oil content less than 15 p.p.m.
- Not from cargo, pump room, bilges on oil tanker
- Not mixed with oil cargo residues

C ships less than 400 GT in all areas except Antarctic

- May retain oil and oily mixtures on board to go to reception facilities; or
- Discharge if all items above are met except that substitute for oil filtering equipment allowed if approved by Administration

Regulation 17. Oil record book

Regulation 18. Segregated ballast tanks and protective location for such spaces

Regulation 19 and 20. Double hull and double bottom requirements for oil tankers delivered on or after 6 July 1996, and those delivered before that date

Regulation 22.
– Double bottom requirements for pump room

Regulation 27. Intact stability

Regulation 28. Subdivision and damage stability

Regulation 29. Slop tanks

Regulation 31. ODMACS for oil tankers 150 GT and above

Regulations 33 and 35. COW requirements and operations for crude oil tankers of 20000 DWT and above
- COW operations and equipment manual

Regulations 34. Standards for operational discharges from cargo area of oil tankers
A (outside special areas)

- Tanker not within a special area
- 15 nm from nearest land
- *En route*
- Instantaneous rate
- No more than 30 l per nm
- Quantity discharged no more than 1/15,000 of total quantity (pre-31 December 1979) and 1/30,000 (post-31 December 1979)

B (in special areas)

- No discharges allowed

Note: discharge restrictions not applicable to clean or segregated ballast

Regulations 38. Reception facilities.
A (outside special areas); B (within special areas)

There are three Appendices to Annex I, one containing a list of oils and the other two containing standard forms for the IOPP Certificate and the Oil Record Book. The text on Unified Interpretations to Annex I contains five Appendices.

Important changes to Annex II are summarized below. Needless to say, to fully appreciate the import and significance of these changes, one must review the whole Annex in light of its previous version.

- No special areas; in effect all seas are special areas
- Chemical tankers must comply with Annex II (environmental regulation and operation) and BCH or IBC Codes (design and other operational requirements)
- Design, construction, equipment and operations (Regulation 11)
- NLS categories are X,Y, Z and "other substances" (Regulation 6)
- Discharge restrictions and standards according to categories (Regulation 13)
- Vegetable oil carriers exempted from Regulation 11 requirements under Regulation 4.3

The OPRC Convention

As can be gleaned from the spectrum diagram above, the International Convention on Oil Pollution Preparedness, Response and Cooperation, 1990 (OPRC), is at once preventive, mitigative and remedial in scope. It sits on the mitigative platform and straddles the preventive regimes of the Intervention and MARPOL Conventions on the one hand, and the remedial regimes of the CLC and Fund Convention on the other.

In 1989, the IMO Assembly, recognized the seriousness of a number of then recent oil pollution incidents and requested the MEPC to draft a convention for consideration at a diplomatic conference. The subject matter was to embrace the development of an international framework for cooperation in combating major oil pollution incidents. These were the large oil spills resulting from serious casualties such as collisions and groundings. The initiative launched was to take account of the experience gained for dealing with these matters, from existing regional institutions such as the Regional Marine Pollution Emergency Response Centre (REMPEC) located in Malta in the Mediterranean region, which was previously known as the Regional Oil Combating Centre (ROCC). Incidentally, this was the first such centre in the world established under the Mediterranean Action Plan (MAP) of the United Nations Environment Programme (UNEP) pursuant to the Barcelona Convention. Subsequently, other similar centres were established in other regions such as REMPEITEC located in Curacao for the Caribbean and Central American region under the Cartagena Convention. These centres are operated by and under the direction of IMO as an executing agency. Eventually, the diplomatic conference for the planned convention was convened at IMO in November 1990, and the OPRC Convention was adopted together with ten Conference Resolutions attached to the Final Act. The salient features of the convention include the following:

The Preamble to the convention refers to "the need to preserve the human environment in general and the marine environment in particular" and to "serious threat by ... oil pollution incidents involving ships, offshore units, sea ports and oil handling facilities". It also refers to the "polluter pays" principle as a general principle of international environmental law and alludes to the connection with the CLC/Fund private law regime.

Articles 1 and 2 contain, respectively, the general provisions and definitions. Article 3 requires the carriage of shipboard oil pollution emergency plans (SOPEP) on ships of state parties. Operators of offshore units are required to have similar plans which need to be coordinated with the coastal state's national system for preparedness and response required under Article 6. The national system must be devised to include a national contingency plan. The procedures to be followed in reporting any event involving a discharge or probable discharge of oil or an observed presence of oil at sea are set out in Article 4. In Article 5 the actions to be taken by states when such a report is received are outlined. International cooperation among state parties for responding to oil pollution incidents is provided for in Article 7. Article 8 calls for cooperation among state parties for research and development activities in relation to preparedness and response. Such cooperation contemplates promotion and exchange of results of research and development of state of the art technologies, surveillance techniques, containment, recovery, dispersion and cleanup of oil pollution as well as mitigation of damage and restoration of the affected marine environment. In connection with the above items, Article 9 calls for technical cooperation among state parties for training and transfer of technology. Promotion of bilateral and multilateral cooperation in preparedness and response is contemplated in Article 10. Article 12 provides for IMO to undertake certain functions and activities; these include providing information, technical services, technical assistance and promoting education and training. Article 14 provides for procedures for amending the convention which include the tacit amendment method.

Other Contemporary Regulatory Law on Ship-Source Pollution

It was indicated at the beginning of this chapter that the focus of discussion is on ship-source pollution, and furthermore, only certain convention regimes have been selected for detailed consideration in the foregoing text. It is recognised, however, that there are a number of contemporary issues that are currently of concern in the field of regulatory ship-source pollution law which need to be mentioned in relative detail even though a comprehensive discussion of them is beyond the intended scope of this chapter. It will be recalled from the spectrum diagram depicted earlier in this chapter that there are some nine convention instruments that fall under the "regulatory" segment of the spectrum. Except for Basel, which is an UNEP convention, the remainder are all IMO instruments. Among them, the original depository of the London Convention on Dumping of Wastes and Other Matter at Sea, 1972 (London Convention) was the Government of the United Kingdom. The Convention was serviced by a separate secretariat although it was physically located in the IMO premises. It was later subsumed into the IMO family of conventions and is presently a part of the IMO in terms of its administrative and secretariat functions.

Dumping of Wastes at Sea

Whereas MARPOL deals primarily with operational discharges, the London Convention, as explained above in the flow chart on marine pollution sources, deals with deliberate dumping of wastes at sea. In the definition of "dumping" in that convention an express distinction is made with "discharge" as defined in MARPOL. It should be noted that a ship carrying wastes from land to be dumped at sea is under a dual regime. It is subject to the rules of the London Convention in so far as dumping is concerned, but it is also subject to MARPOL in terms of its operational discharges. The original London Convention of 1972 underwent a major revision in 1996 through a protocol which reversed the underlying philosophy for the regulation of dumping of wastes at sea. Originally, dumping was subject to the specific prohibitions articulated in the convention; now all dumping is prohibited excepted those substances which are allowed to be dumped under the convention pursuant to a permit regime.

Transboundary Movement of Hazardous Wastes and Ship Recycling

The Basel Convention of 1989, which is an UNEP convention, deals primarily with transboundary movement of hazardous wastes and their environmentally sound management. It is basically designed to control and regulate the export and import of hazardous and other wastes. If wastes are loaded on board a ship from land for disposal at sea, the governing regime is the London Convention; if hazardous wastes are similarly loaded where the wastes are destined for disposal in another country, the Basel Convention is the applicable regime. Both conventions contain similar clauses under which the conventions do not apply to wastes generated on board as a result of normal shipboard operations. Such wastes are obviously governed by MARPOL. One important attribute of the Basel Convention is that in practical terms it is also the current international regime that can govern ship-breaking operations to the extent that a ship on its "end of life" voyage can be treated as a piece of hazardous waste carrying out a transboundary movement. Notably, the newly adopted Hong Kong International Convention for the Safe and Environmentally Sound Recycling of Ships (SRC), 2009, although not yet in force, provides a comprehensive "cradle to grave" regime for a ship's life addressing both environmental as well as human health factors involving ship-recyling.

Anti-fouling Systems

Another important marine environmental phenomenon is the accumulation of marine organisms on a ship's hull while it is traversing the world's oceans through varieties of biological and oceanographic environments. Generically known as "marine growth" or colloquially as "weed", they can cause a reduction in ship speed which in turn can have a serious commercial impact on the ship's earnings. To combat the problem of marine growth, ships have for many decades used anti-fouling paints on ships' hulls which contain organotin compounds acting as biocides that are harmful to the marine environment. Such anti-fouling systems pose a substantial risk of toxicity and other chronic impacts on marine organisms and are ecologically harmful and also detrimental to human health. The International Convention on the Control of Harmful Anti-fouling Systems on Ships (AFS), 2001 was adopted to promote the substitution of such environmentally harmful systems by ones that are less harmful or preferably harmless.

The AFS Convention entered into force on 17 September 2008.

Invasive Alien Species

The phenomenon of alien species travelling in ballast tanks of ships has been recognised as an environmental problem since the advent of steel-hulled vessels over a century ago. While sea water used as ballast is essential for the safety, stability and efficiency of ships, ballasting also results in invasive species entering the ship in one marine environment and being discharged into the waters of another causing serious ecological, economic and health hazards. To combat this problem, scientists, mainly in certain developed countries, have been engaged in research and development on a continuing basis. The traditional method of ballast water interchange has not been entirely successful in resolving the problem. In the absence of a universal regulatory framework to address this issue several states have unilaterally introduced their own legal regimes. Initially a proposal was made at IMO to add a seventh Annex to MARPOL to introduce a regulatory regime that would apply globally, but after considerable debate it was decided that a new and separate convention was the better approach. Thus, the International Convention for the Control and Management of Ships' Ballast Water and Sediments (BWM) was adopted in February 2004. It is not yet in force. IMO initiated the "Globallast" project to provide technical assistance to developing countries to prepare for the legal and practical implementation of the convention when it enters into force for the state concerned.

Ships' Exhaust Emissions

Exhaust emissions from ships have long been viewed as a serious threat to the atmospheric environment and also to the marine environment through their entry to the oceans via the atmosphere. The regulation of pollution emanating from ships' exhausts is regulated by Annex VI of MARPOL which was adopted through a Protocol in 1997. Originally, this Annex regulated the emissions of SO_x and NO_x which primarily cause acid rain but there were no provisions dealing with CO_2, a greenhouse gas (GHG) which is a major contributor to the phenomenon of global warming. Annex VI substantially tightened provisions on the maximum sulphur content allowed in marine fuels. It essentially covers emissions of sulphur oxides (SO_x), nitrogen oxides (NO_x) and other emissions believed to impact the ozone layer. At IMO active debate continues on whether CO_2 and GHG are pollutants and should therefore be included in Annex VI. The following discussion focuses on SO_x, NO_x, GHGs and other airborne pollutants including particulate matter (black carbon) and volatile organic compounds.

Sulphur Oxides (SO_x)

Oxides of sulphur form during the combustion process by a combination of sulphur in the fuel with oxygen, the prime constituent of SO_x being SO_2. The amount of SO_x formed in an engine depends mainly therefore on the concentration of sulphur in the fuel. A study conducted in 2007 indicated that reducing sulphur levels in marine fuels globally could save as many as 40,000 deaths per annum in coastal regions from cardiopulmonary and lung cancer mortalities. The findings were recognised by the IMO in 2008 when a substantial amendment to Annex VI was adopted providing tougher standards for maximum allowable sulphur content in marine fuels.

The regulations pertaining to SO_x emissions from international shipping are laid down in Regulation 14 of Annex VI. It sets a 4.5 % global cap on sulphur emissions by all ships and also makes provisions for specially designated Sulphur Emission Control Areas (SECAs) where the sulphur content in fuel oil must not exceed 1.5 %. The Baltic Sea and the North Sea (incorporating the full length of the English Channel) became SECAs as from May 2005 and November 2007 respectively. A North American ECA (out to 200 nm around the coasts of the USA, including Hawaii, and Canada) came into force in August 2012 and an ECA around Puerto Rica comes into force in 2015.

The 2008 revision of Annex VI set out more stringent limits on sulphur content in fuel:

- Reduction in the global cap to 3.5 % from 1 January 2012 followed by a further reduction to 0.5 % from 1 January 2020 subject to a fuel availability study
- Reduction in SECAs to 1 % from 1 July 2010 and then a further reduction to 0.1 % from 1 January 2015

In the EU, Directive 1999/32/EC established the maxima for sulphur content in marine fuels. The Directive served as the legal instrument for incorporating international sulphur provisions into the EU regional legislation. Once MARPOL Annex VI came into force, the Directive was amended by Directive 2005/33/EC. The EU law, however, went beyond the international instrument and imposed additional requirements. In particular, it introduced:

- 0.1 % maximum sulphur requirement for fuels used by ships at berth in all EU ports from January 2010
- 1.5 % maximum sulphur content for fuels used by all passenger ships in EU waters from August 2006 (in addition to the international requirement of 1.5 % maximum in SECAs prior to 2015)

In 2012 the Directive was once again amended, requiring that all passenger ships operating in EU waters will be required to operate as if in SECAs, i.e. limited to 0.1 % sulphur. To try to ameliorate fuel availability issues, this regulation will be delayed by 5 years and thus come into force in 2020. However, the future global standard of 0.5% will come into force in all European waters in 2020, irrespective of the outcome of the fuel availability study.

Despite the ever tightening SO_x regulations, enforcement is becoming an issue. Dutch authorities released figures for 2010 showing that 46 % of ships failed to meet sulphur standards within the North Sea SECA. It appears this is mainly a reflection of poor fuel standards rather than attempts at evasion by ship operators. However, this clearly needs to be addressed if these regulations are to be rigorously enforced. There are serious concerns within the shipping industry as to how both the SECA (0.1 % in 2015) and global (0.5 % in 2020) regulations are going to be met in terms of cost, fuel availability and accessibility of sufficiently reliable abatement and alternative technologies.

The sulphur content in fuels depends on the sulphur content in the crude from which it was refined. In sweet crude oil, the sulphur content is less than 0.5 %. Heavy fuel oil (HFO) containing less than 0.5 % sulphur is derived from crude with a sulphur content of less than about 0.15 % as most of the sulphur in the crude that is refined ends up in the HFO which is distilled residue oil. However, the average global crude sulphur content is currently about 1.2 % and is expected to rise to 1.4 % by 2020.

Low-sulphur fuels can only be produced by one of three methods;

1. Re-blending very low sulphur HFOs. This is the cheapest option but supplies are limited;
2. Processing sweeter crudes. This is the most cost-effective method but again is constrained by the availability of crude with a sulphur content of less than 0.2 % and by competition with land users (road and power stations);
3. Catalytic hydro-treatment of HFO. This is both expensive and energy intensive.

A number of studies have concluded that the cost of low-sulphur Marine Gas Oil (MGO) is likely to be 80–100 % more than HFO. Though some will be able to pass these costs on, ultimately of course to consumers, some sectors will be very vulnerable, especially short-sea shipping which may see a strong modal shift from sea to land. The consequences of this would be most unwelcome in a broader environmental sense as it would greatly increase the numbers of vehicles on roads, with associated congestion and higher carbon emissions.

Availability of fuel is another key concern; whereas there probably will be enough fuel to meet the 2015 0.1 % SECA requirements, it is almost certain that even by 2020 refining capacity will be nowhere near sufficient to provide the global fleet with 0.5 % low-sulphur fuel. MARPOL Annex VI calls for a fuel availability study in 2018 and if, as expected, it demonstrates a shortfall, the 0.5 % global regulation will be delayed by 5 years until 2025. However, this uncertainty only further exacerbates the reluctance by oil refineries to make the necessary invest-ment to increase capacity for the production of marine distillates. Their reluctance is understandable given the scale of investment required—up to $95 billion according to some analysts.

Availability of reliable abatement technologies and alternative fuel technologies is the third area of concern. A variety of different types of "scrubbers" have been developed to remove SO_x from emissions (they generally also remove NO_x and greatly reduce CO_2 as well) but confidence is low within the shipping industry that any of them are yet reliable enough to meet the regulations 99 % of the time. If a ship is reliant upon a scrubber to meet the regulations, then any malfunction would force the ship into harbour with the associated loss of income and potential contractual penalties. The reliability, therefore, of these units has to be extremely high. This technology is also expensive and therefore ship owners are unlikely to invest until they absolutely have to. However, after the 2015 introduction of the 0.1 % SECA regulation, the price differential of low-sulphur fuel (probably at least $300 or $400 per tonne) will be the spur for owners to make the investment. This, of course, would also suit refiners who will then continue to have a market for off-loading HFO. Alternative fuels (LNG, electric power etc.) suit some sectors (short-sea and local ferries mainly) better than others and some companies are investing heavily in this area, but the global fleet is relatively young and it will take time before this usage becomes significant. There are also regulatory, safety and environmental issues that need to be resolved with LNG in particular.

Nitrogen Oxides (NO_x)

Oxides of nitrogen are formed during the combustion process due to the combination of atmospheric nitrogen and oxygen at the very high temperatures within the combustion chamber. Diesel combustion produces relatively high levels of NO_x and fuel properties only have a minor influence on the amount produced. Atmospheric NO_x leads to the formation of acid rain, the destruction of ozone at high levels as well as the formation of ozone at lower levels, both of which add to global warming, severe respiratory health problems and the eutrophication of seas. Eutrophication is a condition in an aquatic ecosystem where high nutrient concentrations stimulate excessive algael growth leading to oxygen depletion and hence the death of fish. NO_x from shipping represents about 15 % of global NO_x emissions and 40 % of emissions from transport of freight.

The regulations pertaining to NO_x emissions from international shipping are laid down in Regulation 13 of Annex VI. Additionally, there is a NO_x Technical Code (2008) that provides mandatory procedures for the testing, survey and certification of marine diesel engines that enable engine manufacturers, ship-owners and administrations to meet the requirements of Regulation 13.

The IMO NO_x emission standards are commonly referred to as Tier I, Tier II and Tier III and apply retrospectively to new engines greater than 130 kW installed on vessels constructed on or after 1 January 2000, or which undergo a major conversion after that date. The regulation also applies to fixed and floating rigs and drilling platforms. They do not apply to engines intended solely for emergency use. The NO_x emission limits imposed by each Tier are relative to the operating speed (rpm) of the engine concerned, noting that slow-running large engines that tend to be more efficient, also produce more NO_x. The limits are depicted in Fig. 14.3.

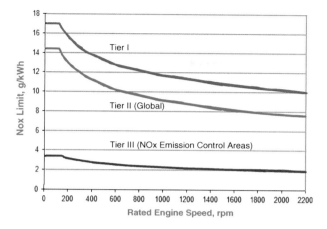

Fig. 14.3 MARPOL Annex VI NO_x emission limits

Tier I applies to the operation of an engine installed on a ship constructed on or after 1 January 2000 but prior to 1 January 2011. This was a weak initial starting point for these regulations and achieves little reduction in overall NO_x emissions, as most modern engines would comply in any event.

Tier II applies to the operation of an engine installed on a ship constructed on or after 1 January 2011. Tier II represents a 16–22 % reduction in NO_x emissions relative to Tier I.

Tier III applies to the operation of an engine installed on a ship constructed on or after 1 January 2016 but only when the vessel is operating within a NO_x Emission Control Area (NECA). Tier III represents an 80 % reduction in NO_x emissions relative to Tier I.

It is apparent that the only NECAs that may be in force in 2016 will be the North American ECA (out to 200 nm around the coasts of the USA, including Hawaii, and Canada, coming into force in August 2012) and an ECA around Puerto Rico which will come into force in 2015. There are also strong moves from HELCOM (Helsinki Commission) countries to get the Baltic Sea which is already a SECA, designated as a NECA as well.

Carbon Dioxide (CO_2) and Greenhouse Gases (GHG)

Through its deliberations within the Marine Environment Protection Committee (MEPC), the IMO has developed standards for ships' operational efficiency and design with the object of further reducing emissions of GHG from international shipping, including CO_2.

In May 2000, the organisation banned the use of perfluorocarbons (PFCs) onboard ships. The 1997 MARPOL Conference adopted Resolution 8 on CO_2 from ships, inviting the IMO:

1. To co-operate with UNFCCC in the exchange of information on the GHG issue;
2. To undertake a study of GHG emissions from ships; and
3. Through the MEPC, to consider feasible GHG emissions reduction strategies.

Following this resolution, the IMO produced a comprehensive study on GHG emissions from ships in 2000 and, after further debate and studies, it was agreed at MEPC 55 in 2006 that the threat from global warming was too serious to be ignored and that the shipping industry must take action. Thus Resolution A.963(23) called for measures to limit or reduce the emissions from international shipping.

In 2009 the IMO GHG study was updated by a second study and this is now widely accepted as the industry benchmark. The study concluded that in 2007 international shipping emitted 870 million tonnes of CO_2, or about 2.7 % of global CO_2 emissions; including domestic shipping and fishing, these figures rise to 1,046 million tonnes, equating to 3.3 % of the global total. Furthermore, mid-range estimates suggest that these emissions will grow by between 150 % and 250 % by 2050 as a result of the predicted growth in shipping. Though 3.3 % sounds small, particularly as shipping carries over 90 % of world trade and is by far the most energy-efficient means of transportation, when compared to emissions from countries, shipping ranks fifth in the world, producing more CO_2 than either Germany or Japan.

The Conference of the Parties (COP) of the United Nations Framework Convention on Climate Change (UNFCCC) has not mentioned shipping in its deliberations so far which may prompt regional action unless the political impasse at IMO is somehow broken.

The 2009 IMO GHG study suggests that, by the application of known technology and practices, shipping could be 25–75 % more energy-efficient, depending upon the ship type and degree of compromise. The challenge therefore is to find the most appropriate policy levers to accelerate new technology and innovation to deliver improvements in energy efficiency. The overall magnitude of CO_2 emissions from a growing shipping industry means that further industry initiatives and international policy action are both inevitable and desirable. The study identified five types of measures that might be implemented to reduce GHG emissions, and most if not all schemes that have subsequently been put forward by states and industry associations are essentially variants and/or amalgams of these five.

1. **Energy Efficiency Design Index (EEDI).** This has been formulated by the MEPC as a measure of the CO_2 emission performance of ships. The ship EEDI is calculated on the characteristics of the vessel at build and incorporates parameters including ship capacity, engine power and fuel consumption.
2. **Ship Energy Efficiency Management Plan (SEEMP).** The purpose of a SEEMP is to establish a mechanism for a company and/or ship to improve the energy efficiency of a ship's operation. This covers a range of operational methods to reduce ship GHG emissions, including slow steaming, virtual

arrivals, weather routing, hull maintenance and optimised ship handling. The plan works through a cycle of four steps; planning, implementation, monitoring and self evaluation.

3. **Energy Efficiency Operational Indicator (EEOI).** Use of the EEOI provides an example of a transparent and recognised approach for the assessment of the GHG efficiency with respect to CO_2 emissions. Simply, it is an expression of efficiency in the form of CO_2 emitted per unit of transport work.

4. **Emissions Trading Scheme (ETS).** An ETS is a cap-and-trade mechanism which establishes cap on net CO_2 emissions and allows market forces of supply and demand to drive the allocation of emission rights so as to achieve reductions in the most cost-effective manner. The aim of any ETS for shipping is to reduce the industry's contribution to atmospheric CO_2 levels by accelerating the cost-effective delivery of improvements in the energy efficiency of individual ship operators.

5. **International Contribution Fund through a Levy.** The fund would collect revenues as a fixed surcharge per tonne of bunker fuels. The primary goal of such a system would be to reinforce incentives for companies to develop and adopt fuel-saving technologies which lead to a reduction of GHG emissions from ships.

Progress within the IMO has been painfully slow. The political divide in the MEPC between developed and developing countries has, at times, been almost unbridgeable and prevented acceptance in 2010 of mandatory implementation of the energy efficiency measures, thus reflecting divisions in the wider UN debates. This has held back progress on environmental and climate change regulation in shipping. At the heart of the dispute is the IMO's fair treatment principle which is at odds with the UNFCCC principle of "common but differentiated responsibilities" (CBDR). Specifically, developing countries have argued that measures could only be mandated in developed countries and left voluntary in developing countries. Such an approach would, of course, lead to a large market distortion.

Frustration is felt by many outside shipping at this lack of progress within the industry to address one of the key issues of our generation. The EU has threatened to go its own way and other countries or regional groupings may do the same. This would be the worst possible outcome for international shipping, skewing world trade and probably leading to large-scale re-flagging and carbon leakage.

After considerable debate, certain control measures relating to CO_2 emissions were agreed at the 62nd session of MEPC held in July 2011. Eventually, these will appear as amendments to Annex VI referred to as the GHG amendments. Among other things, the amendments will make it mandatory for new ships to adhere to the Energy Efficiency Design Index (EEDI) and the Energy Efficiency Operation Index (EEOI) and have a Ship Energy Efficiency Management Plan (SEEMP) which also applies to existing ships. The objective is to adopt best practices for fuel efficiency in relation to ship operations. At MEPC 62 criteria for EEDI and EEOI were adopted which are intended to be mandatory. However, the EEDI formula has proven to be problematic in terms of its application to larger vessels such as VLCCs and Ro–Ro ships because the speed factor has not been taken into account in the current formula. At present, therefore, it will apply only on a voluntary basis to "suitable" ships pending revision of the formula.

The EEDI is non-prescriptive; it is a performance-based mechanism which allows industry to choose an appropriate technology consistent with a specific ship design so as to use the most cost-efficient solution to ensure compliance with the regulations. The SEEMP is a parallel mechanism which enables shipowners and operators to enhance the energy efficiency of a ship. Furthermore, consideration is being given to introduce market-based measures (MBM) to reduce GHG emissions from ships. The proposals being reviewed are recognised to have implications for developing countries in terms of adaptation and capacity building, which, among other issues are on the table for discussion. An expert Group has been established for evaluating proposals submitted by various countries. It is recognised that further in-depth examination of the impact of MBM on developing countries will be necessary. The MBM proposals being reviewed range from the imposition of a levy on CO_2 emissions from ships operating internationally through emission trading systems to schemes based on actual efficiency in terms of efficiency and operation, namely, by application of the EEDI, EEOI and SEEMP mechanisms. Attempts to regulate CO_2 emissions from ships have progressed, no doubt, but the exercise is still incomplete.

It was agreed that the amendments would include a new Chapter IV to Annex VI of MARPOL on energy efficiency for ships to make mandatory the EEDI for new ships and the SEEMP for all ships. The regulations apply to all ships of 400 gross tonnes and above and entered into force on 1 January 2013. However, an Administration may waive this requirement for a period—the waiver may only apply to ships for which the building contract is placed no later than 4 years after the entry into force date of Chapter IV; the keel of which is laid no later than 4 years and 6 months after entry into force; delivery is no later than 6 years and 6 months after the entry into force; or, in the cases of a major conversion, than 4 years after the entry into force date.

The new chapter also includes a regulation on promoting technical co-operation and transfer of technology relating to the improvement of energy efficiency of ships. Administrations, through the IMO, will be obliged to respond to states requesting technical assistance. This, of course, is subject to national laws. There remains much work to be done in terms of developing guidelines for methods of calculating EEDI for new ships, the development of SEEMP, survey and certification of SEEMP and determining minimum propulsion power and speed to ensure safe manoeuvring in adverse weather. There is also the need to include those ship types not already within the EEDI guidelines. There is also no doubt that the proposed chapter is weak, particularly as—given the current commercial pressures (fuel prices etc.)—it is likely that many of the proposed efficiency measures will be incorporated into newbuilds as a matter of course. But that should not diminish the political importance of this first major step towards a global solution for emissions from shipping.

The European Commission has made it clear for some time that it wishes shipping to be included in its carbon targets for the EU. While its public position is that it would prefer a global solution through the IMO, there can be little doubt that it will impose a regional solution if it feels the IMO is not delivering enough sufficiently quickly. The EU Transport White Paper published in 2011 states that:

> In maritime, the need for a global level-playing field is equally pronounced. The EU should strive – in cooperation with IMO and other international organisations – for the universal application and enforcement of high standards of safety, security, environmental protection and working conditions, and for eliminating piracy. The environmental record of shipping can and must be improved by both technology and better fuels and operations: overall, the EU CO_2 emissions from maritime transport should be cut by 40% (if feasible, 50%) by 2050 compared to 2005 levels.

Given that the EEDI will, at best, achieve a saving of about 30 %, it remains a risk that the EU will try to incorporate shipping into a more rigorous European regime, possibly an ETS in line with what is in place already for other European industries. As a first step, the EU intends to introduce a mandatory system of "monitoring, reporting and verifying" (MRV) carbon emissions for all ships operating in European waters.

Though the IMO has achieved at least limited success in getting the EEDI adopted in 2011, this can only be a first step. Efficiency and operational measures alone will only reduce carbon emissions by about 30 % at most. To achieve more will almost certainly require some form of economic instrument—Market Based Measure (MBM), as outlined under policy measures earlier in this Section—in order to raise funds both to further incentivise the industry and for offsetting. Furthermore, if and when the UN High Level Advisory Group on Climate Change Financing introduces a Green Fund and if shipping has to contribute as expected, then this will also require an MBM to raise the required amount. Given the political nature of the GHG debate during recent years within the MEPC, the endeavour to gain consensus to adopt an MBM will ensure that future MEPCs will remain difficult for years to come.

Particulate Matter

Particulate matter mainly refers to what is generally known as black carbon, or soot, which is fine carbon particles emitted from engines. There is increasing environmental concern that black carbon could be having a disproportionately high impact on global warming. The black carbon particles absorb the radiation from the sun and thus while airborne can warm the atmosphere and, if they settle on snow and ice, may increase the speed of melting. Black carbon only remains in the atmosphere for a matter of days or weeks before falling to earth and thus, if reduced, will have a fast impact on global warming. The majority of industries are now being regulated but, while it has been a subject of debate in the IMO since MEPC 58, there is little progress for shipping.

The majority of black carbon is originating from developing countries and this is leading to another impasse within the IMO between developed and developing countries. There was agreement during MEPC 62 (2011) for a sub-committee to develop a definition for black carbon from shipping, consider methods of measuring black carbon and investigate appropriate control methods to reduce black carbon from shipping in the Arctic. This will therefore effectively delay any progress by 2–3 years, achieve little and only address the impact of Arctic shipping whilst it is recognised that the black carbon deposited on Arctic ice can originate from as far away as south of the Equator.

Volatile Organic Compounds (VOCs)

VOCs are organic chemicals that have a high vapour pressure at ordinary, room-temperature conditions. They can be dangerous to both the environment and to human health. Measures to limit VOC emissions from chemical and oil tankers are set out in Regulation 15 of MARPOL Annex VI. Tankers carrying crude are obliged to carry a management plan for VOCs which must be approved by each Administration. However, tankers are only required to use a vapour collection system to return VOCs to shore when undertaking cargo operations in ports that have notified the IMO at least 3 years beforehand. To date no ports have notified the IMO. However, the US Coast Guard Code of Federal Regulations requires that a vapour recovery system be installed, though only a few US ports actually use it. At least one port in Norway also requires its use.

A vapour recovery system is installed in most tankers at build and this has been the case for at least the last 10 years. Few tankers now do not have a vapour recovery system except perhaps those that were constructed with a view that they would never trade in the US.

Chapter 15
The Private Law of Ship-Source Pollution

Introduction

The private law of marine pollution primarily concerns liability for damage caused by pollution and the remedies available to the victim. Indeed, the principal remedy is damages or compensation although a form of remedy in kind is available indirectly as we shall see later in the discussion. In common law legal jargon the term "damages" is not the plural of "damage", and its meaning is the equivalent of "compensation" in ordinary speech. In the continental civil law system and also in international conventions dealing with pollution damage, "compensation" is the term used which makes comprehension simple and easy. As such, in this discussion we are in the realm of liability and compensation for pollution damage which are the two components of the private law of marine pollution.

In conceptual terms, liability is qualitative whereas compensation is quantitative. Liability arises in law when the quality of conduct or standard of behaviour of a person is legally repugnant and unacceptable by reason of it causing damage or injury to another. Damages or compensation, in contrast to liability, is a civil remedy that is quantitative in character. It is the qualitative attribute of liability that dictates the quantum of damages that the wrong-doer must pay according to the law to the person on whom damage, loss, harm or injury has been inflicted. In terms of the private law of pollution, the former is the polluter and the latter is the pollution victim.

In this discussion both these components will be addressed critically. First, the notion of liability will be examined and then the corresponding regime of compensation will be discussed. The private law aspect of ship-source pollution focuses on accidental spills although in theory the principles may apply to pollution damage resulting from operational discharges or deliberate dumping of wastes at sea. It is noteworthy at this juncture that operational discharges are primarily associated with the regulatory aspects of the law of ship-source pollution. It is also to be noted in the present context that the principles of liability and compensation relating to ship-source pollution apply equally to damage caused by accidental oil spills, and also by chemicals and other noxious substances. However, the discussion here will focus primarily on oil spills.

Liability Issues

Marine pollution damage is a maritime tort and liability for it falls within that category. A tort is best defined as a civil wrong as distinguished from a wrong to which penal consequences attach. A ship being maritime property, pollution damage caused by it is a maritime tort (according to *Sir Henry Constable's Case,* i.e., *Constable* v. *Gramble* (1601), 5 Co. Rep. 106, maritime property consists of ship, cargo and freight and the components of ship and cargo, namely, flotsam, jetsam, lagan, derelict and wreck). The damage so caused may be to the marine environment itself or to property that is not maritime in character. Furthermore, aside from damage to physical property that is tangible, the pollution may result in intangible losses as well.

In Fig. 15.1 depicted above, the liability side consists of two elements, namely, the nature of the claim and the basis for liability. The legal connotation of liability must be fully appreciated to understand the two elements. In plain English as well as in law, liability may be succinctly defined as legal responsibility. A person is liable if his or her conduct or behavior is contrary to that which is legally acceptable and another person suffers loss, harm or damage as a result. Not all kinds of conduct relating to some form of responsibility give rise to legal consequences; for example, a responsibility may be moral or ethical but not necessarily legal. In contrast, breach of a legally enforceable obligation does result in liability. In other words, failure of legal responsibility gives rise to liability. Another important point is that the word "responsibility" has different linguistic connotations. When used in French or Spanish, its meaning is identical to that of "liability" in the English language and at English common law. The interplay between these two words is exemplified in Article 235 of UNCLOS. Under the title of "responsibility and liability", this provision addresses damage to the marine environment caused by pollution albeit in the context of public international law.

Nature of the Claim

The characterization of a pollution damage claim depends on the applicable legal system and the jurisdiction in which the claim is pursued. An action for pollution damage may be framed in tort under the common law. In civil law jurisdictions a similar cause of action may lie in delict or other equivalent of tort under the relevant provisions of the national Civil Code. This would be the case if only a national system of law were to apply. However, in respect of ship-source pollution, the regime of liability and compensation is largely governed by international

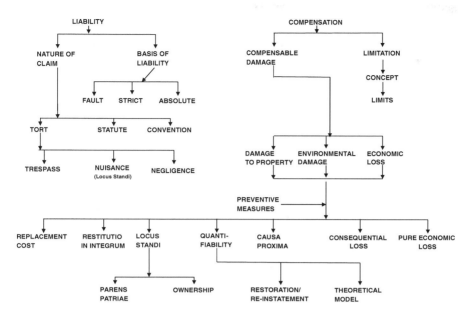

Fig. 15.1 Liability and compensation flow chart

conventions to which most maritime coastal states are parties. In dualistic states which consist of common law jurisdictions in the main except the United States, conventions are given effect through statute. By contrast, in monistic states a convention ratified or acceded to, applies without the need to enact express legislation if the convention is self-executing or directly applicable. Thus globally, there are three basic sources from which the nature of the claim can be derived, namely, unwritten domestic common law, statute law giving effect to relevant conventions and conventions operating directly without corresponding legislation.

In common law jurisdictions tort law is not statute based unlike civil law jurisdictions where the law of delict is to be found in the Civil Code. Thus in common law countries that are not parties to the relevant conventions, the legal regime would ordinarily be based on case law jurisprudence unless there is legislation independent of convention law. Such is the case with the United States which is a singular common law jurisdiction, not a party to any liability and compensation conventions respecting oil but has its own domestic legislation, the Oil Pollution Act, 1990 (OPA 90). It is a comprehensive statute which is the principal source of the applicable law in combination with case law reflecting relevant tort law principles and construing the statute. From a practical perspective it is recognized that national legislation though it be, the impact of this Act is universal because the United States is among the largest oil trading countries in the world. Thus, with respect to the law of liability and compensation for oil pollution damage, a ship plying the world's oceans encounters three different regimes, namely, the convention regime, the non-convention regime, and OPA 90.

In this chapter, the focus is on the current international convention regime relating to liability and compensation for oil pollution at sea. However, there are still several states that do not subscribe to these conventions. Therefore, it is necessary to gain some appreciation of at least the basic principles of the non-convention regime that apply in the common law jurisdictions other than the United States. Before embarking on that discussion, however, the basis of liability in tort must be understood.

Basis of Liability

In private law, liability is based on the premise of fault. Without fault or culpability, as it is understood in the civil law tradition, there is no liability. Thus, it is quality of conduct that determines liability; in other words, conduct must be such that it is reprehensible and repugnant in the eyes of the law. As vile or socially unacceptable as the defendant's conduct might be, unless he is found to be at fault or is culpable he cannot be liable at law. In the absence of fault on the part of the defendant, the plaintiff has no legal recourse and no remedy is available to him. This is the general rule that applies across the board in private law regardless of whether the matter in dispute is one of contract, tort, property or any other area of law.

However, marine pollution is one subject matter in relation to which fault or *culpa* based liability is neither appropriate nor practical. The law and policy justification for not requiring fault in the establishment of liability is the ultra-hazardous or dangerous nature of the activity which in the present context is carriage by sea of large quantities of pollutants. An activity is ultra-hazardous if there is risk of harm that cannot be eliminated even if utmost care is exercised. The rule, now well established in the realm of pollution liability, may thus be expressed in terms of the potentially unpreventable miscarriage of the activity leading to harm even if utmost care is taken to prevent it, the burden of proving which should not be put on the victim. It is to be noted that it is the hazardous or dangerous effect of the activity that is material, not the dangers associated with its conduct which is the concern of regulatory law. Ways of ameliorating the risks involved in the carrying out of the activity, such as prescribing design criteria for tankers, are addressed through regulatory law. The object of such a regime providing for appropriate preventive measures is to ensure as best as possible that no casualty occurs, and further, if it does, then to ensure that damage is contained or mitigated.

It is stated above that private law, specifically tort law in the present context, seeks to provide a remedy to a victim of wrong. Where a person wronged by the act or omission of another suffers loss, damage or injury, tort law provides a remedy in apprehension of such eventuality. Where the act or omission of the wrong-doer, referred to in legal jargon as the tortfeasor, is extraordinarily damaging, the basis of liability deviates from the norm requiring the plaintiff claimant to prove fault on the part of the defendant tortfeasor. It is known as strict or no-fault liability. In strict liability, which generally prevails in the realm of pollution liability, certain defences such as act of God, or *force majeure,* if successfully pleaded, can exoner-ate the defendant polluter. In the private law of marine pollution, the notion of strict liability affords the polluter limited defences for cases where the causative factor was demonstrably beyond his control. If the nature and degree of the damage so warrants, no defence may be allowed. In such case, liability is characterized as absolute. In the context of the application of no-fault liability in the domain of international marine environmental law, it has been stated that strict liability "... differs from absolute liability only in the greater range of exculpatory factors which may negative responsibility". (P.W. Birnie and A.E. Boyle, International Law and the Environment, Oxford: Clarendon Press, 1992)

In interstate litigation under the rubric of public international law, although the cases are of relatively recent vintage, the basis for pollution liability is strict. The classic case in this field is the *Trail Smelter Arbitration* (1941) III *RIAA* 1905 which was an air pollution case. Nuclear damage, however, attracts absolute liability although decided cases are virtually absent. In the private law domain, as far as international conventions are concerned, examples of strict liability regimes are the Civil Liability Convention, 1992 and the Hazardous and Noxious Substances Convention, 1996. But notably, in the Civil Liability for Maritime Carriage of Nuclear Material Convention, 1971, the regime is one of absolute liability. In terms of national legal regimes, Canadian marine pollution legislation provides for strict and absolute liability regimes for different circumstances of pollution damage based on the vulnerability of the environment in question. Under Part XXI of the Canada Shipping Act strict liability applies generally to cases of marine pollution damage in waters south of 60° north latitude, but under the Arctic Waters Pollution Prevention Act, 1970, a regime of absolute liability prevails in ice-covered waters north of the sixtieth parallel where the waters are considered to be more ecologically fragile.

It is notable that under international convention law, strict liability has evolved as the basis of liability for ship-source pollution damage, but in national common law jurisdictions where convention regimes do not apply because of the state being a non-party, liability is based on fault in compliance with the established norm.

Application of Tort Law Independent of Conventions

The Common Law Approach

While international conventions largely govern and dominate the field of liability and compensation for marine pollution damage, the value and significance of the law outside the perimeters of the conventions are no less important simply because there are still numerous states that are not parties to the conventions. In common law jurisdictions where conventions do not apply, relevant areas of the law of torts and the associated legal principles govern marine pollution liability. Pollution as a tort can be characterized as unjustifiable interference with the possession and enjoyment of property. In the case of ship-source pollution, the damage caused is associated with maritime property since a ship is maritime property at law. The relevant torts that are likely to apply are trespass, public and private nuisance, and negligence. The first two have limited application for reasons that will unfold as the discussion proceeds.

Trespass and Nuisance

Trespass as a tort is described as intentional and unjustifiable interference with the plaintiff's right to enjoy property. It is actionable *per se*, which means that the plaintiff need not prove damage but only that the act of trespass was committed. There is a requirement for directness, i.e., the plaintiff must show that the polluter or polluting agent *directly* caused the pollution which damaged the plaintiff's property. Damage to vessels, fishing boats, nets, or other property situated at sea or on land, or fixtures on land bordering the polluted waters caused by a ship-source spill are considered marine pollution damage. If oil as the polluting agent emanating from a ship becomes waterborne and drifts into contact with the property, the pollution damage would be indirect or consequential. By contrast, damage caused by the spilled oil to the body of water itself would be direct damage. A cause of action in trespass would arise if the body of water was somebody's property. Where oil pouring out of a leaking vessel falls directly on to the property without being carried afloat, the damage would be direct and would qualify as trespass.

Indirect damage would not be properly characterized as cases of trespass but rather "trespass on the case" or "action on the case" which in previous times, were terms used to denote what is today known as the tort of nuisance. Liability in trespass is clearly fault-based; and while trespass is actionable *per se*, the plaintiff still carries the burden of proving that the defendant polluter was at fault.

Nuisance as a tort can be public or private. Public nuisance is normally a regulatory offence which attracts a penal sanction but it can also be a tort if it affects a sufficient number of individuals constituting the public. Thus it can be the basis for class actions. If an individual can show that he suffered damage more than others within the relevant public, he can have a valid cause of action in public nuisance and can obtain damages. Private nuisance is unjustifiable interference with the use and enjoyment of land and can apply to cases of ship-source pollution damage. In nuisance, whether public or private, directness is not a required ingredient but the plaintiff victim must prove reasonable foreseeability on the part of the polluter defendant.

Negligence

The tort of negligence may also be applicable to cases of marine pollution damage. Where the cause of action is framed in negligence, liability is fault based. To succeed in a negligence action, the plaintiff must prove that the defendant owed him a duty of care; that the defendant was in breach of the duty, and that the plaintiff suffered damage that was reasonably foreseeable by the defendant and was proximately caused by such breach. These are the necessary ingredients of the tort of negligence.

The concept of duty of care is a legal principle that was established by Lord Atkin in his decision in the House of Lords in the classic case of *Donaghue v. Stevenson* [1932], A.C. 562. Prior to this case, the common law seemed only to recognize a contractual relationship or a fiduciary nexus between the parties as grounds for liability for a civil wrong.

Liability for negligence is clearly fault-based. In ship-source pollution cases, the plaintiff claimant must prove on a balance of probabilities that it was the fault of the defendant that was the proximate cause of the pollution damage suffered. In certain instances, the burden to prove negligence may be alleviated if the plaintiff successfully invokes the doctrine of *res ipsa loquitor* meaning literally, "the thing speaks for itself"; in other words, the facts are so clear that there is no need to prove anything.

The Evolution and Application of Convention Law

The Torrey Canyon *Disaster*

In March 1967, the Liberian tanker *Torrey Canyon* ran aground on Seven Stones Reef off the coast of southwest England in waters that were then part of the high seas. The vessel was fully loaded with a cargo of 119,328 tons of Kuwaiti crude oil, some 80,000 tons of which spilled into the sea. The vessel owned by Barracuda Tanker Corporation, was bareboat chartered to Union Oil Company of California, U.S.A., which operated out of Bermuda. The master and crew were of Italian nationality.

The incident was environmentally catastrophic, the magnitude of the spill being unprecedented. Its global impact was shocking both for the British Government as well as the international maritime community. Both were unprepared and rendered temporarily helpless. The British Government eventually caused the wrecked vessel to be towed out to sea, bombed it to destruction and sunk it in the high seas. The legal and environmental implications were far-reaching but the incident had a catalytic effect by spawning the international legal regimes of public and private law in terms of pollution from mega spills of which this was the first.

IMCO, as it then was, quickly went into action. A diplomatic conference was convened in Brussels out of which emerged the Intervention and Civil Liability Conventions of 1969. A Legal Committee was established to supplement the predominantly technical orientation of IMO, and "cleaner seas" became entrenched as the second prong of its mandate. The legal dimension took shape out of necessity albeit in a reactive rather than a proactive way. The law making role of the Organization which was hitherto concerned primarily with technical and regulatory matters, assumed a new function, i.e., the development of a private law regime governing civil liability pertaining to damage from oil spills.

The Civil Liability Convention

Within 2 years following the *Torrey Canyon* disaster, the international maritime community assembled in Brussels under the auspices of IMCO to establish an international regime for marine pollution casualties. The deliberations of the diplomatic conference eventually bore fruit in the form of the two multilateral treaty instruments mentioned above. It was apparent that the *Torrey Canyon* oil spill provided the impetus for decisive global action in relation to preemptive and preventive measures by coastal states as well as development of a liability and compensation regime for pollution damage.

The object and purpose of the Civil Liability Convention (CLC) was primarily to establish a uniform liability and compensation regime for victims of ship-source oil pollution damage resulting from oil spills. It has been suggested, however, that claims for pollution damage caused by operational discharges are not precluded from the application of the CLC of 1969 as well as its successor the CLC of 1992. But operational discharges, except tank washings, do not appear to fall within the definitional ambit of oil in the CLC which is limited to oil carried as cargo or in the bunkers of a tanker. In practical terms, operational discharges are hardly amenable to private law claims for loss or damage suffered because the source of the discharge cannot be easily identified and linked with the area of contamination. This may be possible only in instances where a polluting vessel is on a continuous, regular short sea run over an extended time period. If the polluted area can be precisely identified and the damage quantified, it may be possible to advance a claim for compensation under CLC but only in respect of pollution from tank washings of a laden tanker.

Operational discharges admittedly cause serious harm to the health of the oceans regardless of compensability. Indeed, the marine environment itself is the victim. It is evident that pollution from operational discharges is more harmful to the marine environment than oil spills including mega disasters. One reason is that the detrimental effects of operational discharges are prolonged. Regulatory preventive measures designed to control operational discharges are more appropriate for dealing with this menace. MARPOL is therefore the proper vehicle.

Salient Features of CLC 1969

Liability and its attendant remedy in the form of compensation revolve around three issues; namely, the basis of liability, who should be liable, and whether liability should be limited, and if so, what should be the limits. At the Brussels diplomatic conference the issue of basis for liability engendered protracted debate. Unsurprisingly, traditionalists supported fault based liability. Those of common law persuasion naturally looked to the familiar civil liability regime of torts and its principles entrenched in the associated case law. Under strict liability the plaintiff need only prove damage. Once damage is established, the defendant is liable regardless of fault. The claimant's burden of proof is obviously less onerous. The conference delegates ultimately chose strict liability subject to certain prescribed defences. This is a hallmark of the CLC.

Who should be liable emerged at first as a contentious issue at the diplomatic conference. Traditionally in private maritime law, where the instrument of damage is the ship, or the tortious act is committed by the master or crew, the shipowner or operator is liable, if at the material time navigational control of the ship was in the hands of the master and crew. In juxtaposition to that notion is the so-called "polluter pays" principle which immediately raises the question of who, at law, is the polluter. Under the traditional view, the owner or operator being vicariously in possession of the pollutant would be considered the polluter; alternatively, the owner of the pollutant cargo could be held to be the polluter, the cargo being the *causa proxima* of the damage. In the case of traditional non-pollutant cargoes, the extant law and practice posed no problem because those cargoes were no threat to the marine environment. But with oil tankers carrying huge amounts of oil, a universal perception of serious threat to the marine environment became real. The vulnerability of the oceans to pollution damage increased rapidly with supertankers and very large and ultra large crude carriers (VLCCs and ULCCs) plying the oceans. Through the 1971 Fund Convention, cargo owner responsibility was eventually established.

The question of limitation was the last of the three major issues. The concept of limitation of liability evolved historically as a privilege accorded to shipowners, without whom, seaborne commercial trade, the economic lifeline of every community, could be seriously impeded. Limitation, as the illustrious Lord Denning stated in *The Bramley Moore* [1963] 2 Lloyd's Rep. 429, CA. 29, is more a matter of public policy than of law. In the past, therefore, the onus was cast on the defendant invoking limitation to show that in the given circumstances he was entitled to it. It is arguable that limitation of liability in the current world economic climate is an outmoded concept; an anachronism that is better placed in maritime history than in practice. But it has remained a distinctive feature of shipping; and indeed under the "conduct barring limitation" test in current convention regimes, the position of the shipowner has been strengthened. The onus is now on the plaintiff claimant to show that the defendant shipowner is not entitled to limit liability. The traditional privilege has been converted to a right.

Where liability is limited, the liable shipowner is not obliged to pay the whole amount of the damages but only a stipulated amount calculated on the basis of the ship's tonnage. The plaintiff must bear the balance of his loss. It was originally thought that a shipowner should not be liable for any amount in excess of the value of his ship. The rationale for tonnage-based limitation rests on the now disputable premise that a ship's value is directly proportional to its size. Nevertheless, tonnage remains the basis for determination of limits. As a point of clarification, limitation, it is to be noted, is not in respect of liability which is qualitative, but in respect of the quantum of damages which is quantitative. The expression "limitation of liability" is thus arguably a misnomer.

At the diplomatic conference the question was raised as to whether the limits for pollution liability should be the same as those in the prevailing international regime of global limitation or should those limits be raised through a new regime given the sensitivity of environmental concerns aggravated by the *Torrey Canyon* disaster. Under the International Convention on Limitation of Liability for Owners of Sea-Going Ships, 1957, then applicable in respect of all maritime claims, the limit was 1,000 poincare (gold) francs per ton of the ship's limitation tonnage. In terms of 1969 U.S. dollars, this was approximately equivalent to USD 67 per ton of limitation tonnage of the ship which was considered to be woefully inadequate by some delegations. The near deadlock situation was eventually broken through a compromise and the Civil Liability Convention, 1969 was adopted with its own set of limitation figures which were considerably higher than those of the 1957 global limitation convention.

The three principal issues discussed above were resolved for the time being with the shipowner alone being liable within a strict liability regime with newly established limits. The regime was modified in 1971 through the adoption of the Fund Convention, a complementary companion regime under which cargo owners were made indirectly responsible for pollution damage through the creation of a fund by levies exacted on importers of oil. The limitation amount was set at 2,000 poincare francs per ton of limitation tonnage (net tonnage calculated as per the International Tonnage Convention, 1969) of the vessel with a maximum set at 210 million poincare francs per incident, which was equivalent to USD 134 per ton and USD 14 million, respectively.

Among its other features, the CLC of 1969 provides for all claims to be channeled through the shipowner who is defined as the registered owner of the vessel at the time of the pollution incident. In practice, the ship's third party liability insurer, usually the P & I Club, handles the claims. Every vessel carrying over 2,000 tons of cargo oil in bulk must provide evidence of financial responsibility. Every tanker must carry a certificate attesting to compliance with this requirement. A claimant can have direct access to the insurer. A potentially liable shipowner may invoke limitation by constituting a fund in the forum court in the amount of the applicable limit which then stands as security against claims.

To successfully invoke limitation, the shipowner must show that there was no actual fault or privity on his part. The Convention is applicable to any pollution incident occurring within the territorial sea (now of 12 nautical miles breadth under

UNCLOS) of a state party regardless of whether or not the flag state of the polluting ship is a party to the convention. Thus the convention is geographical in its application in relation to a state party and is not a typical flag state convention such as MARPOL which applies to every ship of the flag state that is a party regardless of the ship's location. The CLC of 1969 applies only to persistent oil carried in bulk as cargo or in the bunkers of a laden tanker. Pollution from bunker oil of a non-tanker is not covered.

Salient Features of the Fund Convention, 1971

The object of the International Convention on the Establishment of an International Fund for Compensation for Oil Pollution Damage, 1971 (Fund Convention), through the establishment of the International Oil Pollution Compensation (IOPC) Fund is to provide additional compensation to victims of oil pollution damage beyond the CLC limits if the compensation under CLC is inadequate or unavailable. Inadequacy of compensation can arise in three circumstances set out in Article 4 (1) of the Fund Convention. These are—(1) where there is no liability under CLC, by reason of successful invocation of an Article III defence; (2) where the shipowner is insolvent or otherwise incapable of paying compensation under CLC; (3) where the quantum of CLC compensation exceeds the shipowner's limitation under CLC. Compensation under the above circumstances is subject to the "exoneration" provided in Article 4(3).

The CLC and Fund Convention together provide an integrated two-tier scheme of compensation (a third tier has been added; see below) that is functional in scope and is so designed that to be a party to the Fund Convention a state must also be a party to CLC. But the reverse is possible. In such cases, however, securing full recompense by all pollution victims may be limited considerably. The contribution of oil cargo interests is not liability in a traditional sense but can be characterized as a kind of functional responsibility in the nature of an ethical or moral obligation in a sociological context.

The IOPC Fund is an entity with legal personality established under the Fund Convention as an intergovernmental organization to administer the regime. Through this mechanism the non-legal notion of responsibility has been transformed into a legal obligation. The IOPC Fund is the *alter ego* of the cargo interests who, it was agreed, should bear some responsibility for damage from oil spills. Since it can be sued, the Fund can be liable for paying compensation under the Fund Convention just like any other litigant even though it is not the polluter *per se*. In the CLC/Fund scheme, it is apparent that the purity of the "polluter pays" principle is substantially modified through a functional approach to the issue of liability and compensation for oil pollution damage.

The Fund consists of an Assembly, an Executive Committee and a Secretariat and is physically located in London. Representatives of all state parties to the Fund Convention are entitled to be members of the Assembly. The Executive Committee comprises representatives of one third of the member states who are elected by the Assembly. The principal task of the Executive Committee is to consider and approve the settlement of major claims made against the Fund. The Secretariat has a Director as its head and is staffed by a cadre of professionals including lawyers, economists and technical personnel with expertise and experience in matters of marine pollution. The Fund is financed through the exaction of an annual levy imposed on importers in state parties to the Fund Convention of crude oil and heavy fuel oil transported by sea.

Changes to CLC 1969 and Fund 1971

An important change effectuated through protocols to both the conventions in 1976 was a change in the unit of the limitation amounts from poincare gold to the "unit of account" or "monetary unit" which is the special drawing right (SDR) defined by the International Monetary Fund (IMF). The need for this change was triggered by the fluctuation and instability in the price of gold to which the poincare franc was pegged. The SDR is a stable unit the value of which is pegged to a basket of major currencies by the IMF. As a result of the 1976 Protocols, the limitation amount under the CLC was 133 SDR per limitation ton up to a maximum of 14 million SDR

The *Amoco Cadiz* disaster which occurred off the coast of Brittany in March, 1978, sparked renewed concerns regarding pollution damage from mammoth oil spills. The extent of damage caused by the incident and the attendant claims in monetary terms far exceeded those relating to the *Torrey Canyon*. Up to that point in time the *Amoco Cadiz* oil spill was the worst of its kind. The country that suffered the most was France and the French Government therefore sought to reopen the issue of adequacy of compensation under the CLC/Fund convention package. As well, the oil and tanker industry feared that states would move in the direction of unilateral liability and compensation regimes for pollution damage if immediate action was not taken by the international community through IMCO.

A diplomatic conference was eventually convened and protocols to the two conventions adopted in 1984. The Protocols were so designed that the scheme consisting of a tiered system of compensation with significantly raised aggregate amounts of compensation could only work meaningfully if the world's largest importers of oil would join the conventions. Unfortunately, the United States, the world's largest oil importer was a not a party to CLC or the Fund Convention, and Japan, the second largest importer did not accept the Protocols.

The CLC and Fund Convention of 1992

Adoption and Entry into Force

It took another 8 years before a significant revision of the conventions particularly the raising of the limits could be achieved. Meanwhile, the *Exxon Valdez* disaster occurred in Prudhoe Bay, Alaska in 1989. The damage and ensuing claims were far in excess of those associated with the *Torrey Canyon* and *Amoco Cadiz* incidents. The incident provided the impetus for the enactment of the United States Oil Pollution Act, 1990, which spelt the end of any possibility of the United States ever joining the international liability and compensation regime. Despite persuasive efforts by the IMO, the United States refused to alter its unilateral stance.

The international community under the auspices of IMO went ahead and adopted the 1992 Protocols to the CLC and the Fund Convention. Much of the scheme of the failed 1984 Protocols was maintained with some further revisions and updating. The totality of the revision resulted in virtually two new conventions and provision was made for the denunciation of the old conventions by parties once the requisite number of states accepted the new conventions which were called CLC 1992 and Fund Convention 1992.

Salient Features of the New Regime

The scheme as a whole is sound and rational both legally and functionally. Among the substantive provisions, the geographical scope of application has been increased to 200 nautical miles, i.e., up to the outer limit of the exclusive economic zone under UNCLOS. The coverage of the conventions is still limited to pollution damage from persistent hydrocarbon mineral oils. Thus non-persistent oils such as aviation fuel, gasoline, light diesel oil and kerosene fall outside the conventions. Previously the regime applied to pollution damage from laden tankers only; tankers on a ballast voyage were thus not covered. This has been modified. The 1992 conventions apply to non-laden tankers within certain limits as is apparent from the new definition of "ship" which is:

> ...any sea-going vessel and seaborne craft of any type whatsoever constructed or adapted for the carriage of oil in bulk as cargo, provided that a ship capable of carrying oil and other cargoes shall be regarded as a ship only when it is actually carrying oil in bulk as cargo and during any voyage following such carriage unless it is proved that it has no residues of such carriage of oil in bulk aboard.   (Article 2(1) of CLC 1992)

The new definition thus covers combination carriers on a ballast voyage after discharging a cargo of oil with residues of the oil cargo on board. The definition does not cover such a vessel after tank cleaning operations have been completed and the vessel is ready to load a non-oil cargo. Another issue relevant to the notion of the laden or unladen tanker is the definition of "oil" which, after a description of the examples of persistent oil, contains the words "whether carried on board a ship as cargo or in the bunkers of such a ship". This means that pollution caused by bunker oil of a tanker, whether laden or unladen, so long as the definition of "ship" is met, is covered by the convention, but pollution from bunker oil of a non-tanker is not. Incidentally, this lacuna in the law is now addressed by the International Convention on Civil Liability for Bunker Oil Pollution Damage, 2001.

The definitions of "pollution damage", "preventive measures" and "incident" are inter-related. The new definition of "pollution damage" has been carefully drafted but still lacks clarity. It provides for costs of "preventive measures" as an element of compensable damage. The definition of "preventive measures" has not changed, but the definition of "incident" which features in the unchanged definition of "preventive measures" has been altered in the 1992 CLC to mean any occurrence or series of occurrences having the same origin, which causes pollution damage *or creates a grave and imminent threat of causing such damage.* Costs of preventive measures are compensable even if there is no oil spill, provided there was grave and imminent threat of pollution damage.

The registered owner of the polluting ship is strictly liable but is entitled to the enumerated defences characterised as exceptions to strict liability remain unchanged. Claimants are precluded from making claims against servants or agents of the owner, crew members, pilot, charterer, salvor or any person taking preventive measures, including servants and agents of all of the above-noted persons, unless it is proved that the damage resulted from the *personal act or omission of any of those persons, committed with intent to cause such damage, or recklessly and with knowledge that such damage would probably result.*

The new formulation of words in the "conduct barring limitation" clause makes limitation virtually unbreakable and was strongly supported at the international level by the insurance industry. This *quid pro quo* of significantly higher limits is now accepted by most maritime countries.

The aggregate amount of compensation payable under the conventions for one incident is 135 million SDR inclusive of the amount paid by the shipowner under CLC 1992. The IOPC Fund is liable for the balance. The 1992 scheme has also introduced the two-tier system of compensation pursuant to which the maximum amount of 135 million SDR can be increased to 200 million SDR for an incident that occurs during a period when in respect of three parties to the convention, the combined amount of contributing oil received in those states was at least 600 million tons in the preceding calendar year [Article 6 (3)(c) which is a new provision].

The Supplementary Fund

In October 2000 the IMO Legal Committee adopted two resolutions to raise the limits of both conventions by about 50.37 %. As a result, the aggregate amount of compensation payable is now 203 million SDR. Subsequently, an optional third tier of compensation was established through a Protocol known as the Supplementary Compensation Fund 2003 (SCF). This has resulted in a change characterized by a significant increase in the limits of liability for pollution damage emanating from tankers. It is notable that during the period 2000–2003, when the above-noted developments were taking place, two major oil spills occurred; the *Erika* and the *Prestige* incidents. There is no doubt that the system as it stands on the whole has worked considerably well since its inception, and particularly as a result of the periodic revisions including increases in the total amounts of available compensation.

Thus, inbuilt limitations in the Conventions have precluded the possibility of further increases until 2011. The main provisions of the Supplementary Compensation Fund are as follows:

- An optional third tier of compensation for states party to the Fund Convention, funded by oil importers to provide additional payments where the Fund Convention ceiling is exceeded;
- Maximum compensation of SDR 750 million payable by the Supplementary Fund, inclusive of the CLC and Fund Convention amounts; and
- Entry into force 3 months after ratification by eight states with total contributing oil imports of at least 450 million tons.

As of January 2012, 110 States are party to both CLC 1992 and the Fund Convention 1992, 19 States parties only to CLC 1992 and 28 States party to the third tier Supplementary Fund.

Compensation Issues

Compensable Damage

Not all injury, loss or damage suffered is compensable at law. In the common law system a claimant must have *locus standi* in respect of the damage claimed and in the court where the case is brought. It is also a fundamental requirement that the court in question must have jurisdiction over the subject matter brought before it. The court acquires jurisdiction usually through statute. It can then assert jurisdiction and be seized of the case. But even if a court has jurisdiction it cannot proceed with the case if the claimant does not possess *locus standi* in respect of the subject matter and in the forum. Thus the court must have jurisdiction and the litigant must have *locus standi* or standing before litigation can proceed.

Whether or not convention law applies, the compensability of a particular species of claims will be considered in terms of domestic law where the convention is either silent or domestic law applies impliedly or under the terms of the convention itself. This situation can potentially result in the convention regime not being applied uniformly by courts in different jurisdictions. Also, a national court may treat compensability of a particular claim in quite a different manner from the way the relevant IOPC Fund may deal with it under what is loosely called "Fund jurisprudence".

Pollution Damage and Preventive Measures

For damage to be compensable under the convention regime, it has to fall within the definition of "pollution damage". The relevant parts of the twofold definition are as follows:

(a) Loss or damage caused outside the ship by contamination resulting from the escape or discharge of oil from the ship, wherever such escape or discharge may occur, . . .etc.;
(b) The costs of preventive measures and further loss or damage caused by preventive measures.

Paragraph (a) above consists of three distinct elements. First, the loss or damage must be outside the ship; damage caused by contamination inside the ship is not compensable. Secondly, only loss or damage resulting from contamination generated from a ship is covered; in other words, oil pollution that is land based or from the sea-bed is outside the scope of the definition. Thirdly, so long as the pollution is ship-generated and the damage occurs outside the ship, the location of the escape or discharge is immaterial; however, the word "wherever" must be construed within the limitation of the geographical scope of application of the conventions.

Paragraph (b) of the definition expressly provides that costs of preventive measures constitute pollution damage and are therefore compensable. The term "preventive measures" is defined and must be construed by courts and the IOPC Fund within the perimeter of its definition which is "any reasonable measures taken by any person after an incident has occurred to prevent or minimize pollution damage" [Article I (7) of CLC 1969].

Damage to Property

Damage to physical or tangible property is clearly compensable so long as it meets the above definition of "pollution damage". Typical examples of such damage include a claim for loss of or damage to a fisherman's boat, nets and other fishing gear. Damage to a fisherman's physical property may occur in a variety of ways. Oil spilling out of a polluting ship may directly enter into a fishing vessel located near the ship when the spill occurs. This may cause the fishing vessel to sink or be severely damaged. The fishing vessel may not be close to the polluting ship but may be situated within the polluted waters and thereby suffer pollution damage. In such case the damage is not directly caused by the polluting ship but indirectly through the medium of the polluted water. In such case, the fishing vessel together with its fishing gear, i.e., its nets, lines or trawls spread at a distance may suffer pollution damage. Damage to physical property can also be suffered by other vessels plying or located in the polluted area. Examples of physical damage to other kinds of property include fixed objects such as buoys, beacons, transponders, navigation markers, *etc.* at sea, and structures such as breakwaters, pipelines, pontoons and jetties connected to the shore. Pollution damage suffered by beaches and shorelines can be extensive and far-reaching. In all the above cases, the claimant must show that he has a legal interest in the property that is recognized at law; without it he will likely have no *locus standi*.

Economic Loss

Liability and compensability in relation to economic loss is one of the most problematic issues in the law of torts. Economic loss is a topic that poses a dilemma to lawyers, jurists and legal scholars alike, partly because of its practical implications. If it is allowed, it opens the floodgates of litigation. An eminent American jurist, Cardozo J. once described liability for economic loss as "...liability in an indeterminate amount for an indeterminate time to an indeterminate class" [*Ultramares Corporation* v. *Touche* (1931), 255 NY 170 at p. 179]. If it is not allowed, it may cause undue hardship in certain cases and justice may not be served. Generally, claims for economic loss are not entertained by courts, but exceptions are made depending on the facts of a particular case. There is an element of subjectivity no doubt, but there are judicial guideposts as well that serve as principles to be applied in determining whether a claim for economic loss should be allowed in a particular case.

Economic loss can be simply defined as a financial loss sustained by one as a result of a wrongful act or omission of another. There are basically two types of economic losses, one is usually compensable, at least in the context of pollution damage as discussed above, the other is generally not.

Consequential Loss

Financial loss that is a direct consequence of damage to physical property is described as consequential loss. Where property damage is compensable under the conventions as discussed above, financial loss consequential to it is also compensable so long as the financial loss meets the proximate cause test. If the financial loss is too remote from the property damage caused by the pollution, the claim will usually not be allowed. Remoteness in such instances is a question of fact. A good example of consequential loss in the present context is the loss of income of a subsistence fisherman resulting from loss of his fishing boat or nets, gear and other equipment. Other examples of consequential loss would be the loss of profits of a beachfront hotel or restaurant arising from pollution damage suffered by the premises. The proximate cause test will usually be met in such a case.

Pure Economic Loss

Even though it is perhaps fair to say that *prima facie*, pure economic loss is not compensable, there are instances in which exceptions can be made to that rule. Much, however, depends on the viewpoint of the tribunal. The IOPC Fund has been known to admit pure economic losses for compensation in certain cases. It is the inconsistency in the approaches taken by different tribunals that is problematic.

Typical cases of pure economic loss include loss of income, lost profits and loss of opportunity to earn income. Where fishermen and others deriving income from the sea suffer such financial losses, there are many related issues to be considered. Earning of income may be prevented because of regulatory prohibition, loss of access to fishing grounds because of such prohibition or otherwise or falling market conditions. As distinguished from consequential economic loss, pure economic loss is independent of any associated property damage. In other words, it is unrelated to the tortious act other than in terms of a pecuniary loss incidental to it. The directness or remoteness of the loss points to whether the act of polluting was the proximate cause of the claimant's financial loss, which in turn determines its compensability.

Loss of income could also arise as a result of damage to the environment. This could happen in circumstances where loss of property such as the boat, nets or gear of a fisherman has not occurred, but the fisherman faces a loss of income because he is unable to fish in the polluted waters, or, even if he is able to fish, the fish are contaminated and he is unable to sell his catch. In the case of a hotel or restaurant, similar financial loss could arise out of damage to the marine environment in its vicinity. The loss could manifest itself in a number of ways. Patrons and customers could be prevented from coming to the hotel or restaurant, or consumption of fish may decline or stop altogether. In these cases economic loss will be compensated provided the proximity/remoteness test is met.

Relational Economic Loss

In the common law system, relational economic loss is a species of economic loss that is not compensable at law. Relational economic loss is considered to be secondary to the object of the compensation regime, which is primarily to provide recompense for losses arising from physical contamination caused by the pollutant. It is arguable that a fisherman's claim for loss of income is not relational and is compensable, even though it is an economic loss, because the physical activity of fishing from which he derives his livelihood is inextricably connected to the pollution of the waters where he fishes. In contrast, the loss suffered by a fish processing plant or an exporter of the processed fish is without doubt a secondary or relational loss. Such losses are indirect consequences of the pollution and therefore not compensable. In the final analysis remoteness and reasonable foreseeability of loss or damage are the determinants of compensability.

Environmental Damage

The issue of compensation for environmental damage has remained somewhat incomplete in the CLC/Fund convention regimes. The legal basis on which a right to be compensated for environmental damage may rest is not addressed in the conventions. It would appear that this matter has been left to be dealt with by the domestic law of the given the inconsistency in approaches taken by national courts at best, and lacunae in the law at worst. This is compounded by the fact that the IOPC Fund has had occasion to deal with such claims in only a few situations by applying its own policy without much regard to any national law.

The Convention simply provides that "compensation . . . shall be limited to costs of reasonable measures of reinstatement actually undertaken or to be undertaken". It appears that there is an underlying assumption that environmental damage is compensable regardless of the *locus standi* of the claimant. These words can be alternatively construed as providing for a methodology to be applied where environmental damage is compensable under the domestic law of the forum.

Another issue that frequently poses a problem with regard to environmental damage is quantifiability of the claim. In one case, *s.s. Zoe Colocotroni* v. *Commonwealth of Puerto Rico*, 601 F.2d 39 (1st Cir. 1979), it was held that abstract quantification or use value based on theoretical mathematical models are not acceptable. By contrast, "reasonable measures of reinstatement" can be quantified objectively in terms of intrinsic value which is more acceptable.

Industry Action

Interim Arrangements Following the Torrey Canyon

The grounding of the *Torrey Canyon*, was a defining moment which necessarily changed the industry's approach to the rapidly expanding oil trades and trends towards ever larger tankers. It was quickly realised that existing arrangements covering liability and limitation were inadequate. Immediately following the convening of the Brussels diplomatic conference, it was realized that the envisaged convention regime for liability and compensation would become effective only after considerable elapse of time given the slow pace which is characteristic of entry into force of treaty instruments. Thus, during the interim period following the adoption of the CLC and 2 years later, the Fund Convention, the industry became conscious of public criticism unless some arrangement for adequate compensation was put into place. The shipping and oil industries, therefore, set up their own voluntary arrangements.

The *Tanker Owners Voluntary Agreement concerning Liability for Oil Pollution* (TOVALOP) took effect in October 1969. It provided compensation where CLC 1969 did not apply. Parallel arrangements under CRISTAL (*Contract Regarding a Supplement to Tanker Liability for Oil Pollution*) provided a further layer of compensation in relation to incidents involving cargoes with a widely defined concept of CRISTAL-owned cargo. The two schemes, as amended from time to time, particularly increased compensation levels from February 1987, provided a means of filling any gaps in the international regime. As a result of eventual widespread State acceptance of CLC and the Fund Convention, which as explained elsewhere were revised in the intervening period, TOVALOP and CRISTAL were terminated in February 1997.

Voluntary Action Following Adoption of the Supplementary Fund

Action by Shipowners

The maximum limitation amount of SDR 750 million under the Supplementary Fund Protocol is much in line with the European Commission's COPE proposals for compensation of up to €1 billion. Nevertheless, the Supplementary Fund went beyond the "reasonable" levels advocated by the shipping industry to preserve the underlying internationalism of IMO provisions. It was also significantly higher than the SDR400 million put forward by oil importer interests which would be funding any payments.

P&I Club insurers voluntarily agreed to increase the CLC 1992 threshold payment from the Convention minimum of SDR4.5 million to SDR20 million for all pollution incidents in States Party to the Supplementary Fund. It was hoped that the agreement, called the *Small Tanker Oil Pollution Indemnification Agreement* (STOPIA) would bring an end to calls for CLC revision being examined through a Fund Convention Working Group set up following the *Erika* incident.

Oil Industry

However, the position became more complex with some States continuing to call for greater or lesser degrees of revision. At the same time, oil importers were concerned about their potential commitment in the event of an incident leading to third tier payments, arguing that this would distort the long-term equal sharing of liability, and therefore compensation payments, between shipowners and cargo interests.

It was, therefore, a matter of satisfaction when, at its session in October 2005, the Fund Assembly decided to terminate the Working Group set up to consider a possible revision process. Proposals from 11 states for a "limited" revision to correct shortcomings and administrative provisions, leaving aside overall compensation levels and breakability of shipowner limitation rights, received support from 23 delegations, although it must be questionable whether, once opened, the scope of the discussion could, in fact, have been limited as intended. In contrast, 28 delegations opposed revision and the majority view prevailed. The Working Group was, therefore, disbanded.

Removal of the threat of unpredictable changes enabled the shipping industry to go forward with additional voluntary arrangements to maintain the compensation (liability) sharing formula. This was achieved through binding contractual schemes concluded in discussions between the International Group of P&I Clubs, the Fund Convention Secretariat and oil receivers represented by OCIMF (Oil Companies International Marine Forum). Under the schemes:

- STOPIA 2006 (which originally applied only to States Party to the Supplementary Fund) was extended to apply to all parties to the 1992 Fund Convention and, also, to the handful of CLC States not party to the Fund Convention;
- TOPIA (*Tanker Oil Pollution Indemnification Agreement*) will provide 50 % shipowner sharing in the costs of claims involving the third tier Supplementary Fund; and
- Inbuilt arrangements provide a mechanism for monitoring payments and adjusting the agreements to maintain the long term balance of liability sharing.

Spills, particularly major incidents, are comparatively rare but the amounts of compensation now available should satisfy all bar a difficult to imagine catastrophe. It is hoped that after a period of uncertainty when it looked as though the international system might be called into question, the funds and arrangements now in place will be viewed as providing a viable long-term compensation regime without the need for further review.

Other Ship-Source Pollution

Hazardous and Noxious Substances

The modern world relies on any number of chemical and substances, often with harmful effects if not used or handled properly, in the manufacture of everyday goods. While some are obvious, many others are less well known or lost behind a trade name. They are, nevertheless, potentially dangerous. Strict rules apply to their carriage and, of course, rely on shippers' candour to ensure that details are properly disclosed. Even so, incidents can arise due sometimes to misdeclaration or insufficient details being provided and, from time to time, because of an accident involving a vessel. Pollution arising from chemicals and other cargoes having hazardous properties is not covered by the oil spill conventions. Claimants in a jurisdiction subject to LLMC 1976 or 1996 would have to prove negligence to succeed although, certainly for larger incidents, laid down limits of liability might not adequately cover claims for loss or damage.

Following CLC and Fund Convention, IMO tried to devise parallel provisions for hazardous and noxious substances. This quickly proved to be more problematic than originally envisaged. Draft articles for a Convention were concluded by the IMO Legal Committee in 1983. At the subsequent Diplomatic Conference in 1984, and because of the complexity, the content met with disapproval and the project had to be abandoned. Work started again to develop an international convention to avoid regionalisation and, particularly from shipowners' viewpoint, to maintain shared liability through a two-tier instrument. Following long and complex discussions through IMO, new text was put to a Diplomatic Conference (which also considered the amendments to LLMC 1976) held over a 3-week period in April/May 1996.

At the end of the deliberations at the Diplomatic Conference, the *Hazardous and Noxious Substances (HNS) Convention* 1996, was adopted. However, various compromises necessarily agreed to reflect different governmental and user interests, created later administrative obstacles for many States. The situation came to a head in 2007 when it was acknowledged that without certain changes, the Convention would never take effect in major trading nations. This led to the setting up of a Focus Group through the Fund Convention (which was dealing with the administrative aspects in the lead-up to the anticipated implementation of HNS) to develop proposals. At this stage, it will be helpful to take a step back to look at the content of the instrument adopted in 1996. The main elements of the first tier, shipowner provisions, were:

- Hazardous and noxious substances defined by a reference to IMO instruments and the IMDG Code. Coal was controversially excluded to the disappointment of many governments, but not shipowners;
- Liability for damage due to loss of life and injury (which have priority for payments), property and contamination;
- Application to damage arising in the territory and territorial sea of a State Party and damage by contamination in the Exclusive Economic Zone or equivalent area (up to 200 nautical miles);
- Strict shipowner liability (with only limited exceptions) but with rights of recourse action against third parties;
- Shipowner limitation starting at a minimum threshold level of up to SDR10 million for a vessel not exceeding 2,000 gross tons rising, through graduated payments, to a maximum of SDR100 million for vessels of 100,000 gross tons or more;

- Registered owner of the ship to maintain financial security evidenced by a state-approved certificate of (liability) insurance; and
- Claims for compensation to be brought against the registered owner or directly against the insurer.

It will, thus, be seen that the provisions for strict liability, channelling of claims, limitation rights (lost only in the event of the owner's intentional act or recklessness leading to harm) and compulsory insurance, closely mirror CLC arrangements.

As with CLC, a second tier fund under HNS provides further compensation up to a total (including shipowner payments) of SDR250 million where claims exceed the amount available under the first tier. However, in contrast to CLC where a single cargo type resulted in all importers contributing in the event of an incident, because of the diversity of cargo types, HNS was divided into a general account and separate accounts for oil, Liquid Natural Gases (LNG) and Liquid Petroleum Gases (LPG). The purpose was to meet cargo interests' concerns that there should be no sectoral cross-subsidisation and that each cargo type should provide its own self-standing compensation for damage.

Nevertheless, the complexities of the cargo account for establishing levy contributions in the event of a future incident involving second tier compensation, created practical difficulties in implementing the Convention. Shipowners, while initially hesitant to give endorsement to untested obligations, subsequently recognised the value of an instrument which would be specific and clear in scope and designed for international application, as opposed to the emerging trend towards regionalisation. In contrast, cargo interests were less enthusiastic and, in some cases, openly opposed to the instrument.

Delegates at the October 2007 session of the IOPC Fund Assembly were confronted by a stark choice between further efforts towards implementation and suspending work which, in reality, would have spelled the end of the IMO instrument. Fortunately, it was decided to continue albeit with differing views on how this could best be achieved. The shipping industry was concerned that a proposed Protocol to address problematic issues could lead to wholesale reopening of the Convention and a loss of the principle of shared liability with cargo interests.

The need to concentrate on specific issues was recognised. Tightly defined terms of reference were given to a Focus Group mandated to develop legally binding solutions for approval by the IMO Legal Committee and subsequent adoption at a Diplomatic Conference. The Focus Group put forward proposals to remove reporting requirements for packaged HNS goods thus eliminating what would otherwise have been an administrative nightmare for many States; adjusted arrangements for funding LNG levy contributions; and ensure that States comply with treaty obligations to submit details of HNS cargo imports.

The proposals were adopted at a Diplomatic Conference held at IMO in April 2010. The Diplomatic Conference also addressed the question of adjustments to compensation levels which, as is customary, had been left for decision at the Conference. As anticipated, in order to reflect the potential rebalancing of liability between first tier shipowner and second tier cargo interests following removal of the reporting and contributing requirements for packaged HNS goods, it was agreed that for such cargoes shipowner compensation would be increased by 15 %.

The Convention represents an important element in the mosaic of internationally agreed maritime pollution and liability instruments. It is hoped that the modifications will be acceptable to States and lead to early and widespread ratification.

Ship-Source Pollution Damage from Bunker Oil

As we have already seen cargo, and bunker, spills from oil tankers have for many years been subject to internationally agreed liability and compensation arrangements under CLC and Fund Convention. However, there was no parallel regime for bunker spills from non-tankers although many bulk carriers and medium sized container vessels carry up to 2,500 tons of fuel.

Many States already had domestic legislation imposing strict liability for bunker spills. Given that an estimated 90 % of world tonnage is already covered for such liabilities through P&I club entry, it might reasonably be asked why an instrument was required and whether the resulting bureaucracy would detract from the early settlement of claims. Governments' response was that they had, from time to time, experienced difficulties when trying to recover clean-up costs in relation to uninsured vessels.

Work therefore proceeded towards development of the International Convention on Civil Liability for Bunker Oil Pollution Damage, 2001, colloquially referred to as the Bunkers Convention. While there are similarities with CLC and HNS in relation to compulsory insurance, state-certification and direct action, in other respects it is quite different as it is a single tier instrument based entirely on shipowner liability and permits limitation but without specifying a particular limit in the instrument.

The main points are:

- Application to bunker pollution damage in the territory, territorial sea and exclusive economic zone (or equivalent area) of a contracting state and to preventive measures, wherever taken, to prevent or minimise such damage;
- Joint and several liability (with few exceptions) of the owner, including the registered owner, bareboat charterer, manager and operator of a vessel;
- Liability may be limited by reference to an applicable national or international regime. A conference resolution urged States to ratify LLMC 1996 and clearly identify the applicable limitation regime when implementing the Convention although this is a recommendation only and without legal effect;
- Requirement for all ships greater than 1,000 gross tons to maintain insurance covering liabilities under the Convention evidenced by the on-board carriage of a State-approved certificate attesting that insurance is in place;

- Claims for pollution damage compensation can be brought directly against the insurer who has the same defences as the shipowner subject to a defence of wilful misconduct by the shipowner.

Significantly, unlike CLC and HNS, no legal protection is provided for responders or salvors. A resolution was adopted at the Diplomatic Conference urging contracting States to introduce appropriate national laws covering the position. It was agreed, not without controversy, that the entry into force mechanism would be 1 year after acceptance by 18 States, including five States each with ships whose combined gross tonnage was not less than one million.

The necessary ratifications were secured in November 2007 and the Convention took effect internationally on 21 November 2008. However, the lead-up to implementation raised a number of administrative difficulties. The main problem was the sheer volume of certificates required, estimated at some 45,000. As with CLC, contracting States to the Bunkers Convention are required to issue certificates for their own vessels and may issue certification for vessels from non-States Party. At the time, only a limited number of States were in a position to provide the necessary third party certificates although all properly documented requests were understood to have been satisfied when the Convention came into force. Nevertheless, the considerable increase over recent years in the number of contracting States has largely resolved the position.

Unilateral National and Regional Legislation

U.S. Oil Pollution Act 1990

Major incidents of pollution or loss of life inevitably give rise, as has previously been said, to knee-jerk reactions by politicians, to all sorts of solutions by 1-day experts and to pressure for instant solutions by the country or region affected. The US has shown itself particularly prone to this over the years. The *Exxon Valdez* incident in Alaska was a clear and recent example in so far as it gave rise to the Oil Pollution Act 1990 (OPA 90). This had a massive impact on shipping generally—not just tankers—with the result that some companies are no longer prepared to take the risks involved in trading to the US.

Much has been written about the legislation. Suffice it to say:

- It introduced a scheme of virtually unlimited liability in the event of an oil spill, and did not inhibit (as is usually the case) individual states from taking similar or even wider powers. This requirement extends to all vessels, not just tankers, in so far as they might become involved in a pollution incident. The need to provide evidence of financial responsibility has been met by special arrangements and has not proved to be such an impediment as originally feared.

- It required tanker owners to file "response plans" setting out in detail how they would combat a worst case spill. This means that tanker owners have virtually to hand over control to others in the case of spills. A new multi-billion dollar "cottage industry" of "oil spill experts" has thus been spawned.
- All new tankers after 1995 were required to have double hulls. Expert opinion is divided. It may help in some cases but in others the view is that it could well make matters worse.

This legislation by the U.S. alone, which pays scant regard to IMO Conventions, is a clear example of an environmentally driven measure. No one quarrels with its aims, only the methods employed. Whilst it was said at the time that Uncle Sam has "shot himself in the foot" and that tanker (or other) owners would not trade to the US, this has not happened as widely as feared. From the perspective of the US Congress—and the US public—there is little doubt that the legislation has achieved many of its aims. But the cost to the shipping community in time and energy has been immense and it remains, so far as the shipping industry is concerned, a monument to unacceptable unilateralism.

A danger has also been perceived that the EU might, for political reasons, also be forced to take unilateral measures. This the Commission has frequently denied, stressing the importance of working with the IMO. In any event, it is seeking to give a lead in new areas such as routing schemes in environmentally sensitive areas (here the Chamber of Shipping of the UK, post *Braer*, developed a voluntary code); mandatory EU-wide vessel reporting systems; and the introduction of a "black box" data recorder. The importance of international measures through the IMO and the IMO alone cannot be over-stressed.

As previously explained, the USA did not become party to any IMO Conventions on ship-source oil pollution compensation. Even if ratification had been contemplated, the position changed following the spill from the *Exxon Valdez* in Alaska in 1989 and led to the *US Oil Pollution Act* 1990 (OPA 90). The legislation applies to oil spills from tank ships and dry cargo vessels, with differing limits of liability according to vessel type, and a requirement for shipowners to obtain a Certificate of Financial Responsibility (COFR) to confirm liability cover. In contrast to CLC, limitation is easily broken. Moreover, although a federal Act, OPA 90 does not preclude separate state legislation and many maritime states have introduced their own statutes often with more far-reaching provisions.

The introduction of OPA 90 was questioned by shipowners in terms of substance and workability, particularly the COFR requirements. Over the years the industry has come to live with US requirements and potential exposure to considerable financial risks but the situation remains far from satisfactory.

Unilateral Regional Legislation in the EU

In December 1999, the tanker *Erika* foundered off the coast of Brittany. The experience, together with concerns that the level of compensation in the event of future similar incidents would be insufficient, resulted in resolutions being approved by the IMO Legal Committee, at its meeting in October 2000, to increase compensation. As referred to above this eventually led to the Supplementary Fund being established in November 2003 through the tacit amendment procedure.

Prior to this development, France, in particular, was unhappy with the limitation levels and called for changes to the Conventions to permit more frequent increases. Early in 2001, the European Commission came forward with proposals for a scheme called *Compensation for Oil Pollution in European Waters* (COPE) to provide top-up payments where Fund Convention compensation was insufficient. The shipping industry was alarmed that attempts to reopen the IMO Conventions to amend compensation levels would be likely to lead to more extensive changes to a system which, while not perfect, had functioned reasonably satisfactorily over some 30 years while discrete EU arrangements would be likely to be replicated in other parts of the world leading to uncertainty for shipowners. There was also concern among governments that creeping regionalisation would undermine international uniformity developed through IMO.

Conclusion

Policies, practices and procedures pertaining to environmental protection often vary in different jurisdictions. Needless to say, harmonization in these matters is desirable, particularly on a regional basis, but whether or not that is achievable remains to be seen. Within the European Union, concerted efforts to this end are being made, and it is hoped that the initiatives can serve as a model for others to emulate within their own distinctive maritime cultures. This brings to conclusion the discussion on protection of the marine environment including ship-source pollution prevention, and liability and compensation for pollution damage, all of which is of on-going concern and importance in the maritime field.

Chapter 16
Liability and Limitation of Liability

Introduction

This chapter examines the issues of shipowner rights to limit liability. It does not address the conventions relating to ship-source pollution damage since these have been dealt with in the previous chapter. Conventions have been developed, particularly over the last 40 years, through IMO to be applied on an international basis. This means that the same underlying principles will be applied in all contracting states. It is a matter of regret that with the exception of the oil spill compensation conventions, which have been widely ratified (but not by the USA), other IMO liability and limitation conventions have received more limited acceptance. This, in turn, has encouraged some states and regions to take, or attempt to implement, unilateral solutions as in the case of the U.S. Oil Pollution Act referred to in the last chapter. This undermines global uniformity and creates inefficiencies resulting from differing liability and insurance requirements.

As discussed in relative detail in the previous chapter, the distinction between compensation as a civil remedy and punishment as a penal sanction must be readily appreciated. Compensation responds to liability which must be proved if based on negligence or arises because the incident, regardless of the cause or fault, is subject to strict liability such as in the case of pollution damage. The purpose is to reimburse affected parties for loss or damage which they have suffered. It is not intended to be punitive. The majority of incidents result from the natural dangers of the sea, misfortune or snap judgements in the face of difficulties where the clear view of hindsight might have suggested a different course of action. Any question of criminality or irresponsible behaviour must be dealt with in accordance with other legislative mechanisms. It is unfortunate that regulators in some areas have lost sight of this fundamental separation. As a result, their view that compensation should be used as a financial weapon to control and improve shipowner behaviour does not stand up to scrutiny.

The principle of shipowner rights to limit liability is often viewed negatively because of an inadequate appreciation of the workings of the shipping industry.

Limitation is based on the need to predict liability exposure and purchase insurance to cover the risks which may give rise to such liabilities. As such, there is a defined reference point, regardless of fluctuating vessel values and nature of the risk. This facilitates trade by providing finite values in the event of an incident; represents a *quid pro quo* for high compensation levels; and encourages the settlement of claims by reducing the scope for disputes on liability and the quantum of damages. In contrast, unlimited liabilities are uninsurable and in practice would be capped to the extent of available cover; thereafter, shipowners' assets would be taken into account bringing us back to the flawed notion of punishment, this time through the spectre of financial ruin.

A Brief History of Limitation Rights

Limitation in England can be traced to *The Responsibility of Shipowners Act 1733* which quantified a shipowner's maximum exposure as the value of the vessel and freight. It follows that this would be of little practical use where a vessel was lost. *The Merchant Shipping Act 1854* introduced a tonnage-related valuation which, other than in relation to liabilities to passengers and goods, remains the basis for determining compensation. In the United States, limitation legislation was enacted by Congress in 1851 but the US has not subscribed to any international convention on limitation of liability.

The first internationally agreed instrument was the *International Convention for the Unification of Certain Rules to the Limitation of Liabilities of Owners of Sea-Going Ships 1924*. It was drafted by the Comité Maritime International (CMI) and provided a limitation regime for the acts or faults (which would have to be proved or agreed) of the master, crew, pilot, or any other person in the service of the vessel. The right to limit was lost if the owner was at fault.

A second instrument, the *International Convention Relating to the Limitation of the Liability of Owners of Sea Going Ships*, followed in 1957 although it was not until May 1968 that sufficient ratifications had been secured to enable the convention to enter into force. Compensation was initially set by reference to the gold franc but replaced by the Special Drawing Rights (SDR) through a 1979 Protocol. However, the right to limit was again subject to the proviso that it would be lost if the claim "resulted from the actual fault or privity of the owner". A phrase in such terms invites challenges.

IMO Instruments

Another so-called global limitation regime came into existence through the adoption under the auspices of the IMO (then IMCO) of the *International Convention on Limitation of Liability for Maritime Claims* (LLMC) in 1976. The scope of limitation rights in this convention extends to the owner, charterer, manager and operator of a seagoing ship as well as salvors, with liability insurers, i.e., the P&I Clubs being entitled to the same benefits of the Convention as their assureds. Limitation rights are applied to a defined list of claims covering loss of life or personal injury or loss or damage to cargo and other property, including harbour, dock works and navigational aids. Claims ascertaining to the raising, removal, destruction or rendering harmless of a sunken, wrecked or abandoned vessel and/ or cargo may also be subject to limitation to the extent that they do not relate to a contractual arrangement between the person undertaking the operation and the shipowner. Nevertheless, contrary to the 1957 Convention, contracting States may apply a reservation to exclude wreck and cargo removal from limitation.

Oil pollution damage is outside LLMC Convention as this is separately covered under the Civil Liability Convention as are claims for salvage, general average and nuclear damage. Shipowners are also denied limitation rights against seafarers where seafarer contracts confer more favourable provisions than the LLMC Convention.

This convention has brought about two significant changes to the previous regimes. First, the longstanding "conduct barring limitation" provisions of the 1924 and 1957 Conventions based on "actual fault or privity" of the owner have been replaced by a much more tightly drawn provision whereby the person, i.e. the shipowner as defined, claiming limitation stands to lose that right only if the loss "resulted from his personal act or omission, committed with the intent to cause such loss, or recklessly and with knowledge, that such loss would probably result". This almost unbreakable test has been introduced to remove the uncertainty and accompanying scope for litigation, of the vague "fault or privity" test. The new test requires the shipowner to be shown to have engaged in an activity which was deliberate or clearly wrong. This is a very personal obligation where it is necessary for the claimant to prove that the controlling mind, i.e., the *alter ego* of the shipowner, where it is a corporate entity, had set out to act in such a fashion. Shipowners rarely set out to act in this manner and denial of limitation in such circumstances is a rare occurrence.

The second major change is the considerable enhancement of limitation levels as a trade off for the almost unbreakable right to invoke limitation. The structure of the 1957 instrument was, to some extent, maintained with limitation figures, at much higher levels, incrementally graduated by tonnage in the "general limits" on a 2:1 ratio between claims for loss of life and personal injury and other claims such as collision and property damage. Where the life/injury fund is insufficient, the property fund contributes to the outstanding balance and any concurrent property claims rank *pari passu* with life/injury claims. However, unsatisfied property claims are not settled from any unused amount in the fund for death or personal injury.

At the same time a new, and separate, limit has been introduced for claims for injury to passengers; although in a number of jurisdictions this is superseded by the provisions of the Athens Convention 1974 amended by the Convention's Protocol of 2002. The passenger limit, expressed in SDRs, was originally set at a maximum of 46,666 multiplied by the number of passengers which the ship was authorised to carry. Nevertheless, this figure was subject to an upper limit of SDR 25 million. Individual settlement would, therefore, be reduced *pro rata* where the totality of claims exceeded the global limit. The potential pro-rating of claims would normally only become an issue in the event of a major incident. However, in such event, the implications for individuals involved and political repercussions were such that shipowner limitation rights for passenger claims were frowned upon by many regulators. Detailed provisions set out practical arrangements for invoking limitation rights, constituting and distributing any fund which might be set up; and bars to other actions against the ship or other property. It is for States Party to determine individually whether to apply the provisions to ships navigating in inland waterways and to vessels of less than 300 tons.

Also, it is important to recognise that LLMC is a global limitation instrument. The effect is that, except where liabilities are expressly excluded from the scope such as pollution damage under CLC or nuclear damage under the specialised Nuclear Convention, limitation under LLMC is all-embracing. Thus, liability under other instruments is subsumed within LLMC and claimants may therefore see their actual payments reduced where, for example, claims for cargo loss or damage have to compete with other claims.

LLMC 1976 came into force internationally in December 1986. Further amendments were introduced through a Protocol adopted at a Diplomatic Conference in 1996. The main purpose was to increase compensation limits resulting in an average rise of 240 % but with a much steeper increase for vessels below 2,000 gross tonnage where an entry threshold of up to SDR 3 million was applied. Compensation for passenger loss of life or personal injury was increased to SDR 175,000 multiplied by the number of passengers authorised to be carried. Notably, the 1996 Protocol to the Convention which entered into force in May 2004 has removed the SDR 25 million overall cap on claims arising on passenger vessels. However, depending on the jurisdiction, passenger liability in relation to a seagoing ship may arise under the Athens Convention as discussed below.

Two further provisions should be noted. The first is the option for State Parties to exclude claims for loss or damage from chemical and related pollution under the Hazardous and Noxious Substances Convention 1996. The second point is the introduction of a tacit amendment procedure to allow limits to be increased through the IMO Legal Committee, subject to certain restrictions on figures and intervals between changes. An in-built formula sets a maximum percentage uplift and places restrictions on the intervals between increases while the quantum is to be considered in the light of claims experience, changes in monetary values and the effects on insurance costs. The system enables states to agree compensation increases without the need for a full Diplomatic Conference and, from shipowners' viewpoint, avoids the risk of reopening potentially controversial issues. Revision of other provisions has to follow formal arrangements culminating in a Diplomatic Conference.

As a result of a bunker spill off Queensland in 2009, which resulted in a rare example of limits being exceeded, Australia began to press for a review of compensation levels. At the end of 2010, 20 States co-sponsored a proposal to invoke the tacit amendment procedure to increase rates. At its meeting in April 2012, the IMO Legal Committee adopted increases of 51 % for claims for loss of life/personal injury and property damage. The higher limits take effect from April 2015.

Nairobi International Convention on the Removal of Wrecks 2007

Development of the Convention proved to be the longest running project on the IMO agenda, spanning some 30 years. Work was not continuous but went into a state of semi-suspension when more pressing matters came before the Legal Committee. The shipping industry found it difficult to understand the rationale for an instrument to deal with incidents which are always covered by P&I insurance. Once again, Governments responded emphasising the difficulties of recovering public money when a vessel has no insurance. A further problem was that wrecks cause particular difficulties when an incident arises in a busy or hazardous area beyond territorial seas where a coastal state's actions are limited. Following years of debate and discussion, a Convention was finally adopted in May 2007 which took its name from the city where the Diplomatic Conference was hosted.

The Convention applies where a physical or environmental hazard is created by a wreck, widely defined to include not only ships but, also, objects lost at sea such as containers. The main provisions are:

- Coverage in respect of wrecks in a state party's exclusive economic zone, or equivalent area, with optional extension into a contracting party's territory or territorial sea;
- Measures for reporting, locating, determining hazard and marking a wreck;
- Facilitation of removal by the owner or by the State in the event of non-compliance by the owner or if urgent action is needed;
- Strict shipowner liability under the Convention (*except* where shipowner liability would be in conflict with obligations under CLC, HNS or the Bunkers Convention);
- All ships of 300 gross tons and above to maintain insurance up to LLMC 1996 (but liability may be higher as, for example, in the UK) evidenced by a State-approved certificate of insurance; and
- Claimant rights of direct action against the insurer but only up to the certification level.

The structure of the Convention appears to be much in line with other IMO instruments but two points need to be highlighted.

The first, and most important, relates to the scope of the instrument. Other IMO Conventions apply to a contracting State's territory, territorial sea and exclusive economic zone or equivalent area. The Nairobi Convention applies to the exclusive economic zone and may be applied to the territory or territorial sea. This was because many States already had far-reaching domestic wreck removal legislation for their own seas and did not want to see it compromised by the common denominator of an international convention but, equally, wanted rights of response in areas where they did not have the ability to act. In contrast, the shipping industry questioned the value of such an arrangement since casualties are more likely to occur in the close confines of territorial seas or port approaches and pointed to resulting practical difficulties with insurance cover. It was eventually agreed that contracting states would be able to apply the Convention to their territorial seas if they so wished. Such application would be without prejudice to whatever domestic legislation might already exist but, equally, the Convention's liability and compulsory insurance provisions would not apply to domestic requirements exceeding those in the international instrument.

The second point concerns limitation. The Convention preserves shipowner limitation rights under any applicable national or international regime, such as LLMC 1996. However, some States (including the United Kingdom through a reservation to LLMC 1976/96) exclude limitation rights for wreck removal costs. Nevertheless, P&I cover will respond up to whatever legal liability is established.

A related issue concerns certification. During discussions, the shipping industry proposed that the requirements could be satisfied by a P&I certificate of entry, already carried onboard the majority of vessels. This was not, however, acceptable to governments which insisted on State-approved certification. In that the Nairobi Convention certification provisions apply to vessels of 300 gross tonnage and above, it is estimated that some 70,000 vessels will need certification. This will place a considerable burden on administrations which have already been hard pressed to meet the demand for certification under the Bunkers Convention.

The Nairobi Convention will come into effect internationally 12 months after ten States have agreed to be bound by its provisions.

Adoption of the Convention marked the completion of IMO's work to develop a broadly comprehensive mosaic of liability and compensation regimes responding to third party claimants. A number of States have already indicated an intention to accept the provisions.

Convention Relating to the Carriage of Passengers and Their Luggage by Sea

So far those instruments have been mentioned which have conferred rights on outside third party claimants whose interests are prejudiced by a maritime incident covering, *inter alia*, collision, pollution and wreck removal. Passenger rights are secured through an international Convention which lays down carrier liabilities and compensation levels.

The IMO Convention Relating to the Carriage of Passengers and their Luggage by Sea 1974 entered into force in April 1987. It applies to contracts for the international carriage of passengers. Under its provisions, carrier liability for passenger death or injury is fault-based against claimant proof but with a rebuttable presumption of carrier fault in the event of shipwreck, collision, stranding, explosion or fire, or defect in the ship. Rules were also set out covering loss of or damage to luggage and vehicles. Liability for passenger death or injury (originally stated in gold francs but converted to SDRs through a 1976 Protocol) was limited at SDR 46,666. Nevertheless, contracting parties were permitted to set higher levels for their own carriers. Notably, the United Kingdom used this provision on two occasions. The first was after the *Herald of Free Enterprise* disaster in 1987 when the figure was increased to SDR 100,000 per passenger and to SDR 300,000 from 1 January 1999.

In the international sphere, and in recognition of the subsequent period of high inflation and reduction in the real value of compensation levels, an attempt was made through a 1990 Protocol to the IMO Convention to increase the amount for passenger death or injury to SDR 175,000. Increases were also applied in respect of luggage and vehicles. However, the Protocol has never obtained the required ten contracting states to bring it into force. The lack of support may be attributed to the fact that, even by the standards of the time, the revised compensation levels were seen as too low for high cost economies.

Renewed efforts to amend and modernise the 1974 Convention began in earnest in the late 1990s. Discussions continued not only at sessions of the IMO Legal Committee but, also, through inter-sessional correspondence exchanges and in meetings between governments, industry, legal and consumer group representatives. The shipping industry accepted the need for higher compensation limits but voiced concerns about the means to achieve the desired end. Nevertheless, and after intensive, and sometimes passionate, exchanges during a Diplomatic Conference in October/November 2002, the following structure was agreed and set out in a Protocol which, together with the original instrument, is referred to as the Athens Convention Relating to the Carriage of Passengers and their Luggage by Sea 2002 (Athens Convention 2002):

- Continued distinction between strict shipowner liability for "shipping incidents" comprising shipwreck, capsizing, collision or stranding, explosion or fire and defect in the ship (specifically defined as failures in operational and safety systems) and claimant proof of carrier fault for non-shipping incidents usually passenger "slips, trips and falls";
- Carriers required to maintain compulsory insurance of SDR 250,000 per passenger evidenced by State-approved certification with claimant rights of direct action against insurers;
- Overall carrier liability at a *per capita* maximum of SDR 400,000 with strict liability up to SDR 250,000 for shipping incidents and thereafter fault-based liability up to the maximum and "ground up" fault-based liability for non-shipping incidents;

- Carriers exonerated in the event of war but no absolute exoneration for acts of terrorism;
- Increased compensation for loss of or damage to luggage and vehicles;
- Opt-out provision permitting States to set higher maximum compensation limits.

While the content appears to be consistent with the underlying precepts in the liability instruments discussed above, the requirements of the Athens Convention 2002 have proved problematic even before the instrument has taken effect.

A particular issue, one which industry had highlighted throughout the lead-up to the Diplomatic Conference, centred on insurability. Arrangements for compulsory insurance and direct action have worked satisfactorily for many years in relation to CLC. However, compensation under the Athens Convention is significantly greater raising questions in P&I circles about the practicalities and balance between the level of exposure in passenger and other trades. At the same time, difficulties were identified in fulfilling the insurance requirements for terrorism cover and, if not resolved, could conflict with the certification requirements. Special arrangements were subsequently concluded setting out the basis of terrorism liabilities and question of compensation. It is hoped that this will facilitate eventual certification arrangements for all liabilities including shipping incidents and carrier negligence or the result of acts of terrorism.

Developments in Europe

The focus of this chapter has been on provisions agreed through IMO for worldwide application. As already explained, instruments agreed at international level offer an efficient means of harmonising and applying the same conditions and requirements. Despite industry reservations about the implications of regional approaches, as part of its Third Maritime Safety Package in response to the *Erika* incident, the European Commission brought forward legislative proposals respectively covering general limitation rights and liabilities to passengers.

A draft Directive on the Civil Liabilities and Financial Guarantees of Shipowners was introduced early in 2006. It purported to harmonise and apply international law in the EU through implementation of LLMC 1996. However, it went beyond the Convention's provisions and raised potential treaty law conflicts, particularly in relation to vessels from third party states.

Reservations were expressed by the majority of Member States leading to intensive discussions between the EU institutions—Council, Parliament and Commission. Agreement was eventually reached whereby Member States, which had not already done so, would ratify LLMC 1996. This would be the reference point for claims not covered by specific instruments such as CLC. Ships would be required to carry evidence of insurance cover to meet claims subject to limitation under LLMC 1996. However, rather than state-approved certificates as originally put forward by the Commission, the requirements would be satisfied by a P&I

certificate of entry or similar cover, thereby reflecting the position advocated by the industry. The provisions must be transposed into Member States' domestic law before 1 January 2012.

The Commission also brought forward measures to give effect within the EU to the Athens Convention 2002. Here again, questions were raised about the added value of a Regulation to implement an instrument which, it was hoped, would in any event be ratified by individual Member States. Nevertheless, the Commission pressed ahead with proposals to apply the Convention but with certain additional provisions including extension of application to certain domestic trades and a requirement for all Member States to agree any increases in compensation levels.

Discussions were protracted. As a result, it was eventually necessary for the provisions to be referred to conciliation where earlier support in the Parliament and Commission for harmonised compensation levels (seen by the shipping industry as a potential benefit of the Regulation) was given up to secure political agreement on this and other elements of the package.

The Regulation will take effect in the EU when the IMO Athens Convention 2002 comes into force internationally (expected to enter into force on 23 April 2014) or by 31 December 2012 at the latest. In order to avoid the likely difficulties of the prior regional application of an international instrument, particularly one with complex insurance and liability provisions, it was hoped that the Convention and Regulation would enter into force concurrently. However, that has not been the case.

Liability and Limitation Regimes for Carriage of Cargo

The final section of this chapter examines liability issues under contracts for the carriage of goods by sea. Unlike IMO instruments which provide a system of redress for unconnected parties covering clean-up costs and compensation, cargo liability regimes have developed to protect the interests of cargo owners, the bill of lading holder for goods.

Up until the early part of the last century, there was no internationally accepted system of minimum liability as between a carrier (not necessarily a shipowner) and the owner of goods carried. This meant that often onerous terms were imposed on shippers while a third party buyer of goods could not be certain about the extent of any obligations or liabilities which might be contained in a bill of lading. This could give rise to later unexpected and unwelcome surprises.

The Hague Rules

In order to facilitate the needs of trade and provide certainty for merchants in their commercial dealings, the issue was taken up by the Comité Maritime International (CMI), which comprised maritime lawyers, shipowners, charterers, cargo owners and their respective insurers and provided a forum where their interests could be represented. After a series of meetings, starting in the Hague in 1921, the International Convention for the Unification of Certain Rules of Law Relating to Bills of Lading (the "Hague Rules") was signed in Brussels in August 1924. The necessary enabling legislation was passed, almost immediately, in the United Kingdom through enactment of the Carriage of Goods by Sea Act 1924. Other jurisdictions also enacted similar legislation. Thus the Rules received widespread endorsement by the major maritime states and entered into force in June 1931.

The Hague–Visby Rules

However, some 40 years later the world was changing. The advent of containers was beginning to have an effect on ship design and, in due course, would lead to a sharp reduction in cargo loss and damage. The need to try to accommodate the changing conditions resulted in the Visby Protocol of 1968 which increased the level of shipowner limitation amounts and introduced an alternative for limitation by reference to weight or per package, whichever was the higher. Other adjustments were also made. The revised convention, known as the Hague–Visby Rules 1968, entered into force in 1977. Effect was given to the revised Rules in the United Kingdom through the Carriage of Goods by Sea Act 1971. Many other jurisdictions also accepted the revisions and continue to subscribe to these Rules. Several states, however, significantly the USA, have continued to apply the original Hague Rules. Several states have introduced domestic legislation reflecting the basis of the Hague–Visby Rules but this is not the same as formal acceptance of the Convention. Be that as it may, it is perhaps fair to conclude that these are the Rules that are most widely followed internationally one way or another.

The main elements of the Hague–Visby Rules are as follows:

The Rules set a minimum standard in relation to the liability elements which can be imposed on the holder of a bill of lading.

- They apply to contracts of carriage evidenced by a bill of lading or similar document of title. The provisions do not apply mandatorily to charterparties but they do have effect where a charterparty bill of lading transferred to a third party governs the relationship between the carrier and the holder;
- They apply on a tackle-to-tackle basis covering the time between loading and discharging of the goods;
- They apply to goods, other than live animals and cargo agreed to be, and actually carried, on deck;
- They require the carrier to exercise due diligence "before and at the beginning of the voyage" to make the vessel seaworthy – which also means cargoworthy. Case law has shown that the courts impose a very high standard;
- They set out a fault-based liability regime which is the central feature. The carrier is not liable for loss or damage arising from:

- unseaworthiness (including "uncargoworthiness") unless this results from failure to exercise the required due diligence;
- a catalogue of listed defences where, in particular, the carrier is not responsible for the "act, neglect or default of the master, mariner, pilot or the servants of the carrier" in the navigation or management of the ship, the so-called "nautical fault" defence. Other defences include fire, perils of the sea, shipper error and losses arising from the packaging or nature of the cargo;
- an all-embracing exclusion for loss or damage arising without the actual fault or privity of the carrier or fault or neglect of the carrier's agents or servants.

The burden of proving or resisting claims, and the existence or otherwise of a causative link between unseaworthiness and loss, will often shift between the parties during settlement negotiations;

• They provide that where fault is established, the carrier may limit liability at SDR 666.67 per package or unit or at SDR 2 per kilo of gross weight – whichever is the higher. The SDR has replaced the gold franc or poincare franc which was previously used as the reference point. However, "unit or package" has not been satisfactorily defined even by case law and has caused many problems over the years with courts almost invariably interpreting the smallest parcel in a larger unit as fulfilling the package criterion.

It should be noted that shippers are, and remain, responsible to carriers for the effects and costs of loss or damage where cargo is or becomes dangerous. Shipper liability is not limited.

Carriers may, voluntarily, give up any of their rights or increase their obligations under the Rules. However, P&I insurance is normally predicated on the compulsory application of Hague Visby Rules (or where compulsorily applicable Hamburg Rules) and any departure would prejudice liability cover. A carrier responding to the additional demands of a powerful shipper would need to purchase separate cover.

There is an argument that for an industry which often, for good reason, is cautious about embracing change, the Visby Protocol was premature. Its architects could not have foreseen how shipping would change beyond recognition over the following two decades in terms of vessel type, size and the demands of shippers for door-to-door services and accompanying logistical integration.

The Hamburg Rules

The Hamburg Rules came about as a result of pressure during the 1970s for a new regime advocated, in particular, by developing countries whose representatives questioned the basis of earlier international provisions and their suitability in terms of the needs of developing economies. The Rules, which were adopted in 1978, have never been widely accepted with few major trading nations having ratified them. Even so, the Convention is in force.

As with the Hague and Hague–Visby Rules, the Hamburg Rules are not applicable to charterparties. However, the scope of application has been widened to extend carrier liability from the time the carrier takes charge of the goods at the port of loading until the goods have been handed over to the consignee or otherwise delivered on his behalf.

While carrier liability is, again, fault-based, the test is altogether more subjective. The carrier is liable for loss or damage unless he proves that "he, his servants or agents took all measures that could reasonably be required to avoid the occurrence and its consequences". The general lack of clarity resulted in the need for an accompanying Common Understanding at the Conference that carrier liability is "based on the principle of fault or neglect" and that, as a rule, the burden of proof rests with the carrier unless otherwise modified by the provisions of the Convention. Limitation was established at SDR 835 per package or unit or SDR 2.5 per kg, whichever is the higher.

The Hamburg Rules also introduced, for the first time, prescriptive measures relating to jurisdiction and arbitration. Such provisions were, however, inconsistent with arrangements which have functioned successfully over the years whereby claimants, wherever located, normally expect to receive compensation direct from their insurers leaving any recourse action to be pursued by underwriters through a single jurisdiction, usually in a carrier's domicile. This was, perhaps, a significant reason for the failure of the Rules to gain acceptance.

United Nations Convention on Contracts for the International Carriage of Goods Wholly or Partly by Sea, 2008 (Rotterdam Rules)

During the closing years of the last century, concerns began to emerge about the perceived diversity of cargo liability regimes across the world. The position might not have been quite as bleak as it appeared on paper but, nevertheless, the different arrangements set out in this section suggest that the objective of a single international regime had been lost. The world's major trading nations were largely using the Hague–Visby Rules, either as parties or through similar domestic legislation, but the USA remained wedded to its Carriage of Goods by Sea Act 1936, which gave continuing effect to the original Hague Rules. While the US began to look at updating its domestic legislation, in 1997 the CMI proposed an ambitious project to try to harmonise and update liability provisions to recognise the expansion of containerisation and increasing level of door-to-door carriage together with the introduction of new technology.

After several years of detailed consideration and much drafting activity, a CMI text was presented to the United Nations Commission for International Trade Law (UNCITRAL) at the end of 2001 for development as an international convention. Discussions were taken forward through a specialist Working Group, comprising

UNCITRAL member and observer government delegations together with representatives from inter-governmental organisations and observer delegations from industry. The Working Group met twice a year between 2002 and 2007 with a final session held early in 2008. The Working Group's recommendations were subsequently accepted, with little change, by UNCITRAL in June 2008 and formally adopted as a Convention by the UN General Assembly the following December.

The resulting instrument is more comprehensive than existing regimes and is, necessarily, much longer. Traditional core issues such as carrier liability continue to be a central feature but new areas have been addressed including inland carriage, shipper obligations and electronic commerce.

In brief outline, the Convention will apply to contracts of carriage involving a maritime leg between different States. Parties will be free to apply the provisions in line with traditional port-to-port carriage used particularly in bulk trades, but in recognition of the need for door-to-door arrangements to facilitate container traffic to and from inland destinations, optional provisions cover pre- and on-carriage outside of the sea transport sector. Charterparties, including slot and space charters will be excluded, as they are under current regimes, from the mandatory coverage but, reflecting existing practice, the Convention will apply where newly termed transport documents, namely, bills of lading and seawaybills, regulate the contractual arrangements between the holder and the carrier. Thus, as at present, liner trade carriage will be subject to the new Convention whereas, in the tramp trade, the provisions will not take effect until documents have been transferred to a third party.

Subject to one important exception, the provisions are mandatory with limited flexibility allowing only cargo interests to demand more favourable terms. The exception relates to liner trades where shippers and carriers will be permitted to agree tailor-made "volume contracts" reflecting individual party needs and allowing wide derogation from the underlying provisions. The term "volume contract" has deliberately not been quantified leaving parties to decide where and when the arrangements will apply. This system is much in line with the present liner service agreements or service contracts in vogue in the US trades.

E-commerce is an important innovation with functional equivalence giving equal status to paper and electronic documentation. It will enable e-systems to be used without the current limitations of shipper demands for paper bills of lading.

Carrier liability continues on the longstanding fault-based principle for loss of or damage to goods, as well as for delay in delivery. The catalogue of carrier defences, now referred to as "presumptions of absence of fault", has been maintained with the important exception of the nautical fault rule which has been removed. This, arguably, is likely to impose greater liability on carriers. In addition, carrier obligations to exercise due diligence to provide a seaworthy, and cargoworthy, ship which currently applies only before and at the beginning of the voyage, will be extended throughout the voyage.

Carrier liability will be in accordance with compensation limits set out in the Convention unless loss or damage is shown to have occurred beyond a maritime sector in door-to-door transport and another international instrument, such as CMR (*Convention on the Contract for the International Carriage of Goods by Road 1956*), would have applied had the carrier and shipper agreed a separate contract for that part of the carriage. By way of example, an incident on cross-border road carriage in Europe would be compensated under CMR limits whereas damage during a sea leg or where the location cannot be identified (sometimes referred to as hidden or concealed damage) or where no international instrument is applicable before or after the maritime sector, will always be compensated in accordance with the Convention limits.

Limitation rights can normally be invoked in the event of carrier fault for breaches of obligations under the Convention, including misdelivery. Nevertheless, and curiously given that the actual loading will be undertaken by sub-contractors or supervised by the master, the carrier is denied limitation where goods are carried on deck in breach of an under-deck agreement. Limitation continues to be based on the longstanding package/weight formula basis but at an enhanced figure of SDR 875 and SDR 3 per kg respectively. Special arrangements apply in relation to claimed economic loss caused by delay.

An innovation is the introduction of laid down obligations for shippers covering delivery of the cargo to the carrier, its suitability for loading and carriage, provision of information and documentation and rules for dangerous goods. Shipper liability is mainly fault based but strict for documentary inaccuracies where errors may result in the vessel being held up or other action taken. It is also strict in relation to dangerous goods where an incident may have wide implications for the carrier, the vessel and third parties. There is no cap on shipper liability which is potentially open ended.

Documentation covers the use and compilation of paper and electronic negotiable and non-negotiable documentation. A comprehensive list of required information is set out while the obligation to insert shipper provided details is balanced by the carrier's right to qualify the accuracy of the information.

Expectations that a solution would be developed for the age-old problem of demands for cargo without surrender of the bill of lading, failed to materialise. A minor theoretical improvement was achieved but is likely to have limited practical benefits. Nevertheless, the ability to use electronic commerce should help to speed up the movement of documentation and may, at least to some extent, ease the problem of delayed paperwork.

Initially onerous prescriptive provisions on jurisdiction and arbitration, which would have restricted courts' rights to recognise exclusive choice of court clauses and entitled claimants to overturn an arbitration agreement, were modified. Moreover, and most importantly, they will apply only where a state positively elects to opt-in to the provisions. Few states are expected to take this up.

Other provisions include evidentiary aspects of documentary statements, delivery of goods to consignees, carrier obligations when goods are not collected, notification of loss or damage to goods, claimant rights of action and time for suit.

The Convention was opened for signature in Rotterdam on 21 September 2009 and is thus known as the *Rotterdam Rules*, with 20 contracting States required for it to enter into force. As of July 2012, the convention has been signed by 24 States, including 10 in Europe and the USA. So far, Spain and Togo are the only states that have ratified the convention which represents the culmination of many years' work to restore international uniformity and avoid the fracturing of harmonised liability arrangements through the development of alternative regional regimes.

Chapter 17
Conclusion: The Current Milieu and Beyond

In this book an attempt has been made to introduce the reader to the subject of shipping which is as vast as the oceans. Shipping is inherently international in scope; hence the caption "international shipping". A kaleidoscopic view of shipping as it has evolved over the recent past has been provided by looking into the current milieu and beyond clustered by numerous issues of imminent and ongoing concern. In the previous editions of this book, the primary focus has been on the shipping industry viewed largely from the private sector vantage point. While many of the same issues continue to exist, some in the same form, others in a new shape, notions and perceptions are changing inevitably.

Over recent times much has been said about the phenomenon of globalisation which has become a buzzword in every sphere of human endeavour and engagement. What perhaps has thus far not been adequately recognised is that shipping is the original globalised industry and continues to be at the forefront of that phenomenon together with the industries associated with it. An activity that is predominantly international in scope and character must be correspondingly globalised to be efficient and successful.

Shipping has traditionally been regarded as a cyclical industry—7 years fat followed by 7 years lean. While there is no indication that the trend is about to change, competition remains regularly fierce and numerous factors and variables continue to impact on the market including advancements in technology, particularly in the field of acquisition and communication of information. This vast new potential is heralding in changes such as paperless transactions leading to instantaneous transformations of legal rights and the commercial status of parties involved in those transactions. Thus it is not just the shipping industry *per se* but also those industries allied to it such as chartering and brokering, logistics, freight forwarding, supply chain management, insurance, ship finance and the multifarious dimensions of human resources associated with shipping are all experiencing radical diversification of interests and consequences stemming from technological progress globally. Whether or not this will continue for the future remains to be seen but all indications seem to be leading to a positive conclusion on this score.

This book in its previous incarnations has always served as a general yet widespread source of information on shipping for readers ranging from students to professionals to captains of industry. The same readership is contemplated for this edition of the book except that extant topics have been dealt with in more detail and new topics have been introduced embracing recent and current developments and taking into account the continuing dynamic state of shipping. The net has been cast much wider in all respects.

Factors Affecting the Shipping Market

There are many factors that are likely to affect the market in future years beyond our current times. These are identified, examined and discussed in as much detail in various chapters as the narrative flow of the book can accommodate. These concluding remarks again highlight the importance of some of these factors.

Regulation and Technological Advancement

Shipping is continually being subjected to new impacts and, correspondingly, increasing regulatory pressures. On the positive side, change has fostered technological growth and development. Issues such as pollution from ships, piracy and other threats to maritime security, and improvement of seafarer welfare have taken centre stage in the development of law and policy. These have triggered the need for innovative shipping strategies from industry.

There is, of course, the danger of regulatory overkill with regard to maritime safety and protection of the marine environment. Where this happens, undue burden is placed on commercial operations which may well prove to be counterproductive. But the danger does not exist solely in those areas. It can—and does—exist, for example, in the activities of the Competition Directorate of the EU as regards co-operation in different shipping sectors. It even extends to "fishing" expeditions and "dawn raids" in pursuit of evidence of contravention of the competition articles of the EU Treaty.

Shipping continues to pass through a period of change as big, if not bigger, than that in the middle of the nineteenth century from sail to steam. Yet the basic hull design of ships has changed little since the days of the clipper ships. Technological changes have been largely in the size and power of the propulsion unit and the design of propellers so as to give greater thrust and efficiency. In the latter half of the last century, anti-fouling paints and coatings have been developed which give a smoother hull form; initially, they produced harmful effects on the marine environment, but this has now been regulated through international convention law. Faster ships, single or multi-hulled, are used today for the carriage of cargo as well as passengers. The question is whether this trend will continue and, if so, what effect it will have on the market. Equally, where ultimately will the balance lie between speed and the imperative of slower steaming imposed by high bunker prices and environmental considerations?

Information technology is also now a major driver of shipping operations—with the use of electronic bills of lading and other transport documentation being provided for in the new Rotterdam Rules. Whether at sea, in ship-to-shore communications or in land-side logistics, information technology has pervaded almost all aspects of transportation, maritime, multimodal or otherwise. There is no doubt that the trend towards electronification will permeate through all strata of safety and navigational technology. It is already evident in the use of equipment such as ECDIS, GPS, ARPA and other aids to navigation as well as EPIRB and AIS.

Carriage of Goods

New rules governing carriage of goods by sea are in the offing, which purport to bring about a more equitable balance between carrier and shipper interests and would link the carriage of goods liability and other rules more closely with the trade dimension of international shipping. Multimodal shipping is once again in the limelight in terms of its regulation through convention law and the respective roles of freight-forwarders, consolidators and other service providers are changing in consonance with the emerging legal regimes—nationally, regionally and globally. The perennial carrier-shipper interaction hitherto characterised by carrier dominance is being tempered by the expanding and innovative strides taken by the different shipper entities.

Overcapacity

Over the years world trade has grown, sometimes slowly, but always on the increase. Current projections are that the years ahead will see a massive increase. This will inevitably require more ships, but history shows that overcapacity—too many ships chasing too few cargoes—is an ever present danger. What has to be achieved is a reasonable balance in the market.

On the whole today, there is a better balance although not in the liner sector. A measure of controlled restraint needs to be exercised on an ongoing basis—by owners in ordering, by shipyards in building, by banks and finance houses in their lending policies and, above all, by governments in their shipbuilding and shipping policies. A policy of protection for one's own shipping has the same effect as a subsidised building programme. It increases the demand for ships, but ships which should not be built and for which there can be only limited employment. Thus there is a heavy onus on governments to act responsively and responsibly; a far cry from the days when governments had little, if any role. But at the end of the day shipowners also have to do their part. It is they, after all, who order ships to be built. But equally it is they who suffer if they get their market forecasts wrong.

There is an endemic danger of overcapacity in the liner trades because of the imperative of guaranteeing a regular service combined with changing trade volume and balance in each direction. This makes for an inherent instability which the conference and consortia systems have tried to balance out over the years. This trend may change with the new regime of volume contracts under the Rotterdam Rules; only time will tell.

Market Players

The days when the traditional (western) maritime states had the largest share by far of the world shipping market have long gone. This has resulted from the eastward swing of the pendulum—away from Europe and the US towards the Far East—and the increasing participation of fleets from other emerging economies.

The world's biggest shipping companies, with few exceptions, are no longer in Europe or the US, but in China and Hong Kong, and other countries in the Far East. The non-traditional shipping countries have come of age and it seems that this trend is set to continue. Thus the market players today are quite different from those of even 20 years ago, let alone 50 years ago. These new players will bring new ideas, techniques and business models—perhaps better ones. But the basic truth remains that stability of the world's trading system is essential if profitability and reliability of service is to be maintained, a point cogently made by the Asian Shipowner's Forum on several occasions; and, as pointed out by them, this is necessary in the bulk and tanker trades as well as container trades.

Ship Finance

The days when shipowners were able to finance their own new ships have also gone for most. The years ahead will therefore see a requirement for finance from banks or other financial institutions which specialise in ship finance. Here again innovation may play a part. Straight loans on the back of a mortgage are not the only approach. Leasing—as in the aircraft industry—is now increasingly popular. New financial packages or devices may equally be on offer. Overall, however, all parties must understand the need for controlled growth so as to maintain that all important balance in the market, whilst not creating a situation where there is insufficient shipping capacity to meet the needs of world trade.

The Unevenness of the Playing Field

It is recognised that fiscal, taxation and other measures available as incentives and designed to encourage investment, employment and the like vary from one country to another. This leads to a dilemma for shipowners who—while committed in principle to free, fair and open competition—nonetheless are, or believe themselves to be, subject to unfair discrimination because of subsidies or advantages available to others. As a result, some press their national authorities for special treatment by way of subsidies, tax or fiscal advantages; whilst others either nationally, or regionally, argue that their governments should press others to level down to make the playing field more even.

Be that as it may, for as long as substantial cost differences apply, or appear to apply between developed and developing countries, governments in the former are likely to succumb to pressures for assistance, if only to preserve seafaring or other essential skills which would otherwise certainly be lost sooner or later (which is already beginning to happen).

Profitability

For a long periods, shipping companies may face insufficient returns on the vast capital invested in their ships. This applies in all sectors, at different points in their different cycles. Shipping markets are notoriously characterised by their volatility. Although the mid 2000s saw a protracted period of good markets across most sectors, that was unprecedented in shipping memory and difficult and volatile times have now returned. Cash and timing are everything. Ships are extremely expensive and too often revenue has been insufficient to cover other than daily running costs. In an age when the bottom line is paramount this is a serious matter and one that explains the general disinvestment from shipping in some previously maritime states.

Levels of freight rates and therefore return on capital depend essentially upon the balance between supply (over which shipowners have some control) and trade volumes (over which they have no control).

The Age of Fleets

Fleet age is essentially a result of the return on investment which, as we have seen, is generally low. It is a fact which has to be faced. Equally there is a point beyond which a fleet cannot age further. On the other hand, care has to be taken not to equate age with inefficiency, poor standards or unseaworthiness. An old ship is not necessarily a bad ship and there are many examples of older ships performing better than much younger ships, since they have been maintained throughout their life to higher standards and their operating processes are better. This applies equally to second-hand ships.

Ethical Standards

In shipping, as elsewhere, standards of behaviour and of ethics have changed. This is in part, but not entirely, as a result of market conditions, especially in the bulk trades in recent decades. There are also many new countries, names and faces involved either as owners, operators or managers of ships; or as charterers; or as both. Their perceptions of standards may be different though by no means necessarily lower than those of the past.

On the other hand, there is evidence of an upsurge in fraud on both a large and a small scale, quite apart from declining standards of business ethics especially in bulk shipping. Traditionally, shipping has operated on the basis of the Baltic Exchange's Code of Practice and motto "Our word our bond". In other words once an agreement has been verbally entered into, that concludes the essentials of the matter and there should be no further argument.

In the present milieu, there seems a marked inclination to seek agreements with "subject to" clauses under which long negotiations can continue, so that the nature of the agreement can be changed or payments due under it can be delayed. For the independent shipowner, late payment of charter hire, disputes about or late payment for the detention of his ship on loading and discharge for longer than agreed or reasonable (demurrage), or other attempts to re-negotiate the agreement are a cause at best of financial embarrassment for the shipping company or, at worst, of disaster. There have also been many cases in recent years of unilateral abrogation of charterparties, with the same acutely harmful effect.

Thus it is not surprising that some of the major shipping organisations have taken steps in order to assist their members and to halt any further decline. Better market conditions from the shipowners' standpoint would help. But that is by no means the end of the matter. Shipowners want a return to the time when a charterer could be relied upon to fulfil his side of the bargain both to the letter and spirit. In short what seems to be needed is a greater emphasis on the term "first-class charterer" and a strong reminder of and adherence to the existing codes of ethics.

National Unilateralism, Regionalism or Internationalism

As frequently explained in this book, shipping can only thrive if such regulation as is necessary for the general good is based on a fully international approach— whether through the IMO, ILO, UNCITRAL or WTO. Yet there is a perceived danger that, because of national and regional politics and pressures, there will be a move away from international solutions despite the growing acceptance of free-market principles world wide. Sufficient has probably been said already for it not to be necessary to dwell further on this aspect.

It is unfortunate that shipping often has little political clout nationally or internationally. This—coupled with the fact that, despite the efforts of many parties in their own ways, the sector has not been successful in getting the message across to the public about the vital service it provides to world trade—translates at best into a public perception that shipping is faceless and, at worst, a negative perception. Contrast the news stories which attach to a major maritime incident and an advance in maritime technology. Increasingly, the industry accepts the need to promote itself on the basis that merchant shipping is:

- Vital for world trade;
- Inexpensive;
- Essentially safe;
- Environmentally friendly; and
- Important for defence.

Much has to be done if that message is to be conveyed to the younger generation who are still students, to decision-makers, diplomats, law makers and the general public; indeed to all those who benefit from the service that shipping provides.

As has already been said, ships without trade are worthless. The reverse is also largely true. But what needs emphasising is the fact that shipping needs and provides business and essential skills for a raft of fascinating and high-value service sectors:

- Arbitrators
- Brokers
- Classification societies
- Ship management
- Technicians
- Insurers (hull, machinery and P&I)
- Lawyers
- Bankers
- Accountants
- Ports
- Educational
- Charitable and welfare,

as well as for manufacturing sectors, shipbuilding, marine equipment and other suppliers. Many of these require the services of those who have acquired professional skills as seafarers. The danger of the supply falling away in the traditional western maritime states is already evident as previously indicated.

The shipping industry may also wish to revisit the current organisational structures to promote and protect its interests nationally and globally. There is a proliferation of international and national associations, which results in too many bodies and needless overlaps in terms of their functions and activities. The existence of multiple voices, often saying similar things but with minor differences, can have the very damaging consequence of confusing the maritime message in the minds of governments, politicians and other observers of our industry. It makes it clear that the industry just "can't get its act together". Somehow, shipping as a sector has to find a way of seeing beyond the differences of the various constituent parts of this great industry to those aspects, qualities, aims and objectives which are, for the most part, common to them all. It needs to build on and unite behind the 90 % or more that its different bodies have in common, rather than obsess about the differences.

Today, more effort is being put into achieving greater policy and promotional cooperation in some countries and internationally. But there is still much further to go.

Priorities for the Future

It requires considerable boldness to look too far ahead into the future in shipping. Nonetheless in this book as a whole, and particularly in this chapter, a number of priorities for the years ahead have been identified. These include:

- *The vital importance of shipping to world trade.* This importance is not readily appreciated by the populace at large simply because ships are not visible in capital cities or major metropolitan centres unless they happen to be ports. This is epitomised by the unthinking who still believe that all goods today are transported by air. Sea transport begins with raw products, wet and dry, and ends up with food on the table, metal and fuel for cars, and power for generating electricity. Without it, as the current parlance goes: "half the world would starve, and the other half would freeze".
- *Competitiveness.* Increasing and continuing emphasis on cost and operational efficiency will be essential for owners and operators who wish to survive and prosper.
- *The lack of sufficient, well-qualified seafarers world wide.* There are many reasons for this, including the high cost of manning of ships, changing patterns of social norms and career alternatives for the younger generation in the western world. The popular perception is that life at sea is hard where a seafarer has to spend lengthy periods away from home and family. While this is true, in many cases nowadays officers can have their spouses accompany them on board. Other positive aspects of a seafaring career include taking on responsibility in one's career much earlier than ashore, and there are several possibilities of advancing later into high-value, shipping-related employment ashore.
- *Seamanship and respect for the sea.* A solid and continuing understanding of the awesome power of the sea in its many moods will always be necessary. This can only be acquired through experience at sea. Whilst much training can be imparted through simulators and in the class room, there is no substitute for "hands on" experience at sea.

- *Size and complexity of ships.* These far outstrip those of yesteryear. This brings the need for much greater sophistication from seafarers; but equally it brings the danger that technical requirements may outstrip the qualifications of those who have to operate today's huge, costly and complex vessels. It also means that, more and more, each ship is different and may require different skills.
- *Long-term commitment.* The business of owning, operating or managing ships needs deep and long-term commitment. It is an all absorbing way of life and not for the fainthearted. As has already been said the rewards can be enormous, but equally the risks can be overwhelming. This has always been the case and will continue to be so. The profit/risk ratio needs to be far more widely understood coupled with the basic requirement that levels of profitability must be such as to allow reinvestment. The danger is that low levels overall, including of profitability lead to low standards and low service.
- *Proper balance between the regulators and the regulated.* There is a real danger of a proliferation of governmental rules and regulations, all demanding, some oppressive, often coming one on top of the other. This produces saturation, lack of comprehension, a contrary effect to that intended, and clashes of both law and implementation. There is a need for this message to be understood at both national and international levels, whether in the context of flag or port state jurisdiction and implementation, or in the application of environmental or competition rules or any other basic policy issues.
- *Research and development.* This is all part of the drive towards safe shipping and clean seas. It could perhaps be undertaken hand in hand with governments and other sectors of the maritime world.

Status of Freedom in Shipping

The ability to trade freely without let or hindrance is a major part of the theme of this book. It is apparent that freedom in its pure sense has been significantly eroded and today, governments are involved in many aspects of shipping including safety, crewing and manning, pollution control, the environment, operational matters and even the commercial and economic aspects. On the other hand, recent years have seen free-market principles being embraced almost on a world wide basis, and there is some diminution in national protectionist tendencies. This is a trend that gives hope for the future.

As we enter the second decade of this century, shipping is a global, largely self-regulated industry characterised by integrity and efficiency, operating increasingly in cooperation with regulators in the public sector as well as with other allied branches of the private sector such as shipyards, logistics providers, charterers, insurers and cargo interests. We expect ships to continue to be managed and crewed by highly qualified, self-motivated professionals with high standards who will earn and be accorded the respect and recognition they deserve in a socio-economic world that is indispensably dependent on shipping. Ultimately, it is people—whether at sea or ashore—who are the beneficiaries.

Bibliography

Books

Anderson P et al (2003) Cracking the code. Nautical Institute, London
Baatz Y, Debattista N et al (2008) Southampton on shipping law. Informa Law, London
Berridge GR (1987) The politics of the South African run: European shipping and pretoria. Clarendon, Oxford
Beth HL, Hader A, Kappel R (1984) 25 years of world shipping. Fairplay Publications, London
Birnie PW, Boyle AE (2002) International law and the environment, 2nd edn. Oxford University Press, Oxford
Boyd SC, Burrows AS, Foxton D (1996) Scrutton on charterparties and bills of lading, 20th edn. Sweet & Maxwell, London
Brierly JL (1963) The law of nations: an introduction to the international law of peace. Clarendon, Oxford
Churchill RR, Lowe VA (1999) The law of the sea, 3rd edn. Manchester University Press, Manchester
Coles MF, Ready NP (2002) Ship registration: law and practice. LLP, London
Coles R, Watt EB (2009) Ship registration: law and practice, 2nd edn. Informa Maritime & Transport, London
Colombos GJ (1959) International law of the sea. Longmans, Green & Company, London
Conway B (1990) Maritime fraud. Lloyd's of London Press, London
Davis R (1962) The rise of the english shipping industry in the seventeenth and eighteenth centuries. Macmillan, London
Deakin BM, Seward T (1973) Shipping conferences; a study of their origins, development, and economic practices. Cambridge University Press, Cambridge
De la Rue CM, Anderson CB (2009) Shipping and the environment: law and practice. Informa, London
Oude Elferink AG, Rothwell DR (eds) (2004) Oceans management in the 21st century. Brill Academic Publishers, Leiden
Fayle E (1937) A short history of the world's shipping industry. With a foreword by Sir Alan G. Anderson. Allen and Unwin, London
Ferguson AR, Lerner EM, McGree JS, Oi WY, Rapping LA, Sabotka SP (1961) The economic value of the US merchant marine. Transportation Center at Northwestern University, Evanston
Gaskell NJJ, Debattista C, Swatton RJ (1987) Chorley & Giles' shipping law, 8th edn. Pitman Publishing, London
Gauci G (1997) Oil pollution at sea. Wiley, Chichester

Gault S, Hazelwood SJ, Tettenborn A (eds) (2003) Marsden on collisions at sea, 13th edn. Sweet & Maxwell, London

Gold E (1981) Maritime transport: the evolution of International Marine Policy and Shipping Law. Lexington Books, Toronto

Gold E, Chircop A, Kindred H (2003) Maritime law. Irwin Law, Toronto

Gorton L, Ihre R, Sandevärn A (1990) Shipbroking and chartering practice, 3rd edn. Lloyd's of London Press, London

Graham MG, Hughes JO (1985) Containerisation in the eighties. Lloyd's of London Press, London

Griggs P, Williams R (eds) (1998) Limitation of liability for maritime claims, 3rd edn. Lloyd's of London Press, London

Grime R (1991) Shipping law, 2nd edn. Sweet & Maxwell, London

Hermann AH (1982) Conflicts of national laws with international business activity: issues of extraterritoriality. British-North American Committee, London

Hodges S, Hill C (2001) Principles of maritime law. LLP, London

Howarth D, Howarth S (1994) The story of P & O: the peninsular and Oriental Steam Navigation Company. Weidenfeld & Nicholson, London

Hughes OE (1998) Public management & administration: an introduction. Macmillan, London

Jackson DC (2000) Enforcement of maritime claims, 3rd edn. LLP, London

Johnson WC (1992) Public administration, policy, politics and practice. Dushkin Publishing Group, Guildford (Brown and Benchmark, 1996)

Johnson LS (2004) Coastal state regulation of international shipping. Oceana Publications, Dobbs Ferry

Kasoulides GC (1993) Port state control and jurisdiction: evolution of the port state regime. Martinus Nijhoff, Dordrecht

King M, Thornhill C (2005) Niklas Luhmann's theory of politics and law. Houndmills, Basingstoke, Hampshire

Kiss A, Shelton D (2007) Strict liability in international environmental law. In: Ndiaye TM, Wolfrum R (eds) Law of the sea, environmental law and settlement of disputes: Liber Amicorum Judge Thomas A. Mensah, Martinus Nijhoff, Leiden

Lauterpacht H (1977) International law. Cambridge University Press, Cambridge

Long A, Long R, Turnbull F (1974) A shipping venture: Turnbull Scott and Company, 1872–1972. Hutchinson Berham, London

McDowell & Gibbs (1999) Ocean transportation. Beard Books, Washington

Mejia MQ (ed) (2005) Contemporary issues in maritime security. WMU Publications, Malmö

Mejia MQ, Xu JJ (eds) (2007) Coastal zone piracy and other unlawful acts at sea. WMU Publications, Malmö

Molenaar EJ (1998) Coastal state jurisdiction over Vessel-Source pollution. Kluwer Law International, The Hague

Mukherjee PK (2002) Maritime legislation. WMU Publications, Malmo

Mukherjee PK, Mejia MQ, Gauci GM (eds) (2002) Maritime violence and other security issues at sea. WMU Publications, Malmö

Muller G (1999) Intermodal freight transportation, 4th edn. Eno Transportation Foundation and Intermodal Transport Association of North America, Washington

Naess ED (1972) The Great PanLibHon controversy: the fight over the flags of shipping. Gower Press, Epping

Nordquist MH, Moore JN (eds) (1999) Oceans policy: new institutions, challenges, and opportunities. Martinus Nijhoff, The Hague

North PM, Fawcett JJ, Cheshire GC (1999) Cheshire and North's private international law, 13th edn. Butterworths, London

Özcayir ZO (1998) Liability for oil pollution and collisions. LLP, London

Özçayir ZO (2004) Port state control, 2nd edn. LLP, London

Parks AL (1994) The law of Tug, Tow and Pilotage, 3rd edn. Cornell Maritime, Centreville

Pauw FD (ed) (1965) Grotius and the law of the sea. Institut de Sociologie, Brussels

Power VJG (1992) EC shipping law. Lloyd's of London Press, London

Reeder J (ed) (2003) Brice on the maritime law of salvage, 4th edn. Sweet & Maxwell, London

Richardson JW (ed) (2003) The merchants guide. P&O Nedlloyd, Corporate Communications, London

Rubin AP (1998) The law of piracy, 2nd edn. Transnational Publishers, New York

Sands P (2001) Bowett's law of international institutions. Sweet & Maxwell, London

Smith HA (1959) Law and custom of the sea. Stevens & Sons, London

Spruyt J (1990) Ship management. Lloyd's of London Press, London

Spurling J, Lubbock B (1972) Sail: the romance of the clipper ships. Grosset & Dunlap, New York

Starke JG (1989) Introduction to international law, 10th edn. Butterworths, London

Stokes P (1997) Ship finance – credit expansion and the boom bust cycle, 2nd edn. LLP Ltd, London

Stopford M (1988) Maritime economics. Routledge, London

Taylor JA (1976) Ellermans: a wealth of shipping. Wilton House Gentry, London

Tetley W (1994) International conflict of laws: common, civil, and maritime. Blais International Shipping Publications, Montreal

Tetley W (1998) Maritime liens and claims, 2nd edn. Blais International Shipping Publications, Montreal

Tetley W (2002) International maritime and admiralty law. Blais International Shipping Publications, Cowansville

Thomas DR (1980) Maritime Liens, vol 14, British Shipping Laws. Stevens & Co., London

Thornton RH (1959) British shipping. Cambridge University Press, Cambridge

White ND (1996) The Law of International Organisations. Manchester University Press, Manchester

Articles

Berlingieri F (2002) Basis of liability and exclusions of liability. Lloyd's Marit Commercial Law Q 336

Falkanger T, Bull HJ, Brautaset L, Mlynarczyk J (1993) Maritime Law – Model Course 6.08. IMO, London

Gold E (2007) Gard handbook on protection of the marine environment, 3rd edn. WMU J Marit Aff 6(1):97–99 (Arendal: Norway)

Grime R (1986) The loss of the right to limit. In: Gaskell N (ed) The limitation of shipowners' liablility: the new law. Sweet & Maxwell, London

Halberstam M (1998) Terrorism on the high seas: the Achille Lauro, piracy and the IMO convention on maritime safety. Am J Int Law 82:269, 285

Jacobsson M (2009) "Bunker Convention in Force" J Intl Mar Law 15(1):21–36

Kraska J (2009) Coalition strategy and the pirates of the Gulf of Aden and the Red Sea. Comp Strategy 28(3):197–216

Llacer FJM (2003) Open registers: past, present and future. Marine Policy 27(6):513–523

McConnell ML (1987) "Business as usual": an evaluation of the 1986 United Nations convention on conditions for registration of ships. J Marit Law Commerce 18(3):435–449

Mejia MQ (2003) Maritime gerrymandering: dilemmas in defining piracy, terrorism, and other acts of maritime violence. J Int Commercial Law 2(2):153–175

Menefee SP (1989) The Achille Lauro and similar incidents as piracy: two arguments. In: Ellen E (ed) Piracy at sea. ICC Publishing, Paris, p 179

Metaxas BN (1974) Some thoughts on flags of convenience. J Marit Stud Manag 1(3):162–177

Mukherjee PK (2000) New horizons for flag states. Maritime Review, 2nd half, London, Pacific Press, pp. 110–114

Mukherjee PK (2003) The Law of Maritime Liens and conflict of laws. J Int Marit Law 9:545

Mukherjee PK (2006) Criminalisation and unfair treatment: the seafarer's perspective. J Int Marit Law 12(5):325–336

Mukherjee PK (2007) The Penal Law of Ship-Source Marine Pollution: selected issues in perspective. In: Max Planck Institute for Comparative Public Law and International Law (ed) Liber Amicorum Judge Thomas A. Mensah: law of the sea, environmental law and settlement of disputes. Martinus Nijhoff, Leiden, pp 463–496

Mukherjee PK (2010) Liability and compensation for environmental damage caused by ship-source pollution: actionability of claims. In: Faure MG, Lixin H, Hongjun S (eds) Marine pollution liability and policy: China, Europe and the U.S. Wolters Kluwer, Alphen aan den Rijn, pp 75–95

Mukherjee PK (2011) Liability issues pertaining to maritime safety. In: Proceedings of the international conference on marine & maritime affairs, University of Plymouth, Plymouth, 4–5 April 2011

Mukherjee PK, Xu J (2009) The legal framework of exhaust emissions from ships: a selective examination from a law and economics perspective. In: Bellefontaine N, Linden O (eds) Impacts of climate change on the maritime industry. WMU Publications, Malmö, pp 69–101

Plant G (1996) The collision avoidance regulations as a regulator of international navigation rights: underlying principles and their adequacy for the twenty-first century. J Navigation 49(3):377–393

Ramberg J (1999) ICC guide to Incoterms 2000: understanding and practical use. ICC Publishing S.A., Paris

Shaw R (1998) The ISM code and limitation of liability. Int J Shipping Law 3:169–172

Srivastava CP (1990) The role of the International Maritime Organization. Marine Policy 14:243–246

Treves T (2009) Piracy, law of the sea, and use of force: developments off the Coast of Somalia. Eur J Int Law 20(2):399–414

White M (2007) Prompt release cases in ITLOS. In: Nidaye TM, Wolfrum R (eds) Law of the sea, environmental law and settlement of disputes: Liber Amicorum Judge Thomas A. Mensah. Martinus Nijhoff, Leiden, pp 1025–1052

Wiswall F (ed) (1988) Bareboat charter registration, legal issues and commercial benefits. International Chamber of Commerce, Paris

Xu J (2006) Theoretical framework of economic analysis of law governing marine pollution. WMU J Marit Aff V(1):75–94

Xu J (2007) The public law framework of ship-source oil pollution. J Int Marit Law 13:416–428

Documents and Miscellaneous Publications

American Shipper
Annual Reports of the Chamber of Shipping of the UK
Annual Reports of the European Community Shipowners' Associations
Annual Reports of the General Council of British Shipping
Annual Reports of the International Chamber of Shipping and International Shipping Federation
Annual Reports of the Maritime Transport Committee, OECD
Annual Reports of the UNCTAD Secretariat on Maritime Transport
British Shipping Laws Series (Stevens & Sons)
Committee of Inquiry into shipping (The Rochdale Report), (HMSO 1970)
Compensation Fund 1992, London: International Oil Pollution Compensation Fund, 2008
Competition Policy and Shipping – 3rd Report of House of Lords Select Committee, Session 1983–1984

Conference Report: International Symposium on Liner Shipping, III (Bremen, 1984: The Institute of Shipping Economics)

Containerisation International

European Shippers' Councils, *Time for Change* (1995)

Guidelines for Maritime Legislation, Bangkok: ESCAP Publications, Vol. I Third Edition, 1991

International Council of Containership Operators, Container Shipping – Backbone of World Trade (1996)

International Maritime Organization (1999) Piracy and armed robbery against ships: guidance to shipowners and ship operators, shipmasters and crews on preventing and suppressing acts of piracy and armed robbery against ships. MSC.1 Circ. 1334

International Maritime Organization (2009) Piracy and armed robbery against ships: recommendations to governments for preventing and suppressing piracy and armed robbery against ships. MSC.1 Circ. 1333

International Oil Pollution Compensation Fund, *Claims Manual: International Oil Pollution Compensation Fund 1992*, London: International Oil Pollution Compensation Fund, 2008

International Risk Governance Council (IRGC), White Paper on risk governance towards an integrated approach, IRGC, 2006 (available online)

Lilar A, van de Bosch C. Le Comité Maritime International *1897–1972*

Lloyd's Ship Manager: Guide to International Ship Registers and Ship Management Services (1997) – produced in association with ISF

Lloyd's Shipping Economist (LLP Ltd)

Singh, N., *UNCTAD I & UNCTAD II* in the field of Shipping and Invisibles

Stockholm School of Economics, Research Institute, Shipping & Ships for the 1990s

The Greenwich Forum IV, Britain and the sea: Future Defence, Future Opportunities

University of Southampton (1990), "The Ratification of Maritime Conventions" Vol.1-4 LLP, ISBN1-95044-301-7

William A. O'Neil (1999) Speech delivered at Seatrade Awards Ceremony Dinner reported in *Seatrade Review*, July/August, 1999 at pp 4–6

World Trade Organisation, WTO–Trading into the Future, 1995

Table of Cases

Table of Legislation

Arctic Waters Pollution Prevention Act, 1970
Brussels Package, 1979 (EC Regulation 954/79)
Carriage of Goods by Sea Act 1936, (US)
CSG Ministers' Resolution, 1963
EU Regulation 4055/86
Flag State Self-Assessment Scheme and the Voluntary IMO Member State Audit Scheme (VIMSAS)
French Acte de Navigation of 1793
IMO Code for the Investigation of Marine Casualties and Incidents (IMO Code). Resolution A.884 (21) (Amendments to the Code for the Investigation of Marine Casualties and Incidents resolution A.849(20)
Jones Act - US Merchant Marine Act 1920
Maritime Transportation Security Act (MTSA), 2002
Ocean Shipping Reform Act 1998 (OSRA) came into force in May 1999
Oil Pollution Act, 1990 (OPA 90)
Regulation 3577/92/EEC
Regulation 4057/86
Regulation 4058/86
Resolution A.787(19) as amended by Resolution A.882(21)
Resolution A.973(24) Code for the Implementation of Mandatory Instruments, 2005
Rules in the United Kingdom through the Carriage of Goods by Sea Act 1971
The Carriage of Goods by Sea Act 1924, (UK)
The Merchant Shipping Act 1854
The Responsibility of Shipowners' Act 1733
U.K. Marine Insurance Act 1906
UK Aviation and Maritime Security Act (AMSA), 1990
United Kingdom Merchant Shipping Act 1894
United Kingdom Merchant Shipping Act 1995
US Shipping Act of 1916
US Shipping Act of 1984

P.K. Mukherjee and M. Brownrigg, *Farthing on International Shipping*,
WMU Studies in Maritime Affairs, Vol. 1, DOI 10.1007/978-3-642-34598-2,
© Springer-Verlag Berlin Heidelberg 2013

Table of Conventions and Other Treaty Instruments

Athens Convention Relating to the Carriage of Passengers and Their Luggage by Sea, 1974 (PAL)

Basel Convention on the Control of Transboundary Movements of Hazardous Wastes and Their Disposal, 1989 (Basel)

Code for the Construction and Equipment of Ships Carrying Dangerous Chemicals in Bulk, 1986 (BCH Code)

Convention for the Suppression of Unlawful Acts Against the Safety of Maritime Navigation, 1988 (SUA)

Convention on Facilitation of International Maritime Traffic, 1965 (FAL)

Convention on the Contract for the International Carriage of Goods by Road, 1956 (CMR)

Convention on the International Regulations for Preventing Collisions at Sea, 1972, (COLREG)

Convention on the Prevention of Marine Pollution by Dumping of Wastes and Other Matter, 1972 (Dumping); Protocol of 1996

Far East Trade, Tariff Charges and Surcharges Agreement (FETTSCA)

Hong Kong International Convention for the Safe and Environmentally Sound Recycling of Ships, 2009 (SRC)

International Code for the Construction and Equipment of Ships carrying Dangerous Chemicals in Bulk, 1985 (IBC Code)

International Convention for the Control and Management of Ships' Ballast Water and Sediments, 2004 (BWM)

International Convention for the Prevention of Pollution from Oil (OILPOL), 1954

International Convention for the Prevention of Pollution from Ships, 1973, as modified by the Protocol of 1978 relating thereto, 1978 (MARPOL 73/78)

International Convention for the Unification of Certain Rules of Law with Respect to Collision Between Vessels, 1910

International Convention for the Unification of Certain Rules of Law Relating to Bills of Lading, Brussels, 1924, as amended by the protocol of 1968 (Hague-Visby Rules)

International Convention for the Unification of Certain Rules of Law Relating to Bills of Lading (the "Hague Rules"), Brussels, 1924

International Convention for the Unification of Certain Rules Relating to the Limitation of Liabilities of Owners of Sea-Going Vessels, 1924

International Convention of Safety of Life at Sea, 1974, (as amended) (SOLAS)

International Convention on Civil Liability for Bunker Oil Pollution Damage, 2001, (Bunkers)

International Convention on Civil Liability for Oil Pollution Damage, 1969 (CLC 69)

International Convention on Civil Liability for Oil Pollution Damage, 1992 (CLC 92)

International Convention on Liability and Compensation for Damage in Connection with the Carriage of Hazardous and Noxious Substances By Sea, 1996, (HNS)

International Convention on Limitation of Liability for Owners of Sea-Going Ships, 1957

P.K. Mukherjee and M. Brownrigg, *Farthing on International Shipping*, WMU Studies in Maritime Affairs, Vol. 1, DOI 10.1007/978-3-642-34598-2, © Springer-Verlag Berlin Heidelberg 2013

Index

Printed by Publishers' Graphics LLC
MLSI130618.15.15.125